MONEY, VALUE AND MARX'S CIRCUIT OF CAPITAL

RESEARCH IN POLITICAL ECONOMY

Series Editors:

Ndongo Samba Sylla

Rosa Luxemburg Foundation, Senegal

Paul Zarembka

State University of New York at Buffalo, USA

Recent Volumes:

Volume 34: Class History and Class Practices in the Periphery of Capitalism – Edited by P. Zarembka

Volume 35: The Capitalist Commodification of Animals – Edited by B. Clark and T. D. Wilson

Volume 36: Imperialism and Transitions to Socialism – Edited by R. Herrera

Volume 37: Polish Marxism after Luxemburg – Edited by J. Toporowski

Volume 38: Imperialism and the Political Economy of Global South's Debt – Edited by Ndongo Samba Sylla

Volume 39: Value, Money, Profit, and Capital Today – Edited by Rémy Herrera

Volume 40: Trajectories of Declining and Destructive Capitalism – Edited by Rémy Herrera

EDITORIAL ADVISORY BOARD

RESEARCH IN POLITICAL ECONOMY VOLUME 41

MONEY, VALUE AND MARX'S CIRCUIT OF CAPITAL

EDITED BY

GUIDO DE MARCO
Association for the Redistribution of Labour, Italy

AND

ALAN FREEMAN
University of Manitoba, Canada

emerald
PUBLISHING

United Kingdom – North America – Japan
India – Malaysia – China

Emerald Publishing Limited
Emerald Publishing, Floor 5, Northspring, 21-23 Wellington Street, Leeds LS1 4DL

First edition 2026

British Library Cataloguing in Publication Data
A catalogue record for this book is available from the British Library

ISBN: 978-1-83549-597-1 (Print)
ISBN: 978-1-83549-596-4 (Online)
ISBN: 978-1-83549-598-8 (Epub)

ISSN: 0161-7230 (Series)

Printed and bound by CPI Group (UK) Ltd, Croydon, CR0 4YY

CONTENTS

INTRODUCTION

Alan Freeman[a] and Guido De Marco[b]

[a]*University of Manitoba, Canada*
[b]*Association for the Redistribution of Labour, Italy*

ABSTRACT

This volume of Research in Political Economy *marks a new phase of scholarship in the theory of capitalism, defined by its focus on the reproduction of total social capital. This responds to a widely-felt need to end the divorce of political economy from real-world phenomena, notably financial crisis, long-term stagnation, poverty, inequality and economic injustice. To this end, this volume seeks a renewed pluralist dialogue involving all currents critical of neoclassical paradigm that dominates political economy, above all those that seek a departure from the equilibrium paradigm that permeates it. The basis for such an engagement is a common agreement that by studying the circuit of capital, fresh light can be shed on the basic concepts of money, price, value and credit by enquiring into their role in explaining capitalism's 'laws of motion'. These include accumulation, capitalism's historical origin and reproduction as such.*

Keywords: Capitalism; capital circuit; value; price; accumulation; social reproduction

This volume of *Research in Political Economy*[1] marks a new phase of scholarship in the theory of capitalism, defined by its focus on the reproduction of social capital. By publishing it, we respond to a widely-felt need (Morgan et al., 2015) to end the divorce of economics from real-world phenomena, notably financial crisis (Rochon and Rossi),[2] long-term stagnation (Freeman), and more widely poverty, inequality and economic injustice.

This divorce exposes, as Hahn puts it, something rotten in the state of economics; the time has come to excise it. This requires a forensic enquiry to identify those flaws in those basic concepts that are responsible for its empirical failures. To this end, this volume presents a new pluralist dialogue about value,

Money, Value and Marx's Circuit of Capital
Research in Political Economy, Volume 41, 1–10

Published under exclusive licence by Emerald Publishing Limited
ISSN: 0161-7230/doi:10.1108/S0161-723020260000041001

price, money and the circuit of capital. The ground for such an engagement is a common agreement that the study of reproduction will shed fresh light on these basic concepts by scrutinising their role in explaining capitalism's 'laws of motion', including accumulation (Timponelli), capitalism's historical origin (Mazzetti, Block) and reproduction as such (Kliman).

Such a focus constitutes a break with a discussion on Marx's theory of value and price, which has lasted over 60 years since Sraffa's (1962) landmark *Production of Commodities by Means of Commodities* and which rested on the earlier interpretation of this theory due to Bortkiewicz (1907). Following Sweezy's (1942) claim that Marx was a theorist of General Equilibrium (Ackerman et al., 2004; Bridel, 1997) and Morishima's (1973) integration of this interpretation into Japanese Marxism, it was adopted not just by Marx's critics but most of his academic supporters.[3]

The Bortkiewicz–Sweezy–Morishima interpretation, which thus became standard, holds that Marx, like Sraffa, defined values and prices as two distinct sets of ratios at which goods must exchange such that supply should exactly equal demand in a single period. This requires that values, prices and technology should remain constant during that period. Along with Sraffa's own system, it thus belongs to a wider family which we will here call 'single-period market-clearing' theories, dating back to Walras and found across the spectrum of economic theory.

We believe that the debate with and within the post-Sraffian tradition has proven sterile for reasons that Mazzetti and Timponelli convincingly dissect. Since the Cambridge Controversy (Harcourt, 1972), it has produced few if any new insights into the process of capitalist reproduction and has indeed diverted attention from a systematic discussion, as Timponelli notes, of how capitalism reproduces or accumulates.

This sterility arises from two defects in single-period market-clearing derivations of price and value. First, the assumptions in which they are grounded do not occur in the real world. Supply and demand do not equalise at any time; neither prices, nor values, nor technology remain constant over any appreciable interval; and neither prices nor values are determined in a single period. This difficulty cannot be wished away by describing such values and prices as approximations. Any such assertion has to be verified or disproved empirically, which compels us to study the second defect: as noted above, the results which flow from market-clearing assumptions do not correspond to the observable behaviour of capitalist societies. These systems predict the opposite of what happens: that money plays no role; that financial crises are impossible and that long-run declines in the return on capital either cannot occur (Okishio, 1961) or play no role in crisis (Heinrich, 2013).

Alternatives to the market-clearing paradigm have long formed a parallel universe within political economy: they include post-Keynesian, Evolutionary, Institutionalist and Austrian contributions (Chick et al., 2014). It is therefore supremely ironic that Marx, vehement critic of Say and pioneer of the theory of capitalist crisis, should be presented not just by detractors but by followers as just another equilibrium theorist. This one of many reasons for this volume's focus on developments in Marx scholarship that take a critical stance towards the standard interpretation.

A final problem is that devotees of single-period market-clearing, just like their neoclassical counterparts, universally adopt an anti-pluralist or 'monotheoretic' approach (Morgan et al. 2015; Fullbrook 2001, 2008) to scientific investigation: they deny that prices or values can be determined in any other way. This has trapped them in a cage of their own making; this volume charts a way out.

The earliest such ruptures examined the monetary character of Marx's treatment of the relation between value and price, resulting in a family of new approaches, which rejected the 'two-system' aspect of the standard reading but did not see it necessary to depart from its market-clearing assumptions. These innovations, which include Moseley, insisted that the value and price of every product is determined within a single process, including both the production of value and its realisation in monetary form, instead of separately, within two distinct equation systems.[4]

These criticisms led to a strand of scholarship known as the Temporal Single System Interpretation (TSSI) of Marx (Freeman & Carchedi, 1996; Kliman, 2007), which argued that the difficulties facing the standard interpretation arose not just from its treatment of price but from the market-clearing approach as such. Scholars pointed out that single-period equilibrium, as Bortkiewicz explicitly states, requires us to suppose that the whole product of society only becomes available at the end of the current period; in consequence, it must be consumed in the next. At what price is it sold? They argued, in common with Kaleckian scholars but for different reasons, that the 'output price' of goods at the end of the period should equal not the 'input price' of the same period but the input price of the next.

This volume presents a further development, which can be regarded as another way of approaching the market-clearing issue, developing out of studies of Marx's Volume II analysis of the circuit of capital. These radically invert the market-clearing problematic through a revived study of *turnover* (Moseley, 2019, and in this volume; De Marco, 2024). They oblige us to answer a primary question, as Tombazos explains, which has to be solved by any adequate theory of political economy: what do we require of our concepts of value, price and money if they are to explain both how capital reproduces, and why it fails to do so?

Both these responses from within Marx scholarship mesh with a crucial contribution from outside it: the notion of stock-flow consistency (SFC) (Godley and Lavoie, 2007), dating back to Morris Copeland's work on the flow of funds in the 1940s, brought to wider attention by Wynne Godley and subsequently developed within the post-Keynesian tradition. They also draw on circuit theory, pioneered by Graziani (1983, 1986) and discussed by Bellofiore and Covery in this volume.

All these contributions set, on a firmer logical foundation, a critical fact: commodities exist in the dual form of flows and stocks. SFC requires that these are properly reconciled; over any interval of time, every stock changes exactly by the difference between what flows into it and what flows out of it. SFC scholars thus sought to eliminate the 'black holes' of neoclassical macroeconomics, within which money simply disappears in the transition from one period to the next. Marx's analysis of turnover in Volume II,[5] which deserves recognition as the earliest formulation of SFC, applies this as an integrated principle not just to money but, as Freeman notes, to use-value or so-called 'physical quantity' and crucially, to value.

The principle that capital enters production in the first instance as a stock emerged from Marx's critique of the apologetic role of 'fixed capital' in the political economy of his day, where it purported to describe a 'factor' of production that the capitalists supplied, justifying their profits.[6] It was critical to his account of classes, to which Volume III is devoted, which he defines not, as Sraffian analysis suggests, by the flow of income to which they are entitled but by ownership of a stock which confers this entitlement, which has no place in Sraffa's system.

The classes of capitalist society are not confined to factory-owners but extend to merchants, money-dealers, financiers, capitalist landlords, rentiers and not least monopolists. Competition between them, arising from the movement of capital driven by both technical change and price movements in search of surplus or above-average profit (Marx, 1981, p. 142), is a chaotic process which forms a general profit rate from the incessant divergences and convergences of individual profit rates; as a result, classes which own value from which nothing is produced nevertheless appropriate shares of surplus value produced elsewhere. As Balardini notes, the resulting account of rent runs directly counter to the theory of 'technofeudalism'; in general, the appropriation of surplus by non-producing classes is the key to the morbid emergence of parasitic financial classes described by Rochon and Rossi.

The question which then immediately arises is 'What is capital a stock of?' For Marx, the answer, not unexpectedly, is 'a stock of value'. However, this answer cannot be grasped without noting that for Marx, value is always outwardly expressed as a sum of money (Ramos, 1995; Ramos & Rodriguez, 1996). The question then arising, namely 'how does a sum of money come to represent a quantity of labour time?', is a preoccupation of all contributions to this volume, arguably the most important.

As noted, this question is cast in a new light when approached via the circuit of capital. In this volume as Tombazos notes, Marx in Volume II studies not one but three circuits: the circuit of commodities, of production and of money. Bellofiore and Coveri, taking inspiration from the Graziani (1983, 1986), argue, as does Moseley, for a macro-monetary reconstruction of Marx's value theory of labour, pointing to Part 7 of *Capital* Volume I in which Marx views capitalist reproduction as a monetary circuit. De Marco, critiquing the place which Graziani assigns to credit, argues that Marx viewed the money capital circuit as the most suitable for analysing the reproduction of individual capitals but inadequate for understanding the reproduction of total social capital. The commodity circuit, he argues, 'plays a pivotal role in Marx's account of the overall accumulation process as well as the connected problem of the monetisation of expanded reproduction'.

A focus on stocks has afforded Marx scholars a fresh look at Volume II of *Capital*, where he enquires how production interacts with circulation in such a way that the goods it requires are always on hand. Stocks of commodities arise because, in order to enter production, a definite amount of each good must be at the disposal of the producer. This amount varies with its physical characteristics, how it is used and how circulation delivers it to the ultimate consumer. Some goods, such as machinery and buildings, are purchased in their entirety before being set to work, the money advanced for them being the owner's 'fixed constant capital'.

However, the same consideration also applies to raw materials, which Marx terms the owner's 'circulating constant capital'. Notwithstanding the appearance that such materials constitute a pure flow, actually a definite mass of each must be owned by the capitalist – for example the iron required to make steel, the fibres required to make cloth or the grains required to make bread – before flowing into production. Moreover, the resulting goods – the steel, the fabric or the finished articles of clothing – also form stocks, awaiting sale or 'realization', as they emerge from production. Whether these are physically stockpiled by the supplier or the user is immaterial, we are studying total social reproduction. These stocks are, hence, an integral part of production.

However, matters do not stop there. Maintaining them in existence obliges the capitalist (De Marco, 2023; Veronese Passarella & Baron, 2015) to maintain hoards of money, a phenomenon which Marx studies at length in Volume II of *Capital*. Here, he shows how the owner must always set aside a definite part of his sales receipts as a fund from which to renew stocks, forming a hoard – aka working capital. Turnover time links the two. Thus at least in part, money hoards arise directly from the requirements of production.

This does not contradict the fact that money hoards also arise outside production, in circulation itself: this is the most familiar form in which political economy encounters them. As Marx and Keynes both insisted in their criticism of their predecessors and contemporaries, commodities do not exchange for each other but for money. This may, or may not, be exchanged for other commodities. It cannot be assumed, as required by one-period market-clearing equation systems, that all produced goods are sold.

Thus unless money is used to fund consumption, whether productive or personal, it accumulates either as mere currency, or as interest-bearing assets, or as other objects whose rising prices yield speculative capital gains. This accounts for the recurrent financial crises that have afflicted capitalism from its birth. Yet hoards in circulation cannot possibly appear if markets are assumed to clear; they are the *expression* of a failure to clear. This is the forensic reason for the explanatory failure of the restrictive assumptions which the standard interpretation wrongly pins on Marx.

Nor is this all. Though speculative frenzies arising from the unchecked growth of idle money hoards account for the mechanism of crisis, it remains to explain how this mechanism is called into action, why its workings become intractable at certain definite stages in capitalist history and why, at other times such as the expansive phases for which capitalism is famed among its worshippers, finance serves more as a catalyst for, than an impediment to, investment.[7]

This problem cannot be tackled by supposing either depressions or booms to be automatic. They are the product of definite historical circumstances integral to capitalism's evolution and which have to be identified. Yet within neoclassical economics, we find a lack of explanation verging on denial. Its apologetic character is incarnated in the concept of equilibrium itself, which inexorably and logically predicts that stagnation cannot arise from within a market system. It can and does, and the question we face is what to do about it.

Among the critics of neoclassical economics, we find two broad, general types of explanation. The first is the idea that capitalism is in some sense incapable of reproducing itself indefinitely – that growth itself creates irreconcilable gaps between what is produced and what is consumed. While the existence of such gaps is undeniable, questions surround their persistence, tractability and causes. A spectrum of views range from Samuelson's claim that all such disparities can be managed to the catastrophism of *Zussammenbruch* theory first advanced by Luxemburg in opposition to Bernstein's reformism and most fully developed by Grossman, addressed by Kliman in this volume.

A second idea is that stagnation arises not from reproduction in general but accumulation in particular. Though Volume II of *Capital* shows that a mismatch between production and consumption is always possible, Volume III introduces a new element: the profit rate, motor of accumulation. Why should capitalists invest at all? In search of profit. But if production ceases to yield a greater profit than mere speculation, why invest in it?

Marx's analysis centres on his theory that surplus value is a deduction from the value created by labour, transformed by the price system into profit. What happens to this profit? A part is consumed by the capitalists. Marx's well-known analysis of 'Simple Reproduction' addresses the special case where the capitalists consume the whole surplus. But under Expanded Reproduction, he studies the more general case in which the remainder is used to purchase additional means of production and hire additional labour power, upon which production resumes on a larger scale: accumulation.

What then happens to the total capital of society? It is at this point that the transition problem rears up. The answer suggested by Freeman is that total capital grows by an amount exactly equal to the value of the unconsumed surplus. This offers the simplest possible proof of Marx's explanation for the observed long declines in the average rate of profit: the employed labour force, hence new value, surplus value and thereby the mass of profit is at worse stable and at best proceeds more slowly than accumulation: the return on capital therefore declines until and unless it is overcome by offsetting forces. Accumulation, in short, negates itself.

As Chick and Freeman (2018) note (see also Desai & Freeman, 2009), Marx and Keynes shared a recognition of this fact, which led to Keynes' call for the 'euthanasia of the rentier' and the 'comprehensive socialisation of investment'. Yet the published text of the *General Theory* pays only nodding acknowledgement to Marx, his most obvious predecessor in the scathing critique of Say's Law with which the *General Theory* opens. The resulting lack of engagement between Keynesians and Marxists is every day less functional in a multipolar world. It is, we suggest, a further casualty of a sterile half-century during which equilibrium thinking has imprisoned them in adjoining concentration camps.

The benefits of a focus on the study of reproduction becomes clearer when we dissect the most common critique of Marx's Law of the Tendency of the Rate of Profit to Fall, initiated by Moszkowska and popularised by Joan Robinson,[8] who argue that the magnitude of capital falls at the same rate as output because the price of its components have fallen, offsetting the effects of accumulation.

Robinson commits a trivial error which SFC makes clear (Freeman, 2000): capital advanced is not equal to the current price of the owner's assets but the sum of advances made in the past. Of course, a business may write these assets down to their replacement value, but the written-down value does not disappear into a Godleyan black hole; it is deducted from profits. The difference exactly accounts for the difference between Marx's profit rate and Robinson's.

A subsidiary difficulty, discussed by Ekeland, is that because capital grows faster than the rate at which new value is created, expanded accumulation can only take place if their proportions – Marx's 'Organic Composition' – also grow. In addition as noted, the unconsumed surplus may remain idle. These considerations, however, do not negate the overriding fact that all unconsumed profit necessarily adds to the total stock of capital. The historical law that capital grows without limit unless and until interrupted or offset by some larger processes, such as crisis, war, imperialism, or other forms of state intervention, is hence a simple logical consequence of accumulation.

Does this lead to the catastrophic conclusion that this process is inevitable? If so, the reasoning must be false, since long phases of stagnation have been reversed at least three times in the past, the two most recent occurring after the Great Depressions of 1870 and 1929. Indeed, the wartime recovery of 1942–1945 spectacularly restored the US profit rate to its highest historical level ever, as well as those of the other Western countries. A complete explanation must account for this reversal, taking into consideration the historical changes that also affected state interventions.

In sketching the basis for such a complete explanation we face a final ghost, which Freeman addresses in proposing that the laws of reproduction, production and accumulation should be formulated in continuous time and which Moseley (2016) addresses by uncovering a further and decisive difference between the post-Sraffian and Marx's treatment of turnover. This is the entire notion that reproduction consists of the *alternation* of production and exchange, which underlies the Walrasian conception – eagerly seized on by von Bortkiewicz, as Timponelli notes – that the entire product of a period is exchanged at the end of the period.

The problem is that this period is imaginary. Actually, products are exchanged throughout the period in tandem with their production, as Marx clearly recognises when he analyses turnover not as something that every capital repeats once a year for all the world like a team of synchronised swimmers but as something which each component of each individual capital passes through in its own time and at its own pace.

The notion of synchronised alternation lies at the heart of the single-period market-clearing construction, compelling its users to suppose (as they do) that during each such imaginary period neither price, value nor technology changes until the climactic instant of transition when all products are exchanged. In parallel, synchronised equal-time turnover abolishes the distinction between stocks and flows, causing Sraffian and Walrasian theory to become stock-flow inconsistent by ignoring the transition from each period to the next. This inconsistency is then transmitted from microeconomists to macroeconomists without passing through the mind of either.

A correction to this fiction radically challenges the assumption that transformation takes place in time. Goods possess prices and values at all times; a car rolling off the assembly line immediately acquires its price and its value not when it is exchanged for money but when it becomes available for sale with a money price – that is, when it joins the general social stock of similar cars, of which it is just one part. In Marx's own analysis of transformation, both the value of each product and its price of production are established when it emerges from production, not when that production commences. Though this relation evolves over time, at each point in time it is a relation between two expressions of a single thing.

This insight re-opens the closed door to a genuinely *political* economy; recoveries from long stagnations were not automatic but the historical result of definite political events. Only by grasping the economic causes of the present great depression may the political solutions be identified.

NOTES

1. A forthcoming colloquium in the *World Review of Political Economy* will include papers regretfully omitted for reasons of space.
2. Where no publication date is given, it is to be understood that the referenced work is in this volume.
3. Freeman (2020) provides a complete account of the standard interpretation. Kliman (2007) introduced the term 'Simultaneous Dual-System' to describe this interpretation.
4. See the New Interpretation advanced by Foley (1982) and independently by Duménil (1983) and the 'Simultaneous Single-System' (SSS) theory of Wolff, Callari and Roberts (1982).
5. See Bryer (2017) for a systematic exposition of the consistency of Marx's accounting.
6. It is worth recalling that the *Grundrisse* consists in essence of just two chapters: on Money and on Capital.
7. See Desai (2020).
8. See Freeman (2000).

REFERENCES

Ackerman, F., Nadal, A., Benetti, C., Gallagher, K. P., & Salas, C. (2004). *The flawed foundations of general equilibrium*. Routledge.

von Bortkiewicz, L. (1907). On the correction of Marx's fundamental theoretical construction in the third volume of capital. 1984. In P. Sweezy (Ed.), *Karl Marx and the close of his system*. Orion Editions.

Bridel, P. (1997). *Money and general equilibrium theory: From Walras to Pareto, 1870–1923*. Edward Elgar.

Bryer, R. (2017). *Accounting for value in Marx's capital: The invisible hand*. Lexington Books.

Chick, V., & Freeman, A. (2018). The economics of enough: A future for capitalism or a new way of living? In Dow, S., J. Jespersen, & G. Tily. *Money, method and post-Keynesian economics for the 21st century*. Edward Elgar.

De Marco, G. (2023). Marx's general rate of profit: How turnover time, accumulation and rate of surplus value affect the formation of prices of production. *Capital & Class*, *48*(4).

De Marco, G. (2024). Turnover time and Marx's decomposition of profit adjustment in the process of equalization. *Research in Political Economy*, *39*, 145–165.

Desai, R. (2020). Finance capital and contemporary financialisation. In Delheim, J. & F. O. Wolff (Eds.), *Rudolf* Hilferding: What do we still Have to Learn from his legacy? (pp. 155–183).

Duménil, G. (1983). Beyond the transformation riddle: A labor theory of value. *Science and Society*, *47*, 4.

Foley, D. (1982). The value of money, the value of labour-power and the Marxian transformation problem. *RRPE*, *14*, 2.

Freeman, A. (2000). *Marxian debates on the falling rate of profit – A primer*. https://www.academia.edu/6997022/Marxian_Debates_on_the_Falling_Rate_of_Profit_-_a_primer

Freeman, A. (2020). What was Marx's method, actually? In Chick, V. & J. Jesperson (Eds.), *Handbook of macro methodology*. Routledge.

Freeman, A., & Carchedi, G. (Eds.). (1996). *Marx and non-equilibrium economics*. Edward Elgar.

Freeman, A., Chick, V., & Kayatekin, S. (2014). Whig History and the Reinterpretation of economic history. *Cambridge Journal of Economics*, *38*(3).

Fullbrook, E. (2001). Real Science is pluralist; An Argument for pluralism in economics. *Post-Autistics Economics Network*, 5.

Fullbrook, E. (2008). *Pluralist economics*. Zed Books Ltd.

Godley, W., & Lavoie, M. (2007). *Monetary economics: An integrated approach to credit, money, income, production and wealth*. Palgrave Macmillan.

Graziani, A. (1983). Let's rehabilitate the theory of value. *International Journal of Political Economy*, *27*(2), 21–25.

Graziani, A. (1986). The Marxist theory of money. *International Journal of Political Economy*, *27*(2), 26–50.

Harcourt, G. C. (1972). *Some Cambridge controversies in the theory of capital*. Cambridge University Press.

Heinrich, M. (2013). Crisis theory, the law of the tendency of the profit rate to fall, and Marx's studies in the 1870s. *Monthly Review*, *64*(11).

Kliman, A. (2007). *Reclaiming Marx's capital: A refutation of the myth of inconsistency*. Lexington Books.

Marx, K. (1981). *Capital volume III*. Penguin.

Morgan, J.(coordinator), Philp, B., Cronin, B., Bigo, V., Chick, V., Desai, R., Ekeland, A., Freeman, A., Hermann, A., Lee, F., Mearman, A., Negru, I., Olsen, W., Reardon, J., & Wells, J. (2015). *Pluralism, Heterodoxy, and the prospects for a new economics curriculum: Assessing the potential of INET, What's the use of economics, and the CORE project*. AHE.

Morishima, M. (1973). *Marx's economics: A dual theory of value and growth*. Cambridge University Press.

Moseley, F. (2016). *Money and totality. A macro-monetary interpretation of Marx's logic in capital and the end of the "Transformation Problem"*. Brill.

Moseley, F. (2019). Marx's economic manuscript of 1867-1868 (excerpt) editor's introduction. *Historical Materialism*, *27*(4), 145–156.

Okishio, N. (1961). Technical changes and the rate of profit. *Kobe University Economic Review*, *7*, 85–99.

Ramos, A. (1995). *The monetary expression of labour: Marx's twofold measure of value*. Mini-conference of the International Working Group on Value Theory (IWGVT) at the Eastern Economic Association. http://copejournal.com/wp-content/uploads/2017/02/Ramos-The-Monetary-Expression-of-Labour-Marxs-Twofold-Measure-of-Value.pdf

Ramos, A., & Rodriguez, A. (1996). The transformation of values into prices of production: A different reading of Marx's text. In A. Freeman & G. Carchedi (Eds.), *Marx and non-equilibrium economics* (pp. 49–76). Edward Elgar.

Sraffa, P. (1962). *Production of commodities by means of commodities*. Cambridge University Press.
Sweezy, P. M. (1942). *The theory of capitalist development: Principles of Marxian political economy*. Modern Reader Paperbacks.
Sweezy, P. M. (1949 [1984]). *Karl Marx and the close of his system*. Orion Editions.
Veronese Passarella, M., & Baron, H. (2015). Capital's humpback bridge: "Financialisation" and the rate of turnover in Marx's economic theory. *Cambridge Journal of Economics*, *39*, 1415–1441.
Wolff, R., Roberts, B., & Callari, A. (1982). Marx's (not Ricardo's) "Transformation Problem": A radical reconceptualization. *History of Political Economy*, *14*, 4.

MONEY, VALUE AND CAPITAL CIRCULATION IN A FINANCE-LED ECONOMIC REGIME

Louis-Philippe Rochon[a] and Sergio Rossi[b]

[a]*Laurentian University, Canada*
[b]*University of Fribourg, Switzerland*

ABSTRACT

This chapter focuses on the circuit of capital in financialized economic systems, where the role played by financial markets, financial institutions and financial motives is a major factor of systemic crises, so much so that there exists a shadow banking system formed by non-bank financial institutions that are less regulated than traditional banks. The first section explains the circuit of money, emphasizing the seminal role of banks in opening credit lines to any kinds of borrowers. The second section expands on this, pointing out the distinction between productive and non-productive bank loans, as the latter inflate a series of credit bubbles that are problematic for both employment and financial stability on macroeconomic grounds. The third section suggests some policy reforms to avoid an unproductive circuit of capital across the global economy, focusing on monetary as well as fiscal policies to reduce financial instability and unemployment, with a view also to support a 'green' circuit of capital.

Keywords: Credit bubbles; financial circulation; financial crises; money and banking

INTRODUCTION

Contemporary capitalism has evolved into a chaotic and disorderly working economic system, characterized by the frequent bursting of financial crises that have a systemic dimension, thereby negatively affecting the whole economy – also at global level. For example, the US subprime bubble that inflated during

Money, Value and Marx's Circuit of Capital
Research in Political Economy, Volume 41, 11–25

ISSN: 0161-7230/doi:10.1108/S0161-723020260000041003

the early 2000s – which burst in 2007, giving rise to the global financial crisis – is the result of banks' provision of huge volumes of mortgage loans to insolvent people: US banks as well as non-bank financial institutions profited from this bubble in so far as they collected fees and interest income from their borrowers until the subprime market collapsed, showing thereby the financial fragility of capitalist speculation.[1] To be sure, as a matter of fact, in the current finance-led capitalist regime, all types of mortgages can be 'packaged' into securities that have different risk categories, with different prices reflecting the risk associated with their underlying mortgages. Investors can thus choose the risk–return combination that suits them best. Financial institutions can thereby earn sizeable commission fees for issuing securities based on these mortgage loans or for pricing their own risks. Stock market operators can then sell different securities based on these mortgages, fragmented and put together as best suits them to meet the demand of investors seeking the desired combination of risk and return. Thus, instead of excluding the poor and minorities from the lucrative market for mortgage loans, the securitization of these mortgages helped to make the opening of credit lines for homeownership apparently more democratic in the US economy.

Securitization also reflected two further developments related to the financialization of economic activities in the United States and other Western countries. On the one hand, it was an element in the process of financial globalization, as it created financial assets free of any national barriers. For instance, German investors with no connection to real estate owners in the United States could buy a part of these assets on the securitization market. These securities, which were 'packaged' with a degree of risk assigned to them by rating agencies, appeared attractive to investors that were looking for a relevant share of US dollar-denominated financial assets in the global economy. In this way, the US subprime mortgage default problems quickly became global problems, starting with a German bank (IKB) that had to be rescued in July 2007, followed by various problems encountered by BNP Paribas (the largest bank in France) in August of the same year, through to the bank run on Northern Rock in the United Kingdom in September 2007, and the extraordinary write-offs made in Switzerland by both UBS and Credit Suisse for billion-dollar losses in 2007 and also in the years following the bankruptcy of Lehman Brothers, an investment bank in the United States that announced its insolvency on 15 September 2008, thereby triggering a global financial crisis.

This chapter focuses on the structural disorder that originates when banks provide loans for so-called 'non-GDP-based transactions' (Werner, 2011, p. 29), that is to say, for financial market activities that produce no new income for the economy as a whole. For instance, when a bank opens a credit line to a non-bank financial institution (such as an insurance company or a hedge fund) in order for the latter to purchase financial assets, this gives rise to a higher volume of debt in the banking system, without an equivalent amount of newly-produced income, which is necessary to repay all this debt eventually. The circuit of financial capital can thereby expand without any endogenous limit, as the inflating debt bubble does not give rise to any corresponding inflationary pressure in the market for produced goods and services – where central bankers and national statistical offices do measure inflation (see Rossi, 2001 for a critique of such a monetary policy framework).

The next section explains the circuit of money, emphasizing the seminal role of banks in opening credit lines to any kinds of borrowers. The third section expands on this issue, pointing out the distinction between productive and non-productive bank loans, as the latter inflate a series of credit bubbles that are problematic for both employment and financial stability on macroeconomic grounds. The fourth section suggests some policy reforms to avoid an unproductive circuit of capital across the global economy, focusing on monetary as well as fiscal policies to reduce financial instability and unemployment, with a view also to supporting a 'green' circuit of capital. The last section concludes, summarizing the main arguments of this chapter on both theoretical and policy-oriented grounds from a political economy perspective.

THE CIRCUIT OF MONEY AND THE ROLE OF BANKS

The circuit of money begins when a bank opens a credit line to any kind of creditworthy borrowers because banks are special as they can provide loans without disposing of any pre-existent deposits: as Schumpeter (1954, pp. 1110–1117) famously noticed, for banks 'loans make deposits'. This is the fundamental essence of money's endogeneity in the economic system, as monetary circuit theorists have explained cogently (see Graziani, 1990, 1994; Parguez, 1975; Parguez & Seccareccia, 2000; Schmitt, 1959, 1960, for example).

The endogenous nature of money is logical, considering that the first deposit recorded in a bank cannot but be the result of a loan granted by any kind of banks. The circuit of bank deposits has indeed a positive duration in chronological time, from the moment the deposit is created within the banking system to the moment when this deposit is spent, allowing the payee to repay his debt to the bank that granted him a credit line. This amounts to saying that money and income are two different magnitudes: banks create money, but income (which exists in the form of bank deposits) must be produced. Hence, rather than assuming the existence of bank deposits, one must explain how it is possible for bank deposits to exist. This implies the payment of wages, in what Keynes (1933) cogently called a monetary economy of production, that is to say, an economic system where money is essential to produce, not just to consume (as it is assumed in mainstream economics, where money is supposed to intervene in order to avert the double-coincidence-of-wants constraint). In fact, as Lavoie (1984, p. 774) points out, '[m]oney is introduced into the economy through the productive activities of the firms, as these activities generate income. There can be no money without production'. Schumpeter (1954, p. 278) also argued that money must be introduced on the 'very ground floor of our analytic structure', which he labelled a 'monetary economy'.

Since the end of the 1980s, however, a relevant number of bank loans have been granted for 'non-GDP-based transactions' (Werner, 2011, p. 29) as we explained above. These loans inflate the 'final finance' phase of the monetary circuit as a result of an array of financial speculations that do not produce an income in the whole economic system. To be sure, income is always and everywhere the result of production through the payment of wage bills because only labour is truly a macroeconomic factor of production – as Keynes (1936, pp. 213–214) clearly explained when he also pointed out that output is measured in wage units on economic grounds. As a result, monetary profit (that is, the remuneration of capital) is an income derived from wages, when these wages are spent in the market for produced goods and services, thereby transforming an income into its 'real content'. Nominal wages (to wit, the number of wage units earned by workers, W) are thereby transformed into real wages, w (namely, consumption goods) and profits, π, which exist in both a real and a monetary form, since there is an unsold output as well as an amount of bank deposits that define these two forms of firms' profits (see Cencini & Rossi, 2023 for analytical elaboration on this subject matter). Income distribution in the market for produced goods and services can therefore be written as follows:

$$W = w + \pi$$

In this framework, capital exists either in the form of bank deposits that are saved (this is the financial capital recorded by banks) or in the form of machines and equipment that are the result of firms' investment (this is the fixed capital recorded by firms). The circuit of capital concerns therefore financial capital, since fixed capital is fixed forever into those capital goods that firms use to produce any kind of goods or services. By way of contrast, financial capital can always be transformed back into an income that his/her holder then spends to purchase either produced output, real-estate or financial assets. In so far as financial capital exists in the form of a bank deposit, it can thereby circulate in financial markets, giving rise to asset bubbles that banks can inflate providing any credit lines they consider profitable for them, even though these bank loans do not generate an income for the economy as a whole. Let us turn to this issue in the next section.

FINANCIAL CIRCULATION AND CREDIT BUBBLES

Financial circulation and credit bubbles have been investigated to a large extent – even before the global financial crisis burst in 2008 – by a number of heterodox economists (see for instance Epstein, 2005; Forges Davanzati & Tortorella Esposito, 2010; Guttmann, 2008, 2009; Passarella, 2014; Seccareccia, 2012–2013, and more recently Tori et al., 2023). The circuit of financial capital does not and cannot produce any new income within the economic system as a whole: when an economic agent spends a bank deposit across the financial markets, s/he just transfers the property right of this deposit to the seller of any kind of financial assets. Financial transactions are indeed a zero-sum game: the income spent by the purchaser of financial assets is transferred to the seller of these assets, who obtains thereby a claim on some bank deposits. However, if the purchase of these assets is financed with a credit line granted by a bank to (say) a non-bank financial institution, this ('non-GDP-based') transaction gives rise to a new deposit to which no new output (that is, gross domestic product, GDP) corresponds. As a result, there is a higher volume of bank deposits, but no higher amount of income in the whole economic system. This 'empty money' (Schmitt, 2021, p. 123) is spent across financial markets, giving rise to 'asset price inflation' that central banks have been ignoring before the global financial crisis burst in 2008 (see Colander, 2015), even though this phenomenon can affect final goods prices as a result of commodity price speculation induced by a loose credit policy (see, for instance, Keen, 2015).

In fact, central banks themselves have been contributing to inflate many asset prices and thereby credit bubbles both before and after the bursting of the global financial crisis. In this regard, we identify three important ways. First, this is clearly the result of inflation targeting strategies, as the latter have been focusing on the rate of inflation measured in the market for produced goods and services, thereby neglecting (or even ignoring) asset price inflation, particularly across financial markets as a result of loose credit strategies banks implemented to maximize their profits as explained above. Secondly, policy rates of interest have been allowing banks to lend at very low interest rates huge volumes of money to their peers as well as to different non-bank financial institutions, particularly after the major national central banks intervened to avoid that systemically relevant banks (or so-called 'too big to fail' financial institutions) go bankrupt. In this regard, quantitative easing (QE) is the third way in which central banks have contributed to asset price inflation: by providing enormous amounts of liquidity (in the form of central bank money) to these financial institutions, they have been inducing a mushroom growth of asset prices since banks and non-bank financial institutions have been spending much of this liquidity across financial markets to buy a variety of assets in order to maximize their profits in spite of the financial crisis and its negative effects on the so-called 'real economy'. For sure, the primary effect of QE is a structural change in the composition of banks' balance sheets: their settlement balances (once upon a time called 'reserves') increase while their volume of financial assets (mainly government bills and bonds) decreases. The higher volume of 'reserves' induces banks to purchase more financial assets, whose demand increases therefore considerably as a consequence of the central banks' balance sheet expansion. The latter makes banks more fragile and pushes them to inflate a variety of credit bubbles in light of their central bank's implicit guarantee of a bail-out in case a financial crisis occurs (see Rossi, 2023).

To be sure, central banks have become independent of governments but are clearly depending on banks, as the latter cannot be left alone when they are close to failure, so that central banks must intervene as a lender of last resort, which is tantamount to 'privatizing the profits and socializing the losses' of any banking institutions – as also the smallest banks follow the leaders' strategies, so much so that all banks are very interconnected across the interbank market: even a failure of a small bank can thereby impact negatively many other banks, giving rise thereby to a systemic banking crisis that central banks must avoid necessarily (see Rossi, 2022 for analytical elaboration).

Hence, before 2008 financial circulation inflated because central banks ignored asset price inflation, while after the bursting of the global financial crisis central banks reduced their policy rates of interest at historically very low (if not negative) levels, inducing thereby banks to increase their lending volumes for unproductive transactions (see in this regard Panzera, 2015; Rossi, 2019). In both these cases, the circuit of financial capital has been expanding in a number of so-called 'advanced' economies, creating thereby many problems for a variety of stakeholders, particularly for the low- and middle-class people who are willing and able to work, but who are involuntarily unemployed since firms have been reducing both output and employment levels in light of a lack of demand in the market for produced goods and services. These problems are indeed the result of financialization, that is to say, the prevailing importance of financial motives, financial markets and financial institutions when firms decide and implement their business strategies, thereby centred on satisfying first and foremost the interests of these institutions (namely, banks, pension funds, insurance companies and so forth) and of their major shareholders (see Rochon & Tropeano, 2025).

For instance, a firm listed in a stock-exchange market will have to record an increasing profit (both as a total and as a percentage of its business volume) in order for it to be in a position to obtain more financial capital. If this capital were to be invested to purchase machines and equipment (fixed capital) or to finance some research and development activities, this would not be a problem: indeed, it could support economic growth and induce an increase in the level of employment, thereby reducing unemployment across the whole economic system. However, since the late 1980s, financialization has been increasingly affecting this system, exerting a downward pressure on production costs (particularly on labour costs) in order to maximize profits and thereby attract a further volume of financial capital, which has been parked into financial markets because no profitable investment in fixed capital will occur if there is already an excess capacity, owing to excess supply in the market for produced goods and services resulting from the downward pressure on labour costs (hence on wages for the middle-class people). Such a situation can then originate an overproduction (or underconsumption) crisis that eventually affects a variety of stakeholders, including firms and financial institutions at both national and global level.

Now, if listed firms' strategies are dictated by financialization, then also other firms will have to follow similar business strategies even though the latter firms are not listed in a stock-exchange market. This is so because non-listed firms must be competitive against listed firms in the same market segment: if a small non-listed firm wants to sell its own goods or services at a competitive price, it must reduce its own production costs (hence, it must exert a downward pressure on the wages it pays, if not reduce its labour force) in an attempt to keep its market share and thereby earn its expected profits. This is even so much so that non-listed firms must obtain bank loans to finance their production activity whereas listed firms can collect funds across the capital market. In this regard, banks – which are a major player in finance-led economic regimes – want also to maximize their own profits by increasing the spread between their lending rates of interest and the rates of interest they pay to depositors. As a result of these two 'exogenous' forces, unlisted firms must compel and follow listed firms' business strategy as well as banks' pressure to be competitive through a reduction of their own productions costs and hence the level of their workers' remuneration and sometimes also the level of employment eventually.

On the other hand, that is, across financial markets, financialization induces a relevant increase in asset prices, namely, the prices of the financial assets that firms issued and sold in order for them to obtain the financial capital they need either to invest (thereby transforming it into fixed capital) or to park on these markets, where they want to earn financial rents according to the short-term expectations of major financial institutions. In this regard, too, firms implement their business strategies first and foremost to sell a volume of produced goods and services that allows them to maximize their profits so as to pay an ever-increasing dividend to their shareholders, including the firms' managers. As a result, the wage share could remain broadly unchanged, but its components can be much affected, in the sense that managers' compensations increase while the bottom of the firms' hierarchy must accept a reduction of their own wages (which is, indeed, what is spent in the market for produced goods and services, as famously noticed by Kalecki; see in this regard Robinson, 1979).

Such a situation also inflates private debt bubbles across those economies (notably the United States) where consumption expenditures are financed by consumers' debt rather than through an income earned by these economic agents. In the US case, for instance, a series of debt bubbles have been inflating since the advent of financialization, notably as regards the real-estate market (recall the so-called subprime crisis that burst in 2007) but also regarding both consumers' and students' loans – even though these two bubbles, to date, have not exploded yet. All this further increases the financial fragility of a number of economic agents (debtors as well as creditors), thereby also affecting the stability of the economic system as a whole eventually.

The discussion above raises important questions about the role of central banks as well as about non-productive bank loans regarding income and wealth inequality across the domestic economy. The next section focuses on these issues with a view to reorient the circuit of capital in the general interest for the common good.

REORIENTING THE CIRCUIT OF CAPITAL FOR THE COMMON GOOD

The analysis presented in the previous sections shows the importance to make sure that the circuit of capital contributes to the common good instead of generating income and wealth inequalities so much so since it has been destabilizing the economic system as a whole through a series of financial crises that have a systemic dimension. Even though history shows that inequalities and wage earners' exploitation existed also in capitalist economies before their financialization occurred, it is possible to avoid at least that the banking system contributes to these social and economic issues. A political economy approach is necessary in this regard, considering the contribution of a policy mix that focuses on the needs of all stakeholders within contemporary capitalism, particularly wage earners and future generations of economic agents confronted with a series of troublesome climate changes. Let us expand on this in the remainder of this chapter.

First, monetary policy strategies and decisions should consider their distributive effects, as regards, in particular, the policy rates of interest. Rather than just focusing on the rate of measured inflation across the market for produced goods and services, the decisions to increase or decrease the policy rates of interest must take into account their impacts on both debtors and creditors across the banking sector and more generally speaking, within the whole financial system, where also non-bank financial institutions have been increasing their business volumes since the advent of financialization. For instance, any increase in the policy rates of interest – meant to reduce inflationary pressures across the goods market – is likely to give rise to further increases of the price level in this market, as firms will have to pay higher rates of interest when they borrow from banks, thereby transferring this higher cost to their selling prices. This is indeed the so-called 'Gibson paradox' (see Levrero, 2023). Further, increasing the policy rates of interest in different steps (as it occurred across Western economies in 2022 and 2023, in the aftermath of the Russian invasion of Ukraine and the resulting increases in the measured price level) can induce some negative wealth effects within the economic system: homeowners who did obtain a mortgage loan that must be renegotiated could have some troubles in doing so – particularly if meanwhile they have been losing their job – and in any case will have to pay higher rates of interest to renew their mortgage loan, thereby possibly reducing their consumption expenditures, which could have a negative impact on employment across the whole economic system. Moreover, generally speaking, these monetary policy hikes induce a downward pressure on real-estate prices, which further reduces the propensity to consume of homeowners, as they consider to be less rich in this regard, even though they are not going to sell their real-estate object. This monetary policy stance could also induce a number of banks and non-bank financial institutions to increase their lending to carry out 'non-GDP-based transactions' (Werner, 2011, p. 29), notably across financial markets, where lenders (as well as borrowers, in several cases) do expect to earn higher profits compared with the (reduced) expected profitability of investment in fixed capital in the so-called 'real economy'. As a matter of fact, it is well known that the most-risky businesses, like financial speculation, attract a relevant share of bank loans since both banks and financial speculators expect to maximize their own profits thereby. This is so much so when central banks increase their policy rates of interest: banks do increase the lending rates of interest so that an increasing number of small- and medium-sized firms reduce their borrowing volumes in light of the lower profitability of their investment in fixed capital goods. As a result, a problematic vicious circle inflates credit bubbles and asset prices across the financial system, where the circulation of financial capital can be profitable for financial institutions but problematic for a number of firms as well as for the majority of wage earners, particularly among the middle and lower classes of people willing and able to work, who suffer for both income distribution and capital allocation in a finance-led economic regime (see Rochon & Vallet, 2022).

Now, in light of the distributional impacts of the policy rates of interest (see Kappes et al., 2023), central banks should use the latter instrument in a much more targeted way, considering also that an interest rate policy must contribute to address climate changes in an appropriate way (Rochon, 2022 argues that to date monetary policies are carbon-biased). For instance, policy rates of interest could be differentiated in light of banks' financing 'green' or 'brown' economic activities, that is, climate-friendly or climate-damaging transactions across either the real or the financial sector of the economic system (see Solari et al., 2024). As a matter of fact, this approach has recently gained mainstream acceptance, as an increasing number of central banks (such as the Bank of England) are openly discussing the possibility of committing to environmental targets (see Network of Central Banks and Supervisors for Greening the Financial System, 2021). Indeed, this could easily be implemented by the European Central Bank, which since 2014 has been carrying out several Targeted Long-Term Refinancing Operations (TLTROs) to support real economic activity after the bursting of the euro area crisis in 2009: green TLTROs can induce the banking sector as a whole to increase its lending more for climate-friendly activities than for climate-damaging ones, particularly in a period when interest rates are increasing owing to several geopolitical tensions across the global economy (see van't Klooster & van Tilburg, 2020; Monnet & van't Klooster, 2023). Further, central banks could differentiate their own lending rates of interest according to banks' green investment policies, considering, in particular, the share of climate-friendly assets in the portfolio of the latter to add a 'climate premium' to the policy rates of interest (Kempf, 2020). This premium would increase the rate of interest that banks must pay to borrow from the central bank, when the former need to refinance some credit lines they granted to any economic agent whose activities pollute the environment, and could thus induce banks to provide more credit lines to support more green economic activities. Banks would thereby have an incentive in avoiding a reputational cost and risk that could affect their profits and solvability eventually. Such an instrument, however, depends on a properly defined green taxonomy and a coherent as well as consistent verification of its strict compliance by any banking institutions (see D'Orazio & Popoyan, 2019; Sawyer, 2022).

Provided that central banks define and agree on such a taxonomy, they could refer to it also when entering into any repurchase agreements with banks in need of liquidity in so far as the latter institutions dispose of enough eligible assets consistent with ecological targets (see Boneva et al., 2022; Couppey-Soubeyran, 2020; Oustry et al., 2020). As a result, greening the collateral that banks use to borrow liquidity from either the central bank or the interbank market will support an ecological transition that goes along with an increasing volume of bank loans supporting green economic activities so that the issue of financial instability will become less problematic when the volume of carbon-intensive assets will be irrelevant eventually (see Kedward et al., 2022). This is so much so that central banks could also implement 'green' QE monetary policy interventions, targeting thereby climate-friendly economic activities when banks and non-bank financial institutions need huge volumes of liquidity to avoid bankruptcy in the aftermath of a financial crisis such as it occurred in 2008 at the global level (see Dafermos et al., 2020; van't Klooster & Fontan, 2020; Schoenmaker, 2021). In a period of monetary policy tightening, these interventions could also discard first high-carbon financial assets and orienting any corresponding (partial) reinvestment to low-carbon economic activities (Baer et al., 2021; Claeys, 2023; Thiemann et al., 2023). In the currently highly financialized capitalism, to be sure, central banks have the capacity to steer and shape financial markets, which can and should be used to address social as well as ecological concerns in the general interest for the common good, providing the financial stability framework that is currently lacking (see Valsangiacomo, 2022).

Even though a number of central banks are independent of their country's government, particularly in so-called 'advanced' economies, this does not mean that monetary and fiscal policy should not be coordinated to satisfy the general interest of all those agents that are part of the economic system in the relevant country. This policy coordination is indeed necessary and important to make sure the policy mix is not contradictory – such as in the case of Greece after the bursting of the euro area crisis, where monetary policy interventions by the European Central Bank were meant to support economic activities, while a restrictive fiscal policy (namely, austerity) did exactly the opposite in fact – but also to provide an appropriate policy mix that distributes its costs and benefits correctly across the whole economic system. To be sure, rather than using a supposed 'one-size-fits-all' monetary policy instrument like the central bank's rate of interest as explained above, policymakers should consider using fiscal policy because the latter can operate in a more targeted way, thereby reducing the costs and increasing the benefits of policy interventions across the whole economic system (see Saraceno, 2023). For instance, as Baunsgaard and Vernon (2022) suggest, the general government sector can introduce a tax on 'extra profits', which are those profits that firms earn as a result of their market power (like in the energy sector in the aftermath of the war in Ukraine) or because they benefit from huge expenditures by the public sector (such as in the health sector during the COVID-19 pandemic).

Further, considering the distributive effects of interest rate policies decided by central banks, income and wealth inequalities can be addressed in a more structural way by a return to a more progressive tax system, which also supports economic activities and reduces financial instability, because poor and middle-class people have a propensity to consume much higher than rich people. Such a fiscal policy may be complemented with a variety of instruments, including price controls in all those sectors (like energy, health, education and foodstuff) where the purchasing power of lower and middle-class people is largely affected negatively at the time of writing. To this end, incomes policies could also contribute to affect the level of wages, profits and public tariffs so that inflationary pressures across the market for produced goods and services are kept under control (see Saraceno, 2023).

As regards fiscal policy, in particular, the general government sector should introduce a taxation on excessive profits to lower the costs of basic goods and services (such as gas and electricity bills, largely consumed foodstuff, and transport for sustainable mobility) and to collect fiscal revenues that can be used to finance public investment in a series of domains supporting an appropriate ecological transition by both firms and households. The public sector should also collect a micro-tax on all cashless transactions (mostly in financial markets) to finance public investment that support low-income households for childcare and elderly care services as well as training and social integration of the most vulnerable people.

Now, a stronger intervention by the State within the economic system should actually go along with rethinking the organization of contemporary capitalism, notably what, how and for whom to produce in the general interest for the common good. This was already pointed out by Robinson (1972) and implies several distributional conflicts to be solved considering the mutual convenience of all stakeholders in distributing across the whole economic system in a well-balanced form the prosperity resulting from both investment and technological progress aiming at an appropriate ecological transition in a not-too-distant future. The circuit of financial capital must be reoriented in this regard, with a series of policy instruments that we put forward and explained in this section.

CONCLUSION

Money and banking are instrumental for the creation of value in the form of income (a sum of bank deposits). As long as income is not spent in the market for produced goods and services, it exists in the form of financial capital, which their owners usually park in a way or another across financial markets, from which they expect to earn a rent without contributing to produce an income within the economic system as a whole. This chapter – and the analysis presented in it – has shown how it is important to reduce the volume of financial transactions as well as the power of financial institutions in order to affect the circuit of capital, with a view to rebalancing its industrial and financial circulation over the long run so that both distributive and climate-related issues can be addressed for the common good.

A crucial step in this regard consists in implementing a monetary–structural reform of banks' book-keeping system of accounts so that the issuance of money and the credit provided by banks are explicitly separated. As shown in this chapter, banks are in a very powerful situation since they can provide any amount of loans to any kinds of agents – most of the time to other financial institutions – without the need to respect any budget constraints because 'loans make deposits' within the banking system. This endogenous nature of bank money rises the need to separate in banks' ledgers the loans they provide for 'GDP-based transactions' (Werner, 2011, p. 29) – which produce an income – from those loans that do not increase national income since they just inflate financial capital. As Ricardo (1824/1951, p. 276) already noticed with regard to his national central bank, '[t]he Bank of England performs two operations of banking, which are quite distinct, and have no necessary connection with each other: it issues a paper currency as a substitute for a metallic one; and it advances money in the way of loan, to merchants and others'. This fundamental distinction occurs also for any other bank, as all banks (not just central banks) do issue money and provide loans. Such a monetary–structural reform is key for making sure that money, value and capital circulation in a finance-led economic regime contribute to the common good, instead of continuing inflating credit bubbles that go against the long-run general interest of all stakeholders in contemporary capitalism (see Rossi, 2015; 2025 for analytical elaboration on this monetary–structural reform). Rather than just regulating bankers' behaviour with *ex-post* liquidity as well as reserve requirements, national governments must therefore adopt a monetary–structural reform that provides an *ex ante* constraint on banks' credit lines. Such a reform is really instrumental in reorienting both bank loans and financial capital away from polluting as well as destabilizing activities, to support green investment in fixed capital, so much so when the fiscal and monetary policy interventions suggested in this chapter will become a reality across the global economy. All this will not just support economic growth for the common good but will also increase the employment level, particularly of lower as well as middle-class people, thereby enhancing social cohesion and possibly reducing several geopolitical tensions that are currently damaging the well-being on social and economic grounds.

NOTE

1. To be sure, China also experienced a housing bubble more recently, but the factors originating it do not result from financial capitalism: this bubble stems from local government incentives for the construction of new residential buildings, limited investment opportunities for households and the Chinese upper-class propensity to expand home-ownership, which increased house prices beyond any reasonable limits.

REFERENCES

Baer, M., Campiglio, E., & Deyris, J. (2021). It takes two to dance: Institutional dynamics and climate-related financial policies. *Ecological Economics*, *190*, 1–11.

Baunsgaard, T., & Vernon, N. (2022). Taxing windfall profits in the energy sector. *International Monetary Fund Note 2022/002*. https://doi.org/10.5089/9798400218736.068

Boneva, L., Ferrucci, G., & Mongelli, F. P. (2022). Climate change and central banks: What role for monetary policy? *Climate Policy*, *22*(6), 770–787.

Cencini, A., & Rossi, S. (2023). Bernard Schmitt and the Dijon–Fribourg School of monetary circuit analysis. *Review of Political Economy*. https://doi.org/10.1080/09538259.2023.2286467

Claeys, G. (2023). *Finding the right balance (sheet): Quantitative tightening in the euro area.* Monetary Dialogue Papers. https://www.bruegel.org/sites/default/files/2023-03/Claeys%20QT%202023%20Final.pdf

Colander, D. (2015). Asset price inflation. In L.-P. Rochon & S. Rossi (Eds.), *The encyclopedia of central banking* (pp. 10–12). Edward Elgar.

Couppey-Soubeyran, J. (2020). *The role of monetary policy in the ecological transition: An overview of various greening options.* Veblen Institute for Economic Reforms. https://www.veblen-institute.org/IMG/pdf/the_role_of_monetary_policy_in_the_ecological_transition_an_overview_of_various_greening_options.pdf

Dafermos, Y., Gabor, D., Nikolaidi, M., Pawloff, A., & van Lerven, F. (2020). *Decarbonising is easy: Beyond market neutrality in the ECB's corporate QE.* New Economics Foundation. https://neweconomics.org/uploads/files/Decarbonising-is-easy.pdf

D'Orazio, P., & Popoyan, L. (2019). Fostering green investments and tackling climate-related financial risks: Which role for macroprudential policies? *Ecological Economics*, *160*(C), 25–37.

Epstein, G. A. (Ed.). (2005). *Financialization and the world economy.* Edward Elgar.

Forges Davanzati, G., & Tortorella Esposito, G. (2010). Low wages, private indebtedness, and crisis: A monetary-theory-of-production approach. *European Journal of Economic and Social Systems*, *23*(1), 25–44.

Graziani, A. (1990). The theory of the monetary circuit. *Économies et Sociétés (Série Monnaie et Production, 7)*, *24*(6), 7–36.

Graziani, A. (1994). Monetary circuits. In P. Arestis & M. Sawyer (Eds.), *The Elgar companion to radical political economy* (pp. 274–278). Edward Elgar.

Guttmann, R. (2008). A primer on finance-led capitalism and its crisis. *Revue de la Régulation*, 3–4. http://regulation.revues.org/index5843.html

Guttmann, R. (2009). Asset bubbles, debt deflation and global imbalances. *International Journal of Political Economy*, *38*(2), 46–69.

Kappes, S., Vallet, G., & Rochon, L.-P.(Eds.) (2023), *Central banking, monetary policy and income distribution.* Edward Elgar.

Kedward, K., Gabor, D., & Ryan-Collins, J. (2022). *Aligning finance with the green transition: From a risk-based to an allocative green credit policy regime.* UCL Institute for Innovation and Public Purpose, Working Paper no. 2022/11. https://www.ucl.ac.uk/bartlett/public-purpose/wp2022-11

Keen, S. (2015). Credit bubble. In L.-P. Rochon & S. Rossi (Eds.), *The encyclopedia of central banking* (pp. 114–116). Edward Elgar.

Kempf, H. (2020). Verdir la politique monétaire. *Revue d'Économie Politique*, *130*(3), 311–343.

Keynes, J. M. (1933). The monetary theory of production. In Clausing, G. (Ed.). *Der Stand und die nächste Zukunft der Konjukturforschung. Festschrift für Arthur Spiethoff* (pp. 123–125). Duncker & Humblot. Reprinted in *The collected writings of John Maynard Keynes. (1973). The general theory and after, Part I: Preparation* (vol. XIII, pp. 408–411). Macmillan and St Martin's Press.

Keynes, J. M. (1936). *The general theory of employment, interest and money.* Macmillan.

Lavoie, M. (1984). The endogenous flow of credit and the post Keynesian theory of money. *Journal of Economic Issues*, *18*(3), 771–797.

Levrero, S. E. (2023). Gibson paradox. In L.-P. Rochon & S. Rossi (Eds.), *Elgar encyclopedia of post-keynesian economics* (pp. 192–193). Edward Elgar.

Monnet, E., & van't Klooster, J. (2023). *Using green credit policy to bring down inflation: What central bankers can learn from history. The inspire sustainable central banking Toolbox.* Policy Briefing Paper, *13*. https://www.inspiregreenfinance.org/wp-content/uploads/2023/07/INSPIRE-Sustainable-Central-Banking-Toolbox_Policy-Briefing-13.pdf

Network of Central Banks and Supervisors for Greening the Financial System. (2021). *Adapting central bank operations to a hotter world: Reviewing some options.* NGFS Technical Document. https://www.ngfs.net/sites/default/files/medias/documents/ngfs_adapting_central_bank_operations_to_a_hotter_world_final.pdf&ved=2ahUKEwiWwYHGsoKQAxUD_7sIHWBOAr8QFnoECCEQAQ&usg=AOvVaw1A4x_pu9hfgKQzhMfirOPV

Oustry, A., Erkan, B., Svartzman, R., & Weber, P.-F. (2020). Climate-related risks and central banks' collateral policy: A methodological experiment. *Revue Économique*, *73*(2), 173–218.
Panzera, F. (2015). Negative rate of interest. In L.-P. Rochon & S. Rossi (Eds.), *The encyclopedia of central banking* (pp. 376–378). Edward Elgar.
Parguez, A. (1975). *Monnaie et macroéconomie*. Economica.
Parguez, A., & Seccareccia, M. (2000). The credit theory of money: The monetary circuit approach. In J. Smithin (Ed.), *What is Money?* (pp. 101–123). Routledge.
Passarella, M. V. (2014). Financialization and the monetary circuit: A macro-accounting approach. *Review of Political Economy*, *26*(1), 128–148.
Ricardo, D. (1824/1951). Plan for the establishment of a national bank. In P. Sraffa & M. H. Dobb (Eds.), *The works and correspondence of David Ricardo, Vol. IV: Pamphlets and Papers 1815–1823* (pp. 276–300). Cambridge University Press.
Robinson, J. (1972). The second crisis of economic theory. *American Economic Review*, *62*(1–2), 1–10.
Robinson, J. (1979). Michał Kalecki and the economic theory of capitalism. In *Collected economic papers* (Vol. V, pp. 184–196). Basil Blackwell.
Rochon, L.-P. (2022). Sesgos inherentes de la política monetaria. In A. Girón (Ed.), *Política fiscal y monetaria. Confinamiento, pandemia y recuperación inestable, Instituto de Investigaciones Económicas* (pp. 35–50). Universidad Nacional Autónoma de México.
Rochon, L.-P., & Tropeano, D. (2025). Some unexplored financial issues in the monetary circuit since the financial crisis. *Review of Political Economy*, *37*(5).
Rochon, L.-P., & Vallet, G. (2022). The institutions of the people, by the people and for the people? Addressing central banks' power and social responsibility in a democracy. *PSL Quarterly Review*, *75*(301), 83–102.
Rossi, S. (2001). *Money and inflation: A new macroeconomic analysis*. Edward Elgar. (reprinted in 2003).
Rossi, S. (2015). Structural reforms in payment systems to avoid another systemic crisis. *Review of Keynesian Economics*, *3*(2), 213–225.
Rossi, S. (2019). The dangerous ineffectiveness of negative interest rates: The case of Switzerland. *Review of Keynesian Economics*, *7*(2), 220–232.
Rossi, S. (2022). Central bank independence from banks rather than governments. In S. Kappes, L.-P. Rochon, & G. Vallet (Eds.), *The future of central banking* (pp. 360–372). Edward Elgar.
Rossi, S. (2023). The banking crisis of Credit Suisse: Origins, consequences, and reform proposals. *Investigación Económica*, *82*(325), 21–36.
Rossi, S. (2025). A monetary–structural reform to guarantee financial stability. In A. Arauz & S. Kappes (Eds.), *Central banking, monetary policy and financial in/stability* (pp. 5–17). Edward Elgar.
Saraceno, F. (2023). *Inflazione: strategie di policy mix globale*. Istituto per gli Studi di Politica Internazionale. https://www.ispionline.it/it/pubblicazione/inflazione-strategie-di-policy-mix-globale-132334
Sawyer, M. (2022). Monetary policy, environmental sustainability and the climate emergency. In L.-P. Rochon, S. Kappes, & G. Vallet (Eds.), *Central banking, monetary policy and the environment* (pp. 54–71). Edward Elgar.
Schmitt, B. (1959). L'équilibre de la monnaie. *Revue d'Économie Politique*, *69*(5), 921–950.
Schmitt, B. (1960). *La formation du pouvoir d'achat*. Sirey.
Schmitt, B. (2021). Inflation. In X. Bradley & A. Cencini (Eds. and Trans.), *Unemployment and capital malformations*. Routledge.
Schoenmaker, D. (2021). Greening monetary policy. *Climate Policy*, *21*(4), 581–592.
Schumpeter, J. A. (1954). *History of economic analysis*. George Allen & Unwin.
Seccareccia, M. (2012–2013). Financialisation and the transformation of commercial banking: Understanding the recent Canadian experience before and during the international financial crisis. *Journal of Post Keynesian Economics*, *35*(2), 277–300.
Solari, M., Le Bloc'h, A., & Rossi, S. (2024). Ecological transition in a monetary economy of production: A heterodox approach. *Eurasian Economic Review*, *14*(1), 13–37.
Thiemann, M., Büttner, T., & Kessler, O. (2023). Beyond market neutrality? Central banks and the problem of climate change. *Finance and Society*, *9*(1), 14–34.

Tori, D., Caverzasi, E., & Gallegati, M. (2023). Financial production and the subprime mortgage crisis. *Journal of Evolutionary Economics*, *33*, 573–603.

Valsangiacomo, G. (2022). Climate change, financial instability and central banking. In L.-P. Rochon, S. Kappes, & G. Vallet (Eds.), *Central banking, monetary policy and the environment* (pp. 135–154). Edward Elgar.

van't Klooster, J., & Fontan, C. (2020). The myth of market neutrality: A comparative study of the European Central Bank's and the Swiss national bank's corporate security purchases. *New Political Economy*, *25*(6), 865–879.

van't Klooster, J., & van Tilburg, R. (2020). *Targeting a sustainable recovery with green TLTROs*. Positive Money Europe & Sustainable Finance Lab. http://www.positivemoney.eu/wp-content/uploads/2020/09/Green-TLTROs.pdf

Werner, R. (2011). Economics as if banks mattered: A contribution based on the inductive methodology. *The Manchester School*, *79*(2), 25–35.

A GENERAL THEORY OF VALUE, MONEY AND THE STATE

Alan Freeman

University of Manitoba, Canada

ABSTRACT

This paper shows how to represent the production and exchange of commodities by private owners, using the real-world principle of stock-flow consistency (SFC), extended to values and in continuous time. It deduces those general equations of motion, which depend only on how the value is defined, independent of behavioural assumptions. The paper defines three categories or 'genera' of value concept: class production concepts, money price concepts and physical quantity concepts. Members of the first are functionally dependent only on production, of the second only on exchange, while those in the third are functionally independent of both. The paper derives transformations between these value concepts. The authors show that Marx's value concept, a class production concept in which labour is recognised as the sole source of value, furnishes explanations for the three most notable phenomena which General Equilibrium theories fail to account for: prolonged phases of declining output growth, the persistent divergence of money income between the colonial and non-colonial world and repetitive financial crashes.

Keywords: Value; price; money; capitalism; political economy; TSSI

PART ONE: PRODUCTION

Why Is There No Real-World Economics?

Modern economics is widely criticised because it either refuses to explain the real world (ISIP, 2016; Komlos, 2023) or claims to and fails (DeMartino & McCloskey, 2016; Herman & Mouatt, 2020; IEO, 2011; Pierce, 2008). In particular, its accounts of growth, inequality and financial crashes are not confirmed by experience.

Money, Value and Marx's Circuit of Capital
Research in Political Economy, Volume 41, 27–53

ISSN: 0161-7230/doi:10.1108/S0161-723020260000041006

Critical alternatives abound, while new mainstream theories proliferate; yet they either offer limited solutions or address particular problems. This paper tackles a bigger issue: economics is in a state that Colander et al. (2009) term 'systemic failure': it is broken and cannot repair itself. If we are to construct a truly real-world alternative, we need to track down what is wrong about the way modern thinking conceptualises the production and exchange of commodities by private owners, and correct it.

This is a methodological principle, which I term 'forensic'. It informs this paper.

Stock-Flow Consistency and General Equilibrium (GE)

The starting point for a forensic enquiry is the GE approach, which dominates economics. A borrowing from physics, to which economists give a different meaning (Mosini, 2007),[1] GE supposes that an economy reproduces itself without change over a definite period with no relation to the previous or following period. The result, sometimes termed Comparative Statics, is a cinematic simulacrum of motion, which expresses, mathematically, the notion of market perfection. It is not a 'school' but a methodology or 'paradigm' (Bachelard, 2002) found as the dominant variant (Freeman, 2008) in every school.

This paper proposes that Stock-Flow Consistency (SFC) (Godley & Lavoie, 2012) offers a paradigmatic alternative to GE. SFC developed from the observation that the size of any stock of money, over any interval, is exactly equal to the difference between what flows in and what flows out. This principle, familiar to any business, applies to any substance whose quantity cannot be changed by moving it from one place to another – be it water, electrical charge, traffic, population or whatever: it is an uncontestably real-world principle. GE theories, because they violate SFC, are 'Exchange-inconsistent': the money received by sellers in one period is different from that which purchasers pay them for their output in the next.

If the divergences are small, GE can produce empirical short-run approximations, which could be ignored if they balanced over time. However, if the discrepancies are all in the same direction, then they add up like snow on distant peaks until avalanches discharge them. This, I will argue, is the forensic reason that the neoclassical theories of growth, trade and monetary theory produce empirical failures.

Stock-Flow Consistency and Value

SFC is a huge step forward in correcting these errors. However, I will argue that it requires two further developments: it should be applied to the category of value and in continuous time.

I choose the word *category* very carefully; it is an idea on which a theoretical system depends. Though economists of all stripes, including even many Marxists (Steedman, 1971), deny that they need the category of value; in fact, they all use it, but unreflectingly, because they contain the idea that production creates a measurable substance, which is then distributed. If this idea, however defined, is to make sense, then stocks of this substance should be consistent with flows. Anything else supposes that something can be produced from nothing.

Economic theory does not conceptualise value explicitly and indeed tiptoes around it for fear of letting Marx's ideas in by the back door. Yet all economists recognise that nominal or price measures are inadequate due to 'inflation'. Inflation relative to what? Students are taught to fall back on ideas such as 'real output', without reflecting on why they need them. The actual reason is neither the theory of production alone nor distribution alone, but the relation between the two. We cannot ask 'how much is produced' without a measure of it, such as real GDP independent of prices; neither can we ask 'how much did somebody receive' without a measure such as 'real wage' that is also independent of price changes. These are thus nothing but measures of value under euphemistic names.

However, they are subject to a vital constraint, obeyed only in the breach; if the value in the economy, so measured, can increase in circulation, it will then appear that it was created in production, when no new thing was produced. Any such theory then contains the contradictory conclusion that we can produce value without actually changing anything except who owns it and what it is priced at. The idea that finance is productive is best known, but it is only one of many.

To clarify this, we consider three genera of value concept. Quantity concepts are functionally independent of both production and exchange; price concepts are functionally dependent only on exchange; 'class production' or 'factor' concepts are functionally dependent on production alone.

Value Concepts and Their Properties

This paper employs the axiomatic method, which (I argue) is either ignored or abused by economists. It has been maligned by critical economists (Dow, 1990; Lawson, 2006) as *deductivist*: subordinating truth to doctrinal principles. But economics alone is responsible for this abuse (Freeman, 2020b); properly applied, the axiomatic method, subordinated to the forensic principle and to assertive pluralism (Denis, 2008; Fullbrook, 2001), offers an inductive foundation for the study of real market phenomena. Axiomatisation simply means making clear the suppositions on which the conclusions of a theory depend. Experience, guided by observation, then investigates if the results correspond to the real world. If not, this pinpoints the source of error, which is what we mean by 'forensic'.[2]

What properties do economists look for when speaking of something that is produced or distributed? The most basic is that it *measures an amount*. Given any stock of commodities, a value concept should say 'how much' of that stock there is. Measures are therefore additive. If we combine two stocks to make another, its value should be the sum of the values of the two. Non-additive measures such as subjective utility are not Stock-Flow Consistent, because utility can be increased by changing a stock's owner, as if a mass of liquid could be increased by decanting it. Additivity is therefore a conclusion of SFC, important enough to state formally:

D1: An **SFC Value Concept** is a stock-flow consistent measure of sets of commodities.

This is not a dogma. We can and do study non-SFC concepts precisely in order to compare them with SFC concepts. However, to make the comparison, we have to make the distinction.

A Bit of Math

We will use the concept of a *set* – a collection of commodities – which is easier to follow than complex algebraic formulae, which start from the price of single items. Suppose two distinct stocks, *A* and *B*, are combined to make a third. This is written as $A \cup B$, where the U-like symbol is a shorthand for 'Union' and means the set that contains everything in either set.[3] If v is a candidate value concept, $v(A)$ means 'the value of A according to the concept v'. As a convenient abbreviation, we will write this as $\boldsymbol{A}$ in bold case, where it is necessary to distinguish the value of a stock clearly from the stock itself. We may also call v a 'metric' or measure. Then:

D1: Let *A* and *B* be two distinct stocks and v an SFC value concept. Then

$$v(A \cup B) = v(A) + v(B) \tag{1}$$

And that's it. Combined with calculus, it yields a neat definition of a flow: let *A* be a stock at time *t*, and suppose after an interval Δt, it becomes a new stock *B*. The **flow of value** defined by v is then $\Delta \boldsymbol{A} = \boldsymbol{B} - \boldsymbol{A}$. The *average* flow rate **during** Δt is then

$$\frac{\Delta \boldsymbol{A}}{\Delta t} \tag{2}$$

D2: The **instantaneous flow rate**, in the limit as $\Delta t \to 0$, is

$$\frac{\mathrm{d}\boldsymbol{A}}{\mathrm{d}t} \tag{3}$$

which we will abbreviate to $\dot{\boldsymbol{A}}$, and we have SFC in continuous time.

This way of thinking about economic change is different but not difficult; indeed, it brings economics into line with most other branches of knowledge that study the passage of time. An instantaneous flow rate expresses the idea of 'rate of change at any given time'. The speed of a car or the slope of a hill means the average distance or height over an indefinitely small interval.[4] Though initially unfamiliar, it is a very natural way to talk about flows; Marx (Baksi, 2021) understood it perfectly.

Now, let's call attention to a few points. First, price is a value measure. It satisfies D1: **if** A and B are two stocks, and p is a price metric, then

$$p(A \cup B) = p(A) + p(B) \tag{4}$$

Another abbreviation: we'll write £A or \$$A$ instead of $p(A)$.

What about 'physical quantity? The difficulty is the 'Apples and Oranges' problem, sometimes called the heterogeneous goods problem: we can't add a box of apples to a box of oranges and ask how big the result is. Nor can we ask which is 'largest'.[5] It is tempting to decree that physical quantities don't qualify as a value concept, but this is precisely what we are trying to avoid. Our axiom says that *if* a theory has an SFC quantity concept, *then* D1–D2a apply to it. Without this stipulation, we cannot answer questions vital to understanding the real difference between Marx's value theory and others that purport to base themselves on physical quantity measures; we have to study how the equations expressing the dynamics of a real economy change if we employ one measure instead of the other. Furthermore, SFC measures of quantity do exist: they include Bentham's Objective Cardinal Utility (still used in Welfare economics) and macroeconomic measures of constant price or 'real' output.

Production, Distribution and the Axiom of Separation

Ricardo (1817) opens his signature work with the words "To determine the laws which regulate … distribution is the principal problem in Political Economy". We will define a *complete* value concept as one that fully *distinguishes production from distribution*. This leads to a formal mathematical definition:

A1: Axiom of separation. A value concept is **complete** if any change in a stock, so measured, can uniquely be attributed to one of two causes: production and distribution.

Social Classes as Agents of Production

I have opted to include consumption in production because production *involves* consumption; it turns objects into other objects. It is a change in form, transforming one stock into another. While not a source of error, a hard separation creates complication at the cost of clarity, violating Ockam's Razor. This may be counter-intuitive, insofar as economic theories often present production as something business does and consumption as something humans do; they then present personal or household consumption as an endpoint and call it 'final demand', suggesting that the flow of products stops once food, housing, and clothing reach their destination.

But the circular flow does not stop when we take our rest. Human consumption produces humans. It is every bit as much a change in form as industrial production. To be precise, it produces classes, cohesive social groups defined by what they own. It reproduces the providers of labour and the owners of capital, who are themselves engaged in material production. In mainstream economics, these play an ambiguous role, which lies behind their general aversion to talking about value; once we accept that classes contribute to production, we confront the question 'which class supplies what?' Enter the third genus of value concept: class production.

The best known is widely called the 'labour theory of value'. We will not use this phrase, created by Kautsky (1905) in response to Menger's (1871) distinction between 'objective' and 'subjective' value theories, because it reduces to a lowest common denominator the very different ideas of Smith, Ricardo and Marx.

These are actually very distinct. The difference arises because the notion of a *measure* of value, historically, is mixed up with that of a *factor*. Smith says that the value of a commodity is the sum of the contribution of land, labour and capital, which he equates to the income their owners receive – rent, wages and profit. But he insists that the measure of value is 'the toil and trouble of acquiring' the commodity. Value is therefore, on the one hand, equated to the contribution that this factor makes to production, and on the other, to the revenue its owner receives in exchange. These two ideas cannot be reconciled while maintaining a distinction between production and exchange. The whole of economic theory since Smith is a working out of this contradiction.

Factor theory underpins neoclassical theories of both production (Felipe & McCombie, 2013) and trade (Flam & Flanders, 1991). As every undergraduate knows, it treats output as a function of capital and labour:

$$Y = f(K, L) \tag{5}$$

Y is a euphemism for value. However, who supplies K and L? Smith answers that their owners supply them, but *measures* their contribution by the reward they receive, that is to say as a share of Y. Formula (5) avoids this circularity by treating K and Y as independently determined, but begs the question of how they are determined, eviscerating Smith's theory of its real-world point: inputs to production are supplied by classes. A useful economic theory must therefore measure what each class supplies.

But in that case, (5) simply theorises a concealed proposition about value: that the rate at which value enters production is a function of the rate at which classes supply it. The axiom of separation then tells us that the *magnitude of value added by any class is determined independently of exchange*.

This is a stiff condition. For example, K cannot be determined by its cost of production, nor the profit it receives, nor its price. Capital is just a stock of value: the real question, as with labour, is the contribution its owner makes to production. This brings us to the contested question of what, exactly, is distinctive about Marx's value concept. I suggest that it is a *type* of class production concept; it writes (5) as

$$Y = f(\dot{L}) \tag{5a}$$

which, in the simplest case, reduces to

$$Y = k\dot{L} \tag{5a}$$

where k is some constant. This is not a *definition* of value, in respect of which Marx as yet has no equal: it is the forensic reason for the conclusions it leads to. We can now set out some suggested axioms of production.

D3: **Production** is any process in which humans modify a stock of value by changing its form.

D4: **Value added** is the rate at which the stock's value changes.

D5: A **Class Production** concept is one in which value added is independent of exchange but dependent on the activity of one or more social classes.

D6: A **Temporal Class** concept is a class concept in which value added is a function of time.

Suppose that at time t, a capital stock with a value of $\boldsymbol{K}_t$, measured in some value metric, is used for production. Suppose after a time Δt production converts this into $\boldsymbol{K}_{t+\Delta t}$. We can write this as $\boldsymbol{K}_t + \Delta\boldsymbol{K}_t$, that is the capital, plus the increment resulting from production. This increment, sometimes called gross output, is hence $\Delta\boldsymbol{K}_t$. Divided by time, this gives us a rate of flow

$$\frac{\Delta \boldsymbol{K}_{\mathrm{t}}}{\Delta \mathrm{t}} \tag{6}$$

In the limit as $\Delta t \to 0$, this becomes the **rate of value creation**

$$Z = \frac{\mathrm{d}\boldsymbol{K}_{\mathrm{t}}}{\mathrm{d}t} \tag{7}$$

D7: If the rate of value creation Z is proportional to the flow rate of a class factor, this is a *Time Magnitude* (TM) concept. A *Labour time magnitude (LTM)* value concept **is** a TM concept in which only the class supplying value is labour.[6]

We now deduce a theorem that suggests where this is all going. For notational convenience, we will now use L to represent the flow $\dot{\boldsymbol{L}}$ since we do not need to speak of stocks of labour in what follows. The term 'rate of value creation' separates the effects of production, which causes the stock $\boldsymbol{K}$ owned by a capitalist to grow, from distribution, which re-allocates it to classes, usually by selling it. Define the *rate of self-expansion* as the ratio of value added to the value of capital.

$$R = \frac{Z}{\boldsymbol{K}} \tag{8}$$

It can be thought of as the 'maximum rate of return' on $\boldsymbol{K}$; it is what the rate of profit would be if wages were zero. For an LTM concept

$$R = \frac{L}{\boldsymbol{K}} \tag{9}$$

How does this change over time? It depends on how fast $\boldsymbol{K}$ grows. Now, though this is slower than R, it is not in general zero because the remainder after distribution is added to $\boldsymbol{K}$. We will call this 'accumulation'. Note that unconsumed value accumulates whether or not its owners put it to productive use. It remains in their books, whether as productive assets, hoards of idle money, inventories, unused capacity of fixed capital or stockyards full of unsold merchandise.[7] This algebraic consequence of SFC expresses itself in many real phenomena, not least financialisation. It merits a definition:

D8: The **Rate of Accumulation** is the rate at which $\boldsymbol{K}$ actually expands, combining the effects of production and distribution. We will write this as $\dot{\boldsymbol{K}}$, distinct from the rate of self-expansion.

We can now calculate how **R** changes by differentiating (9) with the calculus rule for a quotient:

$$\dot{R} = \frac{\mathrm{d}}{\mathrm{d}t}\left(\frac{Z}{\boldsymbol{K}}\right) = \frac{\dot{Z} - \dot{\boldsymbol{K}}}{\boldsymbol{K}^2} \tag{10}$$

Now, a key difference arises between class and quantity concepts. For an LTM concept, $Z = L$. But unless the working population grows, for society as a whole $\dot{L} = 0$ (the rate of creation of new value is constant). So

$$\dot{R} = \frac{-L}{\boldsymbol{K}^2} \tag{11}$$

This sets an upper bound on the profit rate being the maximum achievable, being that which could theoretically be realised by a capitalist paying no wages. Later in this paper I generalise this result to study the impact of the wage on the profit rate. This equation shows that the maximum profit rate falls as long as accumulation proceeds, confirming Marx's derivation.

Responses (Heinrich, 2013, see Kliman et al., 2013) in effect argue that, though this ceiling is falling, its effects can be postponed indefinitely by countermeasures such as cutting wages. This hypothesis should not be dismissed. Experience (Flores, 2018) shows that wage cuts can offset the fall in corporate profits, which is the logic of neoliberal assaults on living standards. But how far can this go? Let $\boldsymbol{A}$ stand for accumulation and first suppose all profit is accumulated, so wages are simply L–$\boldsymbol{A}$. Can the falling trend be offset by reducing this? Only by increasing $\boldsymbol{A}$: cut wages, and accumulation rises. Replacing Z with $\boldsymbol{A}$ in (8) gives an 'adjusted' rate of return

$$R_{\text{adj}} = \frac{\boldsymbol{A}}{\boldsymbol{K}} \tag{12}$$

Differentiating:

$$\dot{R}_{\text{adj}} = \frac{\dot{A}\boldsymbol{K} - \dot{\boldsymbol{K}}A}{\boldsymbol{K}^2} = \frac{\dot{A}\boldsymbol{K} - A^2}{\boldsymbol{K}^2} \tag{13}$$

because $\dot{\boldsymbol{K}} = A$. To offset the falling trend requires $\dot{A} \geq 0$, hence

$$\dot{A} > A^2 \tag{14}$$

This is an increasing function of A. The lower wages fall, the faster they have to fall. There is thus an absolute limit on what wage cuts can achieve.

Eating the Golden Goose

The only *unlimited* way (Kliman et al., 2013) to raise the profit rate is to disaccumulate: withdraw revenue from production by selling off, or writing down, capital value. This is not the same as physical destruction, which leaves the capitalists with the debt on their hands, which can only be wiped out by liquidation. Spontaneous disaccumulation at the required level has only occurred once historically, in the Great Slump of 1929; it lasted only two years and was insufficient to restore the profit rate. *Organised* disaccumulation occurs when the state displaces the private investor, for example in wartime capitalism, which produced the postwar 'golden age' expansion, rooted in an unprecedented reconstitution of the US profit rate and the United States' rise to industrial pre-eminence.

The tendency can also be offset by transferring value into $\boldsymbol{K}$ from abroad, as Marx notes in the section of Volume III dealing with countervailing tendencies, in his discussion of the role of foreign trade. This is a major function of imperialism. The circumstantial evidence is very strong that the slump of 1870–1890 was overcome by appropriating value from the colonial world. Notwithstanding, the result of Eqs. (8) and (13) is at direct variance with the predictions of all GE theories of production, according to which the profit rate necessarily rises provided only that costs fall.

Productive Consumption, Turnover and the Myth of Fixed Capital

Consumption, though an element of production, plays a specific role within it. This point will lead us to the concept of turnover (Marco, 2023; Veronese Pasarella & Baron, 2015). To pin it down, we must clarify the idea of 'fixed capital'. Though it plays an ideological role in classical political economy as describing a 'necessary factor' that the capitalist supplies, it has a real basis; to produce on any scale beyond hunting and gathering, producers need objects or 'means of production', which Smith calls 'stock'. This stock really is necessary: a factory is a real thing. To rid the notion of 'capital' of its ideological wrapping, we require the real category of depreciation – the technological fact that production consumes objects over time. Marx handles this via the notion of *turnover*.

At any *given* time, a certain productive stock of such objects exists.[8] We can separate any productive capital $\boldsymbol{K}$ into three parts: that which is productively consumed, that which contains the product and that which is simply owned by the capitalist, such as the working money capital or redundant stocks in production. Define X as everything in K, which is used up in production, Y as everything that is created and U (for unproductive capital) as the remainder, so

$$\boldsymbol{K} = X \cup Y \cup U \tag{15}$$

Y is usually called output; X, which Marx calls constant capital, is usually called input. Machinery or raw materials may appear in Y, which represents *new* (that is, distinct) goods, even if of the same type as the inputs. For example, if X is seed corn, Y would be the harvest. We can now define

D9: The rate of productive consumption is $\dot{\boldsymbol{X}}$.

U is only affected by accumulation.[9] $\boldsymbol{Y}$ gives a recognisable expression for the net surplus

$$\dot{\boldsymbol{Z}} = \dot{\boldsymbol{Y}} + \dot{\boldsymbol{X}}, \tag{15}$$

the resultant of the gross rate $\dot{\boldsymbol{Y}}$ at which value is added to the product, and the rate $\dot{\boldsymbol{X}}$ at which productive consumption removes it. $\dot{\boldsymbol{X}}$ is negative because $\boldsymbol{X}$ is being depleted. We now get a neat definition of turnover, first as an aggregate and then decomposed:

D10.1: The rate of turnover of a capital $K = X \cup Y \cup U$, where X is productive consumption, is

$$\frac{\dot{\boldsymbol{X}}}{\boldsymbol{X}} \tag{16}$$

If the value of a stock worth \$100,000 is used up at \$10,000 per year, then it takes 10 years to get used up. We can further decompose this: if X is made up of separate parts $A \cup B \cup C$, we can calculate the turnover rate and time of each part in the same way:

D8: The turnover time of a subset A of productive consumption $X = A \cup B$ is

$$\frac{\boldsymbol{A}}{\dot{\boldsymbol{A}}} \tag{17}$$

Superprofit and Technical Change

The above analysis concerns the average rate of profit for the entire capital of a nation; however, the individual rate of return on a single capital, the focus of business economics, is just as important. As Albarracin (1984) notes, when Marx speaks of a 'general' rate, he means the capital-weighted average of these many rates, which never actually equalise. His focus is the search for a 'surplus' profit rate (Mandel, 1976), which drives most real-world phenomena, including technical progress, financial crisis, imperialism and not least, the formation of prices.

An adequate general theory should focus on the *differences between* profit rates. This yields a *causal* theory of determination, in which the magnitude of prices is established by the movement of capital in search of higher profits, in contrast with GE's *algebraic* theory (Shaikh, 1984), for which these are the solution to a set of simultaneous equations.

A full treatment involves the distribution of values in exchange, studied in part 2, and the role of money and fictitious capital, studied in part 3. However, production itself gives rise to divergences that drive accumulation, so their study belongs here. Their origin is the difference between individual values in a single branch of production, treated in Marx's (1979[1859]) unpublished chapter 'Immediate Results of Production', which Mandel made available in the standard Penguin edition of *Capital* Volume I.

This gives rise to technical superprofit, arising when a producer makes a commodity more efficiently than the others; so the same quantity has a lower individual value. The product then sells above its social value, yielding a higher individual profit rate. The producer's capital then grows faster, because more profit is available in proportion to capital. The new technique will diffuse within the branch as rivals adopt the new methods. Moreover, if the efficient producer's rate exceeds the best obtainable in *other* branches of production, capital will additionally move from branch to branch. This process lies behind capitalism's prodigious revolutions in production.

However, the process is not instantaneous. Before a new technique can be deployed, entirely new plants must be built, production has to ramp up to the scale of the market, new products have to be adopted and rivals have to be displaced. The time scale is thus directly related to the turnover time of fixed capital, which, Marx (1981, Chapter 10) hypothesises, lies behind the 7–11-year alternation of boom and crash (Schumpeter, 1965, p. 41) that has taken place since the dawn of capitalism.

These facts combine to clarify the two related concepts of the 'equalization of the profit rate' and 'socially necessary labour time'. GE, including post-Sraffian theory (Freeman & Carchedi, 1996; Kliman, 2007), supposes that the profit rate is immediately and everywhere equal – indeed otherwise, such theories cannot even calculate prices. They therefore eliminate the mechanism by which its supposed end result is reached, as if an aircraft could jump from one runway to another without taking off or landing.

Such theories then define socially necessary labour time as the labour required by the most advanced technology on hand, the minute this becomes available in even the tiniest quantities. But technology is introduced over time, not all at once: sail barges still plied the Thames in the 1950s. Necessary labour time (Marx, 1981, Chapter 10) is the average of many co-existing techniques.

A Reality Check

This is a good time to take stock. Our dry mathematical results, firstly, give a precise expression for the reasons why capitalism exists. The productive stocks $\boldsymbol{X}$ are necessary for production. A special class of persons – capitalists – secures the exclusive right to dispose of both $\boldsymbol{X}$ and the output $\boldsymbol{Y}$. If production needed no material input ($\boldsymbol{X} = 0$), this class would not be needed.

Our analysis of superprofit explains its prodigious capacity for revolutions in productivity, but also why its expansive phases are relatively short-lived (none has lasted more than 30 years) and why capitalism runs into such dramatic difficulties staying in existence. The owners of capital have no interest in $\boldsymbol{Y}$ unless they can accumulate it, regarding all other expenses as a burden.

Eq. (13) bears out what Marx and Keynes both argued (Chick & Freeman, 2018): whatever an individual capitalist does, accumulation steadily reduces the average compensation his capital brings him. No intrinsic mechanism counteracts the resulting long 'Kondratieff' declines in production seen in Ricardo's day, leading to the 'Long Depressions' of 1870–1890, 1929–1942 and 1974 to the present.

In the purely physical sense, since productivity rises continuously, the quantity of goods remains above the needs of social consumption and even exceeds it, leading to the grotesque phenomenon of mass famine side by side with luxurious plenty. Accumulation, however, is not governed by physical product but value. The opportunities for surplus profit, which Keynes groups under the investment demand schedule, steadily fall (Asimokopulos, 1971; Robinson, 1964, pp. 48–49). As proven above, this continues as long as accumulation continues.

This is unaffected by how much is accumulated productively. Every unconsumed part of Y comes to rest as a stock of some kind; the less is deployed in new production the more is retained as unproductive hoards. Ever more catastrophic financial crashes are merely the end result of ingrained stagnation from which, historically, the only road out so far seen is war. This provides a sufficient empirical basis to place some reliance on the results so far.

These tendencies, however, do not assert themselves unilaterally and fatalistically but intersect with classes, nations and states, which is why 'pure economics' (Desai, 2015) is so fraught. A complete theory should integrate the mechanical effects of capitalist production with the social workings of distribution to lay bare the options open to its classes, the struggles which result and their possible outcomes.

PART TWO: DISTRIBUTION

Exchange, Value and the Problem of Time

Exchange achieves two distinct results: the product reaches its consumers, and its value reaches its owners. However, these do not happen at the same time. Trade itself – an actual transfer of stocks – is not the same as price formation.

This is probably the most radical conclusion that arises from a genuinely stock-flow-consistent treatment of value in continuous time. But it follows, completely logically, from the simple fact that exchange goes on all the time, and not as in GE formalisation, in one apocalyptic moment at the end of a period. Once we accept this real-world fact, we have to separate the effects of trading and price changes.

The conundrum turns on what exchange itself consists of. Trade does not physically move goods; it changes their owners. Consider the sale of land; this is not dug up with spades and shipped in buckets. Goods purchased do not 'pass' from one person to another in trucks, trains and ships, but rather through a transfer of legal ownership. Now consider what happens when a price changes. If no trade takes place, everyone owns exactly what they owned before. Yet the change alters the state of things: if the price of my property doubles, I become twice as rich; if it collapses, I become a pauper. Once we examine how this happens, a class production concept is revealed to be indispensable.

Price, which mediates exchange, is a ratio between quantities, namely sums of money and masses of goods. Hence, if we identify value with it, we arrive at the tautology that price mediates itself. But if we identify value with quantity, there is nothing to mediate, since unless actual trade takes place, all stocks contain the same things. This is why a complete theory of political economy requires a class value concept.

If the price of a stock falls, it loses value; if it rises, the stock gains. If a miser owned an ounce of gold on 11 April 2024, it was worth £1861; next day, it was worth £1954. This is a flow. He gained £93, though he didn't even take it out and gloat over it, let alone try to sell it. Where did the miser's £93 come from? This is not a small problem: the Bank of England owns 300 tonnes of gold; between February 12 and 12 April 2024, gold rose by £400 an ounce, so the bank became richer by half a day's GDP without lifting a finger. The axiom of separation matters: if a theory cannot distinguish genuine production from price rises, sooner or later it will depart from experience. A real-world theory cannot ignore the question 'When stocks undergo gain or losses arising from price changes, *what* do they gain or lose?'

This value cannot be reduced to physical quantity: a tonne of gold is a tonne of gold whatever it costs. 'Constant price' output is also inadequate; it would tell the national accountants that England got richer by four billion pounds. Yet nobody *did* anything. Nobody *produced* the new value.

The magnitude of value created in production must therefore depend not on the quantity of a product or its price, but on a magnitude distinct from both: the contribution of classes.

Price, Value and Transformation

When money price changes, what happens to the distribution of value? The problem thus stated enters the history of economic thought as the 'transformation problem' (Freeman & Carchedi, 1996; Kliman, 2007), but its origins lie earlier, in Ricardo and Smith's preoccupation with the magnitude of price. If this deviated from the value, the differences were either random or cancelled out over time. Ricardo then noted that capital movement influences prices independently of the conditions of production, giving rise to stable, non-random deviations. In summary, the problem arose from a failed attempt to equate the magnitude of price with that of value. As Marx (1979, p. 198) notes, 'The possibility, therefore, of a quantitative incongruity between price and magnitude of value, i.e. the possibility that the price may diverge from the magnitude of value, is inherent in the price-form itself'.

Like the illusion that the sun rises and sets, the idea that price equals value is rooted in reality but does not explain it. The labour required to produce a commodity exerts a real influence on its price, but that influence is *causal.* It arises not from the nature of value but from capital's yearning for the greatest possible return. It is therefore *contingent:* it depends on the extent to which capital's desires are requited. Price never equals value, and such statistical correlations as do exist are manifested over substantial periods of time.[10] The attempt to derive prices directly from values was, in short, defeated by reality.

An analogy is the way gravity really works: the famous phrase 'what goes up must come down' is not true. Throw an object in the air, and its movement depends on the wind and all manner of things. Throw it hard enough, and it will burn up or go into orbit. If it gets stuck in a tree, it may stay there for centuries. The law of gravity explains why gravity *affects* its motion – and nothing else. The law of value tells us how labour time *affects* prices – and nothing else.

The causal mechanism (Mandel, 1976) is capital movement driven by the search for surplus profit: investment rectifies shortages by migrating to industries yielding higher returns, increasing supply and depressing the price. It rectifies oversupply by the converse mechanism. The resulting fluctuations create an average with an apparent centre, just as a flock of birds forms a coherent whole.[11] It is the flock that forms the centre, not the centre that forms the flock.[12] Post-Keynesian critiques of ISLM Keynesianism focused on ergodicity (Davidson, 1991) make the same point: there is no necessary relationship between the real movement of economic variables and the hypothetical state of a static economy.

A general empirical relation between values and prices arises because production is an 'alternative of last resort'; if it is cheaper to make something, buyers will produce instead of exchanging, just as exchange substitutes for production when the converse holds.

Stock-Flow Consistent Exchange and the Formation of Classes

When does exchange 'happen'? All economic theories that treat it as an instantaneous act combining price formation with trade also treat it as happening 'after' production. But exchange proceeds *during* production. Products, when they leave production,[13] enter the market with a price and a value which they acquire as soon as they are offered for sale.

As analysed in part 1, values are a prevailing average. But this average is mediated by price, because competition drives towards a single price, and individual values form a social average. The effect of production on prices is limited to its effect on supply, which in turn determines prices causally. The direction of causation is hence the opposite of what Smith, Ricardo and too many interpreters of Marx suppose. This inverts the so called 'transformation problem': values do not determine what commodities sell for; prices determine who gets the value.

This sheds light on the actual function of the rate of profit in *Capital* Volume III: only 16 chapters (Freeman, 2019) deal with its formation, while the remaining 37 examine how this is distributed to property owners. This is not a theory of how prices are formed but how they bring classes into existence. Each form of property determines specific rights: landed capital receives rent, money capital receives interest, merchant capital receives a mark-up and so on. Capital movement brings about a tendency for the return on each form of capital to equalise: it flows out of those property forms whose return is low and into those where it is high.

The Equations of Transformation

With the problem stated, let us turn to the math. We start with the simplest example possible, supposing an economy with two distinct stocks A and B. The total stock of society C is then $C = A \cup B$, from which follows a value equation and a price equation:

$$\boldsymbol{C} = \boldsymbol{A} + \boldsymbol{B} \tag{18}$$

$$\pounds C = \pounds A + \pounds B \tag{19}$$

recalling that $\boldsymbol{C}$ in boldface type means the value of C and $\pounds C$ means its price. Now, suppose $\pounds A$ falls to £5 while $\pounds B$ rises to £15. Intuitively, the owner of B now has three times as much value as the owner of A. Hence:

A2: **Axiom of distribution**: the value of any stock is proportional to its price.

This does not tell us what the value actually is, only what it is proportional to. What is its actual, absolute value? It doesn't just depend on its price but on all other prices. If, thus, $\pounds A$ rises to £10 while $\pounds B$ becomes £30, then $\pounds A$ hasn't changed: it is, and was, £10. But if we trust A2 alone, its value has halved. We therefore need a common factor that 'normalises' prices to eliminate this distortion caused by a general rise in prices. Economists tend to use index numbers (Diewert, 2016) using quantity as a measure of value. But the results are approximate and misleading because of the Apples and Oranges problem.

Class production values alone offer a general and exact solution, because they alone conform to the axiom of separation. The total value is unaffected by price changes: mathematically, it is an invariant of exchange. This lets us define a common coefficient m such that

$$\boldsymbol{A} = m\pounds A;\ \boldsymbol{B} = m\pounds B \tag{20}$$

and so on. Since total value $\boldsymbol{C}$ is unchanged, $\boldsymbol{C} = m\pounds C$; hence

$$m = \frac{\boldsymbol{C}}{\pounds C} \tag{21}$$

the total value of all marketable stocks in society[14] divided by their price. The inverse of this coefficient, the 'Monetary expression of Value' was first identified by Aglietta (1979, p. 25), and was made rigorous by Ramos and Rodriguez (1996). Ramos (1995) developed the concept in common use, being the Monetary Equivalent of Labour Time (MELT). Foley (1982b, p. 42) and Duménil (1983) independently discovered the coefficient m, the *value of money*, which we will use when the math is easier to follow:

D9: The *Value of Money m* is the ratio between the value of all exchangeable stocks and the price of these same stocks. It is the inverse of the *Monetary Expression of Value (MEV) e*. For an LTM concept, the MEV is the *Monetary expression of Labour Time (MELT)*. We can then define the *Inflation Rate relative to value*:

$$\frac{\dot{m}}{m} \tag{22}$$

The **value transformed in exchange** of a stock K is $m\pounds K$ and the **transformed value flow rate** is

$$\dot{\boldsymbol{K}} = \dot{m}\pounds \boldsymbol{K} + m\pounds\dot{\boldsymbol{K}} \tag{23}$$

In plain language, when prices change, it causes value to flow between stocks, with two factors involved: general and relative price changes. This is an exact expression; it has no index number problems; it can be empirically calculated (Freeman, 1998); and it 'transforms' price changes into value flows.

This restates the relationship between price and value in a way that puts both in their proper place. Prices are no longer 'determined' solely by values, but by all circumstances that affect every actual capitalist economy, restoring them to the role that GE denies them, as the mediator of the causal determination of value distribution by means of capital flows.

Distribution and the Rate of Profit

We can now combine the effects of exchange and production to derive general equations for the rate of return on any capital. First, we extend equations (8) to (13) to give the rate of profit in price terms recalling that, as already noted, e is the inverse of m.

$$\pounds R = \frac{\dot{\pounds\boldsymbol{K}}}{\pounds\boldsymbol{K}} = \frac{\dot{e\boldsymbol{K}}}{e\boldsymbol{K}} = \frac{\dot{e}\boldsymbol{K} + e\dot{\boldsymbol{K}}}{e\boldsymbol{K}} = \frac{\dot{\boldsymbol{K}}}{\boldsymbol{K}} + \frac{\dot{e}}{e} \tag{23}$$

$$= R + \frac{\dot{e}}{e} \tag{24}$$

– the value rate of profit plus the rate of inflation of money relative to value. Among other things, this shows that inflation cannot rescue an economy from a declining profit rate: this would require *accelerating* inflation, which is what happened in the 1970s. Second, we can account for the effects of price changes on the rate of return:

D10: The *Speculative rate of return* on any stock is the value rate of return arising from pure price changes. If $\boldsymbol{m}$ is the value of money (the inverse of e), this is

$$r_E = \frac{m\dot{\pounds K} + \dot{m}\pounds K}{\boldsymbol{K}} \tag{25}$$

The first term gives the effect of a relative change in the price of K alone, and simply shows, as should be expected, that a stock accumulates value if its price is rising compared with others.

Combining this with (8) yields the value rate of profit on any stock of capital, as modified by exchange. Supposing $m = 1$ (whence $\dot{m} = 0$), this gives

$$\frac{Z}{\boldsymbol{K}} + \frac{\dot{\pounds K}}{\boldsymbol{K}} \tag{26}$$

Capitalist Competition and Causal Determination

Eqs. (25) and (26) present competition's essence: they express the rate of return in value terms. R is what mathematicians term canonical: the difference between any two price rates of return is the difference between the value rates, regardless of inflation. Value magnitudes in this way directly express themselves in the real world.

If we can ascertain empirically, for any given economy, how capital movements respond to these differences, we can specify differential equations stating how production in each branch responds to changes in technology. If we can further ascertain how prices respond to changes in supply, our system governs the response of that economy to changes in demand, in turn governed not just by technology but also by the gamut of social and political circumstances, including the action and interaction of states.

This assigns a fundamentally different meaning to the concept of 'determination' than GE, which conceives it *algebraically* (Shaikh, 1984) as the solution to a set of simultaneous equations. Conceptually, this conflates calculation and causation. GE Prices are 'determined' if, and only if, there is only one solution for any set of exogenous variables. But observation testifies that prices fluctuate all the time, regardless of the exogenous variables, with causal effects that GE cannot account for. In particular, if a commodity's price is rising, its owners get a higher rate of return than if it is stable or falling. Capital flows then increase the supply and decrease the price. Conversely, if a price is falling, capital flows out.

GE in effect supposes that discrepancies between supply and demand are corrected at the instantaneous moment of exchange, discounting all causal effects of capital movement. Temporal approaches do recognise that discrepancies between supply and demand persist from one period to the next; but when confined to a sequential or difference equation form, they are confined to an antithesis created by the mental fiction that production and exchange alternate, when actually, they both take place all the time. The passage to continuous time frees theory from this self-imposed prison.

This is by no means all. In order for a GE solution to exist, whether in the marginal form first stated by Walras (1984[1874]) and axiomatised by Arrow and Debreu (1954), or the anti-marginalist form specified by Sraffa (1962), the profit rate must be everywhere equal. Without this supposition, no GE theory can actually determine prices: that is, GE has *no* concept of determination at all.

But in the real world, individual rates of profit diverge widely (Wells, 2007). Each individual capitalist receives a profit rate higher or lower than his rivals. Moreover, without these divergences, prices cannot be causally determined because the divergences drive the movement of capital. Marx (Freeman & Carchedi, 1996; Kliman, 2007) clearly adhered to a causal theory and should be credited with its discovery. In this light, the most fruitful line of advance is to seek rigorous and general formalisations of a causal theory of price determination. Formula (26), by quantifying superprofit in value terms, lays the ground for so doing.

We will describe a system as *causally determined* if it contains verifiable mappings from the distribution of individual rates of profit onto rates of capital flow, and from divergences of supply from demand, as measured by inventory levels, onto individual price levels.

A Second Reality Check

Part 1 of this paper showed how production based on private ownership can take place, provided the classes that supply its factors exist. This part has shown how these classes can be maintained in existence by exchanging the results of production.

A further achievement arises. This analysis of exchange provides a basis to account for the empirical fact (Freeman, 2024) that, contrary to neoclassical trade theory, the divergence between Southern and Northern economies increases with trade liberalisation and decreases when states intervene to protect their national economies.

The centre of this explanation is the phenomenon of unequal exchange, a concept that has fallen out of use only because GE theory failed those who knew it existed but could not explain it, notably Amin (1979, 2010). Unequal exchange does not arise from trade itself, but from the formation of prices – a distinction that GE cannot make, since it supposes all transactions take place at one instant in time. This is why the Heckscher-Ohlin trade theory (Feenstra, 2004) and its predecessor, the Samuelson factor-price theorem, both derived from Haberler's reformulation of Ricardo's theory of comparative advantage as a factor theory,[15] predict that the price mechanism at the international level should iron out the technical advantage of the advanced economies.

In the real world, this does not happen: technically advanced products, which the advanced economies monopolise, appear on the world market at prices whose magnitude deviates systematically more from the labour engaged in producing them than those of the primary and low-wage products in which the global South is compelled to specialise. This occurs independent of whether trade takes place. A business in a poor country, in need of advanced equipment, finds it more expensive to produce at home than to buy from abroad, frustrating any movement of capital into advanced production in those countries and compelling them to purchase instead of investing. This explains why, when the state intervenes to override the profit rate investment criterion, it has empirically been capable of setting production on a basis that can compete. China is the clearest illustration; there are others.

PART THREE: THE UNITY OF PRODUCTION AND DISTRIBUTION

We are now in a position to assess how production and distribution sustain each other in existence. This brings us immediately to money, which mediates the interaction between them.

Money

So far, all we have said is that a price metric assigns an SFC magnitude to any set of commodities. However, any such metric is part of a 'family', which yields the same relative prices. If hats cost £10 and coats cost £100, then 10 hats are worth one coat, but this is equally true if hats cost £10,000 and coats cost £100,000. The unit of currency, called the *numéraire*, selects one member of this family and converts a ratio into an absolute number.

The issue does not arise for class production values, which have an independent measure, typically time. Nor does it arise for quantity metrics, whose measure is some natural unit – pounds, litres, inches, items, journeys or whatever.

The nub of the matter is that there is no measure of price independent of exchange. A UK banknote bears an inscrutable inscription that the bank 'promises to pay' its face value, clarified by the Bank's website as follows:

> However, the value of the pound has not been linked to gold for many years, so the meaning of the promise to pay has changed. You can no longer exchange banknotes for gold. You can only exchange them for other Bank of England banknotes of the same face value.

In the United States, matters are clearer: a dollar note states that it constitutes *a means of payment:* it is a legal tender. The nub of the matter is that though money exists in a variety of forms, including bank deposits, electronic records or fiat and credit money, a complex discussion of liquidity is not needed to establish its essential nature, hence:

D11: A *money commodity*[16] is anything that can be exchanged for any arbitrary set of commodities. A *money price concept* is a metric $p(K)$ that maps any stock K onto the quantity of money for which K can be exchanged.

In general, p depends on the money commodity. Rules (18)–(23) must, however, be modified for two reasons. First, unlike any other commodity, money can be created entirely outside of production. Second, money itself has no price; it enters transformation directly as a quantity. We will now elaborate on the consequences.

Money as a Store of Value

The prices that result from GE's simultaneous equations are relative, which means goods might just as well exchange for each other. There is no difference between these fictitious economies and a barter economy. As a consequence, in neoclassical microeconomics, money is added post hoc, and in post-Sraffian theory, it does not exist.

Yet in the real world, as both Marx and Keynes insisted, goods are not exchanged for each other but for money. A money price, therefore, measures a stock in terms of a real thing. This real thing forms stocks, from which value flows in and out in response to price changes. A money hoard thereby becomes a store of value, with a rate of return, whether or not interest is charged on it. While this is generally negative (because the purchasing power of money, in modern times, falls over time), in times of crisis when all commodity prices fall, this purchasing power rises sharply and the demand for money becomes paramount.[17]

Credit and fictitious capital add further layers of complexity; however, the foundation of any more complex treatment is the basic question 'how does a means of exchange acquire value?' A trivial answer, wrongly attributed to Marx, is the idea that when money rests on a commodity base, it acquires value from production. This fact is undeniable, but misses the point. The very existence of prices transfers value to all exchangeable things; money is no exception. As Marx (1979, pp. 226–227) makes clear, when a precious metal functions as money – when its 'functional existence absorbs its material existence' – its use as metal is irrelevant. It becomes currency. If, and only if, we are clear on how currency becomes a store of value, do we have an adequate foundation for the study of any other monetary instrument, including credit money, fiat money and fictitious capital.

That said, the principal source of confusion arises because money only acts as a store of value when it forms a stock. The need for an SFC treatment of both money and the value it represents in exchange now becomes paramount. Suppose M is a stock of money: the value it acquires in exchange, like any other exchangeable thing, is given by (20):

$$\boldsymbol{M} = m£M \tag{27}$$

What meaning can we attach to $£M$ when M consists of money? Money cannot purchase itself: this lies behind the dictum that 'money has no price'. In this unique case, the place of the price magnitude $£M$ is taken by a quantity magnitude: the amount of money. We can then replace $£M$ with M itself, giving

$$\boldsymbol{M} = mM, \tag{28}$$

that is, the value of the hoard is equal to its size multiplied by the value of money.

Where does this value come from? Since total value is an invariant of exchange by the axiom of separation, it must arise from a loss of value in the rest of the economy. How does this depend on M? Let us divide total social stocks into two parts: money and other commodities, which we will call M and K. The total value in society is then

$$mM + \boldsymbol{K} \tag{29}$$

and the total price is

$$M + £\boldsymbol{K} \tag{30}$$

How does a change in the size of money hoards affect their value? Differentiating (28) gives

$$\dot{\boldsymbol{M}} = \dot{m}M + m\dot{M} \tag{31}$$

To isolate the pure effect of changes in the size of money hoards, we can suppose $\dot{m} = 0$ giving

$$\dot{\boldsymbol{M}} = m\dot{M} \tag{32}$$

That is, as is to be expected, if prices do not change, the value of hoards varies based on the size of the hoard. If, on the other hand, the hoard stays fixed, we can isolate the effect of price changes:

$$\dot{\boldsymbol{M}} = \dot{m}M \tag{33}$$

Recall now that the denominator of m is the total value of all stocks in the economy, and the numerator of m is the total price of these same stocks. Recall also that value is an invariant of exchange. The value of a money hoard therefore grows when prices fall, and falls when prices rise, expressing the intuitive idea that when prices rise, money becomes less valuable – its purchasing power falls.

The idea that money can become value because it has purchasing power is not at all alien to economic thinking, though it encounters resistance among Marxists, chiefly because of the attachment to the 'commodity money' concept. Marx himself (1844, p. 260) writes:

> By value of money, is here to be understood the proportion in which it exchanges for other commodities, or the quantity of it which exchanges for a certain quantity of other things. In Marx's later work, when he has clarified the relation between value, price and exchange value, it is clear that the phrase 'value of money' refers to the value of the things it exchanges for.

The Return On Money

The effect of hoarding on the value of stocks is the reverse of its effect on the value of the hoards; when money acquires value, stocks lose value, explaining Keynes's speculative motive for acquiring money. The change in the value of stocks arising from hoard formation is:

$$\dot{K} = -\dot{m}M - m\dot{M} \tag{34}$$

Thus, when money hoards grow or prices rise, commodity stocks lose value *pro tanto,* while when money prices fall or hoards shrink, they gain. How does this affect reproduction as a whole? It is always, through the movement of capital in pursuit of a higher rate of return. Let us therefore denote the rate of return on money, in value terms, by r_{m}. Dividing (32) by (27) gives

$$r_{£} = \frac{\dot{m}M}{mM} = \frac{\dot{m}}{m} \tag{35}$$

that is, the rate of change of the value of money relative to itself – the inverse of inflation. The higher the inflation, the lower the return on money, and vice versa.

At first sight, since modern inflation is normally positive, $r_{£}$ is negative, so there appears to be little reason for a capitalist to hoard money beyond the transactional requirement to pay for the renewal of used-up inputs. However, matters are not so simple for four reasons.

First, capital movements are driven not by the absolute level of individual profit rates but by the difference between alternative rates. If a manufacturing venture is operating at a loss, it makes sense to run it down and keep the money. Second, prices fall sharply in crises, leading to a rush to get means of payment. Third, most hoarding takes the form of *monetary instruments*: metals, minerals, imperishables, collectibles or real estate; though not currency, these are easily sold to obtain it. Finally, the return on 'fictitious capital' like bonds, equity or sliced and diced credit instruments is boosted by income streams, especially when tied to the general interest rate. This produces what Keynes termed 'Animal Spirits' because the rate at which capital can flow into them is not limited, like technical superprofit, by the time of production.

Speculative returns (Hudson, 2015) become irrationally high (Shiller, 2000) as the demand fuels further price rises, creating asset bubbles which then burst in the next crash. The returns on all such instruments are, however, simply additions to the return on means of payment.

Money and Production

Thus far in this part, we have studied only movements of value due to exchange. Equations 27–35 apply for any value measure that is constant in exchange, including 'real output'. In production, however, the effect of money depends on the value concept. In what follows, we assume the rate of self-expansion of capital L to be given by a class concept.

The general rate of profit is then $\boldsymbol{L}$ divided by total capital. However, total capital is a constant in exchange; the general rate is therefore unaffected. The effect of hoard formation is felt in accumulation. This can be seen by calculating the value return on productive capital $\boldsymbol{K}$ resulting from the combination of production and exchange

$$r = \frac{L - mM}{\boldsymbol{K}} \tag{36}$$

Accumulation can alter both the numerator and the denominator of this rate: if M is growing, the numerator will shrink, but $\boldsymbol{K}$ will not rise as quickly. Recall, however, that the rate falls if $\boldsymbol{K}$ grows at all, as shown in (11). Hoarding amplifies, rather than offsetting, the long-term fall in the industrial profit rate. This is the fundamental mechanism underlying financialisation (Lapavitsas, 2009).[18] Moreover, if M grows, that is if new value is hoarded, rather than adding to $\boldsymbol{K}$, the rate of return on $\boldsymbol{K}$ will fall.

This explains why the 'slaughter of values' in crashes does not rescue the profit rate from the effects of accumulation. Unless the state becomes an investor, capitalist economies are damned if they let slumps run their course, and damned if they don't. In the first case, the growth of $\boldsymbol{K}$ drives the profit rate down regardless of the slaughter of asset values, and in the second, it declines yet faster as new value is shunted off into hoard formation, leading to the ever-deeper crashes and ever-shallower booms which characterise post-1974 industrialised economies.

Interest, Financial Instruments and Fictitious Capital

We now turn to finance capital. In this case, the divergence between essence and form of appearance is especially large because it has no relation to the circuit of commodity capital, which is why Marx called it 'fictitious capital'. We will try to explain as much as possible in the simplest terms, adding complexity only when simplicity falls short. We therefore start by asking why a money-dealing class exists at all.

As Marx (1981, Ch 19) notes, early in capitalist history, managing money becomes a separate branch of the division of labour, and is conducted by a distinct class of money dealers. The class sustains itself by charging a fee – interest. Money capital, when managed by this class, then enters, as do commercial and landed capital, into competition with all other capitals. That is to say, it participates in the equalisation of the profit rate.[19]

Banks also may make loans. They don't have to: many early banks were just glorified safe deposits. Thus, when they make loans, they spawn yet another specific class: capitalist moneylenders. These, Marx insists, are not the same as feudal and pre-feudal usurers because they do not lend out their own money, but rather money that others have lent to them.

Money capital thus separates itself into parts conforming to the various functions of money (de Brounhoff, 1976; Nelson, 2018) – currency, means of payment, store of value and so on. When commoditised – converted into an alienable and exchangeable object – credit mutates into fictitious capital, the legal right of an arbitrary owner to a stream of income.

Fictitious capital becomes the characteristic form of accumulation as the return on productive capital sinks, which accounts for its domination in modern neoliberal capitalism. Financial instruments acquire a price independent of their face value, and financial profit takes the dual form of payment of interest and capital gain. However, unlike all other forms of capital, there is no constraint on the speed at which capital can migrate. The market in securities becomes divorced entirely from the production of useful goods, leading to all the morbid consequences we live through today. This very modern fact constitutes our final reality check.

NOTES

1. Equilibrium conveys the idea of balance, as when a pendulum comes to rest. Economists more often use GE in the sense of thermodynamic equilibrium, when a changing system exhibits constant properties because inflows equal outflows this borrowing, too, is inappropriate because there are no flows in GE.
2. Axiomatics relate directly to pluralism (Fullbrook, 2001). As its critics point out, economics is *monotheoretic*; it does not study alternatives. It compares its candidate theories with the 'null hypothesis' that reality is random. But science tests one theory against another; and to this end studies both candidates.
3. Throughout this paper, sets are 'non-intersecting' meaning that each item is distinct. Hence if A is three coats and a button, while B is a coat and a song, $A \cup B$ is four coats, one button, and one song.
4. If time is quantised, the instantaneous rate means that the interval is as small as possible.
5. Mathematically, sets of quantified objects are in general partially ordered.
6. Complex labour adds more value than the average. Its dimension is still therefore time. Consider the expression 'she does the work of two men'. See Meng (2017).

7. Some writers distinguish 'genuine' consumption from losses when stocks are destroyed without use. We treat this as a wasteful consumption.

8. Foley (1982) discusses the connection between a flow and the stock of it which implicitly exists at any time. We part company from his attempt to extend this to distribution.

9. Accumulation can be negative, as when unutilised capacity, which is part of U, is put to use and so consumed.

10. Normally, the length of the business cycle.

11. Marx's (1920, pp. 26–27) critique of Proudhon's theory of 'proportionality', in which he cites Ricardo's recognition of the causal character of capital movement, gives an early and clear account of this process.

12. The equilibrium concept of a 'centre of gravity' (Moseley, 2018) is rooted in this fallacy.

13. In not a few cases such as houses or subscription products they are sold even before they are produced.

14. To be precise, these totals should refer to all commodities directly exchangeable for a money commodity. See later.

15. As Wikipedia delicately puts it: 'In 1930 Austrian-American economist Gottfried Haberler detached the doctrine of comparative advantage from Ricardo's labor theory of value and provided a modern opportunity cost formulation. Haberler's reformulation of comparative advantage revolutionized the theory of international trade and laid the conceptual groundwork of modern trade theories'.

16. In this paper, I use the word 'commodity' for any exchangeable thing. This diverges from Marx (1979, Chapter 3), for whom a commodity is also a product of labour. The reason for my choice of words is that in its function as means of purchase, there is no essential difference between paper and any other exchangeable thing. Marx's distinction is important, but leads to circumlocutions which, for simplicity, I try to avoid in this paper.

17. Every crash is accompanied by a 30–50% fall in commodity prices, as a vast literature testifies. Consumers do not usually experience this, because the goods most affected are means of production, raw materials, and intermediate goods. Capitalists rarely pass the benefits on to the final consumer.

18. It is not, of course, the *cause* of financialization, which arises from the accumulation of fictitious capital (financial instruments). It does however explain the damaging *effect* of financialization, when it takes place.

19. This is why (Freeman, 2013), money capital including financial instruments must be included in the denominator when calculating the profit rate empirically. Standard calculations (Basu and Manolakis, 2012) that omit money capital yield the contradictory conclusion that a completely financialised economy has an infinite profit rate.

REFERENCES

Aglietta, M. (1979). *A theory of capitalist regulation: The US experience*. New Left Books. Spanish language version Aglietta, M. (1979). *Regulacion y Crisis Del Capitalismo*. Mexico: Siglo XXI.

Albarracin, J. (1984). Constant returns and uniform profit rates: Two false assumptions. In E. Mandel & A. Freeman (Eds.), *Ricardo, Marx, Sraffa*, Verso.

Amin, S. (1979). *Imperialism and unequal development*. Monthly Review Press.

Amin, S. (2010). *The law of worldwide value* (2nd ed.). NYU Press.

Arrow, K. J., & Debreu, G. (1954). Existence of an equilibrium for a competitive economy. *Econometrica*, 22(3), 265–290.

Bachelard, G. (2002). *The Formation of the scientific mind*. Clinamen, trans. by M. McAllester Jones. (*La formation de l'esprit scientifique*).

Baksi, P. (2021). *Karl Marx and mathematics*. Routledge.

Basu, D., & Manolakos, P. T. (2012). Is there a tendency for the rate of profit to fall? Econometric evidence for the U.S. Economy, 1948–2007. *Review of Radical Political Economics*, 45(1), 76–95.

Chick, V., & Freeman, A. (2018). The economics of enough: A future for capitalism or a new way of living? In S. Dow, J. Jespersen, & G. Tily. *Money, method and post-keynesian economics for the 21st century*. Edward Elgar.

Colander, D., Foellmer, H., Haas, A., Goldberg, M., Juselius, K., & Kirman, A. (2009). *The financial crisis and the systemic failure of academic economics*. http://www.debtdeflation.com/blogs/wp-content/uploads/papers/Dahlem_Report_EconCrisis021809.pdf

Davidson, P. (1991). 'Is probability theory relevant for uncertainty? A post Keynesian perspective', *The Journal of Economic Perspectives*, 5(1), Winter 1991, 129–143.

DeMartino, G. F., & McCloskey, D. N. (2016). *The Oxford handbook of professional economic ethics*. Oxford University Press.

Denis, A. (2008). Pluralism in economics education. Editorial Introduction to the special issue on pluralism of International Review of Economics Education (pp. 8–22).

Desai, R. (2015). *Geopolitical economy: The discipline of multipolarity*. Valdai Papers #24 | July 2015. https://valdaiclub.com/files/10943/

Diewert, W. E. (2016). Index numbers. In J. Eatwell, M. Milgate, & P. Newman (Eds.), *The new palgrave: A dictionary of economics* (Vol. 2, pp. 767–780).

Dow, S. C. (1990). Beyond dualism. *Cambridge Journal of Economics*, 14(2), 143–157.

Duménil, G. (1983). Beyond the transformation riddle: A labor theory of value. *Science & Society*, 47, 4.

Feenstra, R. C. (2004). The Heckscher–Ohlin model. *Advanced international trade: Theory and evidence* (pp. 31–63). Princeton University Press.

Felipe, J., & McCombie, J. S. L. (2013). *The aggregate production function and the measurement of technical change: Not even wrong*. Edward Elgar Pub.

Flam, H., & Flanders, J. (Eds.). (1991). *Heckscher-ohlin trade theory*. MIT Press.

Flores, M. (2018). *Yyyy Paper on Mexican profit rate (Have written asking for reference)*.

Foley, D. (1982a). Realization and accumulation in a Marxian model of the circuit of capital. *Journal of Economic Theory*, 28(2), 300–319.

Foley, D. (1982b). The value of money, the value of labour-power and the Marxian transformation problem. *Review of Radical Political Economics*, 14(2).

Freeman, A. (1998). *Time, money and the quantification of value*. MPRA paper 2217. Munich Personal RePEc Archive. https://mpra.ub.uni-muenchen.de/2217/

Freeman, A. (2008). An invasive metaphor: The concept of centre of gravity in economics. In *MPRA paper 6812, presented to the AHE conference 2006*, posted 21 January 2008. https://www.academia.edu/11692549/An_Invasive_Metaphor_the_Concept_of_Centre_of_Gravity_in_Economics

Freeman, A. (2013). The profit rate in the presence of financial markets. *Journal of Australian Political Economy*. Number 70, Summer 2012, 167–192.

Freeman, A. (2019). Class. In M. Vidal, T. Rotta, T. Smith, & P. Prew (Eds.), *The Oxford handbook of Karl Marx*. OUP.

Freeman, A. (2020b). A general theory of value and money (Part 1: Foundations of an axiomatic theory). *World Review of Political Economy*, 11(No. 2).

Freeman, A. (2024). The geopolitical economy of international inequality. *Development and Change*, 55, 3–37.

Freeman, A., & Carchedi, G. (Eds.). (1996). *Marx and non-equilibrium economics*. Edward Elgar.

Fullbrook, E. (2001). Real science is pluralist; an argument for pluralism. In *Economics*. Post-Autistics Economics Network.

Godley, W., & Lavoie, M. (2007). *Monetary economics: An integrated approach to credit, money, income, production and wealth* (1st ed.). Palgrave McMillan.

Heinrich, M..(2013). Crisis theory, the law of the tendency of the profit rate to fall, and Marx's studies in the 1870s, *Monthly Review*, 64, 11.

Herman, A., & Simon, M. (2020). *The heterodox perspective in economics: Implications for theory and policy action*. Routledge.

Hudson, M. (2015). *Killing the host*. Islet Press.

IEO [Independent Evaluation Office of the International Monetary Fund]. (2011). *IMF performance in the run-up to the financial and economic crisis: IMF surveillance in 2004–2007* January 10, 2011.

ISIP (International Student Initiative for Pluralist Economics). (2016). *An international student call for pluralism in economics*. http://www.isipe.net/open-letter/

Kautsky, K. (1905). *The economic doctrines of Karl Marx*. Hyperion.

Kliman, A. (2007). *Reclaiming Marx's capital: A refutation of the myth of inconsistency*. Lexington Books.

Kliman, A., Freeman, A., Potts, N., Gusev, A., & Cooney, B. (2013). *The unmaking of Marx's capital: Heinrich's attempt to eliminate Marx's crisis theory*. https://doi.org/10.2139/ssrn.2294134

Komlos, J. (2023). *Foundations of real-world economics what every economics student needs to know*. Routledge.

Lapavitsas, C. (2009). Financialised capitalism: Crisis and financial expropriation. *Historical Materialism*, 17(2), 114–148.

Lawson, T. (2006). The nature of heterodox economics. *Cambridge Journal of Economics*, 30(4), 483–505.

Marco, G. D. (2023). Marx's general rate of profit: How turnover time, accumulation and rate of surplus value affect the formation of prices of production. *Capital & Class*, 0(0). https://doi.org/10.1177/03098168231179975

Marx, K. (1844). *Excerpts from James Mills's political economy*. Penguin.

Marx, K. (1920). (Translated by Harry Quelch) *The poverty of philosophy*. C. H. Kerr.

Marx, K. (1979). *Capital: A critique of political economy* (Vol. I). Penguin.

Marx, K. (1981). *Capital: A critique of political economy* (Vol. III). Penguin.

Menger, C. (1871). *Grundsätze der Volkswirthschaftslehre, Erster, Allgemeiner Theil*. Wilhelm Braumüller.

Moseley, F. (2018). *Money and totality: A macro-monetary interpretation of Marx's logic in capital and the end of the transformation problem*. Haymarket Books.

Mosini, V. (Ed.) (2007), *Equilibrium in economics: Scope and limits*. Routledge.

Nelson, R., Dosi, G., Helfat, C., & Winter, S. (2018). *Modern evolutionary economics: An overview*. Cambridge University Press.

Pierce, A. (2008, 5 November). *The Queen asks why no one saw the credit crunch coming*. Daily Telegraph.

Ramos, A. (1995). The monetary expression of labour: Marx's twofold measure of value. *Mini-conference of the international working group on value theory (IWGVT) at the Eastern Economic Association*. https://copejournal.com/wp-content/uploads/2017/02/Ramos-The-Monetary-Expression-of-Labour-Marxs-Twofold-Measure-of-Value.pdf

Ramos-Martínez, A., & Rodríguez-Herrera, A. (1996). The transformation of values into prices of production: A different reading of Marx's text. In A. Freeman & G. Carchedi (Eds.), *Marx and non-equilibrium economics*. Edward Elgar.

Ricardo, D. (1817). *The principles of political economy and taxation*. John Murray.

Robinson, J. (1964). *Essays in the theory of economic growth*. Palgrave McMillan.

Schumpeter, J. (1965). *Capitalism, socialism and democracy*. Unwin.

Shaikh, A. (1984). The transformation from Marx to Sraffa. In E. Mandel & A. Freeman (Eds.), *Ricardo, Marx, Sraffa* (pp. 43–85). Verso.

Shiller, R. J. (2000). *Irrational exuberance*. Princeton University Press.

Sraffa, P. (1975[1962]). *Production of commodities by means of commodities*. Cambridge University Press.

Steedman, I. (1971). *Marx after Sraffa*. New Left Books.

Veronese Pasarella, M., & Baron, H. (2015). Capital's humpback bridge: 'financialisation' and the rate of turnover in Marx's economic theory. *Cambridge Journal of Economics*, 39(5), 1415–1441.

Walras, L., & Jaffe, T. W. (1984 [1874]). *Elements of pure economics, or the theory of social wealth*. Orion Editions.

Wells, P. J. (2007). *The rate of profit as a random variable*. PhD thesis The Open University. http://oro.open.ac.uk/22347/

ON THE BEGINNING OF CAPITAL

Till Hahn

Leuphana University of Lüneburg, Germany

ABSTRACT

This chapter addresses the question of the logical unity of Capital *through an examination of* Capital's *three beginnings: The commodity, the primitive accumulation and merchant and usurer's capital in the historical stages before the capitalist mode of production – namely Aristotle's account of chrematistics. It thereby refutes Althusser's claim that the chapter on 'primitive accumulation' falls outside of this logic. It shows furthermore that we have to read these beginnings through a logic of the 'uncanny', which builds on a dialectic of the inside/outside split, to reveal their true unity.*

Keywords: Value-form; wealth; capital; primary accumulation; uncanny

A good book may have three openings entirely dissimilar and inter-related. – Flann O'Brien

'As in Hamlet, the Prince of a rotten State, everything begins by the apparition of a spectre. More precisely by the waiting for this apparition. The anticipation is at once impatient, anxious, and fascinated: this, the thing ("this thing") will end up coming. The *revenant* is going to come' (Derrida, 1994, p. 2). Although Jacques Derrida is speaking of the apparition that is the spectre of communism that opens the *Manifesto*, it is noteworthy that also Marx's magnum opus *Das Kapital* opens with an apparition: 'The wealth of societies in which the capitalist mode of production prevails, *appears* [erscheint][1] as an "immense accumulation of commodities," its unit being the single commodity' (Marx, 2010a, p. 45).[2]

Like the *Wiedergänger* (revenant) that Derrida is speaking of, we find *a thing* – or rather *e pluribus unum* a multitude of things gathered into one – at the beginning of capital: an immense accumulation of commodities. But also, in a quite literal sense we find a *Doppelgänger* (double): The beginning of *capital* itself is doubled. It is doubled in the sense that the entity, that *Das Kapital* is occupied with, the capitalist mode of production, has two beginnings. A logical one, which is found in the first chapter of vol. I of *Das Kapital*, the commodity, and a

Money, Value and Marx's Circuit of Capital
Research in Political Economy, Volume 41, 55–73

ISSN: 0161-7230/doi:10.1108/S0161-72302026000041008

historical one, found in the concluding part on primitive accumulation (*ursprüngliche Akkumulation*). But the beginning of *Das Kapital* is also doubled in a literary sense, in the sense that the very first sentence, the sentence that opens the book *Das Kapital*, is also the first sentence of the *Contribution to the critique of political economy*.

The historical beginning of capital on the other hand, again, splits in two: the beginning of the *capitalist mode of production* as described in the final chapter of vol. I on *primitive accumulation* and an origin-story of the *entity* that is called capital, self-valorising value, M-M^{I}, that is found in the Chapters on interest bearing capital in vol. III.[3] It is by virtue of this split that the entity *capital* predates the development of the *capitalist mode of production* by millennia.[4] How is it possible that capital has existed for thousands of years before its according mode of production could prevail? The answer to this, according to Marx, lies in the historical encounter of the entity capital with its other, the free worker – free, again, in the double sense of 'free to sell his labour-power' and 'free from the possession of his means of production' (Marx, 2010a, p. 705). It is only in this historical encounter that capital finds the possibility to *produce* its own increment, surplus-value and thus produce the potentially infinite 'immense accumulation of commodities' as which the wealth of societies, in which this particular mode of production prevails, appears.

This doubling, finally, is by no means unproblematic. It points, as Louis Althusser claims (Althusser, 2006, pp. 38–40), towards a discontinuity within Marx's 'order of exposition': This 'dialectical' order of exposition is set from the *logical* beginning at the beginning of the *book, Das Kapital*, the beginning with the 'simplest' and most *abstract* forms active within the entity and mode of production of *capital* – abstract value and abstract labour – and is supposed to *philosophically* 'ascent from the abstract to the concrete' (Althusser et al., 2015, p. 37; Pokrytan, 1981, p. 145 ff.; Stiehler, 1961). This logical order of exposition is, according to Althusser, undermined by chapters on the history of the conditions, that stand *outside* of this logical order: 'the working day, the labour process, manufacture and big industry, and' above all 'the extraordinary chapter on primitive accumulation' (Althusser, 2006a, p. 39). We thus ask the question with Althusser: 'Why did Marx *think that he had to begin with the ultimate abstraction of value*?' (Althusser, 2006a, p. 41).

Althusser, of course, answers his own question: 'Nothing, however, requires that we start out from it, unless the aim is to overcharge this concept with meanings that are difficult to keep under control' (Althusser, 2006a, p. 41). But what if this is precisely the goal of the beginning of *Capital*? Didn't Marx himself define this concept as 'overcharge[d] [. . .] with meanings that are difficult to keep under control'? 'A commodity appears, at first sight, a very trivial thing, and easily understood. Its analysis shows that it is, in reality, a very queer thing, abounding in metaphysical subtleties and theological niceties' (Marx, 2010a, p. 81).[5] Why else, finally, are we supposed to come to it through this eerie play of revenants and doubles? Two entities, one might add, that, according to none other than Sigmund Freud, are the acme of the 'uncanny' (Freud, 2003, pp. 142–149). And indeed, he characterizes 'this thing' whose appearance begins *Das Kapital*, as uncanny: For the 'immense accumulation of commodities' that, according to translators Moore and Aveling, is found at the beginning of capital is not just immense in a quantitative sense. According to the German original, it is also *ungeheuer*, monstrous (Marx, 1962, p. 49). It is not just a mere etymological nicety to investigate this further (Lezra, 2018, p. 3): Like the German word *unheimlich* (uncanny), the word *un-geheuer* is the negation of the familiar. The familiar, though, explicitly taken in the sense of the household, the oikos – of which the science of *economy* famously describes the laws. We must, then, take the negation inherent in the word *un-geheuer* in its full dialectical sense: It is not something that simply does not belong to or is outside of the oikos, but it is something different or uncanny at the very heart of it (DWDS: "Ungeheuer"; Freud, 2003, p. 127). Again, this is no mere indulgence in a literary *goût* for paradoxes and ambiguities. On the contrary, the monstrous appearance that lies at the beginning of *Capital* is the first trace that there is 'something off' within capital. It marks the beginning of the critical process, which deciphers a mundane act of commodity exchange as an ideological process, through which the exploitation of labour, which constitutes capital's profits, appears as a mere exchange of equals.[6]

In the following, I will thus investigate (a) this 'monstrosity' of value, this subversion of its own nature, that lies at the heart of capital, through a return to the forefather of economic analysis, Aristotle, and his interpretation through Marx. I will then show how (b) this 'monstrosity' is central to understand the *logical beginning* of capital, the commodity, as its specific *order of appearance* and (c) analyse it in relation to its historical genesis as mode of social mediation through the historical process of *primary accumulation* – the historical *encounter* of capital as entity and the double-free worker, thereby challenging Althusser's verdict on the undermining of *capital's* logic of exposition through the reconstruction of historical events *exterior* to it.

BEFORE THE BEGINNING OF *CAPITAL*: MONSTROUS ACCUMULATION, A FORM AGAINST ITSELF

Before we tackle this 'monstrosity' that is at the heart of Marx's concept of value, let us tarry a bit with the first *Doppelgänger* that has crossed our path on our way into *Capital*: Why is it this sentence that has survived the otherwise radical revisions and reworkings of Marx's late economic manuscripts? Let us begin with stating the obvious: It begins with a category, that is common to *all* modes of production, namely *wealth*. By stressing the appearance as 'immense accumulation of commodities', it already operates on a historical plane: the connection between wealth and commodity marks the historical perspective of the beginning of capital (Eichler, 2015, p. 120). By this operation, the commodity is not just marked as elementary form (*Elementarform*) of wealth under capitalism, it is also marked as elementary form of the contradictory and conflictuous logic of capital. But like with every good *Doppelgänger*, we start to find slight differences between the two sentences: In the *Contribution*, for example,

Marx talks about 'the wealth of bourgeois society' (Marx, 2010c, p. 269)[7] – note the singular – instead of 'societies in which the capitalist mode of production prevails'. Also, in the German original we find two slightly different connotations of the *unit*, the single commodity. Being presented *elementary form* (*Elementarform*) in *Capital* (Marx, 1962, p. 49), it is deemed the *elementary being* (*elementarisches Dasein*)[8] in the *Contributions* (Marx, 1961, p. 15).

In *Capital*, Marx thus presents us with a more refined form of this historical indication, that is placed at the heart of the *logical* beginning: In the *Contributions*, we are presented with an already historically specific form of wealth – bourgeois wealth. The beginning of *Capital* insists on the transhistorical generality of the *category* of wealth, which only *appears* in a special way *if* the capitalist mode of production prevails (Heinrich, 2021, p. 51). In other words: where the first sentence of the *Contributions* presents us with a historical fact, the first sentence of *Capital* presents us with a logical conjunction. A logical conjunction, moreover, that operates on the ontological distinction between essence (*Wesen*) and appearance (*Schein*) (Eichler, 2015, p. 121).[9]

So, what makes this appearance of wealth in societies, in which the capitalist mode of production prevails, so monstrous? To understand this, we (ironically) have to go back to Aristotle, a thinker who wrote long before the capitalist mode of production prevailed. A thinker, nevertheless, who, according to Marx, was the first thinker to have theorized the problem of value (Marx, 2010a, p. 69). In his *Politics*, Aristotle talks about trade as a means to fulfil the needs that occur in the Polis. In the course of his investigation into this practice, he engages in a critique of chrematistics (χρηματιστική), the craft of making money through money, i.e. the craft to buy cheap and sell dear (Aristotle, 1912, p. 1257b). In the third Volume of Capital, describing interest bearing capital, Marx acknowledges this practice – under the name of merchant's capital – as one of the early stages of existence of the *entity* that *Das Kapital* by its name is occupied with: capital, value breeding more value, M-M[1] (Marx, 2010b, p. 588). Aristotle's critique aims at the fact that this practice alienates a means to the public good (money) to a private end (individual wealth). Through this transformation, this mere medium for the satisfaction of the needs of the citizens of the Polis into an end in itself, this medium is deprived of its nature. This critique draws heavily on the Greek differentiation between the science[10] of the good leading of the household, namely the *oiko-nomia*, and the science of the good institution of society, namely *politkē* (Nielsen, 2013; Priddat, 2014).[11] In this distinction, money (*nómisma*) is linked to the sphere of the political, defined as means to distribute commodities throughout the society, to enable every member of the community to lead a good (i.e. ethical) life, by supplying him with the means of subsistence (Aristotle, 2014, p. 1133a). The scandal of chrematistics is thus that a public means is alienated from its end by being used to generate private profit (Alliez, 1996, p. 5; Berthoud, 1987, p. 3). Moreover, it subverts the *nature* of *nómisma* because this private profit is, by virtue of this superposition, infinite. And this very subversion of nature is what Aristotle calls *monstrous* (Connell, 2007). This is why Aristotle remains unclear about the status of this chrematistics:

> Now, the quest for a definition of chrematistics undertaken in the *Politics* does not succeed: remaining shapeless, chrematistics will occupy no rank within the hierarchical order of knowledges and acts. Shapeless, because the form of a thing is what it has that can be bound or set upon within a definition *(logos)*. How can the limits of something that has no limits be defined? (Alliez, 1996, p. 4)

chrematistics is thus not a science at all[12] because it does not deal with the general; it only *makes use* of the general to fulfil private interests (Berthoud, 1987, p. 4; Ferrain, 2001, p. 89):

> Here, on the surface of the Aristotelian narrative, arises the untimeliness of a hybrid science, without regards or moorings, distinguishing itself from the *oikonomia* ruled by use-value inasmuch as that circulation becomes the source of a limitless monetary wealth: "money is *the beginning and the end* of this kind of exchange" (emphasis added), the M-C-M cycle. A science of money whose bad infinity haunts the organicity of the body politic by unsettling the postulate of exchange between equivalents. (Alliez, 1996, p. 3)

So, before we take a closer look at Marx's reappraisal of Aristotle's thoughts on exchange and value, let us dive deeper into this conundrum of the monstrosity that is chrematistics. In his 'On the Generation of Animals', Aristotle describes a monstrosity as an excess of matter over form (as opposed to his concept of privation, the failure to *fulfil* a certain form); a monstrosity, in other words, is the failure of formal nature to fully master material nature (Aristotle, 1829, p. 123; Connell, 2007; Pike, 1999, p. 119). Through this excess of matter, which cannot be fully appropriated by form, the monstrosity escapes definition, which is defined by Aristotle as fulfilment of form (*entelecheia*). At first glance, we seem to find such a case of a monstrosity in the chrematistics use of money:

> Money is torn from its political condition of mediating need to become the number of an artificial and convulsive movement. The infinite movement of accumulation is what empties the city of its self-presence by achieving the metamorphosis of goods into commodities [...]. (Alliez, 1996, p. xvii)

But if we look closer, we realize that things lie a little different here: it is not an excess on the side of matter. It is a condition of possibility of chrematistics, that the matter, that constitutes money, i.e. the precious metals that the coins are minted from, really fulfil their function as money. It is an excess of form *against itself*: Only by really fulfilling its function, i.e. buying and selling commodities,[13] it can detach itself from its place within the political order of the polis. Only by fulfilling its entelechy it can paradoxically subvert it. The end (*telos*) of exchange, to supply every citizen of the polis with the means to lead a good life, gets subverted to the mere private end of accumulating more money, in Marxian terms the formula M-M^{I}. But by entering this bad infinity, the *telos* of chrematistics is not an end at all – it is, by its very definition, *endless* (Johnston, 2024, p. xviii).

The wealth that is produced by chrematistics is thus not defined as the host of goods that satisfy the needs of the citizens (nutrition, clothing, housing, etc.), but its capacity to satisfy a certain need (i.e. its use-value) is reduced to the mere bearer of exchange-value. Wealth becomes *abstract*, *individual* wealth (Berthoud, 2003, p. 283). It is precisely in this regard that Aristotle is credited by Marx as being the first thinker to have analyzed the value-form (Marx, 2010a, p. 69). This value-form is, according to Marx, characterized by three crucial characteristics: (a) 'use value becomes the form of manifestation, the phenomenal form of its opposite, value' (Marx, 2010a, p. 66) (b) 'concrete labour becomes the form under which its opposite, abstract human labour, manifests itself' (Marx, 2010a, p. 69); (c) the labour of private individuals (*Privatarbeit*) becomes the form of appearance of labour in its social character (*'Arbeit in unmittelbar gesellschaftlicher Form'*) (Marx, 1962, p. 73). What Aristotle, in his analysis of the act of exchange, according to Marx, has already discovered are the second and the third characteristics of this value form.

> There was, however, an important fact which prevented Aristotle from seeing that, to attribute value to commodities, is merely a mode of expressing all labour as equal human labour, and consequently as labour of equal quality. Greek society was founded upon slavery, and had, therefore, for its natural basis, the inequality of men and of their labour powers. The secret of the expression of value, namely, that all kinds of labour are equal and equivalent, because, and so far as they are human labour in general, cannot be deciphered, until the notion of human equality has already acquired the fixity of a popular prejudice. This, however, is possible only in a society in which the great mass of the produce of labour takes the form of commodities, in which, consequently, the dominant relation between man and man, is that of owners of commodities. (Marx, 2010a, p. 70)

What is implicated by this analysis of the value-form is thus a certain historical form of the separation of labour: only if this separation is organized in a way that the different concrete labours, producing different concrete use-values are individual, private labour mediated through exchange, exchange-value can emerge (Heinrich, 2021, p. 41). This exchange-value, now, is a rather peculiar entity: Aristotle failed to properly analyze it because he thought of production and exchange as two completely different acts: the former taking place in the private sphere of the oikos and the latter in the public sphere of the polis. Aristotle *did*, in other words, fully analyze the division, abstraction and appropriation of labour. What he *failed* to understand is how they manifested in the objective form of the commodity:

> [. . .] Aristotle wants to find an essence which manifests itself only through exchange though it continues the "latent nature" of the thing. Marx showed clearly what precluded Aristotle from comprehending the essence of the exchange relation: the *absence of the value concept.* (Ilyenkow, 1982, p. 95)

But this value concept is based on the existence of abstract human labour, which reifies itself in the commodity. The value-form escapes Aristotelian entelechy of 'pure form' because the commodity-form is not form in an Aristotelian sense of the teleological fulfilment of a thing's becoming. Being a commodity is not what a thing *is* (in a strictly ontological sense) but rather a social relation that appears *as* a thing (Ilyenkow, 1982, p. 119). This value-form as form of appearance of a social relation *as thing* finds its fulfilment in the money-form:

> Marx answers to the (Aristotelian) question (of form), "what it is, to be a commodity," with the (Hegelian) dialectical exposition of an independent "absolute commodity," with the

> genesis of the form of money [*Geldform*], so that the commodity itself, like in reality, does not present itself as "abstract generality" anymore. The form is in this way taken in its own development, or, as Hegel puts it, in its "own movement" [*Selbstbewegung*]. Because being a commodity is precisely this communal *behaviour* of commodities, which designates an independent commodity as the ground and reason [*Grund*] of their individual existence. (Çıdam, 2012, p. 69)[14]

With this in mind, it might get easier to understand what is monstrous about the form in which 'the wealth of societies in which the capitalist mode of production prevails, appears'. By virtue of being composed of single commodities, which are accumulated virtually *ad infinitum*, its own nature is subverted: By being reduced to the role of a mere bearer of exchange-value, the use-values of the single commodities lose their concrete character of usefulness; by being reduced to a mere quantity of pure value, the concrete useful labour producing these commodities is reduced to a general abstraction, whose only use is to feed the ever growing quantity of abstract wealth, which itself is stripped of all positive determinations (Eichler, 2015, p. 121). Wealth as capital becomes a self-sustaining, self-acting entity that subjects its bearers to its own (abstract) will, and the social structures that mediate it are erased (Johnston, 2024, p. xx). It is thus uncanny in the precise Freudian sense of 'doubt [. . .] whether a lifeless object might not be animate' (Freud, 2003, p. 135).

TO BEGIN AT THE BEGINNING: AN EMPTINESS AT THE HEART OF THE COMMODITY

We have stated earlier that, while the first sentence of the *Contributions* presents us with a historical fact, the first sentence of *Capital* presents us with a logical conjunction. A logical conjunction about a historical fact to be precise: That the transhistorical economic category of wealth under the condition of the capitalist mode of production takes on the appearance of an accumulation of commodities. This implies already the historical specificity of the capitalist mode of production, the potential infinity it brings forth and the element on which this infinity draws, namely the commodity. The logical reason to begin *Capital* with the commodity thus lies in its form itself. We have traced the failure to grasp the commodity-form through Aristotelian hylomorphism in order to show the monstrosity that lies at its heart: It carries within itself a whole universe of social relations that can only appear as objectified in the commodity – the division, abstraction and appropriation of labour – but are at the same time, paradoxically, *erased* in this appearance. It is in this sense that the accumulation of commodities is monstrous, *un-geheuer*, for in it, we have the violent return of something 'once familiar and then repressed' (Freud, 2003, p. 147). It is indeed a concept 'overcharge[d] with meanings that are difficult to keep under control' (Althusser, 2006a, p. 41).

It is thus interesting, that this 'haunting' logic, which is active in the beginning of capital, is criticized by Althusser through the insinuation of another haunting, namely the insinuation that 'idealism haunts *Capital*' (Althusser, 2006a, p. 38).

He claims that the idea to begin with that what is most abstract was imposed on him by a certain idea of science – the Hegelian science of logic (Althusser, 2006a, p. 41). He states that this beginning with the 'simplest' and 'most abstract' form, being the commodity and thus the abstraction of value, will become problematic in the deduction of money and capitalist exploitation, by presupposing abstract labour: 'Marx sets out from it as if it were a given: not the result of a terribly complicated historical process but, as it were, the "simplest" original state' (Althusser, 2006a, p. 39). This strictly logical 'order of exposition', he argues, leaves out something that Marx has to discuss outside of it to propose a theory of exploitation outside of his theory of surplus-value, and Marx has to take into account what his 'order of exposition' explicitly forces him to bracket out: the productivity of labour in all its forms, labour-power taken as something else than a mere commodity, the history of conditions under which capitalism arose, etc. (Althusser, 2006a, p. 39).[15] Especially the purely arithmetical presentation (*Darstellung*) of surplus-value as difference between the value of labour-power and produced value can – according to Althusser – lead to 'purely economistic' interpretation of exploitation. But, in order to facilitate class-struggle, exploitation cannot be reduced to the extraction of surplus-value, so we must take into consideration the concrete forms and conditions of exploitation (Althusser, 2006a, p. 43).

We have already – in apparent agreement with Althusser – stated the odd doubling of the beginning of *Capital*. And, indeed, he seems to be right that Marx 'sets out from a given': At first glance, the first sentence of *Capital* confronts us with commonsensical understandings of the categories, wealth and commodity that are derived from our everyday encounters with them (Heinrich, 2021, p. 54). Subsequently, Marx engages in an analysis (not a definition!) of this category, the commodity. Also, labour, although omnipresent throughout the first part *commodities and money,* is only defined *concretely* in the third part on the *production of absolute surplus-value*. Until then, we only encounter it as abstractions: as (abstractly) useful labour, as 'human labour as such'[16] and as the commodity of labour-power. But here the dialectical 'order of exposition', which Althusser critiques so harshly, unfolds its power: Defining the capitalist mode of production as the historical mode of production, in which exploitation takes the form of the appropriation of surplus-value by the owners of the means of production (Marx, 2010a, pp. 196–209), we see why we have to start from the commodity: The commodity is the bearer of exchange-value, and without exchange-value, there would not be surplus-value. But this realization comes *after* the beginning of *Capital*; it comes when the commodity-form is already fully developed, it comes when we enter the analysis of the production process. So, while it is true that we can only fully understand the meaning of the commodity-form from the standpoint of the developed totality of the capitalist mode of production, it is equally true that we can only understand this totality as developed out of the elementary form of the commodity (Ritsert, 1973, p. 11).

To understand what that means, we have to fully understand the scope of abstraction, that is active in the concept of labour, that Marx uses, before we enter the 'hidden abode of production' (Marx, 2010a, p. 186). The first form that we actually encounter labour in, in *Capital*, is the finished product. Marx introduces this category as answer to the question of the 'common "something"' that is the shared by all commodities in order to express exchange value (Marx, 2010a, p. 47). We thus arrive at the category of labour (or the *product* of labour) by negation of all positive properties of use-values:[17]

> If then we leave out of consideration the use value of commodities, they have only one common property left, that of being products of labour. But even the product of labour itself has undergone a change in our hands. If we make abstraction from its use value, we make abstraction at the same time from the material elements and shapes that make the product a use value; we see in it no longer a table, a house, yarn, or any other useful thing. Its existence as a material thing is put out of sight. Neither can it any longer be regarded as the product of the labour of the joiner, the mason, the spinner, or of any other definite kind of productive labour. Along with the useful qualities of the products themselves, we put out of sight both the useful character of the various kinds of labour embodied in them, and the concrete forms of that labour; there is nothing left but what is common to them all; all are reduced to one and the same sort of labour, human labour in the abstract. (Marx, 2010a, p. 48)

The sticking point here is *not* that the labour process finds its end and embodiment in a product; this holds true for every labour process that produces use-values, regardless of the social forms these use-values will take on later. What Marx prepares here is the insight – which, of course will come only once the commodity-form, and thus the commodity of labour-power, is developed – that only in the capitalist mode of production, the process of production is also the process of generating value (*Verwertung*). This is the full scope of the meaning of production as production *of commodities* (Ritsert, 1973, p. 11). Marx thus goes on to investigate this form of labour that appears to us in the commodity:

> Let us now consider the residue of each of these products; it consists of the same *phantom-like objectivity* [*gespenstische Gegenständlichkeit*] in each, a mere congelation [*bloße Gallerte*] of homogeneous human labour, of labour power expended without regard to the mode of its expenditure. (Marx, 2010a, p. 48; Marx, 1962, p. 52)[18]

This is precisely the moment, in which all the elements, that Althusser deems exterior to the 'order of exposition' are bracketed out: by abstracting from the mode of expenditure of labour, taking it only as homogeneous human labour, all the concrete circumstances under which this labour is expanded, the command of the foremen and the manager, the working hours, the inhumane conditions in the factory, etc., all these concrete factors of production under capital are suppressed from the description. In other words: What is absent from this conjuncture is precisely the object of *Capital*: concrete labour and its exploitation. This act of 'bracketing out', which Althusser – not entirely without reason – criticizes as Hegelian nicety, is the act of *beginning* of *Capital* as a *critique* of political economy.

To understand this we have to revisit this supposed analogy between the beginning of Hegels *Science of Logic* and Marx's *Capital*. Marx himself poses this problem in his preface to the first edition: 'Every beginning is difficult, holds in all sciences. To understand the first chapter, especially the section that contains the analysis of commodities, will, therefore, present the greatest difficulty'

(Marx, 2010a, p. 7). It is noteworthy, though, that Marx tells us that 'every beginning is difficult', by hinting back at the *Contributions*, where this beginning *has already been made*. Furthermore, it has been made in an immediate manner, with (bourgeois) wealth. Hegel, on the other hand, arrives at the 'problem of beginnings', which he grapples with in his *Logic,* from the Problem of Agrippa's dilemma: The beginning cannot be set in an immediate, dogmatic way; it cannot be mediated from something other, neither. It therefore seems to be either dogmatic, regressive or circular. Hegel has to abandon all determination of content to make his beginning, where Marx begins with the seemingly unmediated 'appearance of wealth' (Stekeler, 2020, p. 244). Here, this dissection of the analogy has to be precise to the point of the pedantic: Hegel sets forth from the act of abstraction from all positive content, starting from the empty determinations of pure being and pure nothingness, that, in their emptiness, fall into one (Hegel, 1969a, p. 83). He has to start from there because it is his goal to prove the unity of the ontological order of being and the epistemological order of knowing (Rohs, 1969, p. 19). Marx, on the other hand, starts from a certain given: (bourgeois) wealth. This seems to present us with a certain content: the 'immense accumulation of commodities'. It is only in the subsequent analysis of the commodity-form that we learn that this is actually not a (positive) content at all, but, on the contrary, the commodity-form only exists through the negation of all positive content of use-value and thus useful human labour, reducing all products to a 'mere congelation of homogeneous human labour', which we grasp the abstractness of this beginning. In opposition to Hegel, the reason to begin *Capital* with the abstraction that is the elementary form of bourgeois wealth, the commodity, is *not* knowledge:

> Hence, when we bring the products of our labour into relation with each other as values, it is not because we see in these articles the material receptacles of homogeneous human labour. Quite the contrary: whenever, by an exchange, we equate as values our different products, by that very act, we also equate, as human labour, the different kinds of labour expended upon them. We are not aware of this, nevertheless we do it. (Marx, 2010a, p. 84f)

The abstraction that is thus at play here is *real-abstraction*, an abstraction that does not take place in thought but in reality (Sohn-Rethel, 1970, p. 76). The problem here is thus not abstract thought, as in Hegels *Logic,* but the abstract *act* that is commodity exchange according to value, which produces labour as *abstract* labour (Arthur, 2002, p. 157; Fineschi, 2020, p. 63). What is real in this real-abstraction, which appears as 'immense accumulation of commodities', is the abstraction from all positive determination, which renders the individual use-values comparable. It is precisely this absence of all determination, of all historical or cultural *content*, this emptiness, that is the reality *behind* things as commodities, the reality that just *appears* in these things (Toscano, 2008, p. 276). This is the dialectical twist that Althusser misses in his critique of the 'Hegelian' 'order of exposition': these historical and cultural specificities of the individual objects and the labours that produced them are not absent by literary choice of Marx, but they're absent because they are *erased* from the appearance of the commodity. Furthermore, it is precisely the *function* of the commodity-form to erase them, to *bracket them out* in order to facilitate the form exploitation, that is specific to the capitalist mode of production: the extraction of surplus-value.

We thus *have* to start from the single commodity and its value-form because it is precisely the form through which the concealment of exploitation works; thus, its critique has to articulate itself. Only through the dialectical method, that sets being and nothingness as ontological equals at the beginning, can the negativity, that is active in the commodity-form, be brought forth. Other than Hegel, who, in his *Logic*, sets out from pure nothingness, Marx sets out from a determined negation: the negation of the genus of use-value in the commodity form. He then proceeds to generalize this negation until he arrives at the general form of value as the pure presence of this emptiness that manifests itself as the 'phantom-like objectivity' that is value (Arthur, 2001, p. 35). We see how this dialectical twist, again, follows the logic of the uncanny: the violent return of something 'once familiar and then repressed' (Freud, 2003, p. 147):

> Value, its phantom-like objectivity, is strictu sensu uncanny. It conceals precisely that by which it will be haunted. This is probably the most important part of the story that Capital tells. For Capital does not only deal with commodity exchange. It deals with the hidden logics of exploitation and of crisis, too. (Hartle, 2010, p. 61)

Out of this 'uncanny' logic of the negative, that is active in the commodity form, we can explain the metaphorical opposition between 'living' and 'dead' labour that Marx uses to illustrate the function of accumulation (Arndt, 2012, p. 153). 'Living', i.e. concrete, productive labour can only be accumulated as 'dead' labour, by means of the commodity form, because only in the commodity, it can appear as value, which can be accumulated. The labour that is creating exchange-value is not just 'objectified labour' pure and simple but labour objectified as '*abstract general* labour' and only as such producing value (Marx, 2010c, p. 271). 'Living labour' under capital becomes thus a pure means of production for the sake of accumulation, not the satisfaction of (human) needs. 'Living' labour is reduced to a means of the expansion of 'dead' labour (McNally, 2011, p. 141):[19]

> For all its ghostly objectivity, value flourishes only by attaching itself to, by temporarily possessing, entities whose objectivity is appreciably more palpable. But this attachment takes the form of a grotesque doubling, as the soul of value strives to capture the bodies of value, to possess them, and to evacuate them of all sensibility and concreteness, indeed to suck the life from them in the case of living labour. Marx portrays this vampire-like possession as positively demonic. Its consequence is a nightmare-world in which the products of past labour come to dominate living labour. (McNally, 2011, p. 132)

CAPITALS OTHER BEGINNING: 'PRIMITIVE ACCUMULATION' AND THE MAKING OF THE DOUBLE-FREE WORKER

But then, the question still remains if Althusser's reproach holds true that the chapters 'the working day, the labour process, manufacture and big industry, and the extraordinary chapter on primitive accumulation' (Althusser, 2006a, p. 39) stand outside of this 'order of exposition'? And if so, with what *kind* of outside are we dealing here? To investigate this, let us now turn to the *historical* beginning of the capitalist mode of production, the 'extraordinary chapter on primitive accumulation'. Althusser claims, as we have seen earlier, that we have to take into account the concrete forms and conditions of exploitation, if we want to facilitate class struggle. Something that is not given in the purely arithmetical presentation of exploitation as the difference between the value of the commodity of labour-power and the value it produces (Althusser, 2006a, p. 43).[20] This reproach can hardly be made towards the account of the *historical* beginning, that Marx gives us in the chapter on *primitive accumulation*, stating that 'the history of this [...] is written in the annals of mankind in letters of blood and fire' (Marx, 2010a, p. 706). It might still hold true, though, that this chapter answers to a certain lack within the dialectical order of exposition. Why else go through the pains of beginning again something that has already begun, especially given that 'every beginning is hard' (Marx, 2010a, p. 7)? Marx himself seems to confirm Althusser's suspicion, stating that the chapter on *primitive accumulation* answers to the problem of a 'vicious circle':

> We have seen how money is changed into capital; how through capital surplus value is made, and from surplus value more capital. But the accumulation of capital presupposes surplus value; surplus value presupposes capitalistic production; capitalistic production presupposes the pre-existence of considerable masses of capital and of labour power in the hands of producers of commodities. (Marx, 2010a, p. 704)

This problem is by no means new to the science of political economy. Adam Smith already addressed it in his concept of *previous accumulation*, a concept, that Marx – with good reason – disqualifies as nursery tale: 'In times long gone by there were two sorts of people; one, the diligent, intelligent, and, above all, frugal élite; the other, lazy rascals, spending their substance, and more, in riotous living' (Marx, 2010a, p. 704). This tale – apart from its obvious ideological tendency – is logically flawed in so far as hoarding without the possibility to invest into the production of surplus-value, i.e. the exploitation of labour, is mere treasuring. The amount of value one can get hold of in this system is therefore by definition always particular and finite (Read, 2002, p. 28). The viscous circle begins anew. In order to become capital, money and commodities have to encounter its other, the free worker, the seller of labour-power that is to be exploited:

> In themselves money and commodities are no more capital than are the means of production and of subsistence. They want transforming into capital. But this transformation itself can only take place under certain circumstances that centre in this, viz., that two very different kinds of commodity possessors must come face to face and into contact; on the one hand, the owners of money, means of production, means of subsistence, who are eager to increase the sum of values they possess, by buying other people's labour power; on the other hand, free labourers, the sellers of their own labour power, and therefore the sellers of labour. (Marx, 2010a, p. 705)

It thus turns out, that the *historical* beginning of the capitalist mode of production, this other beginning that supplements, haunts its logical beginning, is nothing other than the historical genesis of capital's other: the free labourer. This begs the question: Why does the constitution of the commodity is given by way of logical analysis but the category of the free labourer developed by way of historical reconstruction? The answer lies in the polarization of the capitalist mode of production that completely separates the labourers from the owners of the means of production. On the scale of commodity production, this split only manifests itself as the difference between two owners of commodities, the owner of the means of production and the owner of labour-power. To fully understand the quality of this split – i.e. the class-difference between these two apparently equal owners of commodities – we have to understand the historical specificity of what it is to 'have nothing to sell but ones labour power' (Marx, 2010a, p. 705). But in order to understand this specificity, the logical order of commodities has to be already established so that the category of labour-power-as-commodity can appear in the first place:

> Whereas primitive accumulation reveals the violent operations necessary to constitute a laboring subject, to constitute those who have only their labor-power to sell, the analysis of the commodity form takes this condition as an already accomplished fact. Once the commodification of labor is assumed, surplus value or surplus labor is only the labor in excess of what is necessary to reproduce labor-power: the value of what is produced over the value of what labor-power costs. (Read, 2002, p. 44)

To illustrate what this means, we can go back to Aristotle. We have already said that Marx, although praising him as the first thinker to have theorized the problem of value (Marx, 2010a, p. 69), also states that he could not fully analyze the form of commodity because the second condition of the capitalist mode of production was not there yet: the free labourer. As long as this condition is not fulfilled, capital cannot enter the production process, and it has to stay outside of it as merchant's capital and usurer's capital 'in the pores of [...] society' (Marx, 2010a, p. 90). Although Aristotle, as credited by Marx, has already developed the manifestation of abstract labour in concrete labour and the social character of the labour of individuals (Marx, 2010a, p. 69), he could not develop the value-form because, although labour in his analysis was already abstract, it was not *general* and therefore labour-power did not appear as a commodity. What did appear as commodities, though, were the *bearers* of this labour-power, the slaves:

> By stressing domination and ownership, i.e., political and legal categories, ancient authors overlooked exploitation, i.e., an economic category. Masters certainly knew that buying and sustaining slaves cost money, but they do not seem to have realized that this money actually "belonged" to their slaves. To phrase it differently, the way in which masters exploited their slaves, i.e. by possessing their whole body, concealed the fact that they did not possess all the products of their labour. (Kyrtatas, 2002, p. 142)

What changes between Aristotle and Marx is thus not the fact but only the form of exploitation. But, and this is the crucial point of the logic of the commodity, the form of exploitation that is specific to capital *does not appear* as exploitation, it appears as an exchange of (equal) commodities. It is thus true that the historical development of the free labourer as capital's other stands outside of the (logical) order of exposition of *Capital* because by means of this historical development, his exploitation becomes readable *as exploitation*. But this 'outside' of the order of exposition is a specific outside that is dialectically bound to it: Only because we went through the logical unfolding of the capitalist mode of production out of the single commodity, we can decipher the exploitation of the free labourer by means of commodity-exchange as exploitation that is *specific to this mode of production*. If we thus look closer at this central figure of the 'free labourer', we find that, in his historical genesis, the logical order of the analysis of the commodity is mirrored:

> Free labourers, in the double sense that neither they themselves form part and parcel of the means of production, as in the case of slaves, bondsmen, &c, nor do the means of production belong to them, as in the case of peasant proprietors; they are, therefore, free from, unencumbered by, any means of production of their own. (Marx, 2010a, p. 705)

The freedom that characterizes the labourer is thus, analogous to the abstract-general-labour-turned-commodity that we encounter at the logical beginning of capital, defined by an absence of determinations. Like the logical analysis of the commodity, the historical genesis of the labourer is a subsequent negation of positive and concrete capacities: 'The expropriation of the agricultural producer, of the peasant, from the soil, is the basis of the whole process' (Marx, 2010, p. 707). This expropriation of the means of production is at the same time an expropriation of the determination of labour as agricultural work and of its product as means of subsistence. This definition of freedom as absence of determinations brings Marx – again – in close proximity to Hegel, whose *Philosophy of Rights*, analogous his *Science of Logic*, sets out from a moment of radical indeterminacy, *freedom*. This radical indeterminacy, though, which Hegel sees as condition for the autonomy of spirit, creates at the same time a radical lack of *real* self-relation: The self-relation that the subject can enter in this stadium is as such an external relation (Hegel, 1970, pp. 49–52). Equality is reduced to a lack of difference, and abstraction to a mere lack of determination. These lead to a dysfunctional concept of freedom (Finelli, 2016, p. 90). Marx inverts Hegels project of developing this dysfunctional concept of freedom to a fully realized concept of freedom in the state, to the prove, that fully developed (bourgeois) freedom is the condition of possibility of the total serfdom of the labourer under capital. He does so by blurring the lines of Hegelian *Logic* and *Realphilosophie* (Arndt, 2017, p. 6). It is thus by no means accidental that the mechanism that mints the indeterminate rabble that the expropriation of agricultural workers has left behind into this new subjectivity that is the free labourer, takes the form of the bourgeois state-apparatus, that, according to its own standards, is governed above all by freedom and equality:

> Thus were the agricultural people, first forcibly expropriated from the soil, driven from their homes, turned into vagabonds, and then whipped, branded, tortured by laws grotesquely terrible, into the discipline necessary for the wage system. It is not enough that the conditions of labour are concentrated in a mass, in the shape of capital, at the one pole of society, while at

> the other are grouped masses of men, who have nothing to sell but their labour power. Neither is it enough that they are compelled to sell it voluntarily. The advance of capitalist production develops a working class, which by education, tradition, habit, looks upon the conditions of that mode of production as self-evident laws of Nature. The organization of the capitalist process of production, once fully developed, breaks down all resistance. (Marx, 2010a, p. 726)

We can see here again the effect of the mirroring of the two beginnings of *Capital*: The logical development had to be abstract to the point of emptiness, in order to define the order in which the categories, that define the capitalist mode of production in its historical specificity could appear in the first place. The historical development of the free worker, that fills these categories with content – labour-power – but is, in this very act, erased from it, had to be concrete to the point of overdetermination, to show the lack at the heart of these categories, taken in their own right. Insofar, Althusser was right in stating that this historical beginning is outside of the dialectical order of exposition, but only in the sense that only the outside can really define what it is to be *inside*. 'Value is fundamentally about corporeality, about the labouring bodies without which the spectral and vampiric powers of capital cannot take flight' (McNally, 2011, p. 134).

CONCLUSION: THE BEGINNING(S) OF CAPITAL

'[T]his, the thing ("this thing") will end up coming. The *revenant* is going to come' (Derrida, 1994, p. 2). We have seen above, that *capital* does indeed follow the logic of the revenant, in the precise sense of the German *Wieder-Gänger*, something (or someone) that – although it should be dead and gone – *walks again* to haunt the living. 'Capital is dead labour, that, vampire-like, only lives by sucking living labour, and lives the more, the more labour it sucks' (Marx, 2010a, p. 241). This vampirism of capital works through the split between the abstract and the concrete: it exploits *living* labour as actual, concrete, useful labour but accumulates *dead* labour, objectified in commodities, in which it only appears under the value-form, as abstract general labour. Through this turn, dead labour turned capital comes to dominate living labour (McNally, 2011, p. 132).

We have seen with Aristotle that capital in its basic form as self-valorizing value, M-M^{1}, has existed for Millennia. But in order to take this dominating position, i.e. for the capitalist *mode of production* to prevail, for capital to really *become* capital, it has to encounter its other: the double-free labourer who has nothing to sell but his labour-power. To understand what it means to 'have nothing to sell but ones labour power', the category of the commodity has to be developed, so the historical specificity of the capitalist mode of exploitation, which works through the buying and selling of this special commodity, can come forth. These are the three beginnings of *Capital*: The historical beginning of the entity *capital*, self-valorizing value, that in its monstrous form was already known to Aristotle; the historical beginning of the *capitalist mode of production* that is set in the encounter of capital with its other, the double-free labourer and finally the logical beginning of capital, which is the dialectical analysis of the commodity, the form of objectivity in which all these historical developments find their specific *order of appearance*.

The *critique* of political economy in this sense had to begin with an act of 'bracketing out' (Althusser, 2006a, p. 39): concrete labour and its exploitation had to be bracketed out of the dialectical unfolding of the category of the commodity because it is precisely the function of the commodity-form in the capitalist mode of exploitation to erase the function of exploitation of concrete labour by turning concrete and specific labour into the commodity of (abstract and general) labour-power and the function of its exploitation into the an exchange of equal commodities. The abstraction that takes place here is *real*-abstraction, abstraction in the sense that, once turned into the commodity-form, the labour expended in it *really is* abstract general labour. These two beginnings then, the logical one of the commodity-form, on the one hand, and the historical one of the double-free labourer, on the other hand, mirror each other: They are both unfolded as a subsequent negation of determinations, and both sets of negation take place in the *real*. Only in this structure of the mirroring, the critique of political economy can unfold its full power. The logical analysis showed the lack that is found at the heart of the commodity form. The historical reconstruction showed this lack to be the history of violence that formed the capitalist mode of exploitation. It is in this sense that the critique of political economy makes use of the logic of the uncanny: it unveils the violent return of something 'once familiar and then repressed' (Freud, 2003, p. 147).

It is in this sense that the accumulation of commodities, from which we started, is monstrous, *un-geheuer*: On the first glance, it seemed to be a rather mundane object found in the centre of every household, but its analysis revealed that in its heart it is 'overcharge[d] [...] with meanings that are difficult to keep under control' (Althusser, 2006a, p. 41). In its heart, we find an emptiness that conceals a whole world of violence and exploitation. Moreover, this emptiness seems to develop its own life, reducing all difference in concrete usefulness to a homogeneous quantity of abstract value, whose only end is its infinite accumulation of ever more abstract value. It becomes an end – or rather an end-*less* – as accumulation for its own sake, unbound from any restriction that actual *human* needs might impose on it. The 'wealth of societies, in which the capitalist mode of production prevails', is thus indeed a monstrosity: a self-servicing entity that breeds at the very heart of our society, something supposedly made by us, that broke free of our control over it and took itself control over us. Something that is supposedly inanimate that develops a life beyond us, beyond our control, serving only its own ends, degrading us to pure means to these ends.

NOTES

1. Although the English language distinguishes between apparition and appearance, I will continue to use it synonymously, since, in Marx, they both refer to the (Hegelian) category of *Erscheinung*.
2. Translation amended, my italics. The dialectical connection between these two apparitions might be worth exploring.

3. Described by Marx as the 'mother of all crazy [*ver-rückte*] forms' (Johnston, 2024, p. 175). For this metaphor of crazy/dis-placed forms, see also Backhaus (2011, pp. 299–333).

4. This is a fact that has led to much confusion in the history of political economy, tempting especially bourgeois economists to place the beginning of the capitalist *mode of production* in some stage of early history, Babylonia or Greece, in order to present it as 'natural order of things' (Milios, 2019, p. 9).

5. Michel Heinrich has pointed towards the fact that these 'metaphysical subtleties and theological niceties' are by no means inherent to the *appearance* of the commodity but have to be unveiled by analysis (Heinrich, 2021, p. 164).

6. Althusser claimed that it is Marx's own mania for a logical exposition that forced him to bracket out the exploitation of labour at this point and only let him introduce it at a later point in *Capital* (Althusser, 2006a, p. 39). But my point here is that it is the *ideological function* of capital *itself* to bracket this out: To present the act of exploitation (the appropriation of surplus-labour) *as* an act of exchange of equal commodities (money vs labour-power). I will come back to this argument below (b).

7. The German original even speaks of *bourgeois wealth* (*bürgerlicher Reichtum*) tout court... (Marx, 1961, p. 15).

8. If we want to embrace the Heideggerian connotation, one could even translate it as *elementary being-there*....

9. For all intense and purpose, lets stick to Hegels definition of appearance (*Schein*) as being without essence (*wesenloses Sein*) (Hegel, 1969b, p. 17) – a definition which brings this *appearance* in close proximity to the *revenant* we started with.

10. Science taken in the Greek sense of *technē*.

11. Giving the bourgeois science of *political economy* an oxymoronic character...

12. According to his definition of science in the *Metaphysics* (Aristotle, 1924, pp. 1025b–1026b).

13. I use the term 'commodity' here in the broadest possible sense of 'a thing infused with exchange value' for a closer discussion of the problem of the commodity form in Aristotle see Hahn (2025).

14. My translation.

15. Althusser relies here on a critique of Marx's theory of the transformation of surplus-value into profit, uttered by Piero Sraffa in his *Production of Commodities by Means of Commodities* (1960).

16. Though it should be kept in mind that Labour 'as such' itself as a historically specific abstraction as Marx has already stated in the *Introduction* of 1857 (Marx, 2010d, p. 40).

17. It is, in this context, not without interest, that the first subject to actually *work* in *Das Kapital,* is *history*: 'To discover the various uses of things is the work of history' (Marx, 2010a, p. 45).

18. Translation amended.

19. Adrian Johnston thus goes so far as to define the formula of capital M-C-M^{I} as 'death-drive-like *Wiederholungszwang*' (Johnston, 2014, p. 77).

20. Beverly Best has shown recently that this arithmetical presentation of exploitation is not a mere error of Marx's method but is intrinsic to capitals own material ideology, through which productivity as such is reduced to a mere arithmetical difference between capital and profit (Best, 2024, p. 113).

REFERENCES

Alliez, E. (1996). *Capital times – Tales from the conquest of time*. University of Minnesota Press.

Althusser, L. (2006). Marx in his limits. In G. M. Goshgarian, F. Matheron, & O. Corpet (Trans.), *Philosophy of the encounter – Later writings, 1978–87*. Verso.

Althusser, L., Balibar, É., Establet, R., Macherey, P., & Rancière, J. (2015). *Reading capital*. tr. Ben Brewster. Verso.
Aristotle. (1912). *Aristotle: Politics – A treatise on government* tr. William Ellis. J.M. Dent & Sons.
Aristotle. (2014). *Aristotle: Nicomachean ethics*. Oxford UP.
Arndt, A. (2012). *Karl Marx – Versuch über den Zusammenhang seiner Theorie*. Akademie.
Arndt, A. (2017). Hegels Begriff des Begriffs und der Begriff des Wertes in Marx' Kapital. *Zeitschrift für kritische Sozialtheorie und Philosophie*, *4*(1–2), 3–22.
Arthur, C. (2001). The spectral ontology of value. *Radical Philosophy*, *107*, 32–42.
Arthur, C. (2002). *The new dialectic and Marx's capital*. Brill.
Backhaus, H. G. (2011). *Dialektik der Wertform – Untersuchungen zur Marxschen Wertkritik*. Ca ira.
Aristotle. (1829). *De Generatione Animalum Libri Quinqi*. Ed. Immanuel Bekker. Akademie.
Berthoud, A. (1987). Argent et Désir d'Argent chez Marx et Aristote. *Cahiers d'Economie Politique*, *13*, 3–17.
Berthoud, A. (2003). La Richesse et ses Deux Types. *Revue du MAUSS, 2003/1*, *21*, 276–287.
Best. (2024). *The automatic fetish – the Law of Value in Marx's capital*. Verso.
Çıdam, V. (2012). *Die Phänomenologie des Widergeistes – Eine Anerkennungstheoretische Deutung von Marx' normativer Kritik am Kapitalismus im Kapital*. Nomos.
Connell, S. (2007). Aristotle's explanations of monstrous births and deformities in generation of animals 4.4. In A. Falcon & D. Levebvre (Hg.), *Aristotle's Generation of Animals – A critical guide* (pp. 207–223). Cambridge UP. https://eprints.bbk.ac.uk/id/eprint/21954
Derrida, J. (1994). *Spectres of Marx – The state of the debt, the work of mourning and the new international*. tr. Peggy Knauf. Routledge.
Digitales Wörterbuch der deutschen Sprache. (Ed.). Berlin-Brandenburgischen Akademie der Wissenschaften. https://doi.org/dwds.de/wb/ungeheuer. https://doi.org/dwds.de/d/zitieren#z-dwdswb-eintrag. Accessed on October 19, 2025.
Eichler, M. (2015). *Von der Vernunft zum Wert – Die Grundlagen der ökonomischen Theorie von Karl Marx*. transcript.
Ferrain, A. (2001). *Hegel and Aristotle*. Cambridge UP.
Finelli, R. (2016). *A failed parricide – Hegel and the Young Marx*. Brill.
Fineschi, R. (2020). Real abstraction: Philological issues. In A. Oliva, Á. Oliva, & I. Novarra (Eds.), *Marx and contemporary critical theory – The philosophy of real abstraction* (pp. 61–78). Palgrave McMillan. https://doi.org/10.1007/978-3-030-39954-2_4
Freud, S. (2003). *The uncanny*. Penguin.
Hahn, T. (2025). Gesellschaftliche Synthesis und Archaische Wertform – Für eine Archäologie der Abstraktion. In C. N. Szász (Hg.), *Kritische Philosophiegeschichte*. Diaphanes. (In appearance).
Hartle, J. F. (2010). Phantom-like objectivity (Gespenstische egenständlichkeit). *Krisis*, *2010*(2), 60–65.
Hegel, G. W. F. (1969a). *Die Wissenschaft der Logik I*. (GW 5). Suhrkamp.
Hegel, G. W. F. (1969b). *Die Wissenschaft der Logik II*. (GW 6). Suhrkamp.
Hegel, G. W. F. (1970). *Grundlinien der Philosophie des Rechts*. (GW 7). Suhrkamp.
Heinrich, M. (2021). *Wie das Marxsche "Kapital" lesen – Leseanleitung und Kommentar zum Anfang des Kapitals, Teil 1*. Schmetterling.
Ilyenkow, E. (1982). *The dialectics of the abstract and the concrete in Marx's capital*. Progress.
Johnston, A. (2024). *Infinite greed – The inhuman selfishness of capital*. Columbia UP.
Kyrtatas, D. J. (2002). Domination and exploitation. In P. Cartledge, E. E. Cohen, & L. Foxhall (Hg.), *Money, labour and land – Approaches to the economies of ancient Greece* (pp. 140–155). Routledge.
Lezra, J. (2018). *On the nature of Marx's things – Translation as necrophilology*. Fordham UP.
Marx, K. (1961). *Zur Kritik der Politischen Ökonomie*. (MEW Bd. 13). Dietz.
Marx, K. (1962). *Das Kapital – Kritik der Politischen Ökonomie, Bd. 1 die Kapitalistische Produktion*. (MEW Bd. 23). Dietz.
Marx, K. (2010a). *Capital Volume I*. (MECW Vol. 35). Lawrence & Wishart.
Marx, K. (2010b). *Capital Volume III*. (MECW Vol. 37). Lawrence & Wishart.

Marx, K. (2010c). *A contribution to the critique of political economy.* (MECW Vol. 29). Lawrence & Wishart.

Marx, K. (2010d). *Grundrisse.* (MECW Vol. 28). Lawrence & Wishart.

McNally, D. (2011). *Monsters of the market – Zombies, vampires and global capitalism.* Brill.

Milios, J. (2019). *The origins of capital as a social system – The prevalence of an aleatory encounter.* Routledge.

Nielsen, K. M. (2013). Economy and private property. In M. Deslauries & P. Destrée (Hg.), *The Cambridge companion to Aristotle's politics* (pp. 67–91). Cambridge University Press.

Pike, J. E. (1999). *From Aristotle to Marx – Aristotelianism in Marxist social ontology.* Ashgate.

Pokrytan, A. K. (1981). *Das Historische und das Logische in der Ökonomischen Theorie des Sozialismus.* Akademie.

Priddat, B. P. (2014). Aristoteles' Theorie der Wirtschaft: eine frühe politische Ökonomie. In B. Zehnpfennig (Hg.), *Die "Politik" des Aristoteles* (pp. 92–105). Nomos.

Read, J. R. (2002). Primitive accumulation: The aleatory foundation of capitalism. *Rethinking Marxism, 14*(2), 24–49.

Ritsert, J. (1973). *Probleme politisch-ökonomischer theoriebildung.* Athenäum.

Rohs, P. (1969). *Form und Grund – Interpretation eines Kapitels der Hegelschen Wissenschaft der Logik.* H. Bouvier & Co.. (=Hegelstudien Beiheft 6).

Sohn-Rethel, A. (1970). *Geistige und Körperliche Arbeit – Zur Theorie der gesellschaftlichen Synthesis.* Suhrkamp.

Sraffa, P. (1960). *Production of commodities by means of commodities.* Vora.

Stekeler, P. (2020). *Hegels Wissenschaft der Logik, Ein dialogischer Kommentar, Band 1: Die Objektive Logik – Die Lehre vom Sein, Qualitative Kontraste, Mengen und Maße.* Meiner.

Stiehler, G. (1961). Die Methode des Aufsteigens vom Abstrakten zum Konkreten bei Hegel und Marx. *Hegel-Jahrbuch, 2*, 39–52.

Toscano, A. (2008). The open secret of real abstraction. *Rethinking Marxism, 20*(2).

GROSSMAN'S BREAKDOWN THEORY VERSUS MARX'S VALUE THEORY

Andrew Kliman

Pace University, USA

ABSTRACT

Although Henryk Grossman and his followers have claimed that his theory of capitalist economic breakdown is rooted in Marx's value theory, it is shown here that the two theories are actually incompatible. Marx's value theory implies that Grossman's breakdown tendency does not exist, because even though consumed constant capital grows faster than variable capital and surplus-value, the growth rates must eventually converge. Grossman's failure to recognize this is most likely due to an incorrect assumption that an unending rise in the ratio of constant to variable capital must be a limitless one. It is also shown here that Grossman's breakdown condition – insufficient surplus-value to fund capital accumulation – and the breakdown tendency and falling rate of profit of the Bauer–Grossman reproduction scheme have nothing to do with value or value theory. They are all physical phenomena in disguise, produced by Grossman's implicit constraint on the production of physical output and the resulting disappearance of the physical net product. These defects are traced to a methodological problem, Grossman's inversions of cause and effect. The chapter also argues that empirical phenomena that seem to confirm the breakdown theory do not actually do so and that the relevant defects of the breakdown theory are absent from Marx's actual theory.

Keywords: Henryk Grossman; breakdown; value theory; Karl Marx; capital accumulation; expanded reproduction

Money, Value and Marx's Circuit of Capital
Research in Political Economy, Volume 41, 75–95

Published under exclusive licence by Emerald Publishing Limited
ISSN: 0161-7230/doi:10.1108/S0161-72302026000041011

INTRODUCTION

In his 1929 book, *The Law of Accumulation and Breakdown of the Capitalist System,* Grossman (2022) argued that capitalist economies have an inevitable and *purely economic* tendency to break down. He purported to deduce the breakdown tendency (*Zusammenbruchstendenz*) from Marx's value theory and stylized facts regarding growth paths of the relevant variables, and he argued that the breakdown tendency is a necessary implication of Marx's theory. To this day, Grossman's followers reiterate the claim that the breakdown tendency and the theory based on it are rooted in Marx's value theory. However, this chapter will show that Marx's theory is actually incompatible with Grossman's breakdown theory.[1]

Marx (1990, p. 929) certainly did foresee that capitalist development and the system's class antagonisms, including the growing indignation/revolt (*Empörung*) of the working class, were heading towards 'the negation of the negation' in which '[t]he expropriators are expropriated'. When I say that Grossman had a 'purely economic' breakdown theory, I mean something different. He quoted and endorsed an argument that Bernstein (1899) had put forward in a polemic against revolutionary Marxism and for his 'Revisionist' alternative. Bernstein argued that '[i]f the triumph of socialism were truly an "immanent economic necessity", it would have to be grounded in some proof' that capitalism's 'breakdown [is] unavoidable on purely economic grounds', and he denied that '[t]he maturity of the proletarians', 'their power', and 'general indignation (*Empörung*) at the planned cartel economy' qualify as purely economic factors. Grossman (2022, p. 62) commented that 'Bernstein was correct ... and entirely in accord with Marx'.

On the surface, Grossman's purely economic breakdown theory is value-theoretic. He argued that the consumed part of constant capital tends to grow more rapidly than variable capital and surplus-value.[2] Unless an economic downturn disrupts this dynamic, the differential growth of constant capital inevitably leads to a breakdown point. At that point, the prevailing rates of accumulation of constant and variable capital cannot be sustained because the mass (i.e., amount) of surplus-value has become insufficient to fully fund accumulation at those rates.

However, Grossman did not actually deduce his breakdown tendency from Marx's value theory, and I will show it cannot be so deduced. Marx's theory implies, to the contrary, that the breakdown tendency does not exist. Even though constant capital does grow faster than variable capital and surplus-value, this does not lead to a breakdown because the growth rates must eventually converge.

In the first stage of his analysis, Grossman employed – but only critically and provisionally – a one-sector adaptation of a two-department scheme of expanded reproduction that Bauer (2012) had developed in 1913. In both Bauer's original model and Grossman's adaptation of it, continuous technical progress takes place (In this respect, it differs from Marx's (1992, Chapter 21) scheme of expanded reproduction.) Grossman then presented his fully developed theory in a second stage of his analysis. It is based on the Bauer–Grossman model, but it relaxes many of the model's assumptions. Accordingly, the conclusions of the fully developed theory differ in some respects from the provisional conclusions that Grossman had earlier drawn from the model.

Followers of Grossman's breakdown theory have frequently responded (with some justification) to critics by arguing that their criticisms pertain to the provisional model but fail to address Grossman's fully developed theory. However, what I will show below – including the fact that his theory is incompatible with Marx's value theory – cannot be rebutted in that way.

To make this clear, I will use the term *Grossman's breakdown theory* only in connection with his fully developed theory. When I am discussing Grossman's adaptation of Bauer's scheme of reproduction, I will refer to the *Bauer–Grossman model*. I will use the term *Grossman's breakdown tendency* in connection with both the model and the fully developed theory since it is present in both. Although the breakdown tendency operates only in a modified and attenuated way in Grossman's breakdown theory, the existence of this tendency is the key feature of both the model and the theory.

Section 2 of this chapter briefly documents the fact that both Grossman and his followers assert that his breakdown theory is grounded in Marx's value theory. Section 3 discusses the dynamical properties of the Bauer–Grossman model, in particular its implicit constraint on the growth of physical output. It is this *physical* constraint that generates the model's falling rate of profit and its breakdown tendency; they have nothing to do with value or value theory. Section 4 shows that, even after the restrictive assumptions of the Bauer–Grossman model are relaxed, the underlying cause of the alleged breakdown tendency is purely physical. This finding contrasts markedly with Grossman's value-theoretic explanation of the breakdown.

Section 5 shows that Grossman's breakdown theory and Marx's value theory are incompatible, since the latter implies that the growth rate of constant capital must eventually converge on the growth rates of variable capital and surplus-value. It also discusses Grossman's response to the objection that his breakdown tendency can be nullified by the cheapening of means of production that results from technical progress. He argued that constant capital continues to increase more rapidly than variable capital, despite the cheapening of means of production, and that the breakdown tendency is therefore not nullified. However, I will explain why the faster growth of constant capital – and other phenomena, such as the tendency of the rate of profit to fall – does not imply that a breakdown tendency exists.

Section 6 provides a brief summary and conclusions.

CLAIMS REGARDING THE MARX–GROSSMAN RELATION

Grossman and subsequent proponents of his breakdown theory have consistently argued that Grossman made explicit and further developed a theory of breakdown that was implicit, but not fully worked out, in Marx's work. Given economic trends that Marx himself recognized, such as the displacement of workers by machines, the breakdown theory is a natural and inevitable implication of Marx's value theory. At the start of Chapter 2 of his book, Grossman (2022, p. 107) wrote:

> Even if Marx did not delineate the law of breakdown coherently in one place, he did specify all the elements required for it, so that it can be developed as a self-evident consequence of the capitalist accumulation process on the basis of the law of value and is so obvious and clear that, once demonstrated, it needs no further proof.

In Grossman's view, the most important link between Marx's value theory and the breakdown theory is the supposed fact that 'valorization' (creation of surplus-value in capitalist production) becomes insufficient to fund capital accumulation at the prevailing rate:[3]

> the capitalist production process is characterised by [... an] immanent opposition between ... the restricted possibilities for valorisation and the unlimited development of the productive forces, which necessarily leads to overaccumulation and insufficient valorisation, thus to the breakdown, the final catastrophe of the entire system.
>
> It is apparent that the problem is not whether an excess of commodities remains or not .... The difficulty lies rather in the valorisation of capital: surplus value is not sufficient for accumulation to continue at the rate assume[d]! Hence the catastrophe. (Grossman, 2022, pp. 511, 181)

Grossman's followers have continually reaffirmed that his breakdown theory is rooted in Marx's value theory. For example, Kuhn (2005, p. 75) wrote that '[t]he contradiction between capitalist production as a labour process and as a process driven by the creation of value through the exploitation of wage-labour was, for Grossman, the ultimate cause of capitalism's breakdown tendency'. More recently, Kuhn (2021) stated that 'Marx's labour theory of value entailed a theory of breakdown' and that Grossman 'recovered Marx's theory'.

Mattick (2018, p. 232) has recently equated Grossman's breakdown theory and Marx's value theory even more starkly, referring to 'Marx's value-theoretic breakdown tendency'.[4] He also reiterates Grossman's view that the breakdown theory makes explicit and further develops what was implicit in the 'materials' that Marx left: '[W]hile not himself achieving the theory of the crisis mechanism he originally promised ..., Marx provided materials for the construction of such a theory – one first worked out ... by Henryk Grossmann' (Mattick, 2018, p. 256).

The alleged link between Marx's value theory and Grossman's breakdown theory is emphasized by Roberts (2017), who recently wrote that 'Grossman, in my view, made major contributions in explaining and developing Marx's theory of value and crises under capitalism' and that 'Grossman put value theory and Marx's laws of accumulation and profitability at the centre of the cause of recurrent and regular crises under capitalism'.

Reese (2021) also stresses the supposed value-theoretic character of Grossman's breakdown theory: 'To prove that the cause [of crises] stemmed from the mode of production, Grossman had to re-center Marx's labor theory of value, the fact that the source of profit is capital's exploitation of commodity-producing labor ....' In addition, he endorses the claim that Grossman's breakdown theory is a development of Marx's own theory: 'It fell to Grossman ..., on the eve of the Wall Street Crash, to clarify Marx's breakdown theory and to prove its validity' (Reese, 2022, p. 47).

Below, I will show that the claimed link between Marx's value theory and Grossman's breakdown theory does not in fact exist. Furthermore, the claim that his breakdown tendency is value-theoretic in nature is at best highly misleading, since it focuses on the surface appearance while neglecting the essence of the matter.

THE PHYSICAL DYNAMICS OF THE BAUER–GROSSMAN MODEL

Grossman (2022, p. 319) interpreted Bauer's model as one in which prices (or values) are constant. Although Bauer did not stipulate this explicitly, Grossman's interpretation seems reasonable to me.[5] Grossman (2022, p. 110, emphases in original) made the assumption explicit at the start of his presentation of his own version of the model, stating that 'the assumption of *constant* prices, as the *simplest* case, is the one most appropriate for theoretical purposes, on the basis of which ... more complicated cases can be examined later'. It is a 'provisional theoretical fiction'.

Although his verbal discussion of the model refers to multiple prices and commodities, Grossman's (2022, pp. 185–186) algebraic formulation makes clear that its dynamical relations are those of a one-sector (or aggregate) economy. Accordingly, in the analysis below, there is only one commodity and one price (apart from labour-power and its price); the commodity serves as both the means of production and the means of subsistence. It is equally correct, however, to interpret these variables as the aggregate magnitudes of a multi-sector economy, that is, to think of the price as the aggregate price *index* and to think of the physical quantities of output and means of production as quantity *indexes* of aggregate output and the aggregate stock of means of production (i.e., real output and real means of production).[6]

On the surface, the variables of the Bauer–Grossman model are amounts of value – constant capital, variable capital, surplus-value and so forth. Yet because the price of the commodity is held constant, valuation processes (creation of value, distribution of value, devaluation, etc.) play no part in the variables' movements. All changes in the magnitudes of the 'value' variables are caused exclusively by changes in the associated physical quantities (or 'use-values'). If, for example, constant capital increases by 10% per year, it is because employment of physical means of production increases by 10% per year.

To disclose more fully the underlying physicalist character of the Bauer–Grossman model and the implications of the constant-price assumption, algebraic formalization will be helpful. I will employ the following symbols:

Value Magnitudes	
C	(Consumed) constant capital
S	Surplus-value
V	Variable capital
W	Total value (or price) of the product
Physical Quantities	
A	Means of production
X	Total output produced
Other	
g_K	Growth rate of means of production and constant capital
g_L	Growth rate of employed workforce, variable capital and surplus-value
$\overline{p}$	Constant price (or value) of the commodity, per unit
r	Rate of profit
t	Time (used as a subscript and as an exponent)

Note that the time subscript t will refer to a *moment* in time, not to a period of time. Grossman's Year 1 starts at time $t = 0$ and ends at time $t = 1$, his Year 2 starts at time $t = 1$ and ends at time $t = 2$, and so on. To reflect the fact that the model conceives of inputs as entering into production at the start of the year and output as emerging at the end, the initial values of C, V and A are denoted as C_0, V_0 and A_0 while the initial values of W and X are denoted as W_1 and X_1. Since surplus-value is created throughout the year, the initial values of S and r are denoted as $S_{0,1}$ and $r_{0,1}$.

Determination of the Value Magnitudes

Bauer and Grossman assume that C grows by 10% per year while V and S both grow by 5% per year. These specific numbers affect only the rapidity of changes in the variables, not the general dynamical properties of the model. To generalize the model, I will treat the growth rates g_K and g_L as parameters that can take on any finite values as long as $0 < g_L < g_K$. The growth paths of C, V and S are therefore

$$C_t = C_0(1 + g_K)^t \tag{1}$$

$$V_t = V_0(1 + g_L)^t \tag{2}$$

$$S_{t,t+1} = S_{0,1}(1 + g_L)^t \tag{3}$$

In accordance with Marx's theory, the total value (or price) of the product is equal to the sum of these three amounts of value:

$$W_{t+1} = C_t + V_t + S_{t,t+1} = C_0(1+g_K)^t + (V_0 + S_{0,1})(1+g_L)^t \quad (4)$$

We can now express the magnitudes of C and W in terms of physical quantities and the commodity's price. First, note that, because the Bauer–Grossman model assumes that the commodity's price is constant, C is equal to that price times the quantity of the commodity employed as a means of production and W is equal to that price times the total output produced:

$$C_t = \bar{p}A_t \quad (5)$$

$$W_{t+1} = \bar{p}X_{t+1} \quad (6)$$

When $t = 0$, it follows from Eqs. (4)–(6), respectively, that

$$W_1 = C_0 + (V_0 + S_{0,1}) \quad (7)$$

$$C_0 = \bar{p}A_0 \quad (8)$$

$$W_1 = \bar{p}X_1 \quad (9)$$

and these latter three equations together imply that

$$(V_0 + S_{0,1}) = W_1 - C_0 = \bar{p}(X_1 - A_0) \quad (10)$$

Using Eqs. (1) and (8), we find that

$$C_t = \bar{p}A_0(1+g_K)^t \quad (11)$$

and, using Eqs. (4), (8), and (10), we find that

$$W_{t+1} = \bar{p}A_0(1+g_K)^t + \bar{p}(X_1 - A_0)(1+g_L)^t \quad (12)$$

Determination of the Physical Quantities

The time paths of the physical quantities A and X can now be determined. We know, from Eqs. (5) and (11), that

$$C_t = \bar{p}A_t = \bar{p}A_0(1+g_K)^t \quad (13)$$

so

$$A_t = A_0(1+g_K)^t \quad (14)$$

Similarly, we know, from Eqs. (6) and (12), that

$$W_{t+1} = \bar{p}X_{t+1} = \bar{p}A_0(1+g_K)^t + \bar{p}(X_1 - A_0)(1+g_L)^t \quad (15)$$

so

$$X_{t+1} = A_0(1+g_K)^t + (X_1 - A_0)(1+g_L)^t \tag{16}$$

Disappearing Physical Net Product

These last results are quite significant. They tell us that *the Bauer–Grossman model implicitly imposes a strict constraint on the production of physical output: it cannot increase as rapidly as the amount of means of production employed.* Eq. (14) says that employment of means of production increases at the annual rate of g_K, but Eq. (16) implies that physical output increases only at a (variable) rate that is always less than g_K, since $g_L < g_K$.

The disproportionate growth of means of production and output can be seen most clearly by computing the trajectory of the so-called 'capital-output ratio', A/X. Using Eqs. (14) and (16), we find that:

$$\frac{A_t}{X_{t+1}} = \frac{A_0(1+g_K)^t}{A_0(1+g_K)^t + (X_1 - A_0)(1+g_L)^t} = \frac{1}{1 + \left(\frac{X_1 - A_0}{A_0}\right)\left(\frac{1+g_L}{1+g_K}\right)^t} \tag{17}$$

Since $g_L < g_K$, the last term in the denominator of the right-hand-side expression decays over time (i.e., as t increases) and approaches 0. The 'capital-output ratio' therefore increases continually and approaches 1. Since the model assumes that all constant capital is consumed, a 'capital-output ratio' that approaches 1 signifies extreme technical regress: *over time, the net product disappears.* That is, the difference between the amount of the commodity that is produced, X_{t+1}, and the amount of the commodity that was employed as an input and fully used up, A_t, becomes a vanishingly small share of total output. For example, production of a bushel of corn eventually requires almost a full bushel of seed corn (plus some amount of workers' labour).

This technical regress is an immediate consequence of the constraint on the growth of physical output, which is, in turn, an immediate consequence of the assumption that the commodity's price is constant. Together with Eq. (4), which is a proposition of Marx's value theory, the postulated growth paths of C, V and S fix the size of W, the total value of the product. But if the commodity's price were allowed to decline, W would be the total value of a *greater physical volume* of output, and technical regress could be avoided. Indeed, the 'capital-output ratio' could remain constant or even fall.

There seems to be no warrant whatsoever for the constraint on the growth of physical output. It is not a feature of Marx's value theory or something implied by it. I know of nowhere where he even discussed it. I am also unaware of any discussion of it by Bauer, Grossman or Grossman's followers. It seems to be simply an unintentional by-product of the constant-price assumption that has heretofore gone unnoticed.

Yet the constraint on the growth of physical output is most consequential. The disappearance of the net product that results from this constraint is the cause of both the inexorable fall in the Bauer–Grossman model's rate of profit and the breakdown tendency of Grossman's theory. It is hardly surprising that a disappearing net product has these consequences, but nonetheless important to demonstrate this, as I will do in the remainder of this section and Section 4.

Physically Driven Fall in the Rate of Profit

Turning first to the rate of profit, which is surplus-value divided by total (constant and variable) capital, note that we can use Eq. (4) to express it as 'the ratio of total value to total capital, minus 1':

$$r_{t,t+1} = \frac{S_{t,t+1}}{C_t + V_t} = \frac{C_t + V_t + S_{t,t+1}}{C_t + V_t} - 1 = \frac{W_{t+1}}{C_t + V_t} - 1 \tag{18}$$

Also note that the right-hand-side expression in Eq. (18) must be less than or equal to 'the ratio of total value to *constant* capital, minus 1':

$$r_{t,t+1} = \frac{W_{t+1}}{C_t + V_t} - 1 \leq \frac{W_{t+1}}{C_t} - 1 \tag{19}$$

so that, using Eqs. (1) and (4), we can see that the assumptions of the Bauer–Grossman model imply that:

$$r_{t,t+1} \leq \frac{C_0(1+g_K)^t + (V_0 + S_{0,1})(1+g_L)^t}{C_0(1+g_K)^t} - 1 = \left(\frac{V_0 + S_{0,1}}{C_0}\right)\left(\frac{1+g_L}{1+g_K}\right)^t \tag{20}$$

Since $g_L < g_K$, the right-hand-side expression decays as t increases. The maximum value of the rate of profit therefore falls continually and approaches zero.

The model's falling rate of profit thus seems to be produced by the movements of its value magnitudes. However, we already know that their movements are caused exclusively by changes in the associated physical quantities. Specifically, we know from Eqs. (13) and (15) that:

$$\frac{W_{t+1}}{C_t} = \frac{\bar{p}A_0(1+g_K)^t + \bar{p}(X_1 - A_0)(1+g_L)^t}{\bar{p}A_0(1+g_K)^t} = 1 + \left(\frac{X_1 - A_0}{A_0}\right)\left(\frac{1+g_L}{1+g_K}\right)^t \tag{21}$$

The right-hand-side expression is the reciprocal of the physical 'capital-output ratio', $\frac{A_t}{X_{t+1}}$ (see Eq. 17). Thus, using Eqs. (17) and (21), we can restate (19) as

$$r_{t,t+1} \leq \frac{W_{t+1}}{C_t} - 1 = \frac{X_{t+1}}{A_t} - 1 \tag{22}$$

What underlies the falling rate of profit of the Bauer–Grossman's model is therefore the following, *purely physical*, dynamic. The constraint on the growth of physical output causes the net product to disappear, which causes the 'capital-output ratio' to approach 1 (from below). Consequently, its reciprocal also approaches 1 (but from above). But Inequality (22) tells us that the maximum rate of profit is equal to this reciprocal, minus 1. The maximum rate of profit therefore approaches zero (from above).

Grossman did not argue that the rate of profit actually falls inexorably in this mechanical fashion. His fully developed theory includes 'modifying counter-tendencies' (Grossman, 2022, Chapter 3) that attenuate and alter the operation of the Bauer–Grossman model's breakdown and falling-rate-of-profit tendencies. But this means only that the physically driven tendency of the rate of profit to fall is manifested in a somewhat different and weaker way. *The modifications do not turn a physicalist falling-rate-of-profit tendency into a value-theoretic one.* The main reason they do not is that Grossman's fully developed theory did not modify the Bauer–Grossman model's constraint on the growth of physical output or its disappearing net product. He did not even discuss these implicit features of the model, evidently because he failed to recognize their presence.

GROSSMAN'S BREAKDOWN TENDENCY

The central feature of Grossman's breakdown theory is the tendency of capitalist production to reach a breakdown point at which continued capital accumulation at current rates becomes impossible. He did not predict that the economy will actually reach this point. In his view, although the breakdown *tendency* is insuperable, problems that arise as the economy moves towards the breakdown point lead to economic crises and downturns, and they in turn set the stage for renewed economic growth and capital accumulation.

Grossman's fully developed theory relaxes the constant-price assumption of the Bauer–Grossman model (Grossman, 2022, pp. 291–297, 319–325). But his breakdown theory continues to be physicalist because the key underlying determinant of the model's dynamics – insufficient production of physical output – is also the underlying cause of the (alleged) breakdown tendency *even when the commodity's price is allowed to vary.*

This seems to be another implication of his theory that Grossman failed to recognize, since he characterized the cause of breakdown in value-theoretic, not physical, terms: 'surplus value is not sufficient for accumulation to continue at the rate assume[d]!' The breakdown is 'chiefly a breakdown of the *valorisation process* on the basis of the *process of value creation*, the law of value' (Grossman, 2022, pp. 181, 512, emphases in original). His followers have frequently repeated this apparent explanation.

The breakdown point in Grossman's theory is the point in time at which the amount of surplus-value created becomes less than the amount of surplus-value that is needed to fund accumulation, given the current rates of growth of constant and variable capital:

$$S_{t,t+1} < (C_{t+1} - C_t) + (V_{t+1} - V_t) \tag{23}$$

where the differences on the right-hand side are the amounts of constant and variable capital that are newly accumulated. Adding $C_t + V_t$ to both sides of Inequality (23), we obtain

$$C_t + V_t + S_{t,t+1} < C_t + V_t + (C_{t+1} - C_t) + (V_{t+1} - V_t) \tag{24}$$

or, using Eq. (4),

$$W_{t+1} < C_{t+1} + V_{t+1} \tag{25}$$

Because all variables in Inequality (25) pertain to the same moment in time and Grossman derived the breakdown tendency in the context of a one-sector reproduction scheme, all variables have the same price per unit. We can therefore restate (25) as:

$$p_{t+1}X_{t+1} < p_{t+1}A_{t+1} + p_{t+1}B_{t+1} \tag{26}$$

where p is the price of the commodity, X is the physical amount of it produced, and A and B are, respectively, the physical amounts of means of production and workers' means of subsistence that are demanded. Dividing through by the price, it becomes clear that the underlying reason the breakdown (allegedly) occurs is that *production of physical output* is not sufficient to satisfy the demand for physical means of production and subsistence if they continue to accumulate at their current rates:

$$X_{t+1} < A_{t+1} + B_{t+1} \tag{27}$$

Inequality (27) explains, among other things, why the economy of the Bauer–Grossman model breaks down. As the net product disappears, the value of A_t approaches the value of X_{t+1}. And since $A_{t+1} = (1 + g_K)A_t$, the value of A_{t+1} approaches $(1 + g_K)X_{t+1}$, which is greater than X_{t+1}. So, breakdown must always eventually occur even if B_{t+1} were equal to zero. In that case, the economy would break down at the moment when $A_{t+1} > X_{t+1}$. The value of B influences only how much sooner, before that moment, breakdown actually occurs. The fundamental cause of the breakdown itself is the constraint on the growth of output that causes the net product to disappear.

Note, however, that Inequalities (26) and (27) have nothing to do with the Bauer–Grossman model's constant-price assumption. Whether p_{t+1} is equal or unequal to previous and subsequent prices, these inequalities are necessary implications of Grossman's breakdown condition. By clearing away the value-theoretic language he used to express it, they reveal the breakdown condition's underlying meaning and the physical cause of the breakdown.[7]

We have seen that insufficient production of physical output lies at the root of both the dynamical behaviour of the Bauer–Grossman model and Grossman's breakdown condition. In both cases, the insufficient production of output is the result of a methodological problem: Grossman's theory reverses the temporal sequence of causation. Earlier events determine later ones, but Grossman allows later events to determine earlier ones.

One way he allows this is by treating the growth rates of value magnitudes as exogenous. These growth rates are obviously effects of multiple events that precede the variables' growth. But by stipulating the magnitudes of their growth rates in advance – prior to time $t = 0$ – Grossman turns effects into causes and vice-versa. The other way he allows later events to determine earlier ones is by holding the commodity's price constant. The magnitude of a commodity's price is the effect of multiple events that precede its formation, but by stipulating this magnitude prior to time $t = 0$, Grossman turns the price into a cause of these events.

In the context of the model he took over from Bauer, these inversions of causal processes were unavoidable. To study and exhibit that model's implications, Grossman had to adopt Bauer's assumptions. However, Grossman's own, fully developed, theory could have endogenized the determination of the commodity's price and the growth rates, but it did not.

To be sure, in his *verbal discussion* of how the alleged breakdown tendency is manifested in an environment in which 'modifying countertendencies' are operative, Grossman says many things that seem to endogenize the price and the growth rates. But his *theory itself* fails to endogenize them, since it imports the breakdown tendency directly from the Bauer–Grossman model, without modification. The properties of the model that generate its breakdown tendency – the implicit constraint on the growth of physical output and the disappearing net product – are thereby imported without modification as well. But these properties are consequences of the Bauer–Grossman model's growth-rate and constant-price assumptions, so they too are imported without modification into Grossman's fully developed theory, notwithstanding his verbal discussion that gives the contrary impression.

In Section 3, I briefly explained how the constant-price assumption generates the constraint on the growth of output, but it might be helpful here to see the inversion of causality this involves. When supply of a product increases, this causes the product's price to decline. This is not only a matter of market dynamics but of Marx's value theory as well. In his theory, the total value of the product is determined by and equal to the value transferred from means of production (consumed constant capital) plus the new value added by worker's labour. The product's value per unit then depends on this total value and the amount of the product that has been produced. Increases in the amount produced cause the value per unit to fall. But in Grossman's theory (apart from verbal remarks to the contrary), the value per unit is fixed in advance,[8] so it and the total value together determine the amount of the product that is produced.

A different inversion of causality is involved in Grossman's conception of the breakdown point. It is the point in time at which the actual amount of surplus-value becomes less than the amount of surplus-value that is needed to fund capital accumulation, given the current rates of growth of constant and variable capital. In this conception, the growth rates determine the amount of capital accumulation that is needed, and it in turn determines the amount of surplus-value that is needed to prevent economic breakdown.

In the real world, however, the generation of surplus-value precedes the accumulation of part of this surplus-value as additional capital (i.e., the generation of profit precedes investment). Thus, the amount of surplus-value that has been generated, together with capitalists' decisions regarding how much of it they will invest, determines the volume of capital accumulation. In this process, the desired volume of capital accumulation is an effect, not a cause. In other words, it is not a pregiven amount but something determined by how much profit has been generated and by capitalists' investment decisions.

Because the desired volume of accumulation is not a pregiven amount, the whole problem that concerns Grossman – whether the existing amount of surplus-value is sufficient to fund a pregiven volume of desired capital accumulation – is simply a non-problem. Another way of putting this point is that, unless the capitalist class decides to invest more surplus-value than it has (!), the amount of surplus-value is *always* sufficient. The capitalists simply decide to invest some fraction (≤ 1) of their surplus-value and set that amount aside. By doing so, they determine the desired amount of capital accumulation *and fund it* at one and the same time.[9]

WHY THE BREAKDOWN TENDENCY AND MARX'S VALUE THEORY ARE INCOMPATIBLE

To avoid unnecessary complications, the following discussion will refer to the sum of variable capital and surplus-value rather than to each of them individually. Their sum is the new value added by workers' labour, which I will also call N. I will assume that N grows at rate g_L and retain the assumptions that the growth rates are finite and that $0 < g_L < g_K$, but I will now treat g_L as a variable, not as a parameter.

In the Bauer–Grossman model, the ratio of constant capital to new value, C/N, increases without limit over time since the numerator and denominator both grow at constant percentage rates, and the growth rate of constant capital exceeds the growth rate of new value. As a result, constant capital also permanently grows faster than the total value of output, which is the sum of the constant capital and the new value. A point is therefore eventually reached at which the actual volume of output must fall short of the volume of output required for continued capital accumulation at current rates. This is the breakdown point.

What Marx's Theory Implies About Breakdown

It is easy to show that Marx's value theory implies that there is no such breakdown point. Since the total value of output is the sum of the constant capital and the new value:

$$W_{t+1} = C_t + N_{t,t+1} \tag{28}$$

and the share (≤ 1) of this year's total value that is invested as constant capital for the upcoming year is

$$\frac{C_{t+1}}{W_{t+1}} = \frac{p_{t+1}A_{t+1}}{p_{t+1}X_{t+1}} = \frac{A_{t+1}}{X_{t+1}} \tag{29}$$

multiplication of (28) by (29) yields

$$C_{t+1} = (C_t + N_{t,t+1})\left(\frac{A_{t+1}}{X_{t+1}}\right) \tag{30}$$

Dividing Eq. (30) by next year's new value, $N_{t+1,t+2}$, and noting that

$$N_{t+1,t+2} = (1 + g_L)N_{t,t+1} \tag{31}$$

we obtain

$$\frac{C_{t+1}}{N_{t+1,t+2}} = \left(\frac{C_t + N_{t,t+1}}{[1 + g_L]N_{t,t+1}}\right)\left(\frac{A_{t+1}}{X_{t+1}}\right) \tag{32}$$

which can be rewritten as

$$\frac{C_{t+1}}{N_{t+1,t+2}} = \left(\frac{C_t}{N_{t,t+1}} + 1\right)\left(\frac{A_{t+1}/X_{t+1}}{1 + g_L}\right) \tag{33}$$

The first derivative of $\frac{C_{t+1}}{N_{t+1,t+2}}$ with respect to $\frac{C_t}{N_{t,t+1}}$ equals $\frac{A_{t+1}/X_{t+1}}{1+g_L}$, which must be a positive number less than 1. The reason it must be less than 1 is that its numerator cannot exceed 1 (since A_{t+1}, the amount of physical output employed as a means of production, cannot exceed X_{t+1}, the total output) while its denominator must exceed 1 (since g_L is positive). Because the value of the derivative is less than 1, the time path of C/N is convergent.[10] In other words, C/N cannot increase without limit, as it does in the Bauer–Grossman model. It can increase to very high levels and even increase forever, but *there is a finite maximum value that C/N cannot exceed.* I will call this maximum value the Marxian Limiting Value (MLV).[11]

But C/N would eventually exceed the MLV if the growth rate of constant capital permanently exceeded the growth rate of new value (by more than an infinitesimal amount). Hence, the growth rate of constant capital must eventually converge to the growth rate of new value.

While the growth rate of constant capital-value of the Bauer–Grossman model is fixed, exogenously determined and permanently greater than the growth rate of new value, it follows from Eq. (28) – a cornerstone of Marx's value theory – that this is impossible (if g_L is positive). The growth rate of constant capital-value is variable, endogenously determined within the valuation process, and convergent on the growth rate of new value in the long run.

The growth rates converge because of another feature of Marx's value theory, the decline in the commodity's price (or value) that occurs as means of production increase more rapidly than living labour. The quickest way to see this is to note that, when the two growth rates are equal, $\frac{C_{t+1} - C_t}{C_t} = \frac{p_{t+1}A_{t+1} - p_t A_t}{p_t A_t} = \frac{p_{t+1}A_t(1 + g_K)}{p_t A_t} - 1 = g_L$. It follows from the last equality that $\frac{p_{t+1}}{p_t} = \frac{1 + g_L}{1 + g_K} < 1$.

But constant capital and new value are the two components of the total value of output. So if they are growing at the same rate, the total value is growing at this rate as well. Thus, in the limit, constant capital no longer grows more rapidly than the value of output. There is therefore no point in time at which, because of disproportionately rapid growth of constant capital, the actual volume of output must fall short of the volume of output required for continued capital accumulation at current rates. In other words, once we replace the growth-rate assumptions of the Bauer–Grossman model with Marx's value theory, as we have done, Grossman's breakdown point simply disappears. So does his breakdown tendency; capitalist development cannot have an inexorable tendency to approach a nonexistent point.

The Source of Grossman's Error

Grossman was well aware that the Bauer–Grossman model's assumption regarding the growth of constant capital needed to be modified. The model assumes that the commodity's price is constant and therefore that physical means of production and constant capital-value grow at the same rate. When developing his own breakdown theory, Grossman (2022, pp. 291–297, 319) stressed that Marx's value theory implies that constant capital-value cannot grow at that rate, because the commodity's price will not actually remain constant. Owing to the technical progress and rising productivity that the model also assumes, the commodity's value (or price) must instead fall, so constant capital-value will grow more slowly than means of production.

When he modified the Bauer–Grossman model in this manner, what Grossman concluded was that the slower growth of constant capital-value causes the breakdown tendency to operate more slowly, and that this in turn causes the moment of breakdown to be postponed. 'The life span of accumulation is … prolonged. … The breakdown will not occur in year 35, as shown in the table … but at a *later* point'. '[T]he value of the constant capital, *c*, has fallen. … This … postpones the breakdown to a more distant future' (Grossman, 2022, p. 297, emphasis in original; p. 322).

We have just seen that this conclusion is false: when the growth of constant capital-value is endogenized and determined in accordance with Marx's value theory, the moment of breakdown is not postponed; it is eliminated. But *why* is the conclusion false? And *what* is wrong with Grossman's reasoning here? It is important to answer these questions, since Grossman's followers have found his argument compelling and the error it contains seems to have gone undetected. I will try to provide the answers.

In the passages of his book that I have just quoted, Grossman asserted that the slower growth of constant capital-value implies that the breakdown tendency remains operative even though it operates more slowly. He provided no justification for that assertion; apparently, he considered it self-evident.

Shortly after the book was published, however, Helene Bauer and Alfred Braunthal criticized this argument of Grossman's. In response to their criticisms, he drafted an unpublished manuscript that returned to the issue. Using the term 'devaluation of capital' to refer to the fact that constant capital-value grows more slowly than means of production, Grossman (2018, pp. 210, 212, emphases in original) wrote:

> Devaluation overcomes the tendency to break down and not, as Marx argued, only weakens it temporarily? How is that possible? ...
>
> Helene B's and Braunthal's proposition that devaluation of capital abrogates the tendency to breakdown necessarily entails the proposition that there is no development of an ever higher organic composition of capital in contemporary capitalist society! ...
>
> [The issue] cannot be abstractly, deductively decided and has to be decided through *empirical observation. Experience*, indeed experience of more than one hundred years, teaches that the *value* of constant capital, thus also of the total capital, in relation to variable capital grows *more quickly* than variable .... This can be expressed more exactly[: ...] the new value created by living labour ... constitutes a progressively *smaller* part of the annual *value of production* ....

Thus, Grossman now recognized that he needed to justify his original assertion, and he revised his argument accordingly. In his revised argument, Grossman first referred to the organic composition of capital (the ratio of constant to variable capital). He then noted, correctly, that what is at issue is more precisely expressed in terms of a related but somewhat different ratio, the ratio of new value to the total value of output, N/W.

Grossman argued that the slower growth of constant capital-value implies that *N/W falls more slowly; but, because it still falls,* the breakdown tendency remains operative even though it operates more slowly. The italicized part of this argument is the part that is new, not present in Grossman's book.

The revised argument's crucial assertion is that a persistently falling N/W implies that the breakdown tendency remains operative. Grossman provided no justification for that assertion; apparently, he considered it self-evident. But it is neither self-evident nor true.

N/W is a monotonically decreasing function of the ratio studied above, C/N; the persistent decline in the former that Grossman refers to implies a persistent rise in the latter.[12] So in his revised argument, Grossman in effect claimed that a persistently rising C/N implies that the breakdown tendency remains operative. We have seen that this claim is false: even if C/N increases forever, breakdown will not occur if C/N cannot exceed the MLV. A breakdown tendency due to 'insufficient surplus-value' exists only if C/N increases *without limit* (or beyond the MLV).

Why did Grossman fail to recognize this? Why did he mistakenly believe that a persistently rising C/N ensures that the breakdown tendency remains operative? I do not know, but I suspect that he fell prey to an exceedingly common fallacy, the incorrect assumption that something must rise without limit if it rises forever. If that assumption were true, then the persistent rise in C/N would indeed be a limitless rise and Grossman's conclusion that the breakdown tendency remains operative would therefore be correct. Since his reasoning becomes impeccable once persistent rise implies limitless rise, it is likely that he fell prey to this fallacy.

Empirical Evidence

But what about Grossman's appeal to empirical evidence in his response to Helene Bauer and Braunthal? First, I believe I have demonstrated that there cannot be a breakdown tendency due to 'insufficient surplus-value' in Grossman's sense if Marx's value theory is correct. Any valid evidence that would support the breakdown theory would be evidence that Marx's theory is incorrect. And since other aspects of Grossman's breakdown theory rely on Marx's theory, such evidence would call it into question as well.

Second, the evidence to which Grossman appealed, the rising organic composition of capital, is very weak evidence in this context. To support the idea that his breakdown tendency exists, the evidence must indicate that the organic composition (or *C*/*N*, etc.) not only rises but rises *without limit* (or beyond the MLV). Grossman's evidence does not indicate this.

Grossman's followers appeal to additional evidence, but some of their evidence suffers from the same problem. For example, Mattick (2018, p. 228) notes that 'numerous non-marxist researchers' have found that something similar to the organic composition of capital rises. However, this evidence likewise fails to indicate that it rises *without limit* (or beyond the MLV).

In my view, the rest of their evidence suffers from even worse problems. For instance, evidence that the rate of profit tends to fall has frequently been misconstrued as evidence that supports Grossman's breakdown theory (see, e.g., Roberts, 2012; Reese, 2022, pp. 141–142). It is compatible with that theory but equally compatible with a theory that implies that Grossman's breakdown tendency does not exist – Marx's theory. So if the evidence counts as evidence in favour of the breakdown theory, it counts equally as evidence against it!

Mattick (2018, pp. 232, 228) construes 'declining profits, market gluts, and bankruptcies', as well as 'the concentration and centralisation of capital, and the generation of a reserve army of labour' as evidence that 'Marx's [sic] value-theoretic breakdown tendency' is operative. This is another case in which the evidence disconfirms the existence of Grossman's breakdown tendency just as much as it confirms it, since it is equally compatible with both Grossman's and Marx's theories.

In addition, the relation of the breakdown theory to most of the phenomena that Mattick mentions is very indirect. Reese's (2022, Chapter 5) discussion of 'The Final Breakdown' also construes a slew of very indirectly related phenomena – trends in global debt, declining manufacturing costs, automation, exponential growth of global GDP, etc. – as confirmation of the breakdown theory. It is hard to avoid the conclusion that their interpretations of the evidence are displays of confirmation bias. Would anyone not already committed to Grossman's breakdown theory interpret the evidence as they do?

Meaningful empirical tests of the breakdown theory would be ones that test claims and implications of the theory that are unique to it and that thereby enable us to assess the relative explanatory power of this and alternative theories. And they would test matters much more directly related to the theory, such as the Bauer–Grossman model's implications that uninvested profit declines in absolute terms and that the ratio of investment to profit and the ratio of consumed constant capital to total value continually rise. I look forward to the results of such tests.

SUMMARY AND CONCLUSION

I have shown in this chapter that the Bauer–Grossman model and Grossman's breakdown theory, which have always been understood to be value-theoretic, are actually physicalist. Although the model's variables have the names of value magnitudes, this is all value-form, no value-substance: the variables' movements are determined exclusively by movements in physical quantities. In particular, the model's implicit constraint on the growth of physical output and the disappearance of the physical net product to which it leads are the causes of the model's breakdown tendency and its falling rate of profit.

In addition, I have shown that Grossman's breakdown tendency remains physicalist even after the restrictive assumptions of the Bauer–Grossman model are relaxed, because the alleged breakdown problem is a physical problem disguised as a value-theoretic one. The moment when the economy allegedly breaks down, the moment when 'surplus value is not sufficient' (Grossman, 2022, p. 181), is the moment when production of physical output is not sufficient to satisfy the demand for physical means of production and subsistence. And even though Grossman's breakdown theory modifies the model, it remains physicalist because the modifications do not turn the model's physically determined tendencies into value-theoretic ones. What is modified is only the manner in which the physically determined tendencies are manifested.

I have also identified the methodological problem underlying both the alleged breakdown condition and the implicit constraint on the growth of physical output and its consequences. The underlying problem is that the Bauer–Grossman model and Grossman's breakdown theory reverse causal processes by allowing later events to determine earlier ones.

The chapter's most important results are those that demonstrate what happens when we jettison the Bauer–Grossman model's constant-price and growth-rate assumptions and instead permit the commodity's price and the growth of constant capital-value to be determined in accordance with Marx's value theory. The ratio of constant capital to new value no longer rises without limit. The growth rate of constant capital-value converges to the growth rate of new value. The breakdown tendency disappears. Grossman and his followers have portrayed the breakdown theory as the fully developed version of a breakdown theory implicit in Marx's work. These results demonstrate the opposite: Grossman's breakdown theory and Marx's value theory are incompatible.

The chapter has identified fatal defects in the Bauer–Grossman model and Grossman's breakdown theory. It is noteworthy that these defects are not present in Marx's theory. It does not constrain the growth of physical output or say that the net product disappears or say that the falling tendency of the rate of profit is physically driven.[13] It says that the ratio of constant capital to new value rises but not that it rises without limit.[14] It says that constant capital increases more rapidly than new value without denying that the difference between their growth rates may become infinitesimally small in the very long run. It does not say or imply that capitalist economies tend inevitably to develop to a point where they must break down because physical output is insufficient to satisfy an exogenously determined volume of demand for means of production and subsistence.

Hence, none of this chapter's results does any damage to Marx's value theory, his law of the tendential fall in the rate of profit or his theory of capitalist economic crisis. They emerge unscathed. To recognize the fact that they emerge unscathed, however, one needs to understand them on their own terms, not through the lens of Grossman's embellishments.

NOTES

1. Some portions of the chapter are drawn, more or less freely, from Kliman (2021).
2. 'Consumed', or 'used up', constant capital refers to the sum of circulating constant capital and the depreciation of fixed constant capital due to wear and tear (see, e.g., Marx, 1990, p. 321). It is the portion of total constant capital investment that is 'used up' in the production process and that becomes a component part of products' values. Because the Bauer–Grossman model assumes that all constant capital is consumed, subsequent references to 'constant capital' in this chapter pertain solely to consumed constant capital.
3. 'Valorization' is a translation of Marx's term, *Verwertung*. An alternative translation, 'self-expansion of value', more closely conveys Marx's meaning – a process in which value 'begets' additional value, i.e., surplus-value (see Marx, 1990, p. 256).
4. The Paul Mattick quoted here is the son of another prominent follower of Grossman, also named Paul Mattick.
5. Bauer (2012, p. 737) wrote that 'variable capital grows at the same rate as the work-force, and ... constant capital grows faster than variable, to the extent required by technical progress'. This statement seems to suggest that, just as the growth rate of variable capital equals the growth rate of the workforce, the growth rate of constant capital equals the growth rate of means of production. If that is the case, the price of the commodity in Grossman's one-sector adaptation of Bauer's model must be constant.
6. Given Grossman's constant-price assumption, all major quantity indexes (Laspeyres, Paasche, Fisher, etc.) produce the same quantity index series. Between times t and $t + 1$, the percentage change in the quantity index number is the weighted average of the percentage changes in the physical quantities of each item, where the weights are total expenditures on the items as a share of total expenditure on all of the items, at time t.
7. An anonymous referee contends that the contrast between Inequalities (26) and (27) 'does not establish a fundamental distinction between physicalist and value-theoretic perspectives'. It was not meant to do so. The point is rather that Grossman's breakdown condition is physicalist – despite his value-theoretic 'perspective' – because the alleged breakdown problem is a physical problem (Inequality (27)) disguised as a value-theoretic one (Inequality (23)).
8. Since there is only one produced commodity in Grossman's adaptation of Bauer's model, its price, which is held constant, equals its value.

9. The preceding two paragraphs abstract from many complications, such as the existence of credit, savings, and inventories. I doubt that burdening the analysis with them would be helpful, given that the alleged breakdown tendency at issue here is a long-run tendency. For example, while credit may enable investment demand to exceed profit temporarily, I cannot conceive of a plausible scenario in which it does so in the long run.

10. An anonymous referee's alleged 'counterexample' to this result fails because it is not about the case in question. By assuming that '$g_L = 0$', it contradicts the Bauer–Grossman model's assumption, reiterated at the start of this section, and here, that g_L is positive. The referee also challenges the conclusion that *C*/*N* is convergent, on the grounds that increases in $\frac{C_t}{N_{t,t+1}}$ cause $\frac{A_{t+1}/X_{t+1}}{1+g_L}$ to rise. I think this is very implausible, but there is no need to debate the issue here, since *C*/*N* remains convergent despite the presumed functional dependence. The maximum value of $\frac{A_{t+1}/X_{t+1}}{1+g_L}$ must still be a finite number less than 1. Denoting this number as *m*, it follows from Eq. (33) and $m < 1$ that *C*/*N* cannot exceed $\frac{m}{1-m}$, i.e., that it converges to this ratio or to a smaller number.

11. Using Eq. (33), and setting $\frac{C_{t+1}}{N_{t+1,t+2}} = \frac{C_t}{N_{t,t+1}}$, we find that $\text{MLV} = \frac{A_{t+1}/X_{t+1}}{(1+g_L) - A_{t+1}/X_{t+1}}$.

12. $\frac{N_{t,t+1}}{W_{t+1}} = \frac{N_{t,t+1}}{C_t + N_{t,t+1}} = \frac{1}{\frac{C_t}{N_{t,t+1}} + 1}$.

13. For further discussion of the non-physicalist character of Marx's falling-rate-of-profit theory, see Kliman (2007, Chapter 7).

14. An anonymous reviewer contends that 'Marx does not suggest any inherent limit to this increase'. My response: (1) Nor does he suggest the absence of such a limit: absence of evidence is not evidence of absence. (2) As I have shown here, it follows from Marx's *theory* that such a limit is present. (3) Since surplus-value is the source of additional accumulation of constant capital-value, the latter cannot *permanently* grow more rapidly than the former (see Kliman, 2022). (4) For these reasons, the assumption that *C*/*N* rises without limit is not a reasonable 'extension' of what Marx and his theory actually say about the rise.

REFERENCES

Bauer, O. (2012). The accumulation of capital. In R. B. Day & D. Gaido (Eds.), *Discovering imperialism: Social democracy to World War I* (pp. 719–743). Brill.

Bernstein, E. (1899, March 26). Antwort. *Vorwärts*, *16*(3), 9–10.

Grossman, H. (2018). Essays and letters on economic theory. In R. Kuhn (Ed.), D. Balwin, et al. (Trans.) *Henryk Grossman works* (Vol. 1). Brill.

Grossman, H. (2022). *The law of accumulation and breakdown of the capitalist system, being also a theory of crises*. (R. Kuhn (Ed.), J. Banaji (trans.), Henryk Grossman works, Vol. 3). Haymarket Books.

Kliman, A. (2007). *Reclaiming Marx's "Capital": A refutation of the myth of inconsistency*. Lexington Books.

Kliman, A. (2021, October 7). Henryk Grossmann's breakdown model: On the *real* cause of the fictitious breakdown tendency. *With Sober Senses*. https://marxisthumanistinitiative.org/economics/henryk-grossmanns-breakdown-model-on-the-real-cause-of-the-fictitious-breakdown-tendency.html

Kliman, A. (2022, May 27). Review-essay: The end of capitalism: The thought of Henryk Grossman. *With Sober Senses*. https://marxisthumanistinitiative.org/economics/review-essay-the-end-of-capitalism-the-thought-of-henryk-grossman.html

Kuhn, R. (2005). Henryk Grossman and the recovery of Marxism. *Historical Materialism*, *13*(3), 57–100.

Kuhn, R. (2021, February 15). Economic crises are unavoidable under capitalism. *Marxist Left Review*. https://marxistleftreview.org/articles/economic-crises-are-unavoidable-under-capitalism/

Marx, K. (1990). *Capital: A critique of political economy* (Vol. 1). Penguin Books.

Marx, K. (1992). *Capital: A critique of political economy* (Vol. 2). Penguin Books.
Mattick, P. (2018). *Theory as critique: Essays on Capital*. Brill.
Reese, T. (2021, July 15). The importance of Henryk Grossman. *Cosmonaut*. https://cosmonautmag.com/2021/07/the-importance-of-henryk-grossman/
Reese, T. (2022). *The end of capitalism: The thought of Henryk Grossman*. Zero Books.
Roberts, M. (2012, September 12). Crisis or breakdown? https://thenextrecession.wordpress.com/2012/09/12/crisis-or-breakdown/
Roberts, M. (2017, December 5). Grossman on capitalism's contradictions. https://thenextrecession.wordpress.com/2017/12/05/grossman-on-capitalisms-contradictions/

MARX AND PASINETTI VERSUS PROPORTIONAL DYNAMICS: CAUSALITY, SIMULTANEITY AND THE LAW OF VALUE

Luca Timponelli

University of Lausanne, Switzerland

ABSTRACT

This contribution will critically appraise Luigi L. Pasinetti's rehabilitation of causality in economics in its link with a rehabilitation of a labour theory of value. Pasinetti highlighted how the incorporation of accumulation into models of simultaneous equations entailed the assumption of fixed coefficient of productions, an assumption at odds both with 'two centuries of industrialization' (Pasinetti, 1993) and with the classical and Marxian approach to capital accumulation and technological change. In the next section, the author will show how a methodology centred on interdependence was explicitly developed in antithesis to Marx's 'successivist' approach and to core aspects of his critique of political economy. The author will then give an account of von Charasoff's, Cassel's and von Neumann's quasi-stationary growth models. The third section will introduce Pasinetti's re-evaluation of the notion of causality, together with its critique to the models of proportional dynamics. In the last section, the author will discuss some of the limits of Pasinetti's structural dynamics.

Keywords: Accumulation; technological change; Marx; growth; proportional dynamics

Money, Value and Marx's Circuit of Capital
Research in Political Economy, Volume 41, 97–118

Published under exclusive licence by Emerald Publishing Limited
ISSN: 0161-7230/doi:10.1108/S0161-723020260000041013

FROM INTERDEPENDENCE TO PROPORTIONAL DYNAMICS

One of the key arguments raised against Marx's theory of value is its perceived disregard of the interdependence between economic variables, which overlook that value and prices of production, the rate of surplus-value and the rate of profit, input and output prices should all be determined simultaneously as reciprocally influencing factors (Howard and King, 1989; Jorland, 1995). This argument was first set out by Bortkiewicz (1952 [1907]) as a development of Jevons (1871), Walras (1874-77) and Marshall's (1890) critique of Ricardo's interpretation of the profit rate as a residual once that the value of the product, the rent and the wage have been independently determined. According to Bortkiewicz, Marx 'held firmly to the view that the elements concerned must be regarded as a kind of causal chain, in which each link is determined, in its composition and its magnitude, only by the preceding links' (1952, p. 24). To the contrary, for Bortkiewicz modern economics was 'beginning to free itself gradually from the successivist prejudice, the chief merit being due to the mathematical school led by Léon Walras. The mathematical, in particular the algebraic method of exposition clearly appears to be the satisfactory expression for this superior standpoint, which does justice to the special character of economic relations'. The untenability of the 'successivist' logic was traced by Bortkiewicz in the impossibility for Marx to transform the value-prices (i.e. the exchange ratios in accordance to the socially necessary labour time expended in their production) of the inputs employed by an economic system in a state of simple reproduction into their respective production prices (i.e. the exchange ratios in accordance with a uniform rate of profit, a given wage rate and given coefficients of production), a task which could be accomplished only by the employment of simultaneous equations and only at the expense of one of the two equivalences established by Marx, respectively, (i) between the sum of values and prices and (ii) between total surplus-value and the sum of profit. Whereas Bortkiewicz's interpretation has for long remained the standard reading of Marx's theory of value, recent literature (Carchedi, 1991; Freeman, 1995; Kliman, 2006; Moseley, 2015) has put Bortkiewicz's claims into question, showing the absence in Marx of a double system of values and prices, stressing the different phases of the circuit of capital and highlighting that production prices of the inputs, being the result of past processes of value production and inter-sectorial redistribution, must be taken as given for each production period. Rather than seeing economic reproduction as the expansion of a given aggregate of commodities, Marx (1997 [1885], pp. 31–69) presents it in terms of a circuit whose different phases are distinguished in time: at first, money is expended in order to buy means of production and labour power; these means of production and labour power are then employed for producing new commodities; finally, these commodities must be converted again into money with a return over the invested money. This circuit is analyzed through a two-stages perspective (Marx 1965 [1867], p. 362; 1985 [1868], p. 11), addressing first the genesis of surplus-value and then its redistribution among (i) capitalists between the same branch of production; (ii) capitalists between different branches of production; (iii) productive and merchant capitalists; (iv) entrepreneurs and financial capitalists; (v) capitalists and landowners. For the first step, each capital is assumed to be a representative of the social average (Marx 1991 [1861–63], p. 299, Shortall, 1994), and abstraction is therefore made from the differences in the composition of capital and in the turnover time. Socially necessary labour time, with its monetary expression, is essential to the determination of the aggregate value added for each period and, together with the length and the repartition of the working day between necessary and surplus-labour time, allows for the determination of the surplus-value and of its rate. The mass of surplus-value can then be put in relation with the total capital advanced, i.e. the money which has been expended in order to start the production process, in order to derive the general rate of profit, which will be positively affected by the rate of surplus-value, and negatively affected by the social composition of capital and by the average turnover time. Only at a second stage, the redistribution of surplus-value is addressed. Differences between individual capitals must considered: the money expended by each capitalist in buying means of productions and labour power is assumed to be given. In order to secure a single price within branches and a uniform rate of profit between branches, the process of price formation continuously redistribute surplus-value from (i) less productive to more productive firms between branches of production and (ii) branches with lower composition of capital and faster turnover time to branches with higher composition of capital and lower turnover times. This redistribution, rather than leading the system to stably converge towards an equilibrium point, emerges, through a process of under- and overshooting (Shaikh, 2016), as an average value, which, in turn, is constantly shifted by changes in the methods of production across all the sectors. Therefore, Marx's theory does not exhibit any circularity: the necessity to start from given money prices is justified by the temporal and sequential nature of production. This aspect is constitutively obliviated by Bortkiewicz's translation, rooted into the general-equilibrium tradition, of the issue in terms of simultaneous equations. The case for the rehabilitation of such a 'successivist' approach appears even more stronger if we consider, on the one hand, the difficulties incurred by general-equilibrium models in terms of unicity and stability of their solutions, both in their neo-classical versions (as shown by Sonnenschein, 1973, Debreu, 1974; Mantel, 1976) and in their neo-Ricardian formulations,[1] and, on the other hand, of the impossibility, remarked by Pasinetti, to deal with capital accumulation in presence of technological change.

MODELS OF PROPORTIONAL DYNAMICS

Originating in Georg von Charasoff's critical examination of Marx's theory of value (1910) and in Gustav Cassel's reformulation of general equilibrium (1918), models of proportional or quasi-stationary dynamics, especially thanks to the contribution by John von Neumann (1945 [1937]), have become the framework of reference for studying accumulation for all the scholars who reject the employment of aggregated production function. It is noteworthy that the first attempt to extend the general equilibrium framework to an expansionary economy was made by von Charasoff with the aim of evaluating Marx's claim about the historical limits of the capitalist mode of production. Von Charasoff had acknowledged (1909) the role played in Marx's thought by the tendential fall in the rate of profit for the demonstration that the capitalist mode of production was unable to unlimitedly pursue the economization of labour time: since technical progress involved a rising composition of capital which negatively affected the rate of profit, capitalists were forced to prolong the duration and the intensity of the working day to attempt to compensate for this tendency. If Marx's depiction of the capitalist mode of production was right, capitalism's claim to represent the maximum of economic efficiency was refuted by the fact that, in order to counter the fall in the profit rate, an ever-greater quantity of labour power had to be wasted in spite of technical progress. Like Bortkiewicz, von Charasoff (1910, pp. 290–291) also stressed the reliance of this argument on Marx's theory of value, which he criticized on similar methodological grounds.

Whereas in Bortkiewicz's model, the commodities figuring in the system could be reduced to dated quantities of labour, von Charasoff had to assume, in order to preserve the reproduction of an expanding economy, a circular flow of production where the inputs and the outputs must be homogeneous and the proportions between commodities must be preserved over time. This allowed him to introduce a theory of prices which, by fully breaking away from the idea of labour as the substance of value, envisaged the economic process as the expansion of a single composite commodity. However, real systems exhibit plenty of commodities which do not enter all the productive processes both as inputs and as outputs, serving either as intermediate goods or as final consumption goods. According to von Charasoff, a system involving only commodities which figure simultaneously as input and output of each process (*Grundprodukte*, 'basic products', among which he includes also the wage goods) can always be derived from the real system by iteratively removing commodities which figure as final consumption goods. The features exhibited by such a derived system are deemed essential for understanding the real system. If, under the assumption of constant returns, we denote with $\mathbf{x}$ the vector of final products, with $\mathbf{x}'$ the vector of the inputs employed in producing them, with $\mathbf{x}''$ the vector of the inputs employed in producing these latter, etc., we can build the production series:

$$\mathbf{x} \sim \mathbf{x}' \sim \mathbf{x}'' \sim \mathbf{x}''' \sim \ldots \sim \mathbf{x}^* \sim \mathbf{x}^{*\prime} \sim \ldots \quad (1)$$

Some of the products in $\mathbf{x}$ will be lacking in $\mathbf{x}'$ (luxury goods), some products in $\mathbf{x}'$ will be lacking in $\mathbf{x}''$ (first-order capitals) and some products in $\mathbf{x}''$ will be lacking in $\mathbf{x}'''$ (second-order capitals) until a point $\mathbf{x}^*$ will be reached where all the commodities left figure both as inputs and as outputs of the production process: any further upward movement in the production series (towards $\mathbf{x}^{*\prime}$, $\mathbf{x}^{*\prime\prime}$, etc.) will result in finding the same inputs employed in $\mathbf{x}^*$. In this configuration, the ratio between each commodity figuring in $\mathbf{x}^*$ and $\mathbf{x}^{*\prime}$ will be the same for each commodity and will be equal to the gross rate of return of the system:

$$\frac{a}{a'} = \frac{b}{b'} = \frac{c}{c'} = \ldots = \frac{n}{n'} = 1 + R \tag{2}$$

The commodities employed by the system will therefore figure in the same proportions both as components of total capital and of total output.

This system exhibits two important properties: (1) the rate of profit is immediately determined as ratio between physical quantities of commodities, and since the whole profit is reinvested, the rate of profit coincides with the rate of expansion of the system; (2) the different commodities exist as multiples and submultiples of a same composite commodity, and their relative prices are immediately determined by the different proportions in which they figure as elements of the same ever-expanding capital (von Charasoff, 1910, p. 111).

The importance of this result lied for von Charasoff in determining the maximum rate of growth of the original economic system: if the whole surplus were devoted to capital accumulation, without any production of luxury goods, the two systems indeed coincide. Since the maximum rate of the expansion of the system was dictated only by technology and by the wage rate, the limits Marx had seen in capital accumulation had no reason to exist. Once that technical progress necessarily entailed, for a given real wage rate, a rise in the rate of profit, the economization of labour time was always advantageous for capitalists: the capitalist mode of production was no more seen as hindering the full development of the forces of production and as necessarily entailing worsening working conditions.[2] Class antagonism persisted only in the trade-off between a higher real wage and a higher accumulation rate, a choice which socialism would have entrusted to the whole community (von Charasoff, 1910, p. 228).

If von Charasoff's model remained almost forgotten until its rediscovery by Egidi and Gilibert (1984), a similar approach to capital accumulation reappeared in Cassels' *Theoretische Sozialökonomie* (1918). Criticizing, again in the name of interdependence, both the marginal utility theory and the Ricardian theory of value, Cassel advanced an interpretation of production as a circular flow and identified the conditions for equilibrium both for the steady and the progressive state in the persistence of the same proportions between all the commodities making part of the economic system. In an expanding system, this condition could be secured by a uniform growth rate for all the sectors. Cassel's depiction of the progressive state, which was not presented in mathematical terms, was later formalised by John von Neumann (1945). In von Neumann's model, under the assumption of constant returns, there's a given set of m productive processes P_i which consumes the quantities a_{ij} and produces the quantities b_{ij} of the n goods G_j:

$$P_i : \sum_{j=1}^{n} a_{ij} G_j \rightarrow \sum_{j=1}^{n} b_{ij} G_j \tag{3}$$

These processes will have m intensities of production x_i, i.e. the rate of transformation of inputs into output per unit of time; the intensity of a process which won't be employed will be equal to zero. The total production E will therefore be defined as:

$$E = \sum_{i=1}^{m} x_i P_i \tag{4}$$

Von Neumann (1945, p. 2) proposes to study 'those states where the whole economy expands without change of structure, i.e. where the ratios of the intensities $x_1: \ldots :x_m$ remain unchanged, although $x_1: \ldots :x_m$ themselves may change'. In all these cases, all the sectors will expand at a common factor $\alpha = 1 + G$ (where G is the rate of growth), which denote the coefficient of expansion of the whole economy. The model should determine (1) the m intensities of production x_i of the m processes P_i; (2) the coefficient of expansion of the economy α; (3) the n prices y_j of the n goods G_j and (4) the interest factor $\beta = 1 + R$, where R is the rate of profit.

It is then assumed that each good enters every activity at least either as an input or as an output, i.e.

$$a_{ij} + b_{ij} > 0, \text{with } a_{ij} \geq 0 \text{ and } b_{ij} \geq 0 \tag{5}$$

Given that the system cannot consume more of each good than it is being produced and that the price of overproduced goods will be zero, we can write:

$$\alpha \sum_{i=1}^{m} a_{ij} x_i \leq \sum_{i=1}^{m} b_{ij} x_i, \text{with } y_j = 0 \text{ if } \alpha \sum_{i=1}^{m} a_{ij} x_i < \sum_{i=1}^{m} b_{ij} x_i \tag{6}$$

From this, it is possible to see that overproduction will be avoided only when the rate of expansion of the economy is dictated by the sector with the lower output-to-input ratio:

$$\alpha = \min_{j=1,\ldots,n} \frac{\sum_{i=1}^{m} b_{ij} x_i}{\sum_{i=1}^{m} a_{ij} x_i} \tag{7}$$

Since the equilibrium position, in consequence of competition, must erase any profit on any process and that processes which result in losses won't be employed, we also write:

$$\beta \sum_{j=1}^{n} a_{ij} y_j \geq \sum_{j=1}^{n} b_{ij} y_j, \text{ with } x_i = 0 \text{ if } \beta \sum_{j=1}^{n} a_{ij} y_j > \sum_{j=1}^{n} b_{ij} y_j \tag{8}$$

For losses to be avoided, the interest factor must be equal to the largest output-to-input ratio in value terms:

$$\beta = \max_{i=1,\ldots m} \frac{\sum_{j=1}^{n} b_{ij} y_j}{\sum_{i=1}^{n} a_{ij} y_j} \tag{9}$$

Since every good is required for the reproduction of the system, every intensity of production must be positive ($x_i > 0$) and, in order for each good to be produced, so must be the case for each price ($y_j > 0$). This implies that $\frac{\sum_{i=1}^{m} b_{ij} x_i}{\sum_{i=1}^{m} a_{ij} x_i}$ is minimized only when $\frac{\sum_{j=1}^{n} b_{ij} y_j}{\sum_{i=1}^{n} a_{ij} y_j}$ is maximized, and vice versa. It is possible to define a saddle point $\varphi(X^*, Y^*)$, where X^* and Y^* are, respectively, the set of the $x_1, \ldots, x_m$ intensities of production and of the $y_1, \ldots, y_n$ prices that characterize balanced reproduction and ensure the respect of both these conditions:

$$\varphi(X^*, Y^*) = \frac{\sum_{i=1}^{m} \sum_{j=1}^{n} b_{ij} x_i y_j}{\sum_{i=1}^{m} \sum_{j=1}^{n} a_{ij} x_i y_j} \tag{10}$$

Since $\varphi(X^*, Y)$ is minimized for Y only when $Y = Y^*$ and $\varphi(X, Y^*)$ is maximized for X only when $X = X^*$ we have that:

$$\alpha = \frac{\sum_{j=1}^{n} \left[\sum_{i=1}^{m} b_{ij} x_i \right] y_j}{\sum_{j=1}^{n} \left[\sum_{i=1}^{m} a_{ij} x_i \right] y_j} \tag{11}$$

$$\beta = \frac{\sum_{i=1}^{m} \left[\sum_{j=1}^{n} b_{ij} y_j \right] x_i}{\sum_{i=1}^{m} \left[\sum_{j=1}^{n} a_{ij} y_j \right] x_i} \tag{12}$$

$$\alpha = \beta \tag{13}$$

Hence, in an equilibrium of balanced growth, the coefficient of expansion of the system must coincide with the interest factor; therefore, the rate of growth must be equal to the rate of interest. The existence of such a saddle point is then demonstrated by von Neumann through an extension of Brouwer's fixed point theorem. As in von Charasoff, von Neumann's model thus established both the identity at the equilibrium of the rate of growth and of the rate of return of the system and the duality between quantities and prices, a result which he interpreted as an important argument in favour of a market economy: since the 'normal price mechanism brings about – if our assumptions are valid – the technically most efficient intensities of production' (von Neumann, 1945, p. 1), the objections against the efficiency of capitalist production raised by Jakob Marschak and Robert Remak (Carvajalino, 2021; Kurz and Salvadori, 1993; Marchionatti, 2019) were overcome.

Despite these conclusions, models of proportional dynamics were hailed, starting from Champernowne (1945), as a restatement of the classical and Marxian theory of capital accumulation. On the one hand, the absence of demand functions and the assumption of a given real wage represented a break with the neoclassical tradition, dismissing both the employment of preferences and the simultaneous determination of wages and profits. Circular production, as already pointed by Cassel, unvalidated the notion of a uniform period of production at the base of Böhm-Bawerk's explanation of interest. On the other hand, balanced growth allowed to preserve the equality between surplus-value and total profits (Morishima, 1973). Discrepancies between these two magnitudes could be ascribed to the existence of unproductive consumption, a factor extraneous to the pure logic of capital accumulation (Shaikh, 1984). This perspective assumed that at the core of the classical and Marxian approaches to value and distribution lied the problem of determining the prices and the rate of profit in a context of given technology and real wage (Garegnani, 1987; Kurz and Salvadori, 1998). According to this perspective, classical economists, lacking the analytical tools of linear algebra, introduced the labour theory of value as an approximation for generalising the determination of the rate of profit in a multi-commodity system, where it is no more self-evident as a physical ratio. The main difference between the classical and the marginal school was no more seen in the antithesis between causality and interdependence but rather in terms of two different models of simultaneous price determinations: while neoclassical general equilibrium took as data (1) the preferences; (2) the available sets of technical alternatives; (3) the initial endowments and their distribution between individuals, the classical economists started from (1) the real wage rate (or, alternatively, the rate of profit); (2) the available sets of technical alternatives and (3) the size and composition of the social product. Marx's contribution, reduced to the sole demonstration of the existence of a positive surplus-value as a condition for positive profits, could be incorporated into this latter perspective thanks to the so-called Fundamental Marxian Theorem.[3] Pasinetti is one of the authors who must be credited with showing the limits, both historiographic and analytical, of this whole framework.

THE LEGITIMACY OF CAUSALITY

Already in 1964 (Pasinetti, 2019 [1964], p. 358) observed that econometric analysis can be conducted by employing two different logical schemes, whose opposite features bear 'profound implications [...] not only for econometric analysis, but also for economic theory':

$$\begin{cases} \alpha_{11}x_1 + \alpha_{12}x_2 + \alpha_{13}x_3 + \ldots + \alpha_{1n}x_n = a_1 \\ \alpha_{21}x_1 + \alpha_{22}x_2 + \alpha_{23}x_3 + \ldots + \alpha_{2n}x_n = a_2 \\ \alpha_{31}x_1 + \alpha_{32}x_2 + \alpha_{33}x_3 + \ldots + \alpha_{3n}x_n = a_1 \\ \vdots \\ \alpha_{n1}x_1 + \alpha_{n2}x_2 + \alpha_{n3}x_3 + \ldots + \alpha_{nn}x_n = a_n \end{cases} \tag{14}$$

$$\begin{cases} \beta_{11}y_1 = b_1 \\ \beta_{21}y_1 + \beta_{22}y_2 = b_2 \\ \beta_{31}y_1 + \beta_{32}y_2 + \beta_{33}y_3 = b_3 \\ \vdots \\ \beta_{n1}y_1 + \beta_{n2}y_2 + \beta_{n3}y_3 + \ldots + \beta_{nn}y_n = b_n \end{cases} \tag{15}$$

In the first system, the value of the unknowns of each equation does not depend only on its coefficients but also on the coefficients of all the equations of the system. All the unknowns must be determined simultaneously, and a symmetric relationship exists therefore between all the variables of the system. Conversely, the first equation of the second system can be solved autonomously, and equations which follows relies on each of the preceding equations in order to be solved. Here economic magnitudes are hierarchically linked in a causal chain, which can also be formulated in terms of a temporal succession. Pasinetti observes that, despite the second schema exhibits a much greater simplicity for the estimation of parameters in presence of stochastic elements, econometricians have usually given their preference to models built upon interdependent relationships. This preference, which remains unexplainable on the ground of econometrics alone, is deeply rooted in the general equilibrium framework embraced by economic theory, where 'the equilibrium solutions stem from the simultaneous combination of these functions, i.e., the market prices and the physical quantities that have been exchanged' (p. 361). However, this is not the only scheme economic theory makes use of. A causal and sequential relation between distributive variables can be found in Ricardo, who determined 'first wages (based on physiological subsistence needs), then rent (based on the fertility of the land) and finally, as a residual income, profits' and in the Keynesian perspective.[4] Keynes starts from the determination of the rate of interest in the financial markets (once that the liquidity preference schedule and the quantity of available money are known), then moves to the determination of investment (from the rate of interest and the schedule of the marginal efficiency of capital) and, at last, arrives, by taking into account also the marginal propensity to consume, to the determination of 'the global amount of effective demand and of the national income'. Analogously, in Kaldor's model we start from the determination of the long-run rate of profit from the natural rate of growth and the propensity to save. Then, the rate of profit together with the technical conditions of productions allows us to determine the capital-output ratio, from which we can obtain the share of profit in overall income and, at last, wages as a residual income. Despite reversing the causal nexus singled out by Ricardo concerning distribution, the Keynesian revolution reinstates for Pasinetti the employment of a causal chain for analyzing the relationship between economic variables. The controversy between the Marginalist school and 'the Classical-Keynesian school' can ultimately be traced to the antagonism between the logical frameworks of causality and interdependence. According to Pasinetti, the persistence of this opposition is rooted in the existence of two orders of economic relationships, which must be carefully distinguished. To the first order, we can ascribe relationships which 'can be stated in terms of objective efficiency', regardless of the existence of any institutional or political framework. In this sense, they can be expressed in 'natural terms'[5] (p. 362), without any reference to social forces like those which characterize a market economy. Once we incorporate the specifical institutional set-up of a market society, the 'opposite and simultaneous forces' of demand and supply require to be addressed by tools apt to capture their mutual influence: we are now confronted with relations which 'are more immediate than the others, more easily observable, and at the same time influenced by the entire institutional set-up (not even strictly economic) of society'. A causal approach to economic phenomena is necessary for addressing more fundamental relations, which allow for the evaluation of the different social configurations: institutional set-ups 'are justifiable only in as much as they tend to produce positions of objective efficiency, that is, the first relationships'. Simultaneous systems describe the economic reality as it is, causal chains as it can be, addressing the factors which affect its evolution when unhindered by imperfect social arrangements. This difference in points of view is later recast (Pasinetti, 1981) in terms of trade-centred and industry-centred theories. By giving pre-eminence on exchange, economic theories conceive problems in term of allocation of given resources, which 'may be expressed by a mathematical function to be maximized under certain constraints' (Pasinetti, 1981, p. 3). If the analysis of exchange necessarily involves a static outlook, the fact of industry cannot be separated from the consideration of changes in the methods employed by people in order to satisfy their wants: here theory is no more centred upon problems of rationality but rather on processes of learning, which must be expressed in function of time. Simultaneity can be useful for approaching the short-run, where changes in the structure of production might be negligible, but becomes irrelevant in the long-run, where the 'persistent movement' (p. 4) of progress is the dominant feature of the system. Rather than exhibiting a naïve and pre-mathematical way of representing economic relationship, causal reasoning is valuable, also from a mathematical standpoint, to address the changes over time of an economic system, neglected by both the neoclassical and the neo-Ricardian version of the long-period positions method. According to Pasinetti, the classical economists, focusing their analysis on industry, had to embrace a dynamic perspective. The starting point of Adam Smith's *Wealth of Nations* was 'an analysis of "the causes of improvements in the productive power of labour"' (Pasinetti, 1981, p. 5). Economic growth presupposed 'changes in the structure of employment, notably an increase in the share of "productive" work (relative to "unproductive" work)' (Pasinetti, 1993, p. 2). Changes in the methods of production were also a necessary component of the core of Ricardo's analysis: the limited quantity of available land together with 'the growth of overall productions brings about a continuous re-proportioning of the sectors of the economic system, along with well-defined changes in income distribution'. No less important was the dynamic perspective for Marx, according to whom 'the tendency toward an increase in the ratio of 'constant capital' to 'total capital' (an increase in the 'organic composition of capital') brings about a series of changes in the proportions among the various commodities that are produced'. Since the focus of the classical economists and of Marx is not on determining prices given a specific technological and distributive configuration, but rather on the causes and consequences of modern industrial production, the adoption of a labour theory of value must have a different rationale than measuring the rate of profit as a ratio of heterogeneous aggregate of commodities. If production has the power to multiply the available means for the satisfaction of needs and technical progress continuously revolutionizes the quantity and nature of commodities employed as inputs for production, the only real cost incurred by society for its reproduction and expansion is the labour that must be expended in these processes. Prices emerge because of the necessity of 'an extensive division of labour' (Pasinetti, 1986, p. 421), which they secure by reflecting the different costs of commodities in terms of the labour that must be expended for their production. Natural resources are freely appropriated by society, and their productivity in physical terms is irrelevant for the formation of prices and for their variations (Pasinetti, 1981, p. 131).

Pasinetti did not fail to observe the 'inherently sequential' nature of this approach. Production and labour services 'are flows, that is, they have a time dimension' (Pasinetti, 1986, p. 423). Every solution for the problem of value in terms of labour 'refers to a particular period of time' (p. 424). Since 'different periods of time will be characterized by different technical coefficients, and therefore by different solutions', this approach 'naturally leads to the investigation of changes, and movements, through time'. To the opposite, simultaneous approaches do not allow to compare systems over time: here 'one cannot admit that technical coefficients can change: since, if they were to change, one should start over from the beginning on the basis of new technical coefficients, which, in turn, should be considered as data and therefore as constants'

(Pasinetti, 1993, p. 12). The new system would have 'nothing in common with the previously built one'. Attempts from a general equilibrium perspective to address the issue of growth, by incorporating the assumption of constant coefficients of production, have ended up 'omitting deliberately what [...] has been singled out as the basic force responsible for the dynamism of the modern society, namely the process of learning which goes on, both on the technical side and on the demand side' (Pasinetti, 1981, p. 120). The assumption of a given state of technology, 'conveniently though it may be mathematically, has nothing to do with the real world', ends up 'taking the structure of the economic system at a given point of time and crystallizing it, so to speak, for all eternity'. Such a representation of the expansion of the economic system is deeply unrealistic not only because coefficients of production change over time at different pace according to the sector but also because it forgets to incorporate changes in the composition of the real wage. In the logic of von Neumann's model, this can be done once that the assumption of a uniform growth rate of the productivity of labour is assumed, either by adopting increasing consumption coefficients or by treating the wage as a part of the social surplus. In the first case, the model would ensure the constancy of the proportions between sectors only if the real wage grew at the same pace of the productivity of labour, 'an analytically elegant, but extremely special' case (p. 121). In the second case, the maximum rate of growth would be secured only in the case, of no economic significance, where all the wage is reinvested into production. In both the cases, 'the von Neumann concept of a maximum rate of growth, if applied to a system with technical progress, not only may not, but actually *can never* correspond – not even by a fluke – to an optimum pattern of growth' (p. 122). Moreover, since the output is entirely determined by technology, it is assumed that consumers will be indifferent to its composition, a statement of dubious economic meaning. Moreover, von Neumann's model forgets that consumption coefficients evolve with changes in real income. As predicted by Engel's law, an increase in income does not involve a proportional increase in the demand for all commodities. As income increases, consumers shift to goods of better quality and spend a growing proportion of their income in satisfying lower priority wants, and the demand of each good is destined to be saturated at a certain level of income. If consumption is considered, the proportional growth path loses therefore its aura of optimality. The requirement of a uniform rate of growth among sectors implies, moreover, that if a commodity is particularly difficult to produce, it will slow down the growth of the entire economic system. Such an 'unacceptable restriction' (p. 123) ignores that substitutes for expensive or rare products can always be found or invented. Lastly, models where the proportions between sectors remain unchanged with capital accumulation make the description of a multi-commodity system equivalent to the one depicted by a single-sector model, telling us nothing more that can already be found in aggregated models like these by Harrod and Kaldor. Despite these strict limits, incompatible with the fact of 'systematic and irreversible changes' (Pasinetti, 1993, p. 7) in the productive structure which characterize industrialized and industrializing economies, proportional dynamics has remained 'for half of a century' the principal tools for investigate economic growth. An alternative approach can for Pasinetti be developed only on the ground of a 'very logical and indeed complete generalization of the pure labor theory of value' (Pasinetti, 1986, p. 424).

FROM DYNAMICS TO THE THEORY OF VALUE: PASINETTI'S SYSTEM

The first analytical device employed by Pasinetti (1973) to address technical change is the elimination of intermediate commodities from the analysis: only final commodities are considered. All production processes are interpreted as distinguished vertically integrated sectors, where all inputs are reduced to inputs of labour and of services from the stocks of capital goods employed. In this way, it becomes possible to make abstraction from intra-industry interdependency, treating each vertically integrated sector as a relatively autonomous sub-system. Two orders of hypotheses are introduced: the first pertaining to the initial condition of the system and the second to its movements through time.

The initial conditions of the system are defined by the following exogenous variables:

(1) (n-1) stocks of capital goods $K_1(0), K_2(0), \ldots, K_{n-1}(0)$, which result from past productive activity. Capital goods are expressed in terms of units of vertically integrated productive capacity, i.e. with reference to the units of their specific final goods produced. As a simplification, it is assumed that capital goods are produced exclusively by the means of labour[6];
(2) a given population $X_n(0)$;
(3) 2(n-1) technical coefficients $a_{n1}(0), \ldots, a_{n,n-1}(0), a_{nk_1}(0), \ldots, a_{nk_{n-1}}(0)$, representing the inputs of labour required in a unit of time to produce one unit of final commodity;
(4) (n-1) technical coefficients $T_1, \ldots, T_{n-1}$ representing the reciprocal of wear and tear of the capital goods employed in each sector;
(5) (n-1) consumption coefficients $a_{1n}(0), \ldots, a_{n-1,n}(0)$ representing the per capita demand for each consumption good per unit of time;
(6) (n-1) investment coefficients $a_{k_1n}(0), \ldots, a_{k_{n-1}n}(0)$ representing per capita demand for each investment good per unit of time;
(7) the given real wage rate $w(0) = \overline{w}$.

It is assumed that the system at time zero is at equilibrium and that, therefore:

i. the (n-1) stocks of productive capacity must be exactly the size required by demand;
ii. the (n-1) investment coefficients at time zero must be entirely determined by the expansion of demand, with neither underproduction nor overcapacity and

iii. the technical, consumption and investment coefficients must secure a level of demand equal to potential national income:

$$\sum a_{ni}a_{in} + \sum a_{nk_i}a_{k_in} + \sum\left(\frac{1}{T_i}\right)a_{nk_i}a_{in} = 1 \qquad (16)$$

These conditions ensure a stable full employment of the labour force as well of full utilization of the available productive capacity.

Population, productivity, per capita demand for each good and the wage rate are then assumed to change over time:

(1) Population increases at the steady rate g:

$$X_n(t) = X_n(0)e^{gt} \qquad (17)$$

(2) Productivity changes in every sector at different (n-1) rates of changes ρ_j, each of them assumed to be steady:

$$a_{nj}(t) = a_{nj}(0)e^{-\rho_j t} \qquad (18)$$

$$a_{nk_j}(t) = a_{nk_j}(0)e^{-\rho k_j t} \qquad (19)$$

These rates of change will be mostly positive, but some of them will be negative due to the increasing difficulty of producing some goods, i.e. because the exploitation of ever scarcer natural resources.

(3) Per capita demand for each good changes according to (n-1) rates of change r_i. These rates are not constant over time and will evolve in function of exogenous individual preferences, in turn affected by the level of real income and by the structure of prices:

$$r_i(t) = f_i\left\{a_{n1}, \ldots, a_{n,n-1}, a_{nk_1}, \ldots, a_{nk_{n-1}}; \frac{d}{dt}\left[a_{n1}, \ldots, a_{n,n-1}, a_{nk_1}, \ldots, a_{nk_{n-1}}\right], t\right\} \qquad (20)$$

However, for simplicity, the rates r_i are supposed to remain constant over the time stretches of length z. It becomes possible to write the movement in time of demand coefficient as follows:

$$a_{in}(t) = a_{in}(t-\theta)e^{r_i\theta} \tag{21}$$

where $\theta = t\text{-}\eta z$, with η being the greatest integer with, if multiplied by z and subtracted to t leaves θ with a positive value.

(4) The wage rate change at percentual rate σ_w will be steady over time:

$$w(t) = w(0)e^{(g+r_i)\theta} \tag{22}$$

In order to maintain a dynamic equilibrium over time, total new investment in each sector must be balanced with the growth of the corresponding final demand, given by the increase both in consumption per capita and in population:

$$a_{k_in}(t) = (g+r_i)a_{in}(t-\theta)e^{(g+r_i)\theta} \tag{23}$$

This formula, which ensures an adequate expansion in productive capacity, must be complemented, in order to secure full employment and full capacity utilization, with the equality between the growth of total expenditure and the growth of potential national income:

$$\begin{aligned} 1 = {} & \frac{1}{\mu\nu}\sum \alpha_{ni}(t-\theta)a_{in}(t-\theta)e^{(r_i-\rho_i)\theta} \\ & + \frac{1}{\mu\nu}\sum\left(g+r_i+\frac{1}{T_i}\right)a_{nk_i}(t-\theta)a_{in}(t-\theta)e^{(r_i-\rho_{k_i})\theta} \end{aligned} \tag{24}$$

where μ represents the proportion between active and total population and ν is the ratio between working hours and the total hours available in a period of time. However, since technical progress will reduce the labour time needed for producing most of the commodities and the demand for any consumption goods will become saturated after a certain level of income is achieved, full employment will be preserved only if this tendence is balanced with the introduction of new goods and, therefore, of new sectors. We won't have any more a given number of (n-1) sectors but rather an increasing one, e.g., [$n(t)$-1] The above condition is, therefore, corrected as follows:

$$\begin{aligned} & \sum_{1}^{n(t)-1} a_{ni}(t-\theta)a_{in}(t-\theta)e^{(r_i-\rho_i)\theta} + \sum_{1}^{n(t)-1}\left(g+r_i+\frac{1}{T_i}\right)a_{nk_i}(t-\theta)a_{in}(t-\theta)e^{(r_i-\rho_{k_i})\theta} \\ & = \mu(t)\nu(t) \end{aligned} \tag{25}$$

Another countertendency that will reinforce the maintenance of full employment is the decrease over time of the right-side of this equation, given by the increase in labour time or in the diminution of the relative working population.

All these conditions allow for the determination of changes in the quantities produced, in relative prices, in the sectorial production, in the sectorial level of employment and in the sectorial rates of profit.

For the changes in the quantities of consumption goods X_i and in the changes of capital goods X_k, we have:

$$X_i(t) = [a_{in}(t-\theta)X_n(t-\theta)]e^{(g+r_i)\theta} \tag{26}$$

$$X_k(t) = \left(g + r_i + \frac{1}{T}\right)[a_{in}(t-\theta)X_n(t-\theta)]e^{(g+r_i)\theta} \tag{27}$$

Therefore, the relative quantities of commodities produced will be entirely determined by demand and by its evolution.

The dynamics of relative prices will be given by:

$$p_i(t) = \left[a_{ni}(t-\theta)\overline{w}\right]e^{-\rho_i\theta} + \left(\pi + \frac{1}{T}\right)\left[a_{nki}(t-\theta)\overline{w}\right]e^{-\rho_{k_i}\theta} \tag{28}$$

$$p_k(t) = \left[a_{nk_i}(t-\theta)\overline{w}\right]e^{-\rho_{k_i}\theta} \tag{29}$$

Productivity in each sector and its change over time will be the only determinant for relative prices.

By combining the determinants of changes in quantities and prices, we can have the different time paths of sectoral productions for the value at current prices of consumption goods $V_i(t)$ and of capital goods $V_{k_i}(t)$:

$$V_i(t) = p_i(t)X_i(t) = \left[a_{ni}(t-\theta)a_{in}(t-\theta)\overline{w}X_n(t-\theta)\right]e^{(g+r_i-\rho_{k_i})\theta} + \left(\pi + \frac{1}{T}\right)$$
$$\left[a_{nki}(t-\theta)a_{in}(t-\theta)\overline{w}X_n(t-\theta)\right]e^{(g+r_i-\rho_{k_i})\theta} \tag{30}$$

$$V_{k_i}(t) = p_{k_i}(t)X_{k_i}(t) = \left(g + r_i + \frac{1}{T}\right)\left[a_{nk_i}(t-\theta)a_{in}(t-\theta)\overline{w}X_n(t-\theta)\right]e^{(g+r_i-\rho_{k_i})\theta} \tag{31}$$

We can then determine the dynamic of employment in the sectors producing consumption goods ($E_i(t)$) as well as in those producing capital goods ($E_{k_i}(t)$):

$$E_i(t) = a_{ni}X_i(t) = \left[a_{ni}(t-\theta)a_{in}(t-\theta)\nu^{-1}X_n(t-\theta)\right]e^{(g+r_i-\rho_i)\theta} \tag{32}$$

$$E_{k_i}(t) = a_{nk_i}(t)X_{k_i}(t) = \left(g+r_i+\frac{1}{T}\right)\left[a_{nk_i}(t-\theta)a_{in}(t-\theta)\nu^{-1}X_n(t-\theta)\right]e^{(g+r_i-\rho_{k_i})\theta} \tag{33}$$

Given the changing structure of employment within sectors, full employment will be preserved only by a continuous transfer of workers from sectors which are expelling workers in consequence of mechanization and changes in the demand patterns to sectors, which are absorbing them.

The system must be closed with the adoption of a *numéraire*. This involves both setting its absolute value at time zero and its rate of change over time. On the one hand, Pasinetti chooses to employ the wage rate for expressing prices in terms of commanded labour. Moreover, in order not to vary over time of time, this *numéraire* must grow together with the average productivity of the system:

$$\sigma_w = \rho^* \tag{34}$$

In turn, this average productivity is determined by weighting the sectoral change in productivity by the hyper-vertically integrated labour coefficients employed by it, i.e. the proportion of the total labour employed in the production of each consumption good (including both the labour directly employed by the sector and the labour employed by the sectors producing the capital goods necessary to the production of this good):

$$\lambda_i(t) = \frac{1}{\mu\nu}a_{in}(t)\left[a_{ni}(t) + \left(g+r_i+\frac{1}{T_i}\right)a_{nk_i}(t)\right] \tag{35}$$

The average rate of growth of productivity can then be written as follows: where ρ_i' designates the (n-1) rates of changes of the vertically hyper-integrated labour coefficients for the (n-1) commodities.

$$\rho^*(t) = \sum \rho_i' \lambda_i(t) \tag{36}$$

Two are the consequences which lead Pasinetti to draw from this scheme a restatement of the labour theory of value. First, the existence of a rate of profit is due exclusively to the phenomenon of economic growth, which leads to an increase of the share of the working day which must be devoted to the production of additional capital goods. On the one hand, the preservation of dynamic equilibrium demands a constant production per head over time. The existence of a growing population with a given labour productivity requires therefore that some resources must be devoted to expanding the productive capacity through the production of new capital goods. The quantity of goods which will be consumed will become lower than to the situation of a constant population. In absence of technical progress, the rate of profit will be exclusively determined by the rate of growth of population. On the other hand, in presence of technical progress, the increase in the per capita income will lead to unequal growth of the demand for each consumption good. Also in this case, the necessity to expand productive capacity must lead to increase the share of labour devoted to the expansion of productive capacity at detriment of the share devoted to consumption goods. The rate of profit of each sector will consequently be determined by the rate of growth of population and by the per capita demand for the final good it produces. Since this rate is determined in complete abstraction from any institutional set-up (especially, no uniformity among industries is assumed), Pasinetti designates these rates as the natural rates of profit:

$$\pi_i^* = g + r_i \tag{37}$$

By inserting this result in the equation of prices and expressing prices in term of the wage rate, we can write:

$$p_i(t) = \left[a_{ni}(t) + \left(\frac{1}{T_i}\right)a_{nk_i}(t) + (g + r_i)a_{nk_i}(t)\right] \tag{38}$$

Since $a_{ni}(t)$ is the labour directly expended in the production of each consumption good i (direct labour), $\left(\frac{1}{T_i}\right)a_{nki}(t)$ the labour expended in replacing worn-out capital (indirect labour) and $(g + r_i)a_{nki}(t)$ is the labour necessary to expand the production of i (hyper-indirect labour), the price of each commodity is entirely determined by the labour expended in its production.

If indeed the transition from the natural system to a capitalist economy where the rate of profit must be uniform across sectors, by preventing the price structure to reflect the labour time spent in production,[7] is a 'more than just a formal' jump (Pasinetti, 1981, p. 153), the natural system maintains for Pasinetti an invaluable importance both for showing the long-run causes of unemployment if the system is not kept in an equilibrium path and the necessity of public intervention for securing full employment also in the long-run according by criteria discovered by the model.

SOME LIMITS OF STRUCTURAL ECONOMIC DYNAMICS

If the formulation of a system in which all the variables are expressed in function of time is a necessary step for addressing capital accumulation (Chatzarakis et al., 2024; Freeman, 1995) and if the distinction between a 'natural' and an institutional level in order to evaluate the effectiveness of the latter as well as the analytical employment of different levels of abstraction (as in Marx's analysis of capital in general) seem to contain precious insight, Pasinetti's model does not seem to take full advantage of the strengths of the methodological perspective he rightly rehabilitated against simultaneism.

In the first place, the exogeneity of technical progress amounts to a renounce to investigate the factors which determine economic development. The abstract notion of learning does not consider that an investigation of progress cannot be separated by the conditions, both material and institutional, which can foster (and hinder) labour productivity. On the one hand, technical progress is a necessity for capitalists in order to outcompete their rivals. On the other hand, the increase in the composition of capital, acting on the rate of profit, reduces the inducement to invest and makes innovations unprofitable. The materiality of innovation, being embodied in particular sets of machinery and of processes for building up a skilled workforce, prevent their dissemination in all directions which Pasinetti, identifying knowledge and economic progress, sees, at least potentially, as one of the key features of modern production. The abstraction of progress from its capitalistic form (included the inter-sectors transfers of value brought about by the tendential equalization of the rate of profit), moreover, prevents Pasinetti from acknowledging some of the asymmetries of international competition when he denies that technological superiority leads per se to economic exploitation of other countries (Pasinetti, 1981, p. 275).[8]

The interpretation of the origin of profit in the necessity to expand productive capacity for preserving dynamic equilibrium blurs the distinction between the surplus-labour workers can perform beyond the time they spend in reproducing their consumption goods and the surplus-value, whose existence as a freely appropriated revenue follows exclusively from the capitalists' power to prolong the working day in consequence of their control of the means of production, a social relation which can take place also in the case of simple reproduction with a given technology and a stationary population. This social relation is completely lost in the treatment of the wage as the only surplus: on the one hand, profit is interpreted not as the freely appropriated labour time by the capitalists but as the necessary time for the expansion of productive capacity; on the other hand, the wage, which should represent a cost element for the capitalist, is interpreted as the residual which remains 'over and above what has been charged for profits' (Pasinetti, 1981, p. 144). The production and the increase of this surplus is defined as 'the purpose of the whole production process'. It could be objected that, being the analysis conducted at a pre-institutional and normative level, it would have little sense to include class dynamics which belong to a specific social configuration: it is beyond doubt that, from a normative point of view, progress should result in more wealth and leisure for the workers. However, as acknowledged also by Reati (2000), Pasinetti's analysis already contains elements which belong to an institutional level: social labour is distributed through monetary prices, and the product is distributed among profits and wages. The analysis could then either reject every social element and limit itself to the possibilities that could be achieved by either reforming or transforming the current social configuration, or describe conditions which provide meaningful insight also for understanding also some essential features of capitalist societies. For the first task, Pasinetti seems to add too much socially specific elements; for the second task, it remains at a too abstract level.

Moreover, the persistence of an equilibrium path, albeit with changing coefficients of production and of consumption and with a normative orientation, weakens the critique advanced to von Neumann, whose model is partially reappraised as an intermediate step between a stationary and dynamic equilibrium (Pasinetti, 1981, pp. 120–121). A dynamic approach should include the analysis of the causes which, on the one hand, inevitably configure a disequilibrium growth path and, on the other hand, lead to a violent reestablishment of viable conditions of reproduction (Chatzarakis et al., 2024). It remains however true that, on the normative level, the demonstration that the system is incapable to spontaneously maintain full employment remains a significative result.

Finally, the exclusive employment of labour coefficients in abstraction from intra- and inter-sectorial value transfers hides the peculiar features of the circuit of capital. Capitalist production cannot be reduced to the application of human labour for the multiplication of the available resources but involves the continuous transformation of money into capital in order to beget more money for the capitalist. The continuous revolutions in value, both of past and present investment, brought about by changes in the production methods, the simultaneous presence of different methods of productions within the same industry, together with the continuous changes in the relative profitability of the different industries, continuously produce deviations between the individual and the social value of each particular commodity, exposing capitalists to the risk of not realizing, partly or completely, the surplus-value they have extracted and of seeing the value represented by its stock of capital evaporate once that more productive methods have been introduced by competitors (Carchedi, 1991; Freeman, 1995). This complex dynamic of value transfers requires the incorporation of money into the framework not only, as Pasinetti does, to account for credit and debt relations but also to express the share of social labour which commodities come to represent, which is different from the share actually expended in their production.

CONCLUSION

At first we have shown that 1) the substitution of a causal with a simultaneous logic was a key moment in the criticism of Marx's theory, whose logic structure is essentially sequential, and that 2) before becoming the benchmark for non-marginalist approaches to growth, simultaneous models of capital accumulation were mobilized by von Charasoff and von Neumann for justifying the efficiency of capitalist production. We have then highlighted how for Pasinetti 1) studying economic dynamics outside of proportional growth required the rehabilitation of a causal framework, which he correctly ascribed to the classics, Marx and Keynes; 2) comparing systems evolving over time required the rehabilitation of a labour theory of value. We have then singled out three limits of Pasinetti's structural dynamics: the exogeneity of technical progress, the way the distinction between a natural and a social level of analysis is articulated, and the abstraction for value transfers as a peculiarity of capitalist production.

NOTES

1. Schefold (1989) has remarked the impossibility of constructing a standard system for systems which exhibit overproduction when all the surplus is reinvested. Concerning stability, see Steedman (1984). For impossibility of generalizing a tradeoff between the real wage and the rate of profit, see Bidard (1997).
2. This remains true for later Marxist 'dual system' approaches, as in Okishio's (1961) theory of competition. Moreover, these approaches cannot preserve at the same time the equality (i) of total value and the sum of prices and (ii) of surplus-value and profit.
3. See Morishima (1973).
4. This reading of Keynes is further developed in Pasinetti, 1974. See also Lucarelli, 2023.
5. This does not mean that they should be interpreted as merely transhistorical, but rather that they should be seen in abstraction from any socially determined variable (e.g. the existence of a uniform rate of profit): Pasinetti (2019, p. 362) clearly states that these 'natural relationships' pertain only to 'an industrial society'.
6. This assumption will be relaxed in Pasinetti, 1988. See also Lavoie, 1997.
7. The possibility to preserve the natural system's proportionality between labour and prices also in the institutional system has been proved by Wright, 2019. This proportionality is assured in term of 'vertically super-integrated labour coefficients', which include, besides direct, indirect and hyper-indirect labor, also the labour necessary to reproduce the capitalist class for a given level of real income. While this is an important analytical result in bringing Pasinetti's program to full coherence, it still makes abstraction from transfers of value taking place within and between sectors, an important feature, as shown below, of capitalist production.
8. However, in the same passage Pasinetti states that forms of economic exploitation between countries do actually take place.

REFERENCES

Bidard, C. (1997). Pure joint production. *Cambridge Journal of Economics*, *21*(6), 685–701.

Bortkiewicz, L. v. (1952). Value and price in the Marxian system. *International Economic Papers*, *2*, 5–60.

Carchedi, G. (1991). *Frontiers of political economy*. Verso Books.

Carvajalino, J. (2021). Unlocking the mystery of the origins of John von Neumann's growth model. *History of Political Economy*, *53*(4), 595–631.

Cassel, G. (1918). *Theoretische Sozialökonomie*. C. F. Winter.

Champernowne, D. (1945). A note on J. V. Neumann's article on "A Model of Economic Equilibrium". *The Review of Economic Studies*, *13*(1), 10–18.

Charasoff, G. v. (1909). *Karl Marx über die menschlische und kapitalistische Wirtschaft*. Hans Bondy.

Charasoff, G. v. (1910). *Das System des Marxismus*. Hans Bondy.

Chatzarakis, N., Tsaliki, P., & Tsoulfidis, L. (2024). *Economic growth and long cycles. A classical political economy approach*. Routledge.

Debreu, G. (1974). Excess demand functions. *Journal of Mathematical Economics*, *1*, 15–34.

Egidi, M., & Gilibert, G. (1989). The objective theory of prices. *Political Economy*, *5*(1), 59–74.

Freeman, A. (1995). Price, value and profit – A continuous, general, treatment. In A. Freeman & R. Carchedi (Eds.), *Marx and non-equilibrium economics* (pp. 225–279). Edgar Elgar.

Garegnani, P. (1987). Surplus approach to value and distribution. In J. Eatwell, M. Milgate, & P. Newman (Eds.), *The new Palgrave. A dictionary of economics* (pp. 1–26). Macmillan. https://doi.org/10.1057/978-1-349-95121-5_1559-1

Howard, M. C., & King, J. E. (1989). *A history of Marxian economics. Vol. I: 1883–1929*. Princeton University Press.

Jevons, W. S. (1871). *The theory of political economy*. Macmillan & Co.

Jorland, G. (1995). *Les paradoxes du capital*. Odile Jacob.

Kliman, A. (2006). *Reclaiming Marx's capital*. Lexington Books.

Kurz, H. D., & Salvadori, N. (1993). Von Neumann's growth model and the 'classical' tradition. *The European Journal of the History of Economic Thought*, *1*(1), 129–159.
Kurz, H. D., & Salvadori, N. (1998). Understanding 'classical' economics. An introduction. In H. D. Kurz & N. Salvadori (Eds.), *Understanding 'classical' economics. Studies in long-period theory* (pp. 1–21). Routledge.
Lavoie, M. (1997). Pasinetti's vertically hyper-integrated sectors and natural prices. *Cambridge Journal of Economics*, *21*(4), 453–467.
Lucarelli, S. (2023). From the effective demand as a principle to the ownership of the capital as social responsibility. Rereading Luigi Pasinetti. *PSL Quarterly Review*, *76*(307), 353–371.
Mantel, R. (1976). Homothetic preferences and community excess demand functions. *Journal of Economic Theory*, *12*, 197–201.
Marchionatti, R. (2019). Between Berlin and Cambridge: Classical conceptions of the general economic equilibrium in the late 1920s. *Cambridge Journal of Economics*, *43*(5), 1377–1395.
Marshall, A. (1890). *Principles of economics*. Macmillan & Co.
Marx, K. (1991). *Economic manuscript of 1861–1863. A contribution to the critique of political economy (Continuation)*. Vol. 33 of K. Marx & F. Engels. Collected works. Progress Publishers.
Marx, K. (1997). *Capital, Volume II*. Vol. 36 of K. Marx & F. Engels. Collected works. Progress Publishers.
Morishima, M. (1973). *Marx's economics: A dual theory of value and growth*. Cambridge University Press.
Moseley, F. (2015). *Money and totality. A macro-monetary interpretation of Marx's logic in capital and the end of the 'transformation problem'*. Brill.
Neumann, J. v. (1945). A model of general economic equilibrium. *The Review of Economic Studies*, *13* (1), 1–9.
Okishio, N. (1961). *Technical change and the rate of profit* (pp. 85–99). Kobe University Economic Review, VII.
Pasinetti, L. L. (1973). The notion of vertical integration in economic analysis. *Metroeconomica*, *25*(1), 1–29.
Pasinetti, L. L. (1974). *Growth and income distribution: Essays in economic theory*. Cambridge University Press.
Pasinetti, L. L. (1981). *Structural change and economic growth. A theoretical essay on the dynamics of the wealth of nations*. Cambridge University Press.
Pasinetti, L. L. (1986). Theory of value – A source of alternative paradigms in economic analysis. In M. Baranzini & R. Scazzieri (Eds.), *Foundations of economics. Structures of inquiry and economic theory* (pp. 409–431). Basil Blackwell.
Pasinetti, L. L. (1988). Growing subsystems, vertically hyper-integrated sectors and the labour theory of value. *Cambridge Journal of Economics*, *12*(1), 125–134.
Pasinetti, L. L. (1993). *Structural economic dynamics. A theory of the economic consequences of human learning*. Cambridge University Press.
Pasinetti, L. L. (2019). Causality and interdependence in econometric analysis and in economic theory. *Structural Change and Economic Dynamics*, *49*, 357–363.
Reati, A. (2000). The complementarity of the post Keynesian and Marxian paradigms: The case of labour value. *Cahiers économiques de Bruxelles*, *168*(4), 481–510.
Schefold, B. (1989). *Mr Sraffa on joint production and other essays*. Routledge.
Shaikh, A. (1984). The transformation from Marx to Sraffa. In E. Mandel & A. Freeman (Eds.), *Ricardo, Marx, Sraffa, the Langston memorial volume*. Verso.
Shaikh, A. (2016). *Capitalism. Competition, conflict, crises*. Oxford University Press.
Shortall, F. (1994). *The incomplete Marx*. Avebury Press.
Sonnenschein, H. (1973). Do Walras' law and continuity characterise the class of community excess demand functions? *Journal of Economic Theory*, *6*, 345–354.
Steedman, I. (1984). Natural prices, differential profit rates and the classical competitive process. *The Manchester School*, *52*(2), 123–140.
Walras, L. (1874-77). *Éléments d'économie politique pure, ou théorie de la richesse sociale*. Corbaz.
Wright, I. (2019). Marx's transformation problem and Pasinetti's vertically integrated subsystems. *Cambridge Journal of Economics*, *43*(1), 169–186.

AT THE FOUNDATIONS OF THE CRITIQUE OF POLITICAL ECONOMY

Giovanni Mazzetti

University of Calabria, Italy

ABSTRACT

Contrary to common belief, Sraffa sidesteps the real problem in determining exchange ratios, which is the coexistence of independent and indifferent producers whose exchange relationships meet their reproductive needs. Instead, he derives a purely logical solution from imaginary conditions derived solely from algebraic equations. While exchange values based on production costs would indeed provide for reproduction, Sraffa's construction does not show how this outcome would come about. Reproduction cannot be assumed to take place spontaneously; unless concrete forces form and operate, the problem supposedly being addressed and solved does not exist. Sraffa does not spend a single word on this imposition, limiting himself to a unilateral assumption of necessity in the semiotically mute form of algebraic notation. Therefore, analysis should highlight whether and how, through a process mediated by exchange and concealed from human knowledge or volition, as argued by Marx, there 'little by little, from the outside and likewise by chance, regulation of reciprocal exchange arises by means of regulation of reciprocal production, [so that] the costs of production, [impose themselves as] the measure of exchange' (Marx Grundrisse, 205). Only thus can Sraffa's problem be acknowledged as genuine, and sensible discussion had about the conditions for its solution.

Keywords: Prices of production; prices; value; Sraffa's reproduction schemes; methods of production

PRICE: A MEASURE OF FREEDOM OR CONSTRAINT?

Marx's critique of political economy was directed at a specific form of thought, which did not take into account the complexity and the contradictory nature of

Money, Value and Marx's Circuit of Capital
Research in Political Economy, Volume 41, 119–138

Published under exclusive licence by Emerald Publishing Limited
ISSN: 0161-7230/doi:10.1108/S0161-723020260000041016

the capitalist relationships it claimed to analyze. As explained in his postscript to the Second edition of *Capital*, the critique was therefore didactic to guard against an abstract assimilation of the fundamental categories, leading to a 'naturalization' of forms of life comprehensible only in their concrete historical evolution.

If you ask a normal person 'what is a price?', he will probably think you are fussing around. Even a child 'knows' what a price is! This is partly true. At the level of description, it is what is given in exchange for a good, that is, its value expressed in money. But is that all? We should also explore what this statement means: what is the reality behind it? The answer is complex; in the following pages, we will clarify one aspect of it.

HOW DOES THE PROBLEM OF PRICES ARISE?

Napoleoni argues that Sraffa formulated the problem of price determination in a methodologically correct manner, that is, without contaminating it with judgements, which would add to its phenomenological manifestation. To comply with this constraint, we start from Sraffa's (1960) own formulation. Experts may feel that such a basic beginning is too elementary, but it lets us present the argument without the unnecessary complications that both Napoleoni and Sraffa sought to avoid.

Sraffa (1960, p. 3) opens his argument by defining a system based on 'production for subsistence'. This, he says, refers to 'an *extremely simple* [a primitive society] society which produces *just enough to maintain itself* [as it is]'.[1] This refers to the earliest forms of exchange in which things are exchanged directly, that is by barter, but there is not as yet a real price. These things are 'produced by separate industries', a somewhat misleading term in that primitive societies do not contain industries either in the modern sense of large-scale manufacturing or as branches of the division of labour. The idea is that certain organisms proceed independently of each other, without knowing what others are doing nor what overall product results. Those products are then 'exchanged for one another *at a market held after the harvest* [*at the conclusion of the production process*]'.

Here Sraffa enters a contradiction, since, given that the market he supposes simply did not exist, the exchange of products as commodities was so accidental that its impact on reproduction would have been marginal. 'Suppose', he continues,

> that only two commodities are produced, wheat and iron. Both are used, in part for the sustenance for those who work, and for the rest as means of production – wheat as seed, and iron in the form of tools. Suppose that, all in all, and including the necessaries for the workers, 280 quarters of wheat and 12 tons of iron are used to produce 400 quarters of wheat; while 120 quarters of wheat and 8 tons of iron are used to produce 20 tons of iron.

Annual production can then be summarized as follows:

[A] 280 q. wheat + 12 t. iron → 400 q. wheat
[B] 120 q. wheat + 8 t. iron → 20 t. iron

This adds nothing to what society as a whole possesses: it consumes, and produces, 400 q. of wheat and 20 t. of iron. However, each commodity was initially distributed between industries according to their productive needs but ends up entirely in the hands of the industry that produces it. There is a single set of exchange values at which the market will re-establish the original distribution of products, thus creating the necessary conditions for the process to renew itself.

However, by starting from the existence of industries that must renew the means of production at their disposal is, as we will see, a tautological component of the reasoning. Marx in contrast uses the concept of reproduction to express the renewal of production.

Sraffa's values arise directly from the production methods. 'In the particular example we have taken, the exchange value that satisfies this condition is 10 q. of wheat for 1 t. of iron'(Ivi). In fact, industry A *directly uses* 280 quintals of wheat so that it has 120 q. left over; the iron industry *directly uses* 8 t. of iron and has 12 t. left over. Since each of the two organisms *needs the other's product to reproduce itself,* the equilibrium exchange should be between those 120 q. of wheat and those 12 t. of iron.

This algebraic description of the process seems simple and coherently solved. Yet, it is decidedly imprecise to argue that it explains how any such 'primitive society' could actually exchange commodities and so determine the ratios at which products should exchange. Rather, it identifies those exchange relations that express the conditions for the system to reproduce, that is, the abstract constraint which economists metaphorically call a state of equilibrium. However, it does not tell us whether these terms of trade will actually be sought by the members of those communities nor whether or how they can actually be established. In short, Sraffa merely presupposes that things proceed as he describes and, as do many economists that use mathematics, confuses a statement of the conditions for the phenomenon to occur with the reality of its occurrence.

We need to explore this further because historically, prices are not at all determined as the equations suggest. 'Primitive communities' do not reproduce by creating 'industries', with the result that exchange is not internal to them, but appears on their margins, in their contacts with other communities. In addition to being distinct, these communities remain mutually alien and independent.[2]

We will now see that, in the place of an abstract approach which attaches no significance to the superficially insignificant differences between developed mercantile circulation and its predecessors, it is essential to understand how the value relationship emerged and was affirmed with the spread of exchange itself. This is all the truer when we apply Napoleoni's empirico-experimentalist principle of *hypotheses non fingo*.

HARROD'S MISUNDERSTANDING

Harrod's (1961) review of Sraffa's work contains a misunderstanding which throws light on the problem. Sraffa, he writes,

> begins his discussion with the case of two industries and two commodities: industry A can produce a surplus of commodities *a*, beyond the amount of what was used for its own production, and the same thing can happen for commodity *b* produced by industry B. The terms of exchange of *a* with *b* is determined solely by the ratio between the production surplus of *a* and the production surplus of *b*.

If we limit ourselves to this particular numerical example, this seems accurate, since 120 q. of wheat exchange for 12 t. of iron, which are apparently just the 'surpluses' of the two industries, as opposed to what they consume, which must be recreated in production. Misled by this reading, Harrod generalizes the argument: 'If we proceed to a greater number of industries and commodities we have a system of simultaneous equations with the exchange values of commodities will be determined by the same principle'.

This argument appears indisputable if we view mercantile relations as natural because it seems equivalent to the principle that everything not directly used by the producers is exchanged, so demand would be sure to balance supply.

Sraffa (1962) however objects that the reasoning is 'clearly the result of a misunderstanding'. Strangely, he does not feel the need to clarify the nature of this misunderstanding but limits himself to postulating that 'that exchange relations are, *naturally*, determined by the production equations and not by the ratios between the production surpluses of individuals products,' adding:

> Harrod was misled by the fact that the two ratios turn out to be equal in the first example given (a two-commodity system with no surplus being in a reintegrative state). Even in this very simple example, however, if, with the same equations, the two commodities were produced in different proportions (so that the system would cease to be in a merely reintegrative state) the exchange ratio would remain the same, but the ratio between the surplus production of the two commodities would change, so that they would no longer be equal. In the case of a system with more than two commodities the ratios of the surpluses of the productions should not be equal, in general, to the values even in the reintegrative state.

Sraffa is *algebraically* right. Indeed, in his three-industry example which immediately follows the one just discussed, adding pigs as a third product (1960, p. 4):

$$240 \text{ q. wheat} + 12 \text{ t. iron} + 18 \text{ pigs} \rightarrow 450 \text{ q. wheat}$$

$$90 \text{ q. wheat} + 6 \text{ t. iron} + 12 \text{ pigs} \rightarrow 21 \text{ t. iron}$$

$$120 \text{ q. wheat} + 3 \text{ t. iron} + 30 \text{ pigs} \rightarrow 60 \text{ pigs}$$

The terms of trade required to reconstitute the original stocks, according to Sraffa (1960, p. 4), are:

10 q. wheat = 1 t. iron = 2 pigs

But according to Harrod's criterion, they would be:

210 q. wheat = 15 t. iron = 30 pigs

Now, unlike the terms of trade in Sraffa's first example, the system could not then reproduce itself: the wheat producers would be unable to regain possession of the goods they need to resume production, and the producers of iron and pigs would have an untraded surplus.

For example, the wheat 'industry', with a surplus of 210 q. compared to its needs, would need 168 q. of wheat to buy the 12 t. of iron and 126 q. of wheat to buy the 18 pigs. Now, it can only obtain these in exchange, so it would have to part with 168 q. + 126 q. = 294 q. of wheat. But it needs 240 q. of wheat for its own reproduction, leaving it only 210 q. It will therefore be able to buy less iron and fewer pigs than those necessary for replenishment, leading to a lower production of grain in the following period, radically modifying the terms of trade in that period. As a result, the producers can no longer as much wheat as before.

In short, these prices would be neither 'equilibrium', nor 'natural', nor 'necessary' – all these being equivalent expressions which orthodox economics employs to grapple with Sraffa's problem. They would be continuously fluctuating prices, incapable of reproducing the given situation. Instead of equilibrium, a dynamic of recurring imbalances would be established. This actually happens systematically on the market, where the prices fluctuate continuously, in defiance of such orthodox theories.

It might seem that, once the misunderstanding has been clarified, we can however proceed as Sraffa suggests. And yet things are not that simple: Harrod's misunderstanding is not accidental. Rather, it indicates a theoretical divergence on the exchange relationship and the nature of prices which *precedes* the determination of prices and decides the manner of its solution. That is, Sraffa and Harrod 'see' the reproduction of the two communities through opposite theoretical systems even though each appears to confirm part of what the other grasps.

CONSTRAINTS IMPLICIT IN THE DETERMINATION OF EXCHANGE RELATIONSHIPS

Sraffa rejects Harrod's conclusion, maintaining that values must arise 'directly from the methods of production'. But in *Production of Commodities by Means of Commodities*, he presented all this as a logical connection asserted algebraically, not on the basis of the real economic relations that occurred in history. His text argues that 'if' the market adopts these values, 'then' the system would reproduce itself. As the use of 'if' shows, this is a conditional proposition, not a necessary one. Sraffa however introduces this necessity in his reply to Harrod but limits himself to proclaiming it. By a tortuous path, he reaches the conclusion that terms of trade do not arise directly from 'production methods' but only from the quantities offered and demanded. These correspond to the relation between the surpluses and the producers' immediate needs for the goods they produce and hence to the individuals' subjective willingness to sacrifice these immediate needs to obtain the other things they need or want.

Everything could obviously be resolved by simply tracing this divergence back to the difference between the two hypotheses, without regard for their empirical foundation. But there is another path: we can evaluate whether both hypotheses suffer from unnecessary one-sidedness. Each captures an aspect of empirical factual reality, which does not have to be asserted a priori in opposition to what the other captures. Without conflating these two aspects, this opens up the possibility that the actual social processes are not linear but contradictory.

What is the source of Harrod's inaccurate reading of Sraffa's first example? In our opinion, it arises because he does ignore the title of Sraffa's first chapter, namely *Production without surplus* and consequently regards as 'surplus' something that is not. Industry A does produce a surplus of grain compared to the quantity that entered its own reproductive process, a certain quantity of iron *also* entered and must be included in this process. This must also be 'reconstituted' for the process to repeat. Industry A, which Harrod sees in a static, merely material way, cannot really exist without using iron which, together with its use of grain, defines it as an 'industry'.[3] The fact that it is the grain industry does not mean its relationship with its own product is all that matters. Its relationship with the production process itself is also essential, in which the iron consumed to produce must be included.[4]

When the wheat 'industry' exchanges its excess grain in Sraffa's first schema, it does so to reconstitute itself as the organism that it is. The two 'industries' thus depend on each other. To reproduce, each requires what it does not produce directly. In Sraffa's example, which refers to a merely reintegrative state, exactly enough excess grain is available to reconstitute the iron, which the industry needs to reproduce itself as a grain production process. Sraffa is therefore right to insist that the 'industry' take this constraint into account though Harrod escapes this constraint by starting from the mere availability of the products.

Is Harrod's misunderstanding so unjustified? If we suppose a 'primitive society' made up of sectors, which after production consciously exchanged each other's products as conditions for their reproduction, would Sraffa's system thus represented be close to this reality? Does the exchange relationship, and with it the problem of determining the terms of trade (the first forms of price), really emerge as Sraffa indicates?[5] In short, does it really make sense to take, as its starting point, the existence of 'industries' which, though producing independently of each other and belonging to independent social organisms, are mutually integrated and such as compose a single organism whose organicity is the foundation of reproduction[6]?

This issue concerns the way social interconnection is articulated through the exchange of goods and the corresponding division of labour. Those who evaluate representative schemes on the sole basis of logical-formal coherence are likely to see this as a non-existent problem; however, the analytical consequences are serious. As Marx (1990, pp. 471–472) remarks:

> the exchange of products springs up at the points where different families, tribes or communities come into contact; for at the dawn of civilization it is not private individuals but families, tribes, etc. that meet on an *independent footing*. Different communities find different means of production and different means of subsistence in their natural environment. Hence their modes of production and living, as well as their products, are different. It is this spontaneously developed difference which, when different communities come into contact, calls forth the mutual exchange of products and the consequent *gradual conversion of those products into commodities*. Exchange does not create the differences between spheres of production but it does bring the different spheres into a relation, thus *converting them into more or less interdependent* branches of the collective production of a whole society. In this case, the social division of labour arises from the exchange between spheres of production which *are originally distinct from and independent of one another.* (my emphases, as throughout in cited text)

Through exchange, each community establishes only a partial and contingent interconnection with the other, with which it exchanges a marginal part of its product, generally in excess of its normal needs, not to acquire things that are not yet conditions for its reproduction but to enjoy a good that it does not normally produce and for which it has no structural need.

Empirically, hence, neither exchange relations nor their determination emerge as Sraffa proposes. We must therefore start from modes of exchange that precede the interconnection between production and reproduction and eventually constitute their intermediary. The production centres – that is the different communities – do not present themselves at all as industries constituting one and the same social organism of a whole 'society' based on a 'shared' use of products. As Marx (1990, pp. 204–205) puts it:

> The form of barter in which the overflow of one's own production is exchanged by chance for that of others' is only the first occurrence of the product as exchange value in general, and is determined by accidental needs, whims, etc.

In short, in historical reality, Sraffa's reintegrative constraint does not initially exist. Modern anthropology fully confirms, as Lévi Strauss (1990) reminds us, 'the tribes traded among themselves not to procure *usual* consumer products, but luxury items'.

How then should we describe the moment when a 'primitive society' embryonically transcends pre-existing reproductive limits and, through exchange, establishes a relationship with another community?

EXCHANGE IN ITS EARLY FORMS: A FREE RELATIONSHIP

To stay as much as possible within Sraffa's framework, consider a community of farmers who use, in each production period, 10 quintals of wheat (for eating, sowing and producing hoes) and 2 wooden hoes which are replaced at the end to produce 10 quintals of wheat and 2 hoes.

It is doubtful that a push for exchange would arise in these conditions. Products will enter into use through the particular practices that characterize the community, and their use-value will immediately express the subsistence of the community, which is not integrated with producers from other communities, and would not see why its own products should become exchange values and hence commodities.

For human beings to begin selling and buying products, they have to become less useful to the community, in comparison with products it can obtain elsewhere. This can initially affect only that part of their product which exceeds normal reproduction of the community. This makes some sense of Harrod's misunderstanding, in which he treats the means of exchange of each 'industry' as a surplus to what that industry requires to reproduce itself, allowing him to ignore Sraffa's constraint.

In fact, exchange takes shape historically as a casual event in which one gives away one's own surplus, which has no use in community life. Harrod did not seem to realize, however, that these could only be treated as surpluses by repudiating Sraffa's scheme. For him, each nucleus has a 'free' relationship to that part of the product which Sraffa, based on his logical-formal assumptions, makes a *necessary* component of its reproduction, improperly defining it as an 'industry'. In so doing, Harrod attributes to a part of the product a determination that is not only incompatible with that attributed to it by Sraffa, but opposite to it. Here we see how right Einstein was to say that theory 'decides' what we can see. Both Harrod and Sraffa seem blind to the theoretical elements that support the other's approach. Sraffa's reply is contradictory: he speaks of 'surplus' as that part of the product that is exchanged in a situation which he himself defined as pure subsistence.

To explore the analytical relevance of the historical evolution of exchange, let us consider a product that is truly *freely* exchangeable. In our example, when production ends the community must have more than the 10 q. of wheat and the 2 hoes it needs for normal reproduction – say 15 q. of wheat:

$$10 \text{ q. wheat} + 2 \text{ hoes} \rightarrow 15 \text{ q. wheat} + 2 \text{ hoes}$$

There is then a surplus of 5 q. of wheat. This community could then decide to exchange with another community, of fishermen, with, we suppose, a surplus of 4 q. of fish arising from the following process:

$$8 \text{ q. fish} + 2 \text{ canoes} \rightarrow 12 \text{ q. fish} + 2 \text{ canoes}$$

First, there is no reason to conclude, as Harrod does, that any particular terms of trade impose themselves as necessary on other possible ones. Moreover, the surplus, as we will see, is treated completely differently from what Sraffa hypothesizes. Compared to their normal reproductive needs, the first community has a surplus of 5 q. of grain and the second 4 q. of fish. Yet in contrast with both hypotheses, *not all the surplus must be exchanged* precisely because the two communities lead an autonomous existence from the other. In fact, nothing prevents either community from developing internally new ways of using products compared to pre-existing ones. For example, the fishers might conclude that a divine force has caused the catch to grow, requiring it to sacrifice more fish, to secure further interventions in their favour, or it may 'offer' the fish to the deceased by placing it on their tombs. These decisions are made with respect to the *use value* of the product for the community, independent of any social exchange value.

The more this occurs, the less likely is an exchange interconnection with other communities. To become an object of exchange a product must no longer be an element of immediate satisfaction (Marx, 1904, p. 41). The idea that a surplus product spontaneously and primarily takes the form of a means of exchange is an arbitrary simplification, typically conceived by those who share the illusion, specific to the capitalist world, that human products are intrinsically and necessarily exchangeable, so they always and only present themselves as commodities. But precisely because products are not by nature exchange values but become so only when the extent of possible use values for the organism that produced them diminishes, there is no reason to assume that the two communities will establish exchange relationships with a uniquely determined value. All we can say is that the exchange can be written as:

$$x \text{ wheat} = y \text{ fish}$$

$$\text{where } 0 \leq x \leq 5 \text{ and } 0 \leq y \leq 4$$

Indeed, it is always a set of merely random, contingent circumstances that leads to a specific quantitative relationship within these limits.

Since things become exchangeable through particular, contingent evaluations of the social organisms involved, the ratios in which they so do are limited by, and reflect, these evaluations, which thus appear, algebraically, as random (Marx, 1990, p. 156). They will therefore differ from the ratios established in exchanges of similar products between other communities or between the same communities at different times.

A Sraffa-style scheme, which assigns a causal status to the technical components (costs) of some overall reproductive process is completely untenable, given that no stable link has been established and each organism reproduces only on its own basis. This leaves both communities free to practice the ratio they want.

THE CONSOLIDATION OF EXCHANGE

We can still modify these hypotheses. Suppose the surplus ceases be an occasional fact and becomes a structural element of production, perhaps, for example, because cultivation has made bushland more fertile while knowledge of fish behaviour has increased the catch. If exchange has already started, the two communities may well resort to it more frequently. The external goods which entered reproduction only occasionally thanks to exchange – appearing according to Lévi Strauss as luxury or 'festive' goods – now tend to enter structurally. That is, fish producers start eating wheat regularly while wheat producers start eating fish.

Consumption that previously appeared superfluous, and therefore outside the production conditions themselves, will then tend to present itself as necessary. Wheat producers will begin to feel that to reproduce themselves – and therefore produce wheat and hoes – they *must* usually be able to consume fish, and fish producers that to reproduce themselves – and therefore produce fish and canoes – *must* be able to consume wheat. Each community would then steadily allocate to exchange a growing share of whatever it normally uses in an attempt to acquire more goods from others.

This now begins to present itself as a condition of its own reproduction. The limit of this transformation of surplus into exchange value is clearly the size of that surplus itself, for each community. In this limit,[7]

$$y \text{ fish} + (15 - \text{x}) \text{ wheat} + 2 \text{ hoes} \rightarrow 15 \text{ wheat} + 2 \text{ hoes}$$

$$(12 - \text{y}) \text{ fish} + \text{x grain} + 2 \text{ canoes} \rightarrow 12 \text{ fish} + 2 \text{ canoes}$$

Even expressed in these terms, the system remains indeterminate and requires no particular exchange ratio among those we have already seen to be possible. To reach Harrod's conclusion that exchange must yield:

$$x/y = 5/4$$

Thus, a constraint must be introduced from the outside, i.e. it must be assumed that the surplus has no other possible use than being transformed into exchange value. This corresponds to the hypothetical situation, which economists refer to as equilibrium. This hypothesis however presupposes a fact that does not occur historically, namely *that it has become necessary to exchange everything that, according to a community's existing methods, exceeds the direct use of its products.* In Marx's language, we would be in a society 'in which the product *is nothing more* than a huge collection of commodities', which is true only for capitalist society. In Harrod's solution, like Sraffa's, the exchange rates are tautologically contained in the starting hypotheses. But neither explains anything about what happens in reality as society proceeds towards the production and exchange of products as commodities.

WHAT SRAFFA AND HARROD BOTH OVERLOOKED: THE RELATIONSHIP BETWEEN FREEDOM AND NECESSITY IN EXCHANGE

To establish the evolutionary dynamics envisaged by Sraffa, the exchange of products is insufficient. Something *more* is needed. We can try to define it in elementary terms at first, bearing in mind that in our exegesis above, exchange mediated the establishment of a connection between organisms that were and remained independent while for Sraffa, production centres are already in a relationship of stringent mutual dependence, which they reproduce through the exchange relationship. This is unknown in pre-capitalist history.

Economics, we can say, tries to analyze exchange as the quantitative ratio at which products are exchanged. But this changes continually in time and place; beyond this appearance, is it possible to identify a causal principle of determination that denies this apparent randomness? Can we speak of an exchange value, and therefore a price, as *immanent* to the commodity, as *necessary* – in the sense that the classical economists and Marx perceive as *value* – without falling into contradiction?

Sraffa undoubtedly concludes that exchange values are uniquely determined *by the conditions of production*, but he adds, coherently, that this is only because they satisfy presuppositions that he formulated abstractly, constraining the productive process to be renewed only and necessarily through a specific articulation of exchange.

Many economists, taking this condition to be so obvious as to require no substantiation, jumped to the Roncaglia (1998) conclusion that Sraffa had 'demonstrated that it would be possible to determine the value of various commodities *without making any reference to demand*'. But this path necessarily distances us from that empirical approach which, in Napoleoni's opinion, constitutes the essential merit of Sraffa's scheme and leaves us with an ideological assertion. It is not at all true that Sraffa makes no reference to demand. Rather, he introduces specific hypotheses on the way it relates to supply.[8] Both global demand and the individual requirements from which it arises are determined by the *constraint that the system must reproduce*. Sraffa is convinced that, by offering what it sells, each 'industry' demands products with reference both to its own reintegrative needs *and* to those of others.

Harrod, and with him the orthodox economists, presupposes instead that demand is completely autonomous with respect to the conditions of general reproduction and that everyone only pays attention to his own reproduction, even if then, he inexplicably superimposes the constraint that everything not used directly must be exchanged.[9] He therefore attributes, to any product not directly used by the industry that produces it, the dual character of being exchanged freely but having to be fully exchanged.[10] In both theoretical approaches, demand exists but takes shape through social mediations that differ profoundly from those that prevail in real social development.

The one-sidedness of both approaches is confirmed by Harrod's conviction that Sraffa does not refer to the question while Sraffa's own disciples are paradoxically convinced that things are in these terms, implicitly supposing that the question can only be addressed in the manner of Harrod.

Since exchange does not make its appearance as a mutual alienation of the conditions of production, the Sraffian framework requires that we verify whether in the social dynamics there are forces which, as exchange proceeds on an enlarged scale, somehow make demand (and the corresponding supply) concretely assume the conditions which Sraffa simply introduces as a prerequisite. Are producers, at a certain point, actually forced to take into account, in determining values, the production methods from which the products themselves arise? And if so, how would such a phenomenon arise? A 'proof' should not lie in the algebraic correctness of Sraffa's accounts but whether these correspond to what happens in social practice.

When Marx (1990), in the section of *Capital* dealing with relative surplus value, complains that economists struggle to deal with the quantitative aspect of the exchange relationship, but unjustifiably set aside the social conditions without which value cannot logically express the operation of an economic law, he refers precisely to simplifications like Sraffa's.

It is essential, therefore, that when an economic necessity is presumed, we fully understand whether something is involuntarily hidden or omitted whose existence should instead be demonstrated. In its absence, we must admit that the reasoning refers to only one of many possible solutions, its univocal result being an expression of what has been projected onto reality. On the other hand, Luigi Einaudi (1962, p. 18) clearly explains the hypothesis underlying marginalist price theory, which Sraffa declares he wants to criticize (his work is subtitled 'Premises for a critique of economic theory'). The marginalists hypothesize, he explains, that 'there would be a true market only when individuals were free to withdraw from it without harm', thus reversing the situation envisaged by Sraffa. In fact, for Sraffa, were goods alienated in ratios different from those he calculates, this would bring about a failure to reintegrate the industries because it would become impossible to produce what was produced before. Therefore, it would result in impoverishment, that is, in damage.

From this perspective, the wheat producer is *forced* to demand the specific quantity of iron he needs to produce, just as the iron producer is forced to ask for a specific quantity of grain. Such a constraint no longer has the personal character typical of the pre-capitalist world but, operating objectively, has no less impact on the reproductive dynamics of those who exchange. For Sraffa, thus, demand not only exists but appears to be determined and conditioned by forces relating to the reproduction of the system while in the universe of the orthodox, it is represented, in an Einaudian way, as free because each producer sees only to his own interest. Suffice it to recall that for Friedman (1962, p. 14), individuals must be 'effectively free to enter or not to enter into any particular exchange so that *every transaction is strictly voluntary*.'[11]

Orthodox reasoning confuses the two problems of *personal* and *material* constraint. The exchange is 'strictly voluntary' since, under bourgeois relations, no one can be *forced* to give up his products or productive activity. But when exchange is no longer sporadic but normal practice, one *is forced by objective conditions which transform a personally free act into economically necessary behaviour.* Failures to reproduce the system arise precisely from the fact underlined by Keynes: as each tries, perhaps succeeding, to avoid harming himself, he can involuntarily cause harm to others. Precisely because the individual producer is a private owner, he *does not and cannot aim to reproduce the system as a whole.*[12]

In Sraffa's scheme, if global demand for the various products is insufficient to meet needs, producers will be unable to reproduce either wheat or iron, and their lives will worsen. This would not, however, occur if what was exchanged was a truly surplus product, that is one which does not present itself as a 'condition of production' and need not be entirely exchanged to obtain what is necessary.

Sraffa and Harrod reconstruct society's functioning mechanisms – its *structure* – with different, even opposite methods yet are strangely convinced that they refer to the same reality. They do not realize that exchange and price formation do not present themselves in a univocal form, which always repeats in the same way, but have gestated, have changed throughout history and are in continuous transformation. Neither conceives of a third situation, closer to the reality of developed exchange, in which, corresponding to Sraffa's approach, freedom no longer exists: that is to say, in which the possibility of proceeding at one's own discretion, regardless of economic conditions, is lacking.

And for Harrod, in the situation existing at the dawn of mercantile cooperation, subjects inertially continue to feel free towards those they exchange with, *as if they still shared no common life*! So, they attend to their own reproduction but not that of the system as a whole. In consequence, the latter intervenes through forces which appear external, and therefore, incapable of producing the envisaged effects, to individuals. Only Marx offers an in-depth and effective account of the recurrent economic crises, which block the reproduction of society.

HOW PRODUCERS RELATE TO THE TOTAL PRODUCTION PROCESS

In historical reality, our ancestors, living in mutually alien separated communities, produced goods expressing an immediate relationship with their environment. Their products 'circulated' in their community without exchange and without outsiders. The problem of determining the quantitative ratio at which the products should exchange – their value – was therefore unconnected with social reproduction. How can we represent this situation?

Consider a society like Sraffa's first example. Sraffa (1960, p. 3) notes that '400 q. of wheat and 20 t. of iron have been used up in the aggregate and the same quantities are produced'. Thus reproduction has taken place. Therefore, this situation should have been represented as follows:

$$400 \text{ q. wheat} + 20 \text{ t iron} \rightarrow 400 \text{ q. wheat} + 20 \text{ t iron}$$

with the terms on the left representing social inputs and those on the right what results.

If this description is to be rejected, that is if we cease referring to the 'whole' alone, in favour of a representation like Sraffa's, which divides 'production operations' into distinct and separate 'industries', then a substantial and explicit reason for so doing is required.

In the scheme just introduced, wheat production does not at all appear as a disjointed and indifferent activity compared to the iron production nor vice versa. Iron and wheat are not other people's products but articulations of a whole – society reproduction – whose organic operation is, notwithstanding any division of labour, an intrinsic element of the reality expressed in this representation.

The passage of part of the grain from those who produce it to those who participate in reproducing the whole by producing iron through rituals, or other procedures, as well as the converse, is not mediated by the principle of the equivalence of exchange-values. It is codified in intrinsic and characteristic elements of the way the community's social structure, considered a whole, reproduces itself. We cannot say that '10 q. of wheat *is worth* 1 t. of iron' even though, in the normal course of events, wheat and iron flow in the necessary quantities – precisely as in Sraffa's example – where they are needed. Anyone who maintains things have a value by nature, and that therefore the form of value is unproblematic, needs to conduct a detailed critical comparison with the first chapter of *Capital* where Marx explains in depth why things aren't like that.

That is to say, the relationship between producers in reproduction is not expressed in the social form of the (exchange) value of the things produced because the mutually binding nature of the 'circulation' of products is known to the 'producers' and doesn't take the form of a contract between independent individuals. The human beings in such organisms normally know, practically, what to do for their common reproduction, and they just do it, expressing the 'value of things' not in ex post exchanges but in concrete social relationships that bind them as a community through the use of mutual products considered common property. So much that, as numerous anthropologists point out, they shy away from practicing money relationships within the community because this would represent a disconfirmation of the community itself.

In Sraffa's framework, however, wheat and iron are not immediately objective moments of community reproduction as a whole but products that express the separation between their producers. These appear as independent owners of things they have obtained autonomously. This separation then has to be overcome by recognizing a constraint – the certainty of the producers themselves that the community will eventually reproduce through exchange. The representation of productive operations by distinct equations for each product, and the problematization of their relations expressed in the need to identify exchange values as guarantors of the system's reproductive balance, shows that each part of the whole acts as *a disiectum membrum* with respect to the others.

The reproduction of society as a whole does not immediately appear as the subjective aim of those who interact to bring it about. They therefore end up having to discover, having already produced it – how much wheat is 'worth' how much iron and vice versa.[13] This is a value which, precisely because there is then no community, is always and only the one convenient to the individual producers, not one which guarantees the reproduction of everyone. The social reproductive process as a whole does exist, but beyond the intentions and awareness of the individual productive nuclei, and therefore appears external to them. This is why they can feel, contradictorily, 'free' in relation to it.

They produce commodities inasmuch as they produce privately and establish connections limited to the *ex post* exchange of particular products against equally particular products which they 'try to buy' precisely because these are not common property. This is why Marx (1973, pp. 196–197) says:[14]

> As much, then, as the whole of this [reproductive] movement appears as a *social process*, and as much as *the individual moments of this movement* arise from the conscious will and particular purposes of individuals, so much does *the totality of the process appear as an objective interrelation*, which arises spontaneously from nature; arising, it is true, from the mutual influence of conscious individuals on one another, but *neither located in their consciousness, nor subsumed under them as a whole.*

In other words, the producers need to determine the terms of trade of their products only if and because they do not face the system as a reality superordinate to them. If they truly relate to this system as the system of their relationships, the need to attribute an exchange value to these products would automatically disappear. Products needed to reproduce 'industries', and the individuals who produce in them, would be distributed immediately through the explicit recognition of the articulation of this common reproduction, just as a family knows who will cook or clean.

Since the community and its members would then 'know' that 400 q. of wheat and 20 t. of iron make 400 q. of wheat and 20 t. of iron, in the proportions expressed by the production equations,[15] the return of these products into production as a conditions of it – excepting events beyond their control – would not be problematic.

In short, needs would not present themselves in the form of a demand which, proceeding privately, completely ignores supply, and a supply which, in turn, proceeds without taking demand into account. Instead of expressing the need to discover the value of one good in relation to the other, the equations would immediately express the principle of mutual integration.

This principle of integration should not be mistaken for a 'plan'. This would assume individuals who set their common material reproduction as an objective goal while in pre-capitalist reality, they merely aim to reproduce a way of existence which, inherited from tradition, is immanent, just as a parent normally 'knows' they should prepare food for his children. The very problem of determining quantitative exchange ratios disappears because the measure of power corresponding to each production finds its roots in tradition, or conscious decisions of a non-economic nature, rather than being determined *a posteriori* on the supposition that individuals act independently and indifferently towards each other. Things are decidedly different when the product is produced as exchange value with the aim of transforming it into money. This is nothing other than a form of power over a part of the general product, implemented without a prior conscious subordination of the producers to the conditions of their overall reproduction, indeed generally accompanied by an antagonistic interests expressed as 'competition'. This is why exchange ratios must be 'discovered' *a posteriori*. And precisely because this is not normally achieved, while reproduction *is not even intentionally set as a goal*,[16] the result is the continuous oscillation of prices and cyclical crises.

THE REFERENCE TO TOTALITY AS AN INDIRECT PROCESS

The problem of quantitative determination emerges, consequently, on the basis of social conditions under which it cannot be formulated in the manner which Sraffa attributes to it, which is why Marx's expository method, which starts from the exchange relationship alone, without initially involving production techniques, is better. Sraffa purports to represent a reality that is absent from the centre of the consciousness and intentions of social agents. The forces that eventually determine the outcome he presents can only act through an external, objective constraint on individuals, sometimes without even understanding its nature.

Sraffa's result is logically impeccable on an algebraic level – after all it is just the solution of a system of equations – but does not address the real problem of identifying the concrete processes that determine exchange values. Marx (2010, p. 277) warns about the limits of this method. If a phenomenon is in reality articulated through a complex set of practical mediations, resolving it in an immediate way, that is, eliminating the mediations, is equivalent "to present that which does not exist as in fact existing. … Thus no solution of the matter is possible here, only a *sophistic explaining away of the difficulty*, that is, only scholasticism."

Sraffa's solutions are therefore univocal only because each productive act is a priori placed in relation to the others, defining it immediately and exclusively as an articulation of the totality. However, the problem of determining exchange values emerges precisely because, given the private nature of individual production, social dynamics do not and cannot proceed on this basis. If individuals or social organisms happen to act so as to relate their mutual products in the ratio

$$x \text{ wheat} = y \text{ iron} = z \text{ pigs}$$

nothing authorizes us to conclude that their *purpose*, in the exchange, is to lead society to a 'reintegrative state' nor that they have the capacity to do so. Even though exchange values calculated on the basis of prevailing production costs would undeniably guarantee reintegration, it is impossible to identify which forces could impose them. Nor could we show that any such tendency establishes itself on its own, without specifying how such forces are concretely constituted and operate, because this would be tantamount to recognizing that the problem we declare we want to face does not exist.

This dimension of reality – the freedom inherent in not accepting that the totality of the production process is a binding reality for the individual producer – peeps out from Harrod's misunderstanding, even if he doesn't give coherent expression to a real theoretical criticism of Sraffa's *approach*. He limits himself to muttering that it is 'surprising that a price determination system can be derived without any reference to final demand', that is, that those who exchange normally do not refer to the conditions of reintegration of the system when creating their private supply and demand. He is therefore convinced that, in expressing his need, the private owner abstracts from these conditions without even realizing it, precisely because the reproduction of the system is not at the centre of his behaviour, and addresses only the need to reproduce himself. In other words, Harrod departs from Sraffa's approach but makes only a fleeting reference to the one-sidedness and possible indeterminacy of Sraffa's system.

Sraffa conducts an operation of the same type but the opposite character, claiming to describe a system that reintegrates only because certain exchange relationships impose themselves on the contracting parties if and when they try to reproduce. But he spends not a single word on explaining the how and why of this 'imposition' and limits himself to his unilateral assumption of necessity in the semiotically[17] mute form of algebraic annotation.

We therefore find ourselves with a set of empirically verifiable facts about history, which cannot be ignored in theoretical elaboration:

a. when human beings begin practicing exchange (barter) they equate some of their products with each other, thus establishing a specific exchange-value relationship, but no system of relationships in which their products *generally take* the form of exchange value. Therefore, no money appears.

They are hence not united by exchange as a single organism, as a totality; they both feel, and really are, mutually free to exchange or not on the basis of values that merely express subjective preferences. Demand and supply thus move independently and in mutual indifference, and nothing forces the subjects to respect the conditions of their common reproduction. The quantitative exchange ratio – the price of one commodity expressed in the other – is random and therefore different from that calculated with Sraffa's method because the goods in question are exchangeable by a pure act of their owners' will to alienate them mutually not because they *must* be exchanged to reconstitute the conditions of production.

Precisely because the exchange neither mediates the reproduction of the system, nor is intended to do so, Sraffa's scheme does not make sense in this historical context even though this is the way we originally learnt to exchange. But neither does Harrod's conclusion that the excess *must* be exchanged because freedom would then be expressed in the form of a necessity other than Sraffa's:

b. subsequently when mercantile ties thicken, the product takes the form of exchange value to a larger extent, and the process becomes a continuous act, which contains within itself the means of its renewal. But producers do not suddenly fall into an upside-down world in which they openly recognize the constraints described by Sraffa;
c. it is, rather, almost inevitable that even if they exchange everything they do not use, inertially retain their previous orientation. They therefore neither know nor want to know about the system of their general productive relations. For this reason, the given conditions are only rarely

> reproduced, perturbations occur which follow more coherently from Harrod's approach, even if he ends up denying they are inevitable. On the market, producers seek individual freedom to secure the best conditions for their autonomous reproduction, not to submit to the conditions of overall reproduction. The operating principle of their 'common' action, when they express their demand, is *laissez-faire*, that is competition. Of this, Marx (1990, p. 196) rightly argued 'The possibility, therefore, of a quantitative incongruity between price and magnitude of value, i.e. the possibility that the price may diverge from the magnitude of value, is inherent in the price-form itself. *This is not a defect*, but, on the contrary, it makes this form the adequate one for a mode of production whose laws can only assert themselves as blindly operating averages between constant irregularities.'

Sraffa's system could conceivably be applied in this context but only if the behaviour evoked by Harrod is recognised. The first behavioural pattern must therefore be introduced as a prerequisite: since the new pattern cannot be directly attributed to the intentions of the social agents, the motivations for its use are required. Otherwise, planning, or simple cooperation, would immediately impose itself as the only way to close the gap between subjective and objective forces, between individual and social reproduction. Indeed, Napoleoni (1960) captured the close link between Sraffa's scheme and input/output planning systems very well though he did not go as far as to recognize that Sraffa's arguments presupposed conscious coordination between aggregate supply and demand, precluding the possibility of their mutual autonomy.

The actual occurrence of an integration process mediated by exchange, that is the 'regulation of reciprocal exchange arises by means of regulation of reciprocal production, [so that] the costs of production [... *establish themselves as*] the measure of exchange' (Marx, 1990, p. 205), obliges us to recognize that what Sraffa posed is actually *a problem* and sensibly discuss how to solve it.

This calls on us to avoid the usual serious error of orthodox economists, who deny that the productive activity of human beings is the result and expression of a historical–social development, fantasizing about a product that would *by nature be* an exchange value, that is, a commodity.[18] They assume the product is naturally endowed with the attribute of value, *in and of itself exchangeable*, separated from its producers and indifferent to the relations that mediated its production and mediate its use. They end up presuming (Clower, 1971, p. 8) that 'every individual is [by nature] an enthusiastic trader, living originally, in the company of the bizarre snake and tigers, and forced by talent and temperament to look for the goods it doesn't produce.'

In other words, if we attribute to a *human product the characteristic of being a 'commodity' by intrinsic nature*, we are perpetually condemned to *oscillate* between the two determinations of this form of sociality, in which the element of freedom and the element of constraint alternately affect the intuition of this or that researcher, *pushing him to absolutize what he manages to glimpse*. We must then agree both with Harrod against Sraffa and with Sraffa against Harrod, precisely because, *due to the fault of both*, the price *contradictorily expresses the universal mutual dependence of the producers in the form of a mutual personal independence*, which finds the its concrete manifestation in producing privately and in trying to 'make the price' on the basis of one's own exclusive interest. This phenomenon is coherently represented only in Marx's theory of value because it captures not only the phase in which such productive relationships mediate not only the taking shape of a universal form of cooperation but also the contradictory nature inherent in it.

NOTES

1. Emphases in cited text are my own throughout, unless otherwise stated.
2. See Marx (Grundrisse, 239–250) for a splendid critique of such approaches.
3. Sraffa's reasoning is logically coherent: he presupposes that 'originally' a set of means of production are available, and identifies the conditions for their reconstitution. Harrod ignores this presupposition, seeing only the products intended for exchange.
4. A heterodox criticism of neoclassical economists is that they see only products, but not the productive relationships. Harrod confirms this criticism.
5. That this is not a marginal problem is demonstrated by the fact that Marx dedicates one of the first chapters of the First Book of *Capital* to the analysis of the 'Process of Exchange'.
6. 'Organicism' was one of several accusations ferociously leveled against Marxists at the time.
7. From now on we omit the units in which products are measured, where the meaning is clear.
8. Most economists are so accustomed to the orthodox account of demand that they imagine the only possible alternative to heterodox hypotheses about it is to deny it as a determining force.
9. It is obvious that, if any surplus cannot have any other use than that of exchange, exchange appears in a Sraffian way as a condition of reproduction. This explains why Sraffa and Harrod seem to dialogue without fractures. But the fact is that, when certain conditions arise, the products cannot be exchanged or the producers do not want to exchange them, so they exit the reproductive process.
10. The logical connection is simple: if everything in excess of one's immediate needs must necessarily be exchanged, then exchange is a necessary event. Harrod however qualifies its content as free, in the sense that individuals exchange according to their preferences regardless of reproduction. To be sure, this is an element of reality, but the insertion of Sraffa's constraint remains to be justified.
11. Friedman (1962, p. 20) distorts the historical data: 'Since the household *always has* the alternative of *producing directly for itself*, [which implies the availability of the resources necessary to do so] *it need not enter into any exchange* unless it benefits from it.. Co-operation is thereby achieved without coercion.' Analytically this means that since individuals can always act as autonomous producers without exchange, as if all the conditions were present, there cannot be any constraint.
12. Federico Caffè summarized this problem in the concept of 'compositional fallacy'.
13. Within communities, products do not take the form of exchange value—for example, no mother will try to sell dinner to her children—precisely because the productive relations that mediate their appropriation constitute a given presupposition, which is itself reproduced.
14. See also Jervis (2011) for an explanation of how a practiced human behavior can be absent from the consciousness of those who practice it.

15. Even if elaborated in a mystical form.

16. Think only of European society's passive acceptance of mass unemployment for the last 40 years.

17. It could be said of Sraffa that, as an economist, he cannot conceptualize the practical behavior of human beings, and limits himself to 'seeing' the objects they move. This limited form of experience was described by Vygotsky (1966) in relation to children's language development.

18. Unfortunately, Napoleoni also makes this mistake. In *the Lessons* we repeatedly read 'work in its *natural determinations*', which phrase also resurfaces in the *Discourse*. This cardinal error deprives Napoleoni of a coherent exegesis of Marx's analysis.

REFERENCES

Clower, R. (Ed.). (1969). *Monetary economics*. Penguin.

Einaudi, L. (1962). *Lessons in social politics*. Einaudi.

Friedman, M. (1962). *Capitalism and freedom*. University of Chicago Press.

Galapagos. (1998). *In light of the theory of value. Interview with Alessandro Roncaglia*. Il manifesto.

Harrod, R. (1961, December). The production of commodities by means of commodities. *Economic Journal*, 782.

Jervis, G. (2011). *The myth of interiority*. Bollati Boringheri.

Lévi Strauss, C. (1990, November 14). Interview *la Repubblica*.

Marx, K. (1904). *A contribution to the critique of political economy* (Vol. 1). Charles H. Kerr & Company.

Marx, K. (1973 [1857-8]). *Grundrisse*. Penguin Books.

Marx, K. (1990 [1867]). *Capital: A critique of political economy* (Vol. 1). Penguin Books.

Marx, K. (2010 [1861–1863]). *Marx & Engels collected works* (Vol. 32, Digital ed.). Lawrence and Wishart.

Napoleoni, C. (1960). On the theory of production as a circular process. *Giornale degli Economisti e Annali di Economia*, XX Nuova Serie, fasc. 1-2.

Sraffa, P. (1960). *Production of commodities by means of commodities*. Cambridge University Press.

Sraffa, P. (1962, June). Production of commodities: A comment, *The Economic Journal*, 72(286), 477–479.

Vygotsky, L. (1986). *Thought and language*. The MIT Press Cambridge.

INSTITUTIONALISM AND THE MACRO-MONETARY LABOUR THEORY OF VALUE

Niko Block

York University, Canada

ABSTRACT

This chapter proposes a framework for synthesizing the abstract Marxian theory of exploitation with the more empirically oriented tradition of original institutionalist economics (OIE). To do so, it highlights the most literal macroeconomic models from each tradition: Duncan Foley's New Interpretation of the labour theory of value (LTV) and Morris Copeland's Money-flows framework. By first modelling a non-capitalist macro-monetary economy, the author demonstrates that economic value, defined as purchasable goods and services, cannot exist without labour. Unlike the capitalist, labour gets purchased, and unlike commodities, labour also gets paid. Labour is the one thing that can make both claims, and this duality in its identity makes it the fulcrum of a monetized economy. Second, by modelling a capitalist economy, the author focuses not on profit as an upstream flow of income to capitalists but rather on their downstream accumulation of financial assets over time – the essential implication of M'. Here the author shows that capitalists' rate of financial accumulation is ultimately constrained by the size of the workforce. Capitalists' attempts to financially accumulate at a rate that exceeds the growth of workforce's total income will result in an unsustainable escalation of the social debt burden, regardless of productivity gains over time. Monetary visions of exploitation do not, therefore, logically require that money be defined as an expression of human labour ex ante. Rather, the fundamental linkage between money and labour can be demonstrated through their structural relationship to one another.

Keywords: Institutionalism; macro-monetary labour theory of value; exploitation; profit realisation; money flows

Money, Value and Marx's Circuit of Capital
Research in Political Economy, Volume 41, 139–159

Published under exclusive licence by Emerald Publishing Limited
ISSN: 0161-7230/doi:10.1108/S0161-723020260000041019

INTRODUCTION

Heterodox economists are more prevalent within the discipline today than three decades ago, but deep divisions persist among them. In particular, the intellectual priors of Keynesians are difficult to reconcile with those of Marxists. The former group focuses on the business cycle, a topic that allows them to depict capitalism as both relatively cooperative as well as reformable. The latter is devoted to problems of distribution, and the escalation of inequality over the past half century seems to confirm their vision of capitalism as fundamentally conflictual and unreformable. The main ground for conciliation has been found in post-Keynesian and especially Kaleckian economics, which incorporates elements of both visions.

Adjacent is the ground of original institutionalist economics (OIE), a tradition distinguished by its prioritization of observational methods over theoretical priors. Indeed, institutionalists' inductive empiricism extends logically from their acceptance that some areas of the capitalist economy are conflictual while others may be cooperative, or can be made so; the determination must often be made ex post, after empirical analysis, not ex ante (Myrdal, 1978). As such, OIE selectively incorporates Keynesian, Marxist and even neoclassical arguments by evaluating their empirical validity. 'In a sense', wrote Morris Copeland, OIE 'is an invasion of economics by sociologists' (1921, p. 131). OIE's unflinchingly empirical orientation makes it, in my view, uniquely promising for economists who are committed to diagnosing real-world problems and developing pragmatic solutions to them.

One concern, however, is OIE's absence of a theory of exploitation. Whereas Marxian theories of exploitation demand that we identify 'the chimera of an invariable standard of value' (Sraffa, 1951, p. xl), institutionalists have not generally regarded it as a serious question. But the lacuna is more problematic than they realize. The Marxist critique has lasting influence in part because we are witnessing persistent trends that give the labour theory of value (LTV) a powerful intuitive resonance. First, consider that the majority of capitalist states have until recently managed their labour forces to ensure that they grow – a trend that raises questions about neoclassical theory's positing of labour and fixed capital as perfectly fungible. Secondly, despite productivity growth, most workers have not experienced a growth in leisure time that even approximates the predictions of utility-based value theorists (Keynes, 1930b; Marshall, 1890). Third, it is difficult to shake the feeling that the 21st century billionaire class exists by dint of exploitation in some way. As many on the left have pointed out, it is impossible to work for a billion dollars; even a person earning $5,000 a day would have to work for 548 years to earn a billion dollars, let alone the hundreds of billions now controlled by some super-elites.

At the same time, the basic precepts of Marxist economics are difficult to square with the modern capitalist environment, given the absence of a satisfactory explanation for how surplus labour is transformed into profit. While proponents of the LTV have stressed that there is a strong correlation between the labour time invested in a commodity's production and its final sale price, they have also acknowledged that there is no clear empirical relationship between labour time and monetary profits (Cockshott et al., 2014; Shaikh, 1998). Meanwhile, Nitzan and Bichler (2009) pointedly critique the LTV by arguing that the incommensurability of different types of labour renders the theory non-operationalizable and by highlighting radical disjunctures between corporate workforces and market capitalization.

This chapter argues that institutionalist methods can cohere with one particular theory of exploitation: the 'New Interpretation' (NI) of the LTV articulated by Foley (1982; 2000). The NI offers a specific form of the *macro-monetary* LTV (MLTV) which holds that a) money is a material expression of labour time and b) the monetary expression of labour time (MELT) can be defined as the ratio of national income (wages plus profits) divided by total labour time. Hence, an average worker is exploited if they are paid less than the hourly MELT. Below I elaborate the NI concept using the 'Moneyflows' model of national accounting advanced by Copeland (1952). In doing so, I validate the NI's premise that money is the expression of labour time by demonstrating their concrete relation to one another rather than by defining money as such ex ante.

This approach therefore does not need to rest upon Marxian priors, which often presume what they claim to explain (Bowles & Gintis, 1985; Hodgson, 1980). Rather, it can be articulated from broadly accepted definitions of concepts like money, value and labour. It resonates with conventional economic methods insofar as the argument is deductive; but at the same time, it remains sensitive to institutionalist circumspection about ideological bias and does not over-extend the deductive argument into a reified behavioural one.

The claim is therefore more abstract than what we find in most Marxist theories of exploitation. By its nature, the MLTV cannot identify any given worker as exploited. It can, however, identify top-end elites as exploit*ers*, which is what matters most when social problems demand redress through class struggle.

In the following section, I survey the Marxist and institutionalist literature, focusing primarily on the problem of exploitation within the dominant parameters of both schools. I then outline the NI, which posits a definitional linkage between labour and money. In Section 3, my argument comes more sharply into view. First, I comment on how deductive reasoning fits into OIE. Here, I place special emphasis on Copeland's assertion that economic models must carefully distinguish between variables representing accounting identities and those representing behavioural predictions. While the former can be articulated deductively, the latter must be tested empirically.

Second, I offer definitions of key terms. In brief: I define value as *purchasable* goods or services; labour as work that is directed towards the production of exchange value; and capitalism as a state-organized system in which top income earners continuously accumulate financial assets. Contrary to the main current of exploitation studies, then, my focus is not on profit as an upstream flow of income to capitalists but rather on their downstream accumulation of financial assets over time: M…M′…M″.

Third, using a closed monetary circuit model, I show that money can be understood as an embodiment of abstract human labour in structural, not just definitional, terms. Here, there are two key points. The first is that full automation would undermine the purchasability of commodities and thus destroy their value. The second is that if, in a capitalist economy, the rate of elites' financial accumulation exceeds the rate of growth of labour supplied to the economy, then the disjuncture in the allocation of monetary value will manifest as an upward spiral in the aggregate debt-to-income ratio. This will occur regardless of any changes to productivity contributed by fixed capital.

Hence, the argument is not that exploitation generates crisis inherently. In a high profit environment, such debt crises would be averted if capitalists consistently spent their profits and returned to a financial balance of zero. Rather, the argument is that at an economy-wide level and over the long run, capitalist financial accumulation is structurally dependent on the expansion of labour. Unlike the capitalist, labour gets purchased, and unlike commodities, labour also gets paid. Labour is the one thing that can make both claims, and this duality in its identity makes it the fulcrum of a monetized economy.

This principle is at the heart of defenses of the LTV, including Mandel's (1969, pp. 25–26), which represent production on a vertically integrated basis to demonstrate that all true costs in production are labour costs. It is made more vivid by Foley's (1982) argument that if we assume monetary transactions to reflect real flows of economic value, then the latter must necessarily emerge from production; it cannot come from monetary exchange, which has a zero-sum character. It follows that profits are expressions of monopoly power more than they are reflections of the 'productivity of capital' per se. Keynes made this point as well: 'It is much preferable to speak of capital as having a yield over the course of its life in excess of its original cost, than as being *productive*'. Rather, he wrote, the returns on fixed capital are generally determined by the scarcity of capital rather that its physical productive capacity. 'I sympathise, therefore, with the pre-classical doctrine that everything is *produced* by *labour*' (1936, pp. 213–214, emphasis in original).

Before proceeding, I should state that this chapter does not answer most of the questions pertaining to value. Value theory has historically encompassed three distinct questions: how economic development occurs (the central focus for Smith); what determines commodities' relative prices (a question Ricardo's LTV claimed to have answered) and whether capitalist profits embody the exploitation of workers (the central focus for Marx). Although a single definition of value can and should operate across these discussions, the questions themselves should be treated as distinct. In particular, assuming that the questions of exchange value and exploitation have an intrinsically identical answer introduces a form of category error. If we are defining exploitation – as most do – as the discrepancy between the labour power sold by a worker to a capitalist versus the labour power they can purchase with their wages, then we are already approaching the money embodied in their wage as representative of an *average* quantity of labour power that exists for purchase in the economy. By definition, the average value of labour flattens differences in wage rates and cannot in behavioural terms explain the source of those differences, or parallel differences in commodity prices.

VALUE AND EXPLOITATION IN OIE AND MARXISM

While Marxists take labour time as their primary unit of economic analysis, institutionalists typically focus on money and transactions. This section surveys the essential contributions from both schools of thought and concludes by observing that the most literal analyses from both – the NI and the Moneyflows model – overlap significantly.

Institutionalist Concepts of Value

Most OIE discussions of value focus on pricing as a site of social conflict. For Commons (1934), who positioned the transaction itself as the essential unit of economic analysis, prices are formed through the 'negotiational psychology of persuasion, coercion, command, obedience, pleading, and argument, instead of the pleasure and pain of commodities. Each party to a transaction is confronted by his own competitors and by the competitors of the opposite party, and is driven by his needs and alternatives' (pp. 424–425).

Unlike the classicists or neoclassicists who draw a linear relationship, respectively, from labour or utility to economic value, OIE instead argues that the behavioural determinants of prices can have a *recursive* character. Each purchase at a given price validates the expectations of the price setter and reaffirms those expectations for the future. Indeed for Commons, perhaps the most essential ingredient in the psychological process of pricing was what he called 'futurity' – the *expectation* of future costs and revenues.

The absence of linearity in the institutionalist theory of value left many wondering exactly what Commons had in mind when he referred to 'reasonable value' or his 'volitional theory of value' because he gave no strong definition of it (McColloch & Vernengo, 2024; Whalen, 2022). But, as noted in Section 1, recursive theories as such are by no means fallacious; they merely raise the question of how the self-reinforcing patterns emerged historically. Here Commons (1924), like others in OIE, argued that the state is an essential protagonist because it both consecrates private property and establishes the rules under which all economic actors negotiate with each other.

In aggregate, the negotiational approach espoused by OIE's leading thinkers – Commons (1924, 1934); Mitchell (1927); Clark (1926, 1934) and Copeland (1931, 1952) – embeds pricing within a matrix of social forces that is considerably more complex than neoclassical or Marxian theory. Expectations, qualitative forms of market power, government policy and upstream production costs all factor into OIE analyses.

Marxian Visions of Exploitation

For several decades, now the Marxian vision of exploitation has struggled with two problems. The first, as noted, is the absence of an empirical relationship between labour times and profit rates. The second is Sraffa's (1960) intervention, which showed that once variation in the sociotechnical conditions of production is introduced to the model, the value contribution of labour becomes indeterminate.

Sraffa's argument is situated in the trajectory of classical theory running from Ricardo to Marx. Ricardo posited that labour has an objective value, which is expressed in the exchange value of all goods, while the labour content of subsistence goods determines the all-important wage rate. Hence, productivity in ulterior areas of industry may increase, but whether those gains are translated into higher profits 'depends solely on the rise of wages; and the rise of wages...on the facility of producing the food and necessaries of the labourer' (1821, p. 292). Marx (1867) demonstrated that if this were so, then capitalist production is inherently exploitative. Specifically, what has since been deemed the 'fundamental Marxian theorem' (FMT) holds that a surplus of labour is the *sine qua non* for the realization of profits (Morishima, 1974).

Sraffa's intervention reversed the causal relationship between labour and profits. Ricardo and Marx assumed a given level of productivity in the subsistence sector, which in turn determines wages, whereas Sraffa *began* with a given rate of profit. Hence, he approached production from the perspective of the entrepreneur, who may observe different sociotechnical strategies for obtaining that rate. One such strategy may have a high ratio of labour to fixed capital while another may have a low one, yet both might produce the same rate of profit. Therefore, the contribution of labour to the value that the firm obtains becomes indeterminate, at least at the firm level.

The late 1970s and 1980s saw a swell of discourse on the problem this posed for the FMT. Wright (1979) pivoted away from Sraffa to argue that Sraffa's argument did not falsify the FMT but rather invited a reformulation of its determinations. For Wright, the presence of sociotechnical variation imposed a 'structural limitation' in which there could be a range of possible rates of exploitation. From there, a specific point within that range is selected by the determination of real wages, which can be influenced by class struggles.

Shaikh (1977), on the other hand, took an approach that he asserted was more faithful to Marx's original argument. The problem of how surplus value gets transformed into profit cannot, he suggested, 'be derived from a theory which *begins* with prices of production' (p. 134). Rather, the transformation can only be expressed heuristically 'by progressively 'feeding back' the effects of the initial price-Value disproportionalities' (p. 131) – a process that, he suggests, could take place in the real world, as Bortkiewicz first argued, through iterative yet simultaneous price adjustments. The mechanisms of this process remain mystified, however, and Shaikh's more recent work (2016) does not address this issue, nor overcome his own finding (1998) that there is no clear correlation between the labour time invested in commodities' production and their associated profit rate.

The concept of simultaneous price adjustments has garnered considerable criticism. Fundamentally, it can serve as an exogeneity that swoops into profit models in just the right ways to transform surplus value into profit. As Kliman and Freeman (Freeman & Kliman, 2008; Kliman, 2001) have argued, these *deus ex machinas* posit that labour is not the exclusive source of profits and thus contradict the FMT. Rather, for the FMT to hold, production and profit must be modelled within a more linear 'temporal single-system interpretation' (TSSI). By positioning price adjustments as downstream from socio-technical changes in the production process, the theory eliminates the confounding circumstance in which profits change independently of expended labour.

The TSSI thus offers an internally consistent defence of the FMT and does so in the lexicon of classical Marxism (Kliman, 2007). But from an institutional standpoint, it has the drawback of remaining within the method of 'theoretical speculation' (Piketty, 2014, p. 574). That is to say, it assumes a specific behavioural tendency without demonstrating that it actually occurs. Instead, Kliman's empirical analysis focuses on the spuriousness of rival theories' methods. His work on the falling rate of profit (Kliman, 2012) is more empirically oriented and smartly operationalizes the MELT as a deflator in much of the analysis. But it does not overcome the problem of empirical inconsistency between profit and labour time across businesses and commodities. Rather, it offers a framework for reading Marx's original texts as internally consistent and *potentially* descriptive of modern-day capitalist exploitation. It thus responds to the second problem noted at the top of this section (the theoretical problem of labour's indeterminate value) but not the first (the empirical problem).

In sum, the LTV has powerful intuitive resonance and has been conceptualized in highly elaborate ways. But the Marxian discourse cannot seem to overcome the concern expressed by Bowles and Gintis (1985, p. 34) that a monolithic LTV is 'either a rather uninteresting tautology based on the definition of 'labor' and 'produce,' or it is false'. Still, they suggest, capitalist society remains fundamentally unimaginable without labour – a theme that we pick up below.

The MLTV and the New Interpretation

The survey above indicates that there has been a relative absence of money in the main currents of Marxist thinking and a relative absence of labour and exploitation in institutionalist thinking. The most effective schematic linkage of these variables to date has occurred through the various iterations of the MLTV.

The MLTV has been advanced in more than one way. Hodgson, whose work embraces Marxism and OIE perhaps more than anyone else, rightly observes that the search for a 'single substance which would explain prices' has been the result of a 'monistic fallacy' – a misguided assumption that exchange value is reducible to a single abstract variable. Logically, however, workers can be viewed as exploitable because they are living beings, and within the parameters of capitalist labour relations, the purchase of their labour power requires 'the conscious submission of the worker' – something that cannot be said for fixed capital (1980, p. 266). Exploitation cannot be effectively measured at the firm level because of the heterogeneity of both labour and technology but rather should be measured as the share of profits, interest and rent in national income (1980, pp. 269–272; 1982, p. 215).

Bellofiore (1989; 1997) offers another vision of the MLTV, which is more oriented towards the concept of the monetary circuit. A key starting point for him is Luxemburg's assertion that 'The abstract human labour discovered by Marx is, in its developed form, none other than money' (quoted in Bellofiore, 2024, p. 67). He then augments the NI somewhat by offering a 'double valuation' of labour power, one expressing pure labour values and the other expressing money incomes (1997, p. 8). This gives the framework greater flexibility, but also more complexity, and arguably reintroduces the transformation problem that the NI was designed to overcome. Indeed, it typifies Kliman's (2007, p. 33) complaint that the NI, at the micro-level, posits 'two distinct and unequal general rates of profit'. Consequently, 'the remaining aggregate equalities cannot both hold true, contrary to what Marx concluded'.

The most lucid version of the MLTV is Foley's (1982; 2000), which builds on similar ideas from Duménil (1980; 1983). The logical pathway 'begins with the global value produced by the expenditure of labor' and then conceptualizes a unit of money 'as a claim to a certain amount of abstract social labor expended in commodity production' (1982, p. 37). Hence, 'the appropriate definition of the monetary expression of labor time' or MELT is the 'ratio of the net domestic product at current prices to the living productive labor expended in an economy over a period of time' (Foley, 2000, pp. 20–21). The hourly MELT can thus be calculated essentially as the national income divided by the total number of hours worked, and an average worker is exploited if they are paid less than that. This means accepting, as OIE would hold, that the price of any particular commodity can be shaped by a variety of factors.

The other methodological resonance between the NI and the OIE approach is that they both put the monetary transaction at the center of their analyses. In Section 3.3, I return to this theme by arguing that the MELT concept can be operationalized within Copeland's Moneyflows framework.

CAPITALISM AND MONEYFLOWS

Given that the NI and Moneyflows are among the most literal and objective frameworks from their respective traditions, the parallels between them are hardly coincidental. There are, however, a number of remaining questions that must be addressed in order for a coherent synthesis to emerge. This section begins with a brief discussion of how the deductive and ontological claims of the MLTV can fit into the otherwise empirical orientation of OIE. Next, I define some key terms. Finally, I show how the premise of the MLTV – that money embodies abstract human labour – can be demonstrated deductively within the

NI-Moneyflows synthesis; it does not need to be posited directly as a matter of definition.

Methods in OIE

In general, a hypothetico-inferential method that links both inductive and deductive logics is the most reliable process for determining material truths, in particular about cause and effect. The essential steps are as follows: first, defining key concepts and variables; second, making observations; third, formulating a hypothesis that would explain the data and articulating predictions that would logically follow from it; fourth, testing those predictions and finally, validating the hypothesis or, if necessary, revising the process.[1]

While Copeland (1931, 1951, 1952, 1955) was not quite so schematic, this approach is consistent with several of his comments on method, as well as his general view that economic theory should hew as closely as possible to material reality.

His critiques of mainstream economists were not, however, limited to their negligence in observation and testing. Equally important is the ontological work at the very first stage, which shapes the coherence and workability of every subsequent step. The basic decisions about terminology, categories and variables determines their measurability or abstractness and thus determines the types of questions that can even be asked in the subsequent stages. For Copeland, modelling exercises must draw a clear distinction between accounting variables and behavioural ones; only then is it possible to identify which forces are active and which are passive (1952, pp. 29–34). Economists, he suggested, have overly invested in behavioural modelling, and in doing so borrowed from Newtonian physics. Instead they should take a more Euclidean approach, by starting from 'conceptual equations' – especially social accounting equations – that are definitionally stable (1955).

For the sake analytical clarity, the following section conveys definitions of key terms while the next conveys a transactions matrix that systematizes the Euclidean logic at the heart of Copeland's framework.

Definitions

Here, I propose a few definitions that may help reconcile some of the ontological disparities between Marxism and institutionalism.

First, *money* may be defined as the prevailing unitized circulating means of payment. Pre-modern commodity money is easy to identify as the coinage or other circulating tokens expended and accepted by states. Modern credit money has a more complex institutional identity in that it consists of three basic components. Strictly speaking credit money is a liquid financial asset, which can both purchase goods and services and annul formal obligations such as taxes. But institutionally, it possesses two other components: a liability and an indemnity.[2]

Next, *capital* is the forward-moving process whereby the investment of a given sum of money (M) establishes a claim to future monetary returns which must exceed the initial investment (M′), thereby generating a pattern of expanding financial claims (M″ and so on). This process inherently relies upon a complex system of property relations (Levy, 2017; Pistor, 2020).

Capitalism, then, I define as a state-organized system in which elite income earners continuously accumulate financial assets. It follows that there must be a complex institutional structure in place that generates credit, facilitates the accumulation of financial assets and enforces the repayment of liabilities (Ingham, 1996, 2008).

Next, *value* I define as *purchasable* goods and services. It therefore encompasses a vast basket of goods that varies across different societies. Correspondingly, the value of any given thing can be understood as the weight of its exchangeability against all other purchasable goods and services. Hence, for value to exist at all, it is not enough that the exchangeable items are present; rather, value is equally predicated upon the institutions that facilitate those transactions (Commons, 1934).

Labour I define as work that is directed at generating exchange value. This can mean either delivering a service that has use and exchange value *or* manipulating the physical material of the Earth in ways that enhance their use values and thus also their exchange value. In this Smithian conception, the business patron, not the capitalist, is the ultimate purchaser of labour power.

Importantly, management and entrepreneurship both fit this definition of labour. Indeed, both are integral parts of the labour process. To say so is not to say that they contribute more than those who are lower in the business hierarchy or that class struggle cannot occur between workers and their managers. But it does single out a different category of individual because what does not fit the definition of labour is *ownership*.

This in turn relates to the definition of *exploitation*: a situation in which workers receive less value than they produce. Correspondingly, the average amount of labour power that an exploited worker can purchase with their wages must be less than the hours they have worked. As noted, it is not generally feasible to apply this concept of exploitation to any particular worker or manager. Production processes are complex and interdependent, and most businesses would collapse if managers or workers were removed entirely. But it is clear that a distant and inert *owner* of business equity contributes nothing to production. To the extent that such an owner collects revenues from the business, therefore, it is uncontroversial to say that exploitation is occurring.

The arguments in favour of the productive contribution of owners *qua* owners are weak and highly conditional. Owners could abstractly be said to play a role in a corporation's operations by voting for board members even though board members themselves are estranged from day-to-day management. Likewise, one could also argue that owners play some integral role in value production by threatening to legally punish managers for violating their fiduciary duties to shareholders if they fail to maximize profits (Pistor, 2020). To the extent that either of these things can be considered 'management', however, they are quite meagre. In reality the bulk of individuals who own corporate stock do so through intermediating investment funds; they pay no attention to the operations of the firms and are often unaware that they indirectly hold these stocks to begin with. These absentee shareholders are owners in the purest sense, gaining monetary returns without contributing anything to the production process.

The NI-Moneyflows Synthesis

One of Foley's key insights is that the conceptualization of value in macro-monetary terms clarifies that value is *produced*. Consider that each discretionary transaction represents a transfer of value from one party to another and that every expenditure by one party is equivalent income for another – a change in monetary holdings that inherently sums to zero. It follows logically from these premises that value cannot be created in exchange but must be actively produced.

Foley's emphasis on the zero-sum nature of financial transactions resonates with Copeland's (1952) 'Moneyflows' method of macroeconomic analysis, which inspired the Federal Reserve's Flow of Funds Accounts. The Moneyflows approach holds that current payments of money should form the objective baseline framework for macroeconomic analysis. Dividing the economy into sectors and then tracking transactions between them reveals not only that income is equal to expenditure but also that the net financial savings (NFS) for the economy as a whole must equal zero. NFS can be measured either as net income minus expenditure (NIE) or net lending and borrowing (NLB). Using current dollars, both methods should yield the same number, so that NFS = NIE = NLB.

Heuristically, the best way to represent these dynamics is in a transactions matrix similar to those used in stock-flow consistent (SFC) economics (Godley & Lavoie, 2007). However, the SFC approach typically adopts Kalecki's (1971, pp. 78–92) synthetic definition of profit, which includes both monetary surpluses and new fixed capital. By contrast, the Moneyflows approach takes a *monothetic*, i.e. strictly monetary, approach to key variables like profit. Hence whereas SFC takes a Keynes–Kaleckian approach to the transactions matrix by dividing the business sector into current and capital accounts, my adaptation of Copeland's Moneyflows model takes a Marx–Luxemburgian approach by dividing it into Departments I and II. This adjustment allows us to more carefully observe the distinction between financial and non-financial variables, the conflation of which often leads to major misapprehensions of reality (Bezemer & Hudson, 2016). Fixed assets and other accrual variables need not be excluded from the analysis but should be represented in a distinct yet integrated table registering changes in net wealth (CNW).

Table 1. Moneyflows in a Four-Sector Model.

<table>
<tr><th colspan="7">1.1: Net Income Minus Expenditures (NIE)</th></tr>
<tr><th rowspan="3"></th><th rowspan="3">Households</th><th rowspan="3">Government</th><th colspan="3">Corporations</th><th rowspan="3">∑</th></tr>
<tr><th colspan="2">Nonfinancial Corporations</th><th rowspan="2">Banks</th></tr>
<tr><th>Dept. I</th><th>Dept. II</th></tr>
<tr><td>Fixed investment</td><td>$-FI1_{H}$</td><td>$-FI1_{G}$</td><td>$+FI1_{DI}$</td><td>$-FI1_{DII}$</td><td>$-FI1_{B}$</td><td>0</td></tr>
<tr><td>Consumption</td><td>$-C1_{H}$</td><td></td><td colspan="2">$+C1_{C}$</td><td></td><td>0</td></tr>
<tr><td>Government consumption</td><td></td><td>$-GC_{G}$</td><td colspan="2">$+GC_{G}$</td><td></td><td>0</td></tr>
<tr><td>Taxes</td><td>$-T_{H}$</td><td>$+T_{G}$</td><td colspan="2">$-T_{C}$</td><td>$-T_{B}$</td><td>0</td></tr>
<tr><td>Transfers</td><td>$+TR_{H}$</td><td>$-TR_{G}$</td><td colspan="2"></td><td></td><td>0</td></tr>
<tr><td>Wages</td><td>$+W_{H}$</td><td>$-W_{G}$</td><td colspan="2">$-W_{C}$</td><td>$-W_{B}$</td><td>0</td></tr>
<tr><td>Dividends</td><td>$+D_{H}$</td><td></td><td colspan="2">$-D_{C}$</td><td>$-D_{B}$</td><td>0</td></tr>
<tr><td>Interest</td><td>$\pm IN_{H}$</td><td>$\pm IN_{G}$</td><td colspan="2">$\pm IN_{C}$</td><td>$+IN_{B}$</td><td>0</td></tr>
<tr><td>Asset sales</td><td>$\pm AS_{H}$</td><td>$\pm AS_{G}$</td><td colspan="2">$\pm AS_{C}$</td><td>$\pm AS_{B}$</td><td>0</td></tr>
<tr><td>Memo ∑</td><td></td><td></td><td colspan="2">NIE_{C}</td><td>NIE_{B} (0)</td><td></td></tr>
<tr><td>∑</td><td>NIE_{H}</td><td>NIE_{G}</td><td colspan="3">NIE_{K}</td><td>0</td></tr>
</table>

<table>
<tr><th colspan="6">1.2: Net Lending and Borrowing (NLB)</th></tr>
<tr><th rowspan="2"></th><th rowspan="2">Households</th><th rowspan="2">Government</th><th colspan="2">Corporations</th><th rowspan="2">∑</th></tr>
<tr><th>Nonfinancial Corporations</th><th>Banks</th></tr>
<tr><td>Savings deposits</td><td>$+S_{H}$</td><td>$+S_{G}$</td><td>$+S_{C}$</td><td>$-S_{B}$</td><td>0</td></tr>
<tr><td>Household loans</td><td>$-L$</td><td></td><td></td><td>$+L_{B}$</td><td>0</td></tr>
<tr><td>Government loans</td><td>$+GL_{H}$</td><td>$-GL$</td><td>$+GL_{C}$</td><td>$+GL_{B}$</td><td>0</td></tr>
<tr><td>Corporate bonds</td><td>$+CB_{H}$</td><td></td><td>$-CB_{C}$</td><td>$+CB_{B}$</td><td>0</td></tr>
<tr><td>Equity purchases</td><td>$+E_{H}$</td><td></td><td>$-E_{C}$</td><td>$-E_{B}$</td><td>0</td></tr>
<tr><td>Memo</td><td></td><td></td><td>NLB_{C}</td><td>NLB_{B} (0)</td><td></td></tr>
<tr><td>∑</td><td>NLB_{H}</td><td>NLB_{G}</td><td colspan="2">NLB_{K}</td><td>0</td></tr>
</table>

<table>
<tr><th colspan="6">1.3: Accounting Memo: Net Financial Savings (NFS)</th></tr>
<tr><th></th><th>Households</th><th>Government</th><th>Nonfinancial corporations</th><th>Banks</th><th>∑</th></tr>
<tr><td></td><td>NIE_{H}</td><td>NIE_{G}</td><td>NIE_{C}</td><td>NIE_{B} (0)</td><td></td></tr>
<tr><td></td><td>$-NLB_{H}$</td><td>$-NLB_{G}$</td><td>$-NLB_{C}$</td><td>$-NLB_{B}$ (0)</td><td></td></tr>
<tr><td>∑</td><td>0</td><td>0</td><td>0</td><td>0</td><td>0</td></tr>
</table>

Using this adjusted version of the Moneyflows concept to illustrate the NI can help to eliminate some of the longstanding complaints about the latter. Saad-Filho (2012, p. 345), for instance, raises three issues. First, he writes, the NI 'short-circuits' the production of fixed capital by focusing on flows of money.

Table 2. Change in Net Wealth (CNW).

			Corporations		
	Households	Government	Nonfinancial Corporations	Banks	$\sum$
Net financial savings	NFS_H	NFS_G	NFS_C	NFS_B (0)	0
Fixed investment	$+FI_H$	$+FI_G$	$+FI_C$	$+FI_G$	$\sum FI$
Net price change financial assets	ΔFA_H	ΔFA_G	ΔFA_C	ΔFA_B	$\sum \Delta FA$
Net price change nonfinancial assets	ΔNA_H	ΔNA_G	ΔNA_C	ΔNA_B	$\sum \Delta NA$
			CNW_C	CNW_B	
$\sum$	CNW_H	CNW_G	CNW_K		$\sum CNW$

Yet a transactions matrix with intra-business exchange integrates fixed investment comprehensively. (Uniquely, fixed investments are registered both in the NIE matrix (Table 1.1) and in the corresponding matrix for CNW (Table 2). Second, Saad-Filho writes the NI's concept of the MELT overlooks the 'real structures, processes and relations mediating the expression of social labour into money'; on the contrary, however, the articulation of objective money flows can complement any representation of real institutional structures.

Third, Saad-Filho writes, the NI identifies exploitation according to 'one of its effects', that is, 'the inability of the workers to purchase the entire net product'. But for Marx, he argues, 'capitalist exploitation is not due to the unfair distribution of income, and the net product is not 'shared' between the classes at the end of each production cycle. Rather, wages are part of the advance of capital..., whilst profit is the consequence of how much surplus value is extracted'. It is odd to claim that Marxian exploitation is unrelated to the distribution of income, when its basis is precisely about the length of the working day for which workers are paid or unpaid. Moreover, NI offers a way to operationalize the concept of surplus value by means of the MELT identity. The only remaining concern of Saad-Filho's then relates to the inability of wages to fund the entire consumption bill with profit realization for businesses. This too is addressed in the Moneyflows model. Indeed, an important implication of Copeland's approach is its proof that if the corporate sector is accumulating financial assets on net, then other sectors of the economy must necessarily be accumulating net financial liabilities. Hence, although Copeland did not engage directly with what is often called the 'paradox' of monetary profits, his framework grants a certain vindication to what Keynes (1936, p. 370) described as the 'heretical theories of under-consumption' advanced by thinkers like Hobson and Luxemburg.

The inescapable fact that capitalists' financial asset accumulation must be matched by non-capitalists' debt accumulation has been a persistent theme for Smithin (2018; 2023). Though primarily in the post-Keynesian tradition, he also offers a vision of exploitation that is essentially Marxian and rooted in what he calls a 'virtual labour theory of production', which posits income in kind as the number of employed workers multiplied by their average productivity (2018). Hence, while Smithin's perspective overlaps with my own, it posits exploitation through a more direct definitional logic. In the following two subsections, I hope to demonstrate a similar idea through a more vivid logic, showing not merely that exploitation can be defined in terms of average claims to labour power but that the value of money is predicated upon the latter.

The Incompatibility of Value and Full Automation

In general, economists' thought experiments about value have presumed a specific institutional environment in which (a) workers are willing to sell their labour power to capitalists, (b) the fiscal state is absent, so that all transactions have a volitional rather than a coercive character, and (c) commodity markets are competitive. To these, I am adding the additional parameters that the model be (d) a closed macroeconomic system and (e) a monetary economy. To return to Copeland's (1955) comments on model analysis, it would be fair to say that parameters (a) through (c) have a behavioural (or Newtonian) character whereas (d) and (e) combined are conceptual (or Euclidean) and apply social accounting consistency.

With the above parameters in place, value could not exist without labour. Consider what would happen if this type of economy were to become so thoroughly automated that every business owner refused to hire workers and every worker refused to obtain a job. The fulcrum of production and consumption has disappeared, and thus any commodities that may come tumbling out of the unstaffed factories would not be purchasable because no one would be employed, as Mandel (1969) pointed out. The only way to sustain purchasability, as Hodgson (1980, p. 259; 1982, pp. 83–84) suggests, would be welfare payments to the propertyless and unemployed. In a macro-monetary environment, Hodgson's scheme would also require that almost all of the capitalists' surplus revenues be taxed away by the state in order to finance the welfare program. Conceivably, price controls may also play a role in this scenario because the state may wish to sustain the circulation of taxable income and may also wish to promote the consumption of some goods over others. All of these policies would violate the traditional assumption of volitional transactions (b) and market competition (c). But from an institutional perspective, the de-linking of value and labour that has occurred here may not be as 'absurd' as Mandel supposes; taxes, transfers and price controls have all been implemented to some extent in every modern economy (I revisit this problem in the conclusion).

Some of the other attempts to theorize the relation between full automation and value have set particular parameters that render their conclusions somewhat abstract and irrelevant. Dmitriev (1974), for instance, claimed that in a fully automated economy, profits could be generated without any labour whatsoever, but his concept of profit was merely a surplus product in kind, not in money (and hence a violation of (e)). Wright (1978), meanwhile, claimed that a single fully automated factory would be disastrous for its owner because it fails to produce surplus value. But this is a micro-level argument that violates (d) (It is also contradicted by the evidence of existing automated businesses, laundromats for instance, who collect small amounts of rent and whose cost and revenue structures are conditioned by labour dynamics elsewhere in the economy).

Thus, if we maintain all five of the parameters listed above, it is fair to assert that labour is indeed the single underlying variable that renders economic exchange possible and thus represents the *sine qua non* of value production.

Because this model operates at a high level of abstraction and focuses more on conceptual rather than behavioural claims, it is not incompatible with OIE. But because OIE evaluates theory more on the basis of evidence than internal coherence, there may be a few sources of discomfort. More specifically, institutionalists may not contest the analytical points arising from the above thought experiment in which production is fully automated and prices fall towards zero. But they might rightly observe that the parameters of such a thought experiment do not reflect real-world dynamics.

The first major point in this regard is that governmental intervention can in some ways diminish or at least complicate the MLTV, as Hodgson's rejoinder to Mandel insinuates.

Second, the process of mechanization has not in fact generated a secular decline in the demand for labour. In various ways, the 'displacement effects' of automation can be balanced by 'productivity effects' whereby firms enjoying windfall profits actually expand their workforce (Acemoglu & Restrepo, 2019). This is not to suggest that mechanization has inherently equilibrating or progressive tendencies. On the contrary, skill-biased growth has been accompanied by a decline in the real wages of non-college educated American men (Autor, 2019), and the rewards for college education have also declined markedly in recent years (Autor et al., 2020). At a more abstract level, it is fair to say that while firms can do various things with their profits – pay dividends, buy back stocks, purchase other financial assets – they cannot grow without purchasing labour power. The value paid for that labour power can still decline over time, however, depending on the existing institutions and the balance of class forces.

Third, as we have seen in the above section on institutionalist concepts of value, OIE would reject the assumption that markets are competitive. Indeed, profit is inexplicable within a model presuming perfect competition and the sale of commodities at cost. In the present reality, it is more accurate to say that costs may influence price, but the degree to which they do is conditioned by dynamics of market power. Productivity gains can diminish prices over time and vice versa. As Weber et al. (2022) have shown, when markets are oligopolistic, jumps in the price of inputs can lead to price increases for consumers that exceed the initial shock. The coordination effect brought by price shocks can thus deliver a higher rate of profit for oligopolists.

These points all highlight important realities. But for the purposes of the present discussion, they merely caution us against a method in which behavioural patterns are posited ex ante and then reified. They do not undermine the analytical point that in the five-parameter model, value falls to zero in a fully automated economy.

Capitalism: Financial Versus Demographic Growth Rates

Perhaps the biggest critique that OIE would level against the five-parameter model above is not merely that it assumes competitive markets but also that it does not represent profit realization. If we augment the model to become a capitalist economy, adding another conceptual parameter (f) that the business sector continuously accumulates financial assets on net, then the relationship between labour and value is further complicated, but not eliminated.

As noted, for parameter (f) to be fulfilled, the economy must possess credit money, including the institutional capacity to protect financial assets and enforce repayment of liabilities. Foley observes that one advantage of the NI approach is that it is compatible with any monetary regime; in the spirit of institutional accuracy and relevance, let's posit a system of endogenous money creation (Ingham, 2004). The introduction of credit and autonomous demand in particular means that we are no longer presuming each sector returns to a balance of zero at the end of each cycle (Serrano, 1995). Effective demand can thus be larger than the aggregate wage bill, and at first glance, this may appear to break the intrinsic link between the two. But the link remains over the long run because the continuous accumulation of financial profit upon a stagnant quantity of labour is destined to generate unsustainable escalations in the total ratio of debt to income.

Consider what needs to happen for corporations' NFS to be positive in cycle after cycle. The collective NFS of the household and government sectors must all necessarily be in deficit. Over time, this means an accumulation of assets in the corporate sector and an accumulation of debts everywhere else. Because this seems unsustainable, Smithin (2023, pp. 291–292) has suggested that the non-capitalist deficits cannot be a 'permanent fix'; after only a few cycles, the uneven accumulation of assets and liabilities would surely lead to a crisis.

In fact, a scenario of capitalist monetary accumulation and non-capitalist debt accumulation is only unstable if it means that the ratio of debt to income – or the debt burden (*b*) – rises indefinitely. For simplicity, imagine that the government is not undertaking any debts; instead, the household sector is. Whereas $-L_H$ in Table 1 represents a flow of household loans in a single year, *d* represents the total stock of accumulated debts. Household income is equal to average personal income (*i*) times population (*p*). Hence, a basic conceptual formula is as follows:

$$b = d/(i^{*}\mathrm{p})$$

Financial assets can continue to accumulate in the corporate sector while *b* declines under the condition that *d*'s rate of growth < (*i***p*)'s rate of growth. But throughout the Global North *d* is has grown faster than (*i***p*) for the past five decades. This generates what I call a 'growth trilemma' for governments. That is to say, they have three options for preventing *b* from rising inexorably, but none are politically easy. First, they might find ways to reduce *d* although this would involve reducing elite financial asset accumulation. Second, they could find ways to increase *p*, but this has clear political difficulties as social preferences have shifted towards smaller families, and more recently, anti-immigrant sentiment has escalated. Third, they could find ways to increase incomes for the lower and middle classes, but this too risks pushback from elites.

Hence, the arguments made about productivity in the above section on the incompatibility of value and full automation remain equally relevant in a capitalist context. Productivity increases may boost real income, but they will not lead to a smooth or automatic reduction in labour time. If population and wages are stagnant, then b will rise, regardless of the level of productivity. Because personal debt burdens are now growing, most workers will not choose to work less; some may choose to work more than before. In a simple arithmetical model, we can assume that the system finds ways to persuade workers into borrowing, with what might amount to a vague functionalist theory. Yet no such functionalism is required for a real-world application; rather it is clear that escalating housing costs have been serving this exact purpose. It is also clear that housing costs have risen precisely because various actors at the micro-level have been incentivized to lend, borrow, sell and buy at ever-higher levels within the evolving capitalist institutions of the Global North (Adkins et al., 2020). Hence, the trilemma, in its present institutional context, has manifested as a decline in the value of money relative to housing.

Fully operationalizing this articulation of the debt burden would of course demand that we complicate the model somewhat. Once the foreign sector enters the equation, the pressures of the trilemma can be diminished by a trade surplus but exacerbated by a trade deficit. The government, of course, is in reality the main bearer of debt, but this does not obviate the ultimate role of labour. Rather, it means that b must be understood through a more detailed distributional model that accounts for tax burdens and bond ownership as well as income distribution writ large.

The monothetic framework proposed here thus contradicts the Keynesians and neoclassical assumption that productivity growth alone can smoothly propel economic growth over the long run. Rather, there are monetary and demographic dynamics that must be held in balance so that any escalation in d is matched by a commensurate increase in $(i*p)$. The insight that, *ceteris paribus*, population growth is necessary for capitalist growth validates the Marxian argument that the sum of labour must grow in order for the capitalist economy to grow. The income growth solution may at first appear to decouple value from labour, but ultimately, it does not. The value, or output, produced by a fixed population may grow in absolute terms while the dangers of financial accumulation are offset by rising absolute wages. But this means that the rate of accumulation remains fixed because the population is fixed. Capitalists thus cannot sustainably translate productivity gains into a growing rate of financial accumulation. The latter can only be sustained by a growing workforce.

CONCLUSION

The version of the NI proposed here does not define value as labour directly; rather, it accepts a colloquial definition of value and shows its mechanical linkage to labour at a macroeconomic level. I have demonstrated that linkage through a model based on both behavioural and conceptual parameters, none of which are controversial in themselves. That model provides a pragmatic framework for identifying exploitation. It remains admittedly unhelpful for identifying specific workers who are exploited because the MELT is an average, and my approach makes no claims about 'productive' versus 'unproductive' labour. The model does, however, render a clear logic for identifying exploit*ers*.

The parameters capture capitalist reality well enough; at the very least, they capture the ideal type of capitalism. Yet parameters are inherently subject to contestation, and thought experiments resolve nothing on their own. Mandel abstractly posited that full automation would eliminate purchasability and thus destroy economic value. Hodgson responded that a regime of charity could sustain purchasability in this scenario. Elaborating Hodgson's idea a little further, I proposed that such a regime might involve an escalation of the taxes, transfers and price controls already implemented by many states. Any orthodox Marxist would concede that the nature of value, in the latter scenario, would have fundamentally changed from what they initially envisioned. The question, then, must be about which of these models is more reflective of reality. This essay has only gestured toward the empirical question, though at a glance it is fair to say that most capitalist states do not contain strong political mechanisms for transforming labour-saving technology into increased redistributive transfers to the poor.

I have argued that the NI offers a vision of exploitation that is internally consistent and more operationalizable than other versions of the LTV. I have also demonstrated that its operationalizability can be enhanced by Copeland's Moneyflows framework. This synthesis, I hope, can help to expand the common ground between Marxism and OIE so that the insights of both schools can be brought more coherently into conversation with one another. As noted at the outset, OIE offers a promising tradition for intellectual conciliation because its premises are determined by their conceptual integrity as well as their empirical validity; for that reason, it encompasses some key insights from Keynesian economics. Indeed, I hope that the framing offered here can contribute to the growth of a critical institutionalism that accommodates those who both accept and reject the argument that there is an objective basis for the concept of exploitation yet who are nonetheless able to productively discuss the broader social relations of capitalism.

NOTES

1. Godfrey-Smith (2003, p. 236) and others usually refer to this as the hypothetico-deductive method – in my view, a rather slanted label. Nola and Sankey (2007, p. 170) instead suggest, 'a better name might be the *hypothetico-inferential method* to cover both cases of deductive and non-deductive inference'. For more on institutionalist methods see Mayhew (2018) and Schneider (2020).
2. For Keynes, 'money itself' is 'that by delivery of which debt contracts and price contracts are *discharged*' (1930a, p. 3, emphasis in original). By 'indemnity', I refer to the debt contract itself, which can take many forms, ranging from collateralized loans to those

which have been secured through some form of third-party insurance. Ingham (1996) and Pistor (2020) discuss the complexity and variability of indemnification as a legal process.

REFERENCES

Acemoglu, D., & Restrepo, P. (2019). Automation and new tasks: How technology displaces and reinstates labor. *The Journal of Economic Perspectives*, 33(2), 3–30.

Adkins, L., Konings, M., & Cooper, M. (2020). *The asset economy: Property ownership and the new logic of inequality*. Polity Press.

Autor, D. H. (2019). Work of the past, work of the future. *AEA Papers and Proceedings*, 109, 1–32.

Autor, D., Goldin, C., & Katz, L. F. (2020). Extending the race between education and technology. *AEA Papers and Proceedings*, 110, 347–351.

Bellofiore, R. (1989). A monetary labor theory of value. *Review of Radical Political Economics*, 21(1–2), 1–25.

Bellofiore, R. (1997). Marx after Marx, or do we need a credit theory of exploitation? In *International symposium on marxian theory, 1997 mini-conference working papers* (pp. 2–10).

Bellofiore, R. (2024). Absolute value. In R. Bellofiore & T. R. Riva (Eds.), *Marx: Key concepts* (pp. 67–107). Edward Elgar Publishing.

Bezemer, D., & Hudson, M. (2016). Finance is not the economy: Reviving the conceptual distinction. *Journal of Economic Issues*, 50(3), 745–768.

Bowles, S., & Gintis, H. (1985). The labor theory of value and the specificity of Marxian economics. In S. A. Resnick & R. D. Wolff (Eds.), *Rethinking Marxism: Struggles in Marxist theory: Essays for Harry Magdoff & Paul Sweezy* (pp. 31–44). Autonomedia.

Clark, J. M. (1926). *Social control of business*. University of Chicago Press.

Clark, J. M. (1934). *Strategic factors in business cycles*. Printed by H. Wolff.

Cockshott, P., Cottrell, A., & Valle Baeza, A. (2014). The empirics of the labour theory of value: Reply to Nitzan and Bichler. *Investigación Económica*, 73(287), 115–134.

Commons, J. R. (1924). *Legal foundations of capitalism*. Macmillan.

Commons, J. R. (1934). *Institutional economics: Its place in political economy*. Transaction Publishers.

Copeland, M. A. (1921). *Some phases of institutional value theory: Vol. Reprinted from the university of Chicago abstracts of thesis, humanistic series*, (Vol. II, p. 26). University of Chicago.

Copeland, M. A. (1931). Economic theory and the natural science point of view. *The American Economic Review*, 21(1), 67–79.

Copeland, M. A. (1951). Institutional economics and model analysis. *The American Economic Review*, 41(2), 56–65.

Copeland, M. A. (1952). *A study of Moneyflows in the United States*. National Bureau of Economic Research.

Copeland, M. A. (1955). Statistics and objective economics. *Journal of the American Statistical Association*, 50(271), 639–659.

Dmitriev, V. K. (1974). *Economic essays on value, competition and utility*. CUP Archive.

Duménil, G. (1980). *De La Valeur Aux Prix De production*. FeniXX réédition numérique.

Duménil, G. (1983). Beyond the transformation riddle: A labor theory of value. *Science & Society*, 47(4), 427–450.

Foley, D. (1982). The value of money the value of labor power and the Marxian transformation problem. *Review of Radical Political Economics*, 14(2), 37–47.

Foley, D. (2000). Recent developments in the labor theory of value. *Review of Radical Political Economics*, 32(1), 1–39.

Freeman, A., & Kliman, A. (2008). Simultaneous valuation vs. the exploitation theory of profit: A summing up. *Capital & Class*, 32(1), 107–117.

Godfrey-Smith, P. (2003). *Theory and reality: An introduction to the philosophy of science*. University of Chicago Press.

Godley, W., & Lavoie, M. (2007). *Monetary economics: An integrated approach to credit, money, income, production and wealth*. Palgrave Macmillan.

Hodgson, G. (1980). A theory of exploitation without the labor theory of value. *Science & Society*, 44(3), 257–273.

Hodgson, G. (1982). *Capitalism, value, and exploitation: A radical theory*. Robertson.

Ingham, G. (1996). Money is a social relation. *Review of Social Economy*, 54(4), 507–529.

Ingham, G. (2004). *The nature of money*. Polity.

Ingham, G. (2008). *Capitalism: With a new postscript on the financial crisis and its aftermath*. Polity.

Kalecki, M. (1971). *Selected essays on the dynamics of the capitalist economy*. Cambridge University Press.

Keynes, J. M. (1930a). *A treatise on money in two volumes: 1 the pure theory of money* (Vol. 5). Cambridge University Press for the Royal Economic Society.

Keynes, J. M. (1930b). Economic possibilities for our grandchildren. In E. Johnson & D. Moggridge (Eds.), *The collected writings of John Maynard Keynes* (1st ed., Vol. 9, pp. 321–332). Cambridge University Press.

Keynes, J. M. (1936). *The general theory of employment, money and interest* (Vol. 7). Cambridge University Press for the Royal Economic Society.

Kliman, A. (2001). Simultaneous valuation vs. The exploitation theory of profit. *Capital & Class*, 25(1), 97–112.

Kliman, A. (2007). *Reclaiming Marx's capital: A refutation of the Myth of inconsistency*. Lexington Books.

Kliman, A. (2012). *Failure of capitalist production: Underlying causes of the Great Recession*. Pluto Press.

Levy, J. (2017). Capital as process and the history of capitalism. *Business History Review*, 91(3), 483–510.

Mandel, E. (1969). *An introduction to Marxist economic theory*. Pathfinder Press.

Marshall, A. (1890). *Principles of economics*. Springer.

Marx, K. (1867). *Capital: A critique of political economy: Vol. I*. Penguin Books.

Mayhew, A. (2018). An introduction to institutional economics: Tools for understanding evolving economies. *The American Economist*, 63(1), 3–17.

McColloch, W., & Vernengo, M. (2024). From regulation to deregulation and (perhaps) back: A peculiar continuity in the analytical framework. In L. Fiorito, S. Scheall, & C. E. Suprinyak (Eds.), *Research in the history of economic thought and methodology* (pp. 131–153). Emerald Publishing Limited.

Mitchell, W. C. (1927). *Business cycles: The problem and its setting*. National Bureau of Economic Research.

Morishima, M. (1974). The fundamental Marxian theorem: A reply to Samuelson. *Journal of Economic Literature*, 12(1), 71–74.

Myrdal, G. (1978). Institutional economics. *Journal of Economic Issues*, 12(4), 771–783.

Nitzan, J., & Bichler, S. (2009). *Capital as power: A study of order and creorder (1. Publ)*. Routledge.

Nola, R., & Sankey, H. (2007). *Theories of scientific method: An introduction*. Acumen Publishing.

Piketty, T. (2014). *Capital in the twenty-first century*. The Belknap Press of Harvard University Press.

Pistor, K. (2020). *The Code of capital: How the law creates Wealth and inequality (first paperback printing)*. Princeton University Press.

Ricardo, D. (1821). In P. Sraffa (Ed.), *On the principles of political economy and taxation* (Vol. 1). Cambridge University Press.

Saad-Filho, A. (2012). Transformation problem. In B. Fine, A. Saad-Filho, & M. Boffo (Eds.), *The elgar companion to Marxist economics* (pp. 341–347). Edward Elgar.

Schneider, G. E. (2020). Contemporary original institutional economics principles, status, and relationship with other heterodox schools of thought. *American Review of Political Economy*, 14(1).

Serrano, F. (1995). Long Period effective demand and the Sraffian supermultiplier. *Contributions to Political Economy*, 14(1), 67–90.

Shaikh, A. (1977). Marx's theory of value and the "transformation problem". In J. G. Schwartz (Ed.), *The subtle anatomy of capitalism* (pp. 106–139). Goodyear Publishing Company.

Shaikh, A. (1998). The empirical strength of the labour theory of value. In R. Bellofiore (Ed.), *Marxian economics: A reappraisal: Volume 2: Essays on Volume III of capital profit, prices and dynamics* (pp. 225–251). Palgrave Macmillan UK.

Shaikh, A. (2016). *Capitalism: Competition, conflict, crises*. Oxford University Press.

Smithin, J. (2018). *Rethinking the theory of money, credit, and macroeconomics: A new statement for the twenty-first century*. Lexington Books.

Smithin, J. (2023). Profit, interest, and wages in the monetary circuit. *International Journal of Political Economy*, 52(3–4), 282–296.

Sraffa, P. (1951). *Introduction to "the works and correspondence of David Ricardo. Vol. 1: On the principles of political economy and taxation"* (pp. xiii–lxii). Liberty Fund.

Sraffa, P. (1960). *Production of commodities by means of commodities: Prelude to a critique of economic theory*. Cambridge University Press.

Weber, I. M., Jauregui, J. L., Teixeira, L., & Pires, L. N. (2022). *Inflation in times of overlapping emergencies: Systematically significant Prices from an input-output perspective (UMass amherst economics department working paper series 340)*. University of Massachusetts Amherst.

Whalen, C. (2022). *Reforming capitalism for the common good: Essays in institutional and post-Keynesian economics*. Edward Elgar Publishing.

Wright, E. O. (1978). *Class, crisis and the state*. Verso Books.

Wright, E. O. (1979). The value controversy and social research. *New Left Review*, I/116, 53–82.

MARX'S THEORY OF PRICES OF PRODUCTION WITH UNEQUAL TURNOVER TIMES AND A RESPONSE TO DE MARCO'S CRITIQUE[1]

Fred Moseley

Mount Holyoke College, USA

ABSTRACT

The so-called transformation problem, the main reason critics give for rejecting Marx's value theory, concerns its apparent contradiction with the empirical tendency towards equal rates of profit across industries. That theory holds that labour is the only source of new value and hence surplus value (or profit), implying that industries with a higher-than-average proportion of labour to capital should have a higher-than-average rate of profit. This also applies to industries with a shorter-than-average turnover time, reducing the investment required to produce a given annual surplus value. These both contradict the tendency towards equal rates of profit across industries. The debate has largely ignored the problem of unequal turnover times, both because Marx did not discuss it and because it is more complicated. In this article, the author addresses Marx's approach and de Marco's recent critique of it.

Keywords: Turnover times; prices of production; transformation problem; general rate of profit; profit adjustment

INTRODUCTION

In Part 2 of Volume 3 of *Capital*, Marx presented his theory of prices of production to explain this apparent contradiction. Critics, ever since Bortkiewicz

Money, Value and Marx's Circuit of Capital
Research in Political Economy, Volume 41, 161–179

Published under exclusive licence by Emerald Publishing Limited
ISSN: 0161-7230/doi:10.1108/S0161-723020260000041021

(1952) and Sweezy (1942), argued that this failed because he 'failed to transform the inputs of constant capital and variable capital' from values to prices of production. Moseley (2016), in which Part 2 contains a comprehensive critical review of the recent literature, argues that Marx did *not,* in fact, fail to transform the inputs and that Marx's theory of prices of production is logically complete.

The debate has largely ignored the problem of unequal turnover times, both because Marx did not discuss it and because it is more complicated. However, he did note this issue.[2]

> We have now to investigate: (1) differences in the organic composition of capitals; (2) *differences in their turnover times*. (Marx, 1981, p. 243)

> Besides the differing organic composition of capital ... there is another source of inequality between [value] rates of profit: the *variation in the length of capital turnover* in the different spheres of production. (Marx, 1981, p. 250)

> ... we shall ignore for the time being the differences that may be produced here by *variation in the turnover times*. This point will be dealt with later. (Marx, 1981, p. 254)

Unfortunately, he did not return to this in Volume 3. Fortunately, however, it has recently been discovered that he did so in a later manuscript – the *Economic Manuscript of 1867–1868*, published for the first time in German in 2012 in the *Marx/Engels Gesamtausgabe* (MEGA), Volume II/4.3, pages 254–280), which contains his only attempt to address this issue.[3] An English translation, summarised in the next section using different algebraic symbols for greater clarity, was published in *Historical Materialism* in 2019, along with an introduction by myself.

In de Marco's (2024) critique of Marx's decomposition of the profit adjustment in this text and of my introduction, he presents his own alternative decomposition. I appreciate his attention to Marx's excerpt, but disagree with much of his interpretation.

This paper discusses:

- Marx's theory of prices of production with unequal turnover times and his decomposition of the profit adjustment.
- The main takeaways from this excerpt are that the rate of profit, advanced capital and annual cost price are taken as given, and the latter as given in the determination of both values and prices of production; further, prices of production are long-run equilibrium, centre-of-gravity prices.
- De Marco's critique of Marx's decomposition of the profit adjustment and my response to his critique.
- De Marco's alternative decomposition and my critique of it.
- The further meaning of the components of the profit adjustment.
- De Marco's critique of my interpretation of the rate of profit as given.
- De Marco's critique of my interpretation of prices of production as equilibrium prices.

Marx's Theory of Prices of Production With Unequal Turnover Times

According to Marx's theory, the price of production (P_i) of the annual product of an industry i is the sum of its annual cost price plus the annual average profit calculated on its total advanced capital. Algebraically, this is:

$$P_i = K_i + rC_i \qquad (1)$$

where K_i is the *annual cost price* (the *capital consumed* in production in a year = consumed constant capital + variable capital), C_i is the *total advanced capital* in industry i, rC_i is the *average profit received* there, and r is the *general rate of profit*. C_i and K_i are taken as given, and r is also taken as given, being determined by the ratio of the total surplus value produced in a year divided by the total capital in the whole economy ($r = S/C$), as presented in Volumes 1 and 2 and Part 1 of Volume 3 of *Capital.*

A commodity's price of production is the price at which it would have to be sold in order to receive the average profit based on r. Marx did not assume it actually sells at this price, but that there is a *tendency* for its market price to gravitate towards its price of production. This is a theory of these tendential centre-of-gravity prices.

In the 1867–1868 excerpt, Marx decomposed rC_i into two components:

$$rC_i = S_i + A_i \qquad (2)$$

where S_i is the annual surplus value produced in industry i and A_i, which could be positive or negative, is the profit adjustment needed for its rate of profit to equal the general rate. So (1) can be written:

$$P_i = K_i + S_i + A_i \qquad (1^*)$$

which can be compared with the value of that industry's annual product (W_i):

$$W_i = K_i + S_i \qquad (3)$$

Thus, this profit adjustment is the difference between the commodity's price of production and its value:

$$A_i = P_i - W_i \qquad (4)$$

In the 100 pages prior to the excerpt, Marx discussed at length: (1) the reasons for unequal turnover times of the total advanced capital in different industries (mainly different proportions of fixed and circulating capital and other reasons)[4] and (2) the effect of turnover time of the total advanced capital on the annual rate of profit on that capital.[5]

To explain how the turnover time of total advanced capital affects the rate of profit on the total advanced capital, Marx introduced in these pages a new concept of the rate of profit – *the rate of profit on the cost price* (π), which is the ratio of the annual surplus-value to the annual cost price: $\pi = S/K$, as opposed to the rate of profit on the total advanced capital $r = S/C$. This new concept of the rate of profit on the cost price enabled him to decompose this annual rate of profit into two factors: the rate of profit on the cost price and the turnover time of total advanced capital ($T = C/K$):

$$r = S/C = (S/K)/(C/K) = \pi/T \tag{5}$$

The rate of profit on the total advanced capital for the average social capital is the *general rate of profit* with which the rate of profit on the total advanced capital in all industries is compared. The rate of profit on the total advanced capital for an individual industry assumes that the commodity that is produced in that industry is sold at its value and is also called the *value rate of profit*.

Marx usually assumed that the turnover time of the average social advanced capital is one year so that $K = C$ (i.e. $C/K = 1$) and thus $S/K = S/C$ (i.e. $\pi = r$) for the average social capital. For individual capitals, Marx usually assumed that $K_i \neq C_i$ (i.e. $C_i/K_i \neq 1$) and thus $S_i/K_i \neq S_i/C_i$ (i.e. $\pi_i \neq r_i$). Throughout this manuscript, Marx expressed the surplus-value component of the value of the annual product in an industry as the product of the rate of profit on the cost price in that industry (π_i) and the cost price in that industry (K_i), i.e. $S_i = \pi_i K_i$. And the value of the commodity is expressed many times as $W_i = K_i + \pi_i K_i$.

Furthermore, to explain the determination of this new concept of the rate of profit on the cost price, Marx also introduced another new concept – the *composition of the cost price*. The composition of the cost price (θ) is the ratio of the constant capital consumed in one year ($K - V$) (= depreciation of fixed constant capital + circulating constant capital) to the circulating variable capital (V): $\theta = (K - V)/V = K/V - 1$. And the rate of profit on the cost price depends in part on the composition of the cost price:

$$\pi = S/K = (S/V)/(K/V) = (S/V)/(\theta + 1) \tag{6}$$

Marx's excerpt used these new concepts to analyse the effect of *unequal turnover times* of the total advanced capital in different industries on the *prices of production* in different industries. He compared two capitals: (1) an average capital, representing total social capital with average turnover time and the average composition of the cost price, and (2) an individual capital, representing capital in an individual industry with a different turnover time and/or a different composition of the cost price.

He considered three main cases: unequal turnover times (the main case), unequal compositions of the cost price and both inequalities together. Rates of surplus value are assumed to be equal and equal to 1.

The *first case* is *unequal turnover times* between the average social capital and the capital in an individual industry (assuming equal compositions of capital of the cost price and equal rates of surplus-value). Marx usually assumed that the individual industry had a *slower* than average turnover time (e.g. annual $K_i = 440$ and $C_i = 500$). Since the individual industry has a slower than average turnover time, it produces less surplus value in a year (88 instead of 100), and thus its industry rate of profit on the advanced capital is less than the general rate of profit (17.6% instead of 20%). Therefore, to equalise the rate of profit on advanced capital in an individual industry with the general rate of profit, a *profit adjustment* (A_i^t) would have to be added to the surplus-value produced in that industry, and the price of production of the annual product in that industry would be greater than its value.[6]

$$P_i = K_i + S_i + A_i^t \tag{7}$$

The profit adjustment is:

$$\begin{aligned} A_i &= P_i - W_i \\ &= (K_i + rC_i) - (K_i + \pi_i K_i) \\ A_i &= rC_i - \pi_i K_i \end{aligned} \tag{8}$$

Thus, the profit adjustment is equal to the difference between the *average profit received* in an industry (rC_i) and the *surplus-value produced* ($\pi_i K_i$) in this industry[7] Eq. (8) is a very important equation to keep in mind.

Assuming $K = C$ for the social average capital, and thus $r = \pi$, Eq. (8) can be expressed as:

$$A_i^t = \pi C_i - \pi_i K_i$$

Since $\pi = \pi_i$ in this first case (due to equal compositions of the cost price), this equation can be simplified to:

$$A_i^t = \pi_i C_i - \pi_i K_i = \pi_i (C_i - K_i) \tag{9}$$

This equation identifies the cause and determines the magnitude of the divergence between the price of production of a commodity and its value in this first case.

The *second case* is of *unequal compositions of the cost price* between the average social capital and the capital in an individual industry (assuming equal turnover times and equal rates of surplus-value), which Marx discussed only very briefly (presumably because he had already discussed this case at length in the *Manuscript of 1864–1865*, i.e. in Volume 3 of *Capital*). In this case, Marx assumed a second capital with a *higher* than average composition of capital, which implies less variable capital and therefore less annual surplus value, and thus a lower rate of profit on the cost price. Again, to equalise the rate of profit in this industry with the general rate of profit, a profit adjustment should be added to the surplus value it produces (A_i^c), and again its price of production would be greater than its value.[8] Since equal turnover times ($C_i = K_i$) are assumed in this case, the profit adjustment is:

$$A_i^c = P_i - W_i = rC_i - \pi_i K_i = rK_i - \pi_i K_i = (r - \pi_i) K_i \tag{10}$$

This identifies the cause and determines the magnitude of the divergence between a commodity's price of production and its value in this second case.

The *third case* is the combined and more complicated case where both turnover times and unequal compositions of the cost price are unequal. The profit adjustment then consists of three sub-components: one for the separate effect of unequal turnover times (A_i^t), one for the separate effect of unequal compositions of capital (A_i^c) and one for the combined effect of both together ($A_i^{t\,c}$), yielding.

$$A_i^{t\,c} = \pi_i(C_i - K_i) + (r - \pi_i)K_i + (r - \pi_i)(C_i - K_i). \quad (11)$$

Thus, Marx's decomposition of the profit adjustment that transforms the value of a commodity into its price of production *identifies the causes of the deviation of the price of production from the value* – a non-average turnover time, a non-average composition of capital on the cost price and a combination of these two causes; and this equation determines the contribution of each of these causes to the overall profit adjustment – how much is due to unequal turnover times, how much is due to unequal compositions of the cost price and how much is due to the combination of the two.

Takeaways for the Transformation Problem

I argued in Moseley (2019) that Marx's excerpt, beginning a more developed theory of prices of production, provides additional textual evidence to support the 'macro-monetary' interpretation of Marx's theory in Moseley (2016) and has important takeaways for the long-standing controversy over Marx's theory of prices of production as presented in the earlier Volume 3 manuscript (Marx, 2016), as follows:

1. In Marx's theory of prices of production presented in this excerpt and summarized above, the *general rate of profit (r)* (i.e. the rate of profit on the total advanced capital of the social average capital) *is taken as given*, as determined in Volumes 1 and 2 and Part 1 of Volume 3 by the ratio of the total surplus-value produced in a year to the total capital invested in that year. This assumption of a given general rate of profit is stated in the title of this section of the manuscript:

> *General rate of profit given*. How does the equalization of values to prices of production take place, with respect to unequal turnover of capitals in different spheres of production? (Marx, 2019, p. 162)

Throughout the entire excerpt, the general rate of profit of the average social capital is given, as equal to 100/500 = 20%. And the point of the excerpt is to explain how an individual industry with a different turnover time from the total social capital or/and a different composition of capital from the total social capital can nonetheless could receive this predetermined general rate of profit of 20%.

2. The *cost price K and the advanced capital C are also taken as given* throughout this excerpt (along with their two components, constant capital and variable capital), both for the total social capital and for an individual industry. As we have seen above, these given quantities of money capital inputs for an individual

industry, together with the predetermined general rate of profit, determine the price of production of the annual product in that industry ($PP_i = K_i + rC$; Eq. (1)). And the *presupposed cost price is the same* in the determination of both the value and the price of production of the annual product of this industry (as they are in Chapter 9 of Volume 3), and is symbolized throughout this excerpt by the same letter K_i:

$$\text{value} = K_i + S_i$$
$$\text{price of production} = K_i + rC_i = K_i + S_i + A_i$$

Since the cost price = constant capital + variable capital, this excerpt provides further important textual evidence that these inputs to capitalist production are *supposed to be the same* in the determination of both values and prices of production in Marx's theory. The inputs are *not supposed to be transformed*, contrary to the long-standing criticism of Marx's theory of prices of production. Nothing is said in this excerpt about the necessity to transform the inputs in the transformation of values to prices of production.

3. *The prices of production that are determined in this excerpt are long-run center-of-gravity equilibrium prices* because the average profit component of the price of production of each and every individual commodity is determined by rC_i, where r is the general rate of profit.

The Production and Distribution of Surplus Value

To elaborate on this point, I argue that Marx's theory of surplus-value is based on *two main levels of abstraction* – the *production* and *distribution* of surplus-value. The main question at the first level is the *determination of the total annual surplus-value* produced in the economy as a whole, and in the second level, the *division of the predetermined total surplus-value into individual parts* – first the equalisation of the rate of profit across industries and then the further division of the total surplus value into commercial profit, interest, and rent. And the fundamental premise of this logical structure is that *the total surplus value is determined at the first level of abstraction* (production of surplus value) and *is taken as a pre-determined magnitude at the second level of abstraction* (distribution of surplus value), i.e. in the division of this pre-determined total surplus value into individual parts.

Thus, there is a *strict logical sequence* from the first to the second level of abstraction: first, the production and determination of total surplus value; then the determination of the individual parts of this presupposed total. This logical sequence follows directly from Marx's labour theory of value and surplus value, according to which all the individual parts of surplus value come from the same source – the surplus labour of workers. Therefore, the total must be determined prior to its division into individual parts. It is determined by surplus labour and by surplus labour alone. Moseley (2016) presents 75 pages of textual evidence (from all the drafts of *Capital*) and commentary to support this interpretation. I argue further that the distinction between the production and distribution of surplus value is the quantitative dimension of the two main levels of abstraction in Marx's theory: capital in general and competition, which is based on the two levels of abstraction in Hegel's logic of the concept: universality and particularity ('the whole determines the parts').[9]

Taking the general rate of profit as given in this 1867–1868 excerpt is another example of this logical method. As we saw above, the profit adjustment that equalises the rate of profit and transforms the value of a commodity into its price of production is equal to the difference between the *average profit received* in the industry that produces this commodity (which is an element of the distribution of surplus-value) and the *surplus value produced* in that industry (which is obviously an element of the production of surplus value).

De Marco's Criticisms of Marx's Decomposition of the Profit Adjustment

In the Appendix to De Marco's paper, he makes two criticisms of Marx's decomposition. Both criticisms concern Marx's simplifying assumption that $K = C$ for the average social capital, and thus $K/C = 1$, that is advanced capital turns over once annually. I argue that it can be easily generalised to eliminate the 'limitations' alleged by De Marco.

The first criticism is that, if $K \neq C$ and thus $K/C \neq 1$, then Eq. (9) for the profit adjustment for unequal turnover times is incorrect, because if $K_i = C_i$ (i.e. $K_i/C_i = 1$), the industry will have a different turnover time compared to the average capital and thus should have a profit adjustment for unequal turnover times; but according to (9),

$$A_i^t = (C_i - K_i)\pi_i. = 0$$

However, (9) can be easily generalised to allow for $K \neq C$ for the total social capital, as follows:

$$A_i^t = [(K/C)C_i - K_i]\pi_i \qquad (9^*)$$

It can be seen that, if $K/C = 1$, then (9**) reduces to (9). And if $K/C = x \neq 1$ and $K_i/C_i = 1$ (i.e. $K_i = C_i$), then $A_i^t = (xC_i - C_i)\pi_i \neq 0$, as it should, since the two turnover times are different. But if $K/C = x$ and K_i/C_i also $= x$ (i.e. $K_i = xC_i$), then $A_i^t = xC_i - xC_i = 0$, as it should, since the two turnover times are the same. Finally, and most generally, if $K/C = x$ and if $K_i/C_i = y \neq x$ (i.e. $K_i = yC_i$), then $A_i^t = xC_i - yC_i = (x - y)C_i \neq 0$. Thus, in the first case, the adjustment for industry *i* depends on the difference between the number of annual turnovers of the total advanced social capital ($K/C = x$) and that of an individual capital *i* ($K_i/C_i = y$).

De Marco's second criticism concerns Eq. (10). He argues that it 'looks awkward' because it compares the *profit margin* of an individual industry (i.e. rate of profit on the cost price π_i) with the *rate of profit* of the average capital (r). In Marx's example, $K = C$ and thus the profit margin of the average social economy (π) is equal to the general rate of profit of the average social economy (r), so (8) can be considered a comparison of the profit margins of the individual industry and the total social economy ($A_i^c = (\pi - \pi_i)K_i$). However, De Marco argues that, if $K \neq C$, this substitution can no longer be made and Eq. (10) 'looks awkward', which I presume means is incoherent.

It is true that, if $K \neq C$, we could no longer substitute π for r in this equation, but so what? The analysis then just reverts back to Marx's basic non-simplified Eq. (8): $A_i^c = rC_i - \pi_i K_i$. This is based on Marx's theory of the profit adjustment as the difference between the average profit received in an individual industry (rC_i) and the surplus value produced in that industry ($\pi_i K_i$), as discussed above. De Marco does not seem to understand that this equation is not 'awkward', but is instead the basic equation for Marx's analysis of the profit adjustment that is necessary to equalise the rate of profit and transform values into prices of production.

Critique of De Marco's Alternative Decomposition of the Profit Adjustment

De Marco (2024, pp. 153–55) presents an alternative decomposition of the profit adjustment, which he argues is superior to Marx's decomposition because of the alleged 'limitations' of Marx's decomposition (which I have shown do not exist). De Marco's decomposition differs from Marx decomposition in three important respects: (1) he decomposes the *surplus value produced* in an individual industry as $r_i C_i$ instead of $\pi_i K_i$; (2) he defines the *turnover time of capital* in terms of *variable capital* only, rather than the *total advanced capital* (constant capital advanced, including fixed capital + variable capital); and (3) he defines the *composition of capital* in terms of *total advanced capital* rather than in terms of the *capital consumed* in one period.

We have just seen that the profit adjustment is the difference between the *average profit received* in an industry (rC_i) and the *surplus value* it produces ($\pi_i K_i$): $A_i = rC_i - \pi_i K_i$. But De Marco interprets this surplus value produced in an industry as $r_i C_i$ instead of $\pi_i K_i$.[10] This is inappropriate for Marx's theory, according to which surplus value is the result of the *capital that functions in the valorisation process* (K_i), not the total advanced capital (C_i), which includes fixed capital that has not yet functioned in the valorisation process ($C_i - K_i$). We saw above that, earlier in this manuscript, Marx introduced a new concept (π) of the *rate of profit on the cost price* (i.e. on the capital consumed in one period or the capital that functions in the valorisation process) to analyse the effect of turnover time of total advanced capital on the rate of profit on that capital. This new concept disappears in De Marco's interpretation.

Secondly, De Marco's decomposition is based on a different definition of the *turnover* of capital. As we also saw above, Marx defined the turnover time of total advanced capital as the period of time required for this total to be recovered through the sale of the product (C/K). But De Marco defines it as the number of times *the advanced variable capital only* turns over in a year (the inverse of the period of time for one turnover). He bases this on Marx's analysis of the turnover of variable capital in Chapter 16 of Volume 2, which Engels followed in Chapter 4 of Volume 3.[11] De Marco's (2024, p. 154) alternative is expressed in his Eq. (7):

$$A_i^t = s'(n - n_i)Q_i\,C_i \tag{12}$$

where n is the number of times the advanced variable capital of the average capital turns over in a year, and n_i is the same for an individual industry i, s' is the real rate of surplus value for a single turnover of variable capital of the average capital (it is assumed that $s_i' = s'$), and Q_i depends on the composition of the individual capital i, which we discuss next.

This equation is supposed to express the causes of the difference between the price of production and the value of an individual commodity. It specifies that the main cause of this difference is the *difference in the turnover rates of advanced variable capital* between the individual and social average capital. According to it, the *difference between the turnover time of total advanced capital in different industries plays no role in determining the difference between the price of production and the value of individual commodities*. But this is wrong either as an interpretation of Marx's theory or as a description of capitalist reality. In both, these are one of two main causes (along with unequal compositions of the cost price) of the difference between the price of production and the value of a commodity. In the real capitalist economy, *capitalists compete over the rate of profit on the total advanced capital*, not on the rate of profit on the advanced variable capital only; and this rate is thus equalised according to differences in the turnover of *total advanced capital*, not the turnover rates of the variable capital only. The profit adjustment required to equalise the rate of profit depends on the differences in the turnover times of the total advanced capital and of an individual capital, not on the differences in the advanced variable capital only.

We also saw above that Marx defined the composition of capital in this excerpt in terms of the *composition of the cost price* (i.e. the capital consumed in a year). He defined the composition of capital in this way to explain his new concept of the rate of profit on the cost price, in turn, necessary to explain how the turnover time of total advanced capital affects the rate of profit on that capital.

De Marco, however, defines the composition of the *total advanced capital* rather than the composition of the cost price. He chooses this definition[12] because that is how Marx usually defined the composition of capital in *Capital*. However, Marx chose a different definition of the composition of capital in the excerpt for the specific purpose of analysing the effect of the turnover time of the total advanced capital on the rate of profit on the total advanced capital. For this purpose, the new concept of the rate of profit on the cost price is necessary, in turn requiring that the composition of capital be defined as the composition of the cost price.

Further analysis of the effect of unequal turnover times on the prices of production of commodities should be based on Marx's decomposition in the excerpt and should incorporate both of Marx's new concepts to develop this important extension of his theory of prices of production.

Further Meaning of the Components of the Profit Adjustment

We have seen above that the components of Marx's profit adjustment in the excerpt identify the *causes* of the difference between price of production and value in a single period of analysis and thus determine the magnitudes that each cause *contributes* to the overall profit adjustment in this period.

Despite his wrong equation for the profit rate, De Marco agrees in part that these three components (which he calls 'factors') of the profit adjustment identify the causes of the difference between the price of production and the value of a commodity. However, he also argues erroneously that these factors *'generate the need' for changes in future periods* that will tend to eliminate these causes of differences, and thus the value rate of profit in an individual industry (r_i) *will gravitate towards the general rate of profit* (r), *and the values of commodities will gravitate towards their prices of production.*

For example, De Marco argues that, if the turnover time of an individual capital is slower than that of the average capital, then in future periods this turnover time of the individual capital will rise so that the turnover time of individual capitals will gravitate towards that of the average capital. *This will cause the value rate of profit of the individual industry to gravitate towards the general rate of profit*, which in turn *will cause the value of the individual commodity to gravitate towards its price of production.* And he argues that a similar adjustment will occur in future periods with respect to differences in the compositions of capital of the individual capital and the average capital.

The following three passages succinctly express De Marco's interpretation of the factors of the profit adjustment in Marx's theory of prices of production in this excerpt. To begin with:

> Marx's decomposition of Eq. (7) ascribes the differences ($r - r_i$) to three factors: unequal turnover times of capital advanced, unequal compositions of annual production costs, and their combined effect ... *Each of these factors generates the need for the corresponding adjustments* A_i^t, A_i^c, A_i^{tc} *necessary to compensate for the deviation of the value rate of profit* r_i *from the general rate of profit* r ... (De Marco, 2024, p. 152)

This is how he converts Marx's one-period analysis into a multi-period analysis in the future – he assumes that *differences* in Marx's single period 'generate the need' for *changes* in these factors in future periods which will tend to reduce and eliminate these factors. However, these alleged future changes are pure speculation. Marx says nothing about such a 'need' for these changes in future periods, and De Marco provides no explanation of their 'necessity'. These changes are especially unlikely if the turnover of capital is defined in terms of variable capital only, as in his interpretation.

A second passage:

> When $r_i \neq r$, the compensation or curtailment determined by the profit adjustments A's should allow the movement toward equalizing the industry 'i' average 'price' rate of profit to the general rate of profit, because $W_i + A_i = P_i$. (De Marco, 2024, p. 152)

De Marco has confirmed[13] that *industry 'i' average* 'price' *rate of profit* in this sentence is another term for the *value rate of profit*, which moves towards equality with the general rate of profit. However (again), Marx said nothing in the excerpt, nor anywhere else, about the value rate of profit in individual industries gravitating towards the general rate of profit, which would imply that the values of commodities would gravitate towards their prices of production. Rather, Marx argued that the rates of profit of individual industries would equalise through the *difference* between the prices of production and the values of commodities.

And a third passage:

> To determine the profit-adjustment decomposition, the excerpt must assume both a given general rate of profit and the rate of profit of a given industry because this is literally what its definition requires, but *that does not imply that for Marx this decomposition is not intended to describe the changes that occur in profit adjustments during the equalization process.* (De Marco, 2024, p. 156)

Eliminating the double negative, the second part of this sentence states that Marx's decomposition is intended to describe the changes that will occur in profit adjustments during the equalisation process in future periods. Surely, this misinterprets Marx's theory, in which there is *no tendency* for value rates of profit in individual industries to gravitate towards the general rate of profit and no tendency for the values of commodities to gravitate towards their prices of production. Instead, in Marx's theory, there is a tendency for *market prices* to gravitate towards prices of production.

Response to De Marco's Critique of My Interpretation of the Rate of Profit as Given

De Marco acknowledges that Marx takes the general rate of profit as given throughout the excerpt but argues that Marx does not add (as I did) 'as determined by the prior theory of total surplus-value in Volumes 1 and 2 of *Capital*' (p. 155). It is true that Marx did not explicitly state this in the excerpt. However, he also did not provide another explanation of the determination of the rate of profit; how else would he determine the rate of profit that is taken as given in the excerpt, if not by his theory of total surplus value presented in Volumes 1 and 2?

Furthermore, taking the rate of profit as given in Marx's theory of prices of production was a key element of his general logical method of the two levels of abstraction (the production and distribution of surplus-value) discussed in Section 2 of this paper and at length in Chapter 3 of my book. Marx also took the rate of profit as given in the other two drafts of his theory of prices of production in the *Manuscript of 1861–1863* (in the chapter on Rodbertus) and, of course, in Chapter 9 of Volume 3 of *Capital*. The 1867 excerpt is consistent with these earlier drafts in this important respect.

De Marco argues that the rate of profit cannot be taken as given because the factors of the profit adjustment describe changes that occur in future periods, during which these factors will change, and with that, the general rate of profit, which therefore cannot be taken as given, except as a provisional assumption. However, we have seen above that Marx's components of the profit adjustment do not refer to changes that will occur in future periods but to the causes of the differences between the values and prices of production of commodities in a single period. And the rate of profit is taken as given in this single period.

De Marco also acknowledges that, in Chapter 9 of Volume 3, the well-known chapter in which Marx presented his theory of prices of production, Marx took the general rate of profit as given, as determined by the total surplus value produced and the total capital invested in all industries. However, De Marco argues that it is only a *provisional assumption,* which is later relaxed in Chapter 10. He argues that Chapter 10 analyses the *actual equalisation process* of the different rates of profit in individual industries and that this actual process *changes the general rate of profit itself.* So he argues that the general rate of profit that Marx takes as given in Chapter 9 is not the final general rate of profit but changes as a result of the equalisation process discussed in Chapter 10. He makes a similar argument elsewhere.

De Marco argues that I 'undervalue Chapter 10', and places great emphasis on the following passage on the second page of Chapter 10:

> The really difficult question here is this: how does this equalisation of profits or this establishment of a general rate of profit take place, since it is evidently a result and cannot be a point of departure? (Marx, 1981, p. 274)

De Marco interprets this as a question about how the rate of profit is *determined,* arguing that Chapter 10 provides Marx's answer to this question and that Marx's answer is that the actual process of the equalisation changes the general rate of profit.

However, this interpretation is contradicted by Marx's paragraph immediately prior to his question, which states that (1) the *general rate of profit* is determined by the profit on the average capital, which is the same rate as the total surplus value on the total capital; (2) the *total surplus value* is determined by the *total unpaid labour,* (3) the *total profit* is equal to the total surplus value, (4) the *average profit* is a share of the total surplus value that is distributed among the branches of production according to the amount of capital in each industry and (5) prices of production are determined by adding the average profit in each industry to the cost price in that industry. Please read this passage carefully.

> It can also be added here, firstly, that wherever an average profit is established, i.e. a general rate of profit, and *however the result may have been brought about, this average profit can be nothing other than the profit on the average social capital, the total sum of profit being equal to the total sum of surplus-value,* and secondly that the prices produced by adding this average profit onto the cost prices can be nothing other than the values which have been transformed into prices of production... It is clear enough that *the average profit can be nothing other than the total mass of surplus-value, distributed between the masses of capital in each sphere of production in proportion to their size. It is the sum total of the realized unpaid labour,* and this grand total is represented, just like the laid labour, dead and living, in the total mass of commodities and money that accrues to the capitalists. (Marx, 1981, p. 274)

Note that the first sentence in this passage states that, however the result of the equalisation of the profit rate may have been brought about or in reality (i.e. no matter what Marx's answer to his question in the next paragraph might be), the average profit '*can be nothing other than*' a share of the total surplus value that is produced by the total unpaid labour (which is determined by Marx's theory of surplus value in Volumes 1 and 2 and presupposed in Volume 3). And prices of production 'can be nothing other than' adding the average profit to the cost price in each industry. This is the theory of the general rate of profit and average profit and prices of production that Marx presented in Chapter 9, and it is presupposed in Chapter 10 and the rest of Volume 3 (and in the 1867–1868 excerpt).

Thus, Marx's question posed at the beginning of Chapter 10 is not about how the rate of profit is *determined*; that question has already been answered in the previous chapter and summarised in the previous paragraph. Instead, Marx's question is about how the actual rates of profit in individual industries tend to converge in reality to the general rate of profit determined by total unpaid labour and total advanced capital.

Though De Marco suggests that this question is the main subject of Chapter 10, in fact it is hardly discussed at all in this chapter, is not discussed again for the next 22 pages, and when it is discussed towards the end of the chapter, it is only four paragraphs. Most of Chapter 10 is about the *market value* of commodities, not prices of production and the equalisation of the profit rate. The main points of Chapter 10 are (1) market value is a weighted average of the individual values in an industry brought about by competition within each industry and (2) market value is an equilibrium price which assumes that supply = demand and is the centre of gravity of the fluctuations of market prices.[14]

Finally, on pp. 297–298, Marx returns to the question of how the equalisation of the rate of profit takes place in reality. The most important passage is the following:

> If commodities were sold at their values, however, this would mean very different rates of profit in the different spheres of production, as we have already explained, according to the different organic composition of the masses of capital applied. *Capital withdraws from a sphere with a low rate of profit and wends its way to others that yield higher profit. This constant migration, the distribution of capital between the different spheres according to where the profit rate is rising and where it is falling, is what produces a relationship between supply and demand such that the average profit is the same in the various different sphere, and values are therefore transformed into prices of production.* Capital arrives at this equalization to a greater of lesser extent, according to how advanced capitalist development is in a given national society … (Marx, 1981, p. 297)

This is Marx's brief answer to the question posed at the beginning of the chapter: the general rate of profit, determined by total unpaid surplus labour, '*takes place*' in reality through transfers of capital in search of a higher rate of profit. These transfers of capital result in a relation between supply and demand ($S = D$) such that the *rate of profit is the same in all industries,* and prices of production are determined by adding the average profit (determined by the general rate of profit) to the cost price in each industry.[15]

The next three paragraphs are about the speed of this equalisation, which depends on the mobility of capital and labour. Again, nothing is said about this equalisation process changing the rate of profit. De Marco cites these four paragraphs but does not quote the important passage on p. 297 quoted and discussed above. Instead he comments:

> Marx *repeatedly refers to the migration of capital* from less profitable spheres of production to spheres with higher average rates of profit (MMV3, pp. 305–306; KV3, pp. 297–298). (De Marco, 2024, p. 157)

The phrase 'repeatedly refers' is a gross exaggeration. Marx referred to the migration of capitals to equalise the rate of profit in Chapter 10 only in the four paragraphs just discussed,[16] and said nothing about this equalisation process causing the general rate of profit to change.

In sum, Chapter 10 provides *no textual evidence* to support De Marco's interpretation that the rate of profit changes as a result of the equalisation process, which is hardly discussed at all in this chapter, and in the brief discussion of the equalisation process on pp. 297–298, Marx does not say the equalisation process causes the general rate of profit to change. Instead, these four paragraphs are about how transfers of capital equalise individual rates of profit to the general rate of profit determined by the total unpaid labour.

De Marco argues that:

> Indeed, this chapter is *clearly at odds with the idea of a given general rate of profit*, definitively predetermined at the level of abstraction of the first two volumes of *Capital*. (De Marco, 2024, p. 157; underline emphasis by De Marco)

I argue, to the contrary, that Chapter 10 is not at all 'at odds' with the idea of a given general rate of profit. Chapter 10 hardly concerns the rate of profit at all; in it, the main passage concerning the determination of the general rate of profit states that it is 'nothing other than' the total surplus value produced, determined by the total unpaid labour and divided among the different spheres of production according to the capital invested in each industry. I would say that Chapter 10 is clearly at odds with De Marco's interpretation that the general rate of profit changes as a result of the equalisation process.

Response to De Marco's Critique of Prices of Production as Equilibrium Prices

In his introduction, De Marco states:

> I argue that the excerpt does not provide evidence to support Moseley's (2019) long-run equilibrium interpretation in which the equalization of profit rates is achieved through the simple fluctuation of market prices. (De Marco, 2024, p. 146)

It is true that Marx does not say explicitly in this excerpt that prices of production are long-run equilibrium prices, but he assumes throughout this excerpt, in all the cases considered, that the profit component of prices of production is determined by the general rate of profit, which is taken as given and does not change. This is the equilibrium condition for prices of production, which are therefore equilibrium prices in this excerpt.

This is also true of Chapter 9 of Volume 3 and in the first draft of Marx's theory of prices of production in his discussion of Rodbertus in *Theories of*

Surplus-Value, Volume 2. The general rate of profit is determined as the ratio of the total surplus value produced in all industries to the total advanced capital in all industries, and this predetermined general rate is taken as given in the determination of prices of production, which again means that prices of production determined in this way (equal rate of profit in all industries) are long-run equilibrium prices.

As mentioned in the previous section, one of the main points of Marx's theory of market value in Chapter 10 is that *market value is an equilibrium price that assumes that supply = demand* and which is the centre of gravity of the fluctuations of market prices. And Marx said twice in this chapter that what he says about market value in this chapter also applies to prices of production.

> What we have said here of market value holds also for the price of production, as soon as this takes the place of market value. (Marx, 1981, p. 280)

> ... and everything that was said about this [market value] applies with the necessary limitations also to price of production. (Marx, 1981, p. 300)

Marx also explained in Chapter 10 that his theory is about the 'inner laws of capitalist production', which assume that supply = demand, and that political economy assumes that supply = demand '*in order to treat the phenomena it deals with in their law-like form* ...' i.e. to consider them independently of the appearance produced by the movement of demand and supply.

> The *real inner laws of capitalist production* clearly cannot be explained in terms of the interactions of demand and supply ... since these laws are realized in their pure form only when demand and cease to operate; i.e. when they coincide. In actual fact, demand and supply never coincide, or, if they do so, it is only by chance and not to be taken into account for scientific purposes; it should be considered as not having happened. Why then does political economy assume that they do coincide? *In order to treat the phenomena it deals with in their law-like form*, the form that corresponds to their concept, i.e. *to consider them independently of the appearance produced by the movement of demand and supply*. (Marx, 1981, p. 291)

And Marx also stated on the next-to-last page of Chapter 10 that his concept of price of production is 'the same thing' as the price concepts of Smith, Ricardo and the Physiocrats, which, of course, were long-run equilibrium prices with equal rates of profit or the average rate of profit.

> The price of production includes the average profit. And what we call price of production is, in fact, the same thing that Adam Smith calls 'natural price', Ricardo 'price of production' or 'cost of production', and the Physiocrats 'prix necessaire', though none of these people explained the difference between price of production and value. (Marx, 1981, p. 300)

De Marco argues that:

> Indeed, the whole analysis of the redistribution of capital across the various spheres of production developed by Marx in this chapter [Chapter 10] (and elsewhere) would not make sense if Marx had been interested in the long run equilibrium prices of production, as suggested by Moseley. (De Marco, 2024, p. 157)

We have seen above that there is very little analysis of the redistribution of capital in this chapter (only the four paragraphs towards the end), and this brief discussion explains how the redistribution of capital tends to result in a relation between supply and demand such that the average profit is the same in all industries; in other words, the redistribution of capital results in a tendency towards prices of production as long-run equilibrium prices. Not only does the redistribution of capital make sense in Marx's theory of long-run equilibrium prices of production, but the redistribution of capital is also *necessary* to 'bring about' a tendency towards long-run equilibrium prices of production. See Moseley (1999) for further textual evidence from *Theories of Surplus-Value* and Volume 3 of *Capital* that Marx's prices of production are long-run centre-of-gravity equilibrium prices.[17]

CONCLUSION

The main conclusions of this paper are:

(1) Marx introduced two new concepts in this manuscript – the rate of profit on the cost price (π) and the composition of capital of the cost price (θ) – to analyse the effect of unequal turnover times of the total advanced capital on the rate of profit on the total advanced capital and on prices of production. De Marco's paper ignores Marx's new concepts almost entirely.
(2) Marx's simple numerical example in this excerpt of his theory of price of production with unequal turnover times can easily be generalised to remove the 'limitations' that De Marco criticised.
(3) De Marco's alternative decomposition of the profit adjustment in the case of unequal turnover times is clearly inferior to Marx's decomposition because it assumes that the difference between the value and price of production depends on differences in the turnover rates of *advanced variable capital* instead of the turnover time of the *total advanced capital* (including the fixed constant capital), which is clearly not true.
(4) The components of the profit adjustment that transform the value of a commodity into its price of production (equation 11) identify the causes of the difference between the price of production and the value of the commodity and determine the magnitude of the contribution of each of these causes to the overall profit adjustment. Contrary to De Marco, the components of the profit adjustment do not indicate changes that will occur in future periods and will tend to eliminate these causes.
(5) Contrary to De Marco, Marx did not argue that the values of commodities tend towards their prices of production. Instead, Marx argued that the *market prices* of commodities tend towards their prices of production and their values are generally unaffected by the gravitation of market prices to prices of production.
(6) Marx took the rate of profit as given in his theory of prices of production in this excerpt and also in other drafts of his theory of prices of production in the *Manuscript of 1861-63* and the *Manuscript of 1864-65* (i.e. Volume 3 of *Capital*). Marx did not determine the rate of profit as the result of a

multi-period equalisation process that follows the single period that Marx analysed in this excerpt.

(7) Chapter 10 of Volume 3 does not provide textual evidence to support De Marco's interpretation that the rate of profit and prices of production are determined as the result of a multiple-period equalisation process. Chapter 10 hardly discusses the rate of profit and prices of production at all.

I think Marx's excerpt is an important advance for Marx's theory of prices of production. It answers the main remaining question with respect to this theory. It explains how the labour theory of value is compatible with equal rates of profit despite unequal turnover times of the advanced capital; indeed, the labour theory of value is necessary to explain prices of production with equal rates of profit in spite of unequal turnover times of the total advanced capital and unequal compositions of the cost price.

Moving forward, I think future work on Marx's theory of prices of production with unequal turnover times should be based on Marx's decomposition presented in this manuscript. More complicated numerical examples should be constructed, similar perhaps to Marx's tables in Chapter 9 of Volume 3. Empirical work on the extent of the differences in turnover times in different industries would also be useful.

NOTES

1. I thank Guido De Marco for our productive discussions over the last several years, from which I have benefitted greatly despite (and partly because of) our disagreements.
2. Throughout this paper, emphases in quote text are mine.
3. Henceforth 'the exerpt'.
4. Other reasons he briefly discusses are very long labour processes, very long production processes, and greater distances of the market from production. Note there are *two components of the turnover time of the total advanced capital* – that of *fixed capital* and that of *circulating capital*. The former is more than one year, and the latter is usually (and in Marx's excerpt) less than a year. The turnover time of the total is a *weighted average* of these (see Chapter 9 of Volume 2 of *Capital*, 'The Overall Turnover of the Capital Advanced'). Marx chose numbers in his base case such that fixed capital's longer turnover time was exactly offset by circulating capital's shorter time, making the overall turnover time one year (and thus $K = C$). See the Appendix to Moseley (2019) for an explanation.
5. The annual rate of profit assumes that the commodity is sold at its value, so it could also be called the value rate of profit.
6. If an individual capital had a faster than average turnover time (i.e. $K_i > C_i$), then A_t would be negative and the profit adjustment would be subtracted rather than added.
7. 'Average profit received' is shorthand for *profit that would be received if the commodity were exchanged at its price of production.*
8. If another capital had a lower than average composition of capital, then π_i would be greater than r_i and A_i^c would be negative.
9. An anonymous referee objected to this interpretation of the relation between Marx's two levels of abstraction and Hegel's moments of the Concept. I discuss this relation in detail in Moseley (2014).
10. This incorrect substitution of r_iC_i for π_iK_i also results in an incorrect equation for the total profit adjustment: $A_i = rC_i - r_iC_i = (r - r_i)C_i$, which is the basis for De Marco's analysis of the profit adjustment (see his Eq. 7 on p. 152).

11. De Marco does not mention Chapter 9 of Volume 2 on 'The Overall Turnover of the Advanced Capital'.

12. Personal communication.

13. Private correspondence.

14. Thus, market values in Marx's theory in Chapter 10 are clearly equilibrium prices with supply = demand; see especially pp. 286–296. More on this point in the next section.

15. This passage is further evidence that prices of production in Marx's theory are equilibrium prices at which the rate of profit is the same in all industries.

16. His reference looks like a second passage, but both references refer to the same passage in Volume 3 of *Capital*; MMV3 is the recent English translation of Marx's original Volume 3 manuscript in the *Manuscript of 1964–1965* (Marx, 2016), and KV is the Penguin edition of Volume 3.

17. An anonymous referee distinguishes an '*equilibrium*' interpretation of prices of production from a '*tendency*' interpretation and suggests my interpretation is an equilibrium one. However, mine is a 'center-of-gravity' interpretation: there is a *tendency* for market prices to gravitate toward prices of production, determined as explained above. Perhaps by 'equilibrium', the referee means a *stable* equilibrium with no tendency to change. But neither is that my interpretation; this also includes an inherent tendency for prices of production to *change* occasionally as a result of changes in the productivity of labour and other causes which I discuss in Moseley (1999).

REFERENCES

Bortkiewicz, L. (1952 [1906]). Value and price in the Marxian system (Part I). *International Economic Papers*, *2*, 5–60.

De Marco, G. (2024). Turnover time and Marx's decomposition of profit adjustment in the process of equalization. In *Value, money, profit, and capital today* (Vol. 39, pp. 145–165). Research in Political Economy.

Marx, K. (1981 [1894]). *Capital* (Vol. 3). Random House.

Marx, K. (2016 [1864–1865]). Marx's economic manuscript of 1864–1865, edited with an introduction. In F. Moseley (Ed.), *Historical materialism book series* (Vol. 100). Brill.

Marx, K. (2019 [1867–1868]). Marx's economic manuscript of 1867–1868 (excerpt). *Historical Materialism*, *27*(4), 162–192.

Moseley, F. (1999). *Marx's concept of prices of production: Long-run center of gravity prices*. www.academia.edu/27678884/Marxs_Concept_of_Prices_of_Production_Long_Run_Center_of_Gravity_Prices

Moseley, F. (2014). The Universal and the particulars in Hegel's logic and Marx's capital. In Moseley, F. & T. Smith (Eds.). *Marx's capital and Hegel's logic: A reexamination*. Brill.

Moseley, F. (2016). *Money and totality. A macro-monetary interpretation of Marx's logic in Capital and the end of the "transformation problem"*. Brill.

Moseley, F. (2019). Marx's economic manuscript of 1867-1868 (excerpt), editor's introduction. *Historical Materialism*, *27*(4), 145–156.

Sweezy, P. (1942). *Theory of capitalist development*. Monthly Review Press.

CAPITAL AS ORGANISATION OF RHYTHMS AND CRISIS AS ARRHYTHMIA

Stavros Tombazos

University of Cyprus, Cyprus

ABSTRACT

The three circuits of capital are crucial for understanding capitalist crises. The money-capital circuit reveals the rhythm of valorisation of value, the productive capital circuit reveals the rhythm of accumulation and the commodity-capital circuit reveals the rhythm of value realisation. In any individual case, the capitalist crisis results from a disruption of these three rhythms, i.e., their disconnection, which undermines the conditions of economic equilibrium. In other words, the capitalist crisis is an economic arrhythmia, which can result from the deceleration of the process of valorisation or of the deceleration of the process of realisation. The fall in the rate of profit led to the crisis of the 1970s. Under neoliberal policies, in conditions of slow productivity growth, surplus-value recovers at the expense of wage, creating difficulties in the process of value realisation. In the world of advanced economies, if one looks at productive investment in relation to industrial profit one detects a paradox, a peculiarity of the neoliberal era: Although industrial profit is recovering, productive investment does not closely follow. The surplus-value/investment ratio is on an upward trend. Capital is increasingly 'investing', not in production but in the very process of reproducing labour power. For a period of time, the deregulated financial system allowed the overcoming or, rather, the masking of problems in the process of value realisation, by transferring to the present a future demand through lending. With the increase in non-performing loans, the neoliberal schema of capital reproduction, which had an expiration date from the outset, collapsed in 2008.

Money, Value and Marx's Circuit of Capital
Research in Political Economy, Volume 41, 181–195

Published under exclusive licence by Emerald Publishing Limited
ISSN: 0161-7230/doi:10.1108/S0161-72302026000041023

Keywords: Circuit of capital; Marx; capital; economic rhythms; economic crises

INTRODUCTION

Marx's theory of capitalist crises is not systematically summarised in specific chapters in *Capital*. The reader must go through the three volumes of the book and identify in them those parts that are of most interest for the analysis of crises. To understand the historical crises of the system, many Marxist economists concentrate attention on volume three and especially on the tendency of the rate of profit to fall. However, the theory of crises in Marx is not mono-causal. The three circuits of industrial capital, as they appear in the first section of the second volume of *Capital*, are crucial for understanding capitalist crises.

The industrial capital is of course a human relationship based on the exchange of equal values in the framework of the general circulation of commodities, on the one hand, and the exploitation of the working class that produces more value in the production's process than the value of its labour power, on the other hand.

However, Marx explicitly argues that industrial capital is something more than a simple class relation. Analysing its status as an autonomous logic of economic rhythms, one can better understand the theory of capitalist crises in general and the 2008 crisis in particular. The latter is not only a financial crisis but a structural crisis of the neoliberal schema of reproduction, which is caused by the deceleration of the sustainable realisation's process of value.

THE CIRCULATORY PROCESS OF INDUSTRIAL CAPITAL

> Capital, as self-valorizing value, does not just comprise class relations, a definite social character that depends on the existence of labour as wage-labour. It is a movement, a circulatory process through different stages, which itself in turn includes three different forms of the circulatory process. Hence it can only be grasped as a movement, and not as a static thing. Those who consider the autonomization [*Verselbstständigung*] of value as a mere abstraction forget that the movement of industrial capital is this abstraction in action. (Marx, 1992, p. 185)

In the first section of the second volume of *Capital*, Marx analyses the movement of the 'self-valorising value', which can be presented in three interdepended processes or circuits. These are the circuits of money, productive and commodity-capital:

Circuit of Money-Capital: M-C...P...C′-M′

Money (M) is transformed into productive capital (P), through the purchase of commodities (C: material means of production and labour power). The production process, which is also the consumption process of productive capital, produces new commodities of higher value (C′) than those purchased (C), as they include surplus-value. When sold they are converted into money (M′) of equal value. Therefore, M′ − M = Surplus Value. To simplify his presentation, Marx initially considers that each stage of the circuit (M-C, P and C′-M′) is completed before the next one starts whereas, in reality, the three stages run simultaneously.

Marx believes that this circuit shows the capacity of capital to multiply itself through the production process and the exploitation of labour power that takes place in it. Because the quantitative difference between the original M and the final M′ is equal to the total surplus-value produced or the total industrial profit, this circuit pertains to the *rhythm of valorisation of value*. The total profit (surplus-value) of this industrial circuit is not necessarily the profit of the industrialist. Marx calls the latter 'profit of enterprise': the remaining profit after the subtraction of interest, dividend, etc.

Circuit of Productive Capital: P...C′-M′-C(′)...P(′)

Productive capital is transformed into commodities of greater value than the value of the means of production (including labour power) because they include surplus-value. A share of this surplus-value, however, necessarily escapes from the circuit because it is consumed privately by the capitalist. In the case of a simple reproduction of capital, the money (M) that will buy the necessary commodities (C) for the new production (the final P) does not contain any surplus-value since the industrialist entirely consumes it privately. Only in the case of expanded reproduction, apostrophes on the signs for the purchased commodity ($C^{(')}$) and for the new productive capital ($P^{(')}$) are needed. These apostrophes are put in brackets for two reasons: first, because they only apply in case of expanded reproduction and secondly, because the surplus-value to which they refer is only a share of the total surplus-value produced ($C' > C^{(')}$). In other words,

$P^{(')} - P$ = Surplus Value − Share of Surplus Value privately consumed.

Therefore, this circuit does not pertain to the rhythm of valorisation of value but to the *rhythm of accumulation of value*, that is, to the rate of growth of productive capital depending on net investment.

Circuit of Commodity Capital: C′-M′-C(′)...P(′)...C(′)′

In this circuit, as Marx argues, the process begins with the social recognition of the total value (including surplus-value) contained in the commodity (C′), which can be consumed individually or productively. Any problem in the realisation of its value decelerates the process. For this reason, this circuit pertains to the *rhythm of realisation of value*. In case of a simple reproduction of capital, the apostrophes in brackets are not needed for the same reasons discussed above. In the case of expanded reproduction, the apostrophe in brackets in the final commodity ($C^{(\prime)\prime}$) indicates that its value, which contains the new surplus-value produced, is greater than the value of the original commodity (C′).

As we will see, Marx's formal presentation of the three circuits does not correspond to some of its valuable developments in the first section of the second volume of *Capital*. This is because in the circuits with five terms, as presented by Marx, the *functional forms* of capital and its '*passive forms*' appear one after the other without being separated from each other. However, it is not difficult to transform the descriptive circuits with five terms in the functional circuits of capital with three terms:

Marx's formula for the circuit of money-capital is M-C. . .P. . .C′-M′. However, the first C does not function as commodity in this circuit because it will not be sold in its present form. C simply refers to the function of the original M, which buys the means of production from another capital and from the working class. This commodity (C) is 'passive' in our circuit and can be put into a bracket (even as P because the commodity C indicates the purchase of the means of production) or, in a brief version, deleted. M′ can also be put into a bracket or deleted because it simply indicates the function of C′ that consists in its conversion into money. Of course, a part of M′ (not the entire M′) will function again as capital, however not in this specific circuit but in the following circuit of money-capital. For the same reasons, one can eliminate the last term in the other two circuits of capital, as well as the commodity that does not function as such in each of them.

Applying the above-mentioned logic, the functional circuits appear as in the following Table 1:

Table 1. The Circuits of Industrial Capital.

	Descriptive Circuits	Functional Circuits	Functional Circuits (Brief Version)
I	M-C. . .P. . .C′-M′	M(P). . .P(C′)-C′(M′)	M. . .P. . .C′
II	$P\ldots C'\text{-}M'\text{-}C^{(\prime)}\ldots P^{(\prime)}$	$P(C')\ldots C'(M')\ldots M^{(\prime)}\ (P^{(\prime)})$	$P\ldots C'\text{-}M^{(\prime)}$
III	$C'\text{-}M'\text{-}C^{(\prime)}\ldots P^{(\prime)}\ldots C^{(\prime)\prime}$	$C'(M')\text{-}M'(P^{(\prime)})\ldots P^{(\prime)}(C^{(\prime)\prime})$	$C'\text{-}M^{(\prime)\prime}\ldots P^{(\prime)}$

It is clear now that every functional form of capital is necessarily a starting-moment, transitional-moment and end-moment in the process:

> The total process presents itself as the unity of the process of production and the process of circulation; the production process is the mediator of the circulation process, and vice versa. (Marx, 1992, p. 180)

More precisely, in the circuit of money-capital the production mediates the two stages of simple circulation (purchase of the means of production and sale of commodities), in the circuit of productive capital the sale of commodities mediates the production and the purchase of the means of production, and in the circuit of commodity-capital the purchase of means of production mediates the sale of commodities and the production.

The capitalist reproduction thus appears as a continuous sequence of the three functional forms of capital that coexist at each moment because of the total circuit of its transformations. This is exactly how Marx describes, in words and not in symbols, the total movement of capital:

> The total circuit presents itself for each functional form of capital as its own specific circuit, and indeed each of these circuits conditions the continuity of the overall process; the circular course of one functional form determines that of the others. [...] Different fractions of the capital successively pass through the different stages and functional forms. Each functional form thus passes through its circuit simultaneously with the others, though it is always a different part of the capital that presents itself in it. A part of the capital exists as commodity capital that is being transformed into money [$C'(M')$], but this is an ever-changing part, and is constantly being reproduced; another part exists as money capital that is being transformed into productive capital [$M(P)$ or $M^{(')}(P^{(')})$]; a third part as productive capital being transformed into commodity capital [$P(C')$ or $P^{(')}(C^{(')'})$]. The constant presence of all three forms is mediated by the circuit of the total capital through precisely these three phases. (Marx, 1992, p. 184)

The industrial capital appears here explicitly as an organisation of three fundamental rhythms: the rhythms of valorisation, accumulation and realisation of value. These rhythms are of course interdependent. Regular economic growth presupposes that they behave in relative concordance with each other. If the rhythm of valorisation is too fast (i.e., the annual profit rate is too high) in comparison to the rhythm of realisation of value, the rhythm of valorisation is slowed down decelerating also the rhythm of accumulation. In this case, the fall in the rate of profit is the result and not the cause of the crisis: The crisis of 1929 is of course a contested issue, but some important Marxist authors (for example Duménil & Lévy, 2011) argue that this crisis is not due to a fall of the rate of profit.

If, therefore, capitalist growth is based on a concordance of rhythms, the economic crisis is nothing else than the manifestation of an economic discordance of rhythms or an economic 'arrhythmia'. The latter results from a temporary discordance of one fundamental economic rhythm in relation to the other two.

As Marx points out, the industrial capital is a continuous process in which its functional forms manifest themselves as 'fluid forms, and their simultaneity is mediated by their succession'. (Marx, 1992, p. 184). In other words, we must read the three circuits of each individual capital, and certainly of social capital, not only horizontally (as a metamorphosis of each functional form) but also vertically (as the simultaneous coexistence of each functional form). The succession of the functional forms results in their simultaneous coexistence. In times of crisis, the incompatibility of the three rhythms of capital, their 'arrhythmia', manifests itself as a disproportion between the three functional forms of capital that coexist simultaneously.

Every capitalist crisis is the manifestation of a discordance of rhythms, in which the causal relationship can be different: The deceleration of the valorisation rhythm of capital, or the fall in the rate of profit, can cause a deceleration of the accumulation's rhythm of capital and economic growth. In this case, the rate of profit explains the crisis. However, it is also possible that the fall in the rhythm of accumulation and the rhythm of valorisation are caused from a structural deceleration of the rhythm of realisation of value. In this sense, Marx's explanation of the crisis is not mono-causal (Tombazos, 2014).

In the process of reproduction of social capital, some quantitative relations between its three functional forms that co-exist simultaneously must be respected. In the last part of the second volume of *Capital*, in very general terms, Marx attempts to determine these quantitative relations or necessary proportions between these functional forms (money-capital, productive capital and commodity-capital). Thus, a general idea of the schemas of reproduction of industrial capital is formulated. The circuit best suited to the development of such reproductive schemas is the circuit of commodity-capital or the circuit of realisation of value: $C'\text{-}M'\text{-}C^{(\prime)}\ldots P^{(\prime)}\ldots C^{(\prime)\prime}$.

The basic idea is this: A schema of reproduction of capital can perpetuate itself only if the supply of commodity values of the various productive departments is compatible with a distribution of social income that sustains the realisation of the commodities value. This means that distribution of money in the form of income, distribution of productive activities and hence distribution of commodities in a regime of accumulation are interdepended. Let us give a very simple example: If the value of commodities for working class consumption cannot be socially realised because the social distribution of income does not allow their purchase at their value, the rhythm of realisation of value decelerates. The three rhythms of capital are not compatible with each other. The economic crisis is nothing else than this 'incompatibility' or 'arrhythmia'.

The examples developed by Marx divide productive activity into two departments: Department I that produces commodities for productive consumption (the means of production except labour power) and Department II that produces commodities for private consumption.

The value of the annual product of Department I, which produces the material means of production, includes the consumed constant capital (Ic), the consumed variable capital (Iv) and the surplus-value ($Isur$): $Ic + Iv + Isur$.

By analogy, the annual value of Department II, which produces consumer commodities, is written as follows: $IIc + IIv + IIsur$.

In conditions of simple reproduction, to the supply of means of production corresponds the demand $Ic + IIc$ because capitalists should simply replace the productively consumed constant capital. So: $Ic + Iv + Isur = Ic + IIc$. By deleting the equivalent terms appearing on both sides of the equation, we see that the net value added of department I should correspond to the demand for constant capital of Department II: $Iv + Isur = IIc$.

Starting from the supply of Department II and applying the same logic, we end up in the same equation, with reversal of the left and right legs: $IIc = Iv + Isur$.

In conditions of expanded reproduction, part of the surplus-value will be productively invested in constant capital in both department (ic and iic). Therefore, another part of the surplus-value must be invested in additional variable capital (iv and iiv), and only the surplus-value remaining will be consumed privately by the capitalists (ip and iip). Therefore, the surplus-value in each department is now divided into three parts as follows: $Isur = ic + iv + ip$ and $IIsur = iic + iiv + iip$. Therefore, the value of the supply (left-hand leg of the equation) and the value of the demand (right-hand leg) of Department I and Department II can now be written as follows:

Department I: $Ic + Iv + ic + iv + ip = Ic + ic + IIc + iic$ or
$\boldsymbol{Iv + iv + ip = IIc + iic}$.

The part of the value offered by Department I to Department II, including its variable capital, the surplus-value transformed in additional variable capital and the surplus-value consumed privately by the capitalists, must correspond to the demand of Department II in constant capital.

Department II: $IIc + IIv + iic + iiv + iip = Iv + iv + ip + IIv + iiv + iip$ or
$\boldsymbol{IIc + iic = Iv + iv + ip}$.

The part of the value corresponding to the supply of Department II to Department I, including its constant capital and its additional constant capital (the new investment in constant capital), must be equal to the total demand of Department I for consumer commodities.

According to Marx, for capitalist reproduction to be relatively smooth, the reproduction schemas must be close to the above equilibrium conditions.

This not mono-causal explanation of capitalist crises allows a better understanding of the crisis of 2008.

THE CRISIS OF THE NEOLIBERAL SCHEMA OF REPRODUCTION

It is generally accepted that neoliberalism is based on the dogma that markets can regulate themselves. However, neoliberal economists (Alan Greenspan for example) do not hesitate to ask for a more active state intervention, when capital need it (for the stabilisation of the banking system, for avoiding a fast devaluation of private fictitious capital or financial derivative products etc.) For this reason, neoliberalism can be defined as the set of politics aiming at the rise of the exploitation rate of the working power and of the rate of profit. The Tokyo summit of 1979 can be considered the turning point into the neoliberal times.

Well-known Marxist authors attempt to analyse the crisis based on the 'tendency of the rate of profit to fall'. Michael Roberts is a prominent example. It should be noted, however, that even Roberts acknowledges that the rate of profit rose in the neoliberal period, i.e., from the beginning of the 1980s:

> In the G7 economies, the rate of profit fell secularly between 1950 and 2011 because in that period, the organic composition of capital rose much more than did the rate of surplus value [...]. But in the neoliberal period, when profitability rose, organic composition actually fell slightly while the surplus value rose significantly. (Roberts, 2016, pp. 223–224)

Without any doubt, the fall in the rate of profit in the 1970s has something to do with the crisis of 2008. However, if the profitability rose in the neoliberal period, as Roberts writes, one cannot explain the crisis as a direct result of 'the tendency of the rate of profit to fall'.

The research study of many Marxist authors confirms the upward trend of the rate of profit in the neoliberal period for the United States (Brenner, 2016; Duménil & Lévy, 2011, 2016), Germany (Schäfer, 2008; Weiß, 2015) or, more generally, the most important countries of advance economies (Husson, 2008, 2010; Tombazos, 2019).

If every capitalist crisis is a discordance of economic rhythms or an 'arrhythmia' of capital, the 2008 crisis seems to be caused from the structural slowdown of the (sustainable) realisation's process of value.

In the neoliberal times, the productivity of labour rose slowly in comparison to the post-war Keynesian period. However, in the neoliberal period, it rose very fast in comparison to the real wage. In Marxist terms, this is tantamount to the rise of the exploitation rate of the labour power or the rate of surplus-value (Surplus-Value/Wage). The evolution of the organic composition of capital, combined with the significant rise of the exploitation rate, permitted the progressive recovering of the rate of profit.

However, from the beginning of the 1980s in the United States and in European Union and from the mid-1990s in Japan, the rate of accumulation does not closely follow the increase of the rate of profit, as it was the case before: The former lags behind the rate of profit (Husson, 2008, 2010). This divergence between the rates of profit and accumulation is confirmed from the increasing ratio Net Operating Surplus/Net Investment in Fixed Capital or the ratio Surplus-Value/Accumulation: the former ratio approximates the latter (Tombazos, 2019).

If the ratio Surplus-Value/Accumulation is increasing, it is possible to show that the crisis of 2008 relates to the deceleration of the rhythms of realisation, avoiding the debate about the evolution of the rate of profit: The different Marxist estimations of the rate of profit mainly result from the mode of calculation of the stock of fixed capital while for the calculation of the ratio Surplus-Value/Accumulation are used (Tombazos, 2019) only current data (not stocks).

While the ratio Surplus-Value/Accumulation is increasing, the ratio Private Consumption/Adjusted Wage Share in the GDP is also increasing at all three major poles (United States, UE and Japan) of advanced economies. The increase of this ratio can be attributed to various factors, but the most important one for the understanding of the crisis is the increase of working-class household borrowing (Harvey, 2010; Lapavitsas, 2013; Tombazos, 2019). Economic instability arises when profits that are not productively invested are less and less consumed by the classes that appropriate them. If wages freeze while the debt of working-class households is constantly on the rise, wage earners spend some of their future income at the present time. This debt may be sustainable if the working-class ability to service it is not justifiably or unjustifiably challenged by the 'markets'. In the event of such a challenge, the whole regime of accumulation (or the schema of reproduction) collapses because the subjectivities that formed it (the 'markets') realise the fragile nature of its foundations. The ensuing panic leads to a financial crisis with the first obvious cracks in its foundations.

Applying the logic of the reproduction schemas of capital developed by Marx, it is easy to show that a reproduction schema based on an increasing working-class indebtedness is not sustainable in the long run. In the neo-liberal reproduction schema, as it has evolved from the early 1980s, the dynamic driving to the collapse was present from the beginning. It was just a matter of time.

The reproduction of capital that has been already implicitly suggested modifies the schemas developed by Marx as follows: In conditions of expanded reproduction, part of the total surplus-value is granted as a loan to the wage earners. Consequently, to the consumption corresponding to the wages of each period ($Iv + IIv + iv + iiv$), we must add the *consumption corresponding to loans granted to the workers* (*cglw*) in the current or previous periods and deduct the *debt service* (*dsw*) of the current period. Led us suppose for a moment that the real interests are zero, to deal with them separately:

Workers' consumption during the current period can now be written as follows:

$Iv + IIv + iv + iiv + cglw - dsw$. Their total consumption increases so long as cglw is greater than dsw.

The glw-surplus-value (the part of surplus-value granted to the workers as a loan) stimulates the demand for consumer commodities. However, to the extent that the glw-surplus-value is returned to capital, through gradual debt service, the rate of capital accumulation must accelerate in both productive departments, i.e., the productive consumption of constant and variable capital must increase in both departments. The supply and demand equilibrium of consumer goods and means of production is now achieved at a higher level of production.

Let us call the *glw-surplus-value that is returned to the capitalist through the gradual debt service* (for loans of the current and prior periods) *rglw*. This rglw-surplus-value will be invested in the two departments. One part of this amount will be invested in additional constant and variable capital in Department I (*icrglw* and *ivrglw*) and the other part in additional constant and variable capital in Department II (*iicrglw* and *iivrglw*). The equilibrium equation of each department can now be rewritten as follows:

Department I:

$Ic + Iv + ic + iv + ip + icrglw + ivrglw = Ic + IIc + ic + iic + icrglw + iicrglw$ or
$\boldsymbol{Iv + iv + ip + ivrglw = IIc + iic + iicrglw}$

The lending creates an additional supply (*ivrglw*) of Department I to Department II and a corresponding additional demand (*iicrglw*) of Department II for Department I:

$ivrglw = iicrglw$.

Department II:

$IIc + IIv + iic + iiv + iip + iicrglw + iivrglw = Iv + IIv + iv + iiv + ip + iip + glw - dsw$ or
$\boldsymbol{IIc + iic + iicrglw + iivrglw = Iv + iv + ip + cglw - dsw}$

Lending also creates an additional supply in consumer commodities (iicrglw + iivrglw) and a corresponding additional demand (cglw − dsw):

$iicrglw + iivrglw = cglw - dsw$.

Given that ivrglw = iicrglw, we know that ivrglw + iivrglw = cglw − dsw. Therefore,

$IIc + iic + iicrglw + iivrglw = Iv + iv + ip + ivrglw + iivrglw$, or
$\boldsymbol{IIc + iic + iicrglw = Iv + iv + ip + ivrglw}$

Just as in Marx's reproduction schemas, the supply of Department I to Department II corresponds to the demand of Department II for means of production while the supply of Department II to Department I corresponds to the demand of Department I for consumer goods.

Lending acts as a multiplier of production, investment and wages and/or employment. However, such a reproduction schema is only sustainable in the long run if debt service does not undermine wages: In this case, granting loans to workers becomes more and more risky for the capitalists.

Taking all other circumstances as equal, with a positive real interest rate, the schema of reproduction will, sooner or later, necessarily collapse. If we assume, simplifying our presentation, that the exploitation rate (Sur/V) and the share of the surplus-value allocated as a loan to total surplus-value (glw/Sur) do not change and if the time to pay back the loan with its interest (Int) is equal to one period (t), then we will have the following sequence (See Table 2):

Table 2. The Increasing Loan Amount and Dept Service.

Period	t_1	t_2	t_3	$\ldots t_n$
Loan amount	glw_1	$glw_2 + Int_1$	$glw_3 + Int_1 + Int_2$	$glw_n + Int_1 + Int_2 \ldots + Int_{n-1}$
Debt Service*	$glw_1 + Int_1$	$glw_2 + Int_1 + Int_2$	$glw_3 + Int_1 + Int_2 + Int_3$	$glw_n + Int_1 + Int_2 \ldots + Int_n$

*Corresponding to the loan amount, regardless of whether the debt service is not completed in the same period but in the next one.

The loan amount increases disproportionately to the glw-surplus-value from period to period because it includes the accumulated interests of the prior periods. In other words, the increase in the interest from period to period not only corresponds to the increase in glw-surplus-value but also to the cumulative interests of the prior periods. With a fixed interest rate (e), we can write the interest corresponding to the loan amount of each period as follows (See Table 3):

Table 3. The Increasing Interest.

Period	t_1	t_2	t_3	$\ldots t_n$
Interest	e.glw$_1$	e.(glw$_2$ + Int$_1$)	e.(glw$_3$ + Int$_1$ + Int$_2$)	e.(glw$_n$ + Int$_1$ + Int$_2$…+ Int$_{n-1}$)

Consequently, capital gains (interest) added to the surplus-value increasingly undermine the purchasing power of wages. For a reproduction schema to include a transfer of part of the surplus-value to wage earners in the form of consumer loans (including housing loans), the debt service should not rise continuously disproportionately to wages. However, given that debt service rises (in relation to the total borrowed amount) faster than the increase in glw-surplus-value, the Debt Service/Wage ratio rises constantly. In other words, the share of the total wage available for consumption constantly decreases.

Such an unbalanced reproduction schema will exhaust its absolute time horizon as soon as the proportion of disposable wages shrinks to such an extent that the reproduction of labour power is no longer compatible with debt service. It collapses, however, before exhausting its absolute horizon: once the so-called markets start to doubt whether the accumulated rights on future wages will be redeemed. The economic crisis thus manifests itself first in its financial dimension: as the accumulation of unsustainable private debts.

The financial system of the neoliberal period allowed the massive 'transfer' of future working-class demand to the present time through a rising private debt (Lysandrou, 2016), whose service has increasingly undermined the disposable income of wage workers. Hence, the neoliberal reproduction schema had an expiration date from the outset.

This reproduction schema shows, on the one hand, the multiplier effect of glw-surplus-value on production, investment, wage and employment, and, on the other hand, the corrosive impact of interest-bearing capital on economic equilibrium.

The financial 'bubble' (Mian & Sufi, 2008; Moatti, 2008) created before the 2008 crisis was a necessary condition for the accumulation's rhythm, which was to slow in comparison to the accumulation's rhythm of the upwards stage of the post-war cycle, but to fast in comparison to the economic sustainable realisation's rhythm in neoliberal times.

The neoliberal economists used to present the financial derivatives as a rational management of financial risk (Committee on Oversight and Government Reform, 2008). Their common methodological flaw was to implicitly consider the individual risk management as equal to social risk management. However, the continuous shifting of risk to the Generalised Other, instead of being rational risk management, transforms this risk from individual to social, from private to systemic and from local to national and global.

In Marx, money-capital is not an independent entity but part of the industrial capital. And of course, interest is only part of industrial profit. From the point of view of the owner of money-capital, however, the money (m) which he lends to the industrialist appears to exhibit the (meta)physical property to multiply itself over time. The same applies to the owner of money buying shares from the industrialist. The dividend, like interest, is not something different from industrial profit but only a part of it. Industrial profit includes all the subdivisions of surplus-value: profit of enterprise (the profit remaining in the productive business after interest, dividends payments, etc.), interest, dividend, etc.

Nevertheless, from the point of view of the securities purchaser and the lender, the process of valorisation of value is simplified to m-m′. In the phantasmagoria of stock markets and banks, money acquires the capacity to multiply itself by magic. In this metaphysical world thrives what Marx calls 'fictitious capital' (Chesnais, 2016).

Marx's analysis of interest-bearing capital, and more generally of money-capital as a seemingly independent form, emphasises the credit mechanisms linking capitalists to one another. However, in neoliberal times, there is another form of money-capital that is very important for the understanding of the 2008 crisis. When money-capital is used as credit extended to wage earners (Lattanzi-Silveus, 2018), the interest is not any more a part of the industrial profit or surplus-value, but a part of the wage. In this case, money-capital, through credit, leads to the growth of the purchasing power of wage labour in the present time but reduces (to a greater extent, unless the real interest rate is zero or negative) its future purchasing power because the wage earners must service their debt. This is tantamount to an increase in capitalist income through debt servicing. To the surplus-value produced in the process of exploitation of labour, power is added the interest. To the exploitation rate, the interest rate is added as a kind of 'direct exploitation' (Lapavitsas, 2013), which is not mediated by the productive consumption of labour power. The interest-bearing capital seems in this case to facilitate the reproduction of labour power in the present time independently of its reproduction in the future.

In other words, because in the neoliberal times the exploitation rate of the working class is increasing on the one hand while a share of the total surplus-value is 'liberated' to be used as credit to the working class on the other hand, the social surplus-product is not only the surplus-value through the exploitation of labour power in the production process of capital but also the interest through the 'investment' of money-capital in the reproduction process of labour power itself.

However, when the accumulation of rights over future wages, in the form of financial derivatives or classic loans, cannot be redeemed due to unsustainable debt and the collaterals of these loans are not sufficient, then these fictitious rights are, according to market terminology, 'toxic capitals' (Down, 2007): not only they are fictitious because of their seemingly autonomous life but a part of them does not represent any real value.

The impressive rise of fictitious capital in recent decades is also due to the increase in public debt, but it is mainly due to the growth of other forms of money-capital (financial derivatives of all kinds, interest-bearing capital, shares, etc.). The same money-capital appears with multiple faces, i.e. it appears in multiple accounting books (Chesnais, 2013).

The development of finance with the deregulation of the financial system in recent decades has played a double role at the global advanced economy. Firstly, through the increased mobility of money-capital and the more intense competition that has emerged from it, real wage growth has decelerated in favour of profit. Secondly, money-capital offset for a while the negative impact of the downward trend of the adjusted wage share of GDP on private consumption through the increase in private consumption of wage labour based on borrowing.

The industrialists buy shares from each other and from the financial sector, which also buys industrial shares. This is why the 'finance' does not really finance the productive sector through the stock market (Duménil & Lévy, 2000). Therefore, it is a mistake to explain the increase in the ratio Surplus-Value/Accumulation through the increase of the share of surplus-value appropriated by money-capital. The productive capitalists invest less and less in productive activities because there are not new productive activities that promise an 'acceptable' rate of profit (Husson, 2008). This is why they invest a large share of 'their' surplus-value in the financial sector. The rise of interests and dividends as a share of surplus-value is the symptom and not the cause of the increasing ratio Surplus-Value/Accumulation.

This is why the crisis of 2008 onwards is not only a financial crisis. It is the crisis of the neoliberal schema of reproduction, i.e. the crisis of the capitalist response to the crisis of the 1970s that was caused from the fall in the rate of profit (Mandel, 1982, 1995).

CONCLUSION

The possibility of such a crisis, a crisis that does not directly stem from the fall in the profit rate but from a growing part of not productively accumulated profit, is described by Marx himself in the third volume of *Capital*:

> Taking all other circumstances as equal, the amount of profit destined for transformation back into capital will depend on the amount of profit made [...]. But if this new accumulation comes up against difficulties of application, [...] i.e. if branches of production are saturated and loan capital is over-supplied, this plethora of loanable money capital proves nothing more than the barriers of *capitalist* production. The resulting credit swindling demonstrates that there is no positive obstacle to the use of this excess capital. But there is an obstacle set up by its own laws of valorization, by the barriers within which capital can valorize itself as capital. (Marx, 1991, p. 639)

And of course, this over-supplied money-capital 'develops the need to pursue the production process beyond its capitalist barriers: too much trade, too much production, too much credit'. (Marx, 1991, p. 640).

Monetary policies and state interventions, deviating from neoliberal orthodoxy as much as needed (quantitative easing, significant fiscal deficits especially in the United States), saved the neoliberal schema of reproduction from total collapse. Despite quantitative easing, household debt in advanced economies stopped growing after the 2008 crisis. Although it remains at a high level, the trend is rather downward. Quantitative easing has allowed government borrowing at very low or even negative real interest rates during a period of increased fiscal deficits. In contrast to profitability crises, value realisation's crises are characterised by a deflationary tendency. This is why trillions of dollars of quantitative easing have not led to inflation. Even the inflation of the recent period is imported into advanced economies.

Quantitative easing and fiscal deficits prevented a deflationary vicious circle. However, they could not ensure a new period of significant growth of GDP, on the one hand, and created new 'bubbles' in the stock markets, on the other hand.

The 2008 crisis is the crisis of the neoliberal response to the profitability crisis of the 1970s. A general increase in wages would have a positive effect on GDP, but it is not an option for capital. Such a development would change the power relations between the social classes, with the risk that realisation's difficulties would regress into a low profitability like in the 1970s.

Never in post-war history has there been such a long-term and at the same time general stagnation of labour productivity in the advanced economies as in the post 2008 period. This is why the same schema of reproduction survives only through accelerated social regression and crises of political hegemony that are already unquestionable in some countries.

REFERENCES

Brenner, R. (2016). *The economics of global turbulence: The advanced capitalist economies from long boom to long downturn, 1945–2005*. Verso.

Chesnais, F. (2013). The first five years of the on-going world economic and financial crisis. *Social Sciences: Trilingual Revue of Social Research, 2–3*, 148–162.

Chesnais, F. (2016). *Finance capital today. Corporations and banks in the lasting global slump*. Brill Academic Publisher.

Committee on Oversight and Government Reform. (2008). *The financial crisis and the role of Federal Regulators*. https://www.gpo.gov/fdsys/pkg/CHRG-110hhrg55764/html/CHRG-110hhrg55764.htm

Down, R. (2007). *CDOs: Toxic or tonic*. HSBC Global Research.

Duménil, G., & Lévy, D. (2000). *Crise et sortie de crise. Ordre et désordres néolibéraux*. PUF.

Duménil, G., & Lévy, D. (2011). *The crisis of neoliberalism*. Harvard University Press.

Duménil, G., & Lévy, D. (2016). *The historical trends of technology and distribution in the U.S. Economy: Data and figures (since 1869)*. http://www.cepremap.fr/membres/dlevy/biblioa.htm

Harvey, D. (2010). *The enigma of capital: And the crises of capitalism*. Oxford University Press.

Husson, M. (2008). *Un pur capitalisme*. Éd. Page deux.

Husson, M. (2010). *La hausse tendancielle du taux de profit*. http://hussonet.free.fr/tprof9.pdf

Lapavitsas, K. (2013). Profiting without producing. How finance exploits us all. Verso.

Lattanzi-Silveus, L. (2018). Consumer finance and labor exploitation. *Review of Radical Political Economics*, 1–16.

Lysandrou, Ph (2016). Colonization of the Future: An alternative view of financialization and its portents. *Journal of Post Keynesian Economics*, *39*(4), 444–472.
Mandel, E. (1982). *La crise 1974–1982: les faits, leur interprétation marxiste*. Flammarion.
Mandel, E. (1995). *Long waves of capitalist development: A Marxist interpretation*. Verso.
Marx, K. (1991). *Capital: A critique of political economy* (Vol. 3). Penguin Books.
Marx, K. (1992). *Capital: A critique of political economy* (Vol. 2). Penguin Books.
Mian, A., & Sufi, A. (2008). *The consequences of Mortgage credit expansion: Evidence from the 2007 Mortgage crisis*. https://www.moodys.com/microsites/crc2008/papers/cons_morg_cred_exp.pdf
Moatti, S. (2008). *La machine à dette. Alternatives économiques* (Vol. 274).
Roberts, M. (2016). *The long depression: How it happened, what it happened and what happens next*. Haymarket Books.
Schäfer, C. (2008). *Anhaltende Verteilungsdramatik*. WSI-Verteilungsbericht 2008. http://www.boeckler.de/pdf/wsimit_2008_11_schaefer.pdf
Tombazos, S. (2014). *Time in Marx. The categories of time in Marx's capital*. Brill Academic Publisher.
Tombazos, S. (2019). *Global crisis and reproduction of capital*. Palgrave-Pivot.
Weiß, T. (2015). The rate of return on capital in Germany - An empirical study. In *19th FMM conference: The Specter of stagnation? Europe in the world economy*. Berlin-Steglitz. https://www.boeckler.de/pdf/v_2015_10_24_weiss.pdf

THE CIRCULATION OF VALUE, RENT AND CLASS STRUGGLE: A CRITIQUE OF 'TECHNOFEUDALISM'

Fabian Balardini

The City University of New York, USA

ABSTRACT

Recently, several authors have advanced the argument that capitalism is undergoing a number of profound structural changes, leading to its own destruction and its replacement by an even more sinister economic system called 'Technofeudalism'. In this chapter, the author offers a critique of the Technofeudalism hypothesis by contrasting it with Karl Marx's analysis of the circulation of value, his perspectives on rent, and the theory of class struggle inherent in his framework. The author argues that Marx's theoretical contributions offer an alternative interpretation of contemporary capitalism, one that diverges from the claims advanced by proponents of the Technofeudalism thesis. Through a detailed examination and comparison of the conceptual frameworks of Marx and Technofeudalism, particularly concerning the theory of rent and its role in the circulation of value, the author assesses the validity of these competing claims by reviewing key stylized facts related to US capitalism. The author concludes by discussing how Marx's analysis of value circulation and rent provides important insights into the evolving forms of class struggle within the global capitalist system.

Keywords: Technofeudalism; rent; class struggle; value; surplus value; landlords

INTRODUCTION

According to Varoufakis (2023), capitalism has evolved into a new mode of production termed 'Technofeudalism'. From this perspective, traditional capitalist enterprises have been transformed into modern 'vassals', compelled to pay rent in

Money, Value and Marx's Circuit of Capital
Research in Political Economy, Volume 41, 197–209

Published under exclusive licence by Emerald Publishing Limited
ISSN: 0161-7230/doi:10.1108/S0161-723020260000041026

order to access new forms of 'fiefdoms' – digital platforms – owned by contemporary 'feudal lords', namely large technology corporations such as Google, Amazon, Apple and Microsoft. In this framework, workers function as the new 'serfs', continuing to be exploited by these 'vassal' firms. However, the nature of their exploitation has assumed a more insidious form, as they now contribute unpaid labour through voluntary activities such as uploading videos, posting reviews and generating content on digital platforms. Proponents of the technofeudalist hypothesis also identify the state as a key factor in this new mode of production. They argue that central banks, particularly through the implementation of monetary policies such as Quantitative Easing (QE), have facilitated the expansion of technofeudalist firms by providing them with 'free money', thereby enabling their extraordinary capital accumulation and the consolidation of their economic power. Varoufakis (2023) contends that QE policies serve as clear evidence of 'capitalism's emancipation from profits', asserting that 'central bank money has replaced capitalist profits as the system's fuel'.

The present study critically examines the theoretical foundations of the Technofeudalism hypothesis. While scholars advancing this perspective often situate their analysis within a Marxist theoretical framework, I argue that their conception of rent and class struggle diverges significantly from the theories found in Marx. This critique specifically engages with the work of Yannis Varoufakis, who has emerged as a leading proponent of the technofeudalist thesis.[1] By comparing the theories of rent and class struggle in Varoufakis (2023) with those found in Marx's *Capital*, I demonstrate that Varoufakis' interpretation of capitalism's transformation into Technofeudalism is predicated on theoretical assumptions that differ markedly from Marx's own analysis. Following this critique, I evaluate the empirical validity of key claims associated with the Technofeudalism framework by examining stylized facts regarding the evolution of US capitalism since World War II. Finally, I conclude by discussing the continued relevance of Marx's analysis of the circulation of value and rent in shedding light on contemporary forms of class struggle emerging within the global capitalist system.

On the Circulation of Value, Rent and Class Struggle: Technofeudalism vs Marx

Varoufakis on Circulation of Value, Rent and Class Struggle

In *Technofeudalism*, Varoufakis (2023) provides a detailed exposition of the theoretical concepts that underpin his analysis, particularly in Appendix 1. Although he identifies as a Marxist theorist, a close examination of these concepts reveals that his theoretical framework diverges significantly from that of Marx as presented in *Capital*.[2] Notably, two key methodological approaches central to Marx's analysis are absent from Varoufakis' work: the emphasis on class struggle as the primary driver of historical change and the reliance on a theory of value based on socially necessary labour time. Among the theoretical concepts Varoufakis employs, his definition of capital is the most aligned with Marx's understanding, as he describes it as 'a social relation that affords its owners extractive power over non-owners' (Varoufakis, 2023). However, the remainder of his conceptual framework is deeply influenced by Keynesian and Neoclassical economic traditions.[3] The central thesis advanced in *Technofeudalism* is that contemporary technological firms – such as Amazon, Apple, Google and Microsoft – have ushered in the end of capitalism by establishing a new form of capital, which he terms 'cloud capital'. He defines cloud capital as 'the agglomeration of networked machinery, software, AI-driven algorithms and communication hardware crisscrossing the whole planet and performing a wide variety of tasks'. Varoufakis further argues that under this new mode of production, 'the capitalist sector continues (as it did under capitalism) to produce all of the economy's exchange value. However, the capitalist sector is now embedded into, and is subjugated within, the broader realm of cloud fiefs built on cloud capital. As cloud capital accumulates, due to the unpaid labour of cloud serfs and the cloud rents of the vassal capitalists, more and more of the surplus value generated in the capitalist sector is siphoned off in the form of more cloud rent to the cloudalists'. Varoufakis contends that this transformation represents a worsening of capitalism, as it establishes a system of 'universal exploitation', wherein 'cloud serfs work for free to increase the stock of the cloud capital, which allows cloudalists to appropriate more and more of the surplus value that the capitalists extract from employees already converted into cloud proles whose work is guided and sped up by cloud capital'.[4]

A central argument of *Technofeudalism* is that class struggle has undergone a radical transformation: while capitalists continue to exploit workers, they themselves are now exploited by big-tech firms, which function as modern landlords. Furthermore, Varoufakis posits that this technofeudalist structure generates conditions for a persistent state of economic stagnation:

> Now what is happening is that at the center of techno-feudalism you have a capital sector, which is absolutely necessary. The capital sector is the only sector that produces value – exchange value in Marxist terms – but the owners of that capital, of old-fashioned capital, are vassals to the cloud capitalists. Their profits are being skimmed off. So surplus value is withdrawn from the circular flow of income by the "cloudalists". (Varoufakis, 2023)[5]

Regarding the concept of rent, Varoufakis distinguishes between profit and rent by arguing that, unlike profit, rent is insulated from market competition:

> Under capitalism… profit is vulnerable to market competition, rent is not. The reason is their different origins. Rent flows from privileged access to things in fixed supply, like fertile soil or land containing fossil fuels; you cannot produce more of these resources, however much money you might invest in them. Profit, in contrast, flows into the pockets of entrepreneurial people who have invested in things that would not have otherwise existed. (Varoufakis, 2023)

Accordingly, he maintains that rent is determined independently of competitive market forces.

Beyond his theoretical claims, Varoufakis presents a particular interpretation of class struggle, which is implicitly embedded in his historical analysis of the transition from feudalism to capitalism. He asserts:

> Capitalism in the eighteenth century and nineteenth century, when it emerged, overthrew feudalism, but it needed the feudal sector to continue producing food because otherwise we would all have died. That is why I'm saying that capital was parasitic on the feudal agricultural sector. So, it's not that one dies and the other lives. What happens is that capital takes over the hegemony of the system, but it is parasitic on the previous system. (Varoufakis, 2024)

Here, Varoufakis conceptualizes class struggle as a conflict between landlords and capitalists, presupposing that these two classes possess fundamentally irreconcilable interests. This perspective suggests that the advent of *Technofeudalism* represents the culmination of this struggle, in which landowners – now embodied by large technology firms – have prevailed over capitalists by leveraging cloud capital as a new instrument of domination.

The question remains: does this interpretation of capitalism's evolution align with Marx's theoretical framework? The following discussion critically examines this issue.

Marx on the Circulation of Value, Rent and Class Struggle

According to Marx, rent in capitalism fundamentally arises from the historical struggle among three distinct social classes: capitalists, workers and landowners.[6] Marx identified the conflict between capitalists and workers as the principal driving force of the system, wherein individual capitalists compete against each other by seeking to extract the maximum surplus value from their workers. The struggle between capitalists and landowners, on the other hand, revolves around the appropriation of the surplus value extracted from the working class. Additionally, Marx emphasized the conflict between landowners and the working class, characterizing the landowning class as adopting a passive-aggressive stance: it remains passive (and it does not get directly involved) in the process of extracting surplus value from workers, but it turns aggressive in preventing the working class from acquiring and cultivating land.

Marx conceptualized this trilateral class struggle as a consequence of the historical transition from feudalism to capitalism. Contrary to what Varoufakis suggests, Marx argued that landlords actively transformed themselves in response to changing economic conditions, facilitating capitalist farming and increasing rent-based profits. In Part VIII of *Capital, Volume I*, Marx provides a detailed account of the enclosure movement, a violent episode of class struggle that lasted approximately 300 years, during which peasants had their customary land rights deprived and feudal landlords were transformed into capitalist landlords (Marx, 1981). This transformation enabled landlords to replace feudal rents in kind with increasingly valuable money rents by prioritizing sheep farming over traditional agriculture. Instead of being passively exploited, as suggested by Varoufakis, landlords actively integrated themselves into the supply chains of emerging capitalist industries. For Marx, this transformation signified the shift from feudal rent to capitalist rent, wherein land became a non-reproducible means of production incorporated into capitalist accumulation.

Overlooking these historical developments, as Varoufakis does, fails to recognize the transformation of the feudal landowning class into a capitalist landowning class that, while subjected to capitalist imperatives, also benefits from them. In *Capital, Volume III*, Marx further theorized that in a fully developed capitalist mode of production, rent is determined within the competitive capitalist system rather than being an external factor, as Varoufakis suggests. Applying dialectical reasoning, Marx identified rent as both an obstacle to the free flow of capital investment and a facilitator of capital accumulation. He argued that landowners in capitalism play a dual role: as passive appropriators of surplus value and as active providers of non-reproducible means of production to capitalists. Marx stated:

> the landowner does play his role in the capitalist production process, not only by the pressure that he exerts on capital and not simply by the fact that large landed property is a premise and condition of capitalist production, but particularly by the way that he appears as the personification of one of the most essential conditions of production. (Marx, *Capital, Volume III*, Ch. 48)

This dual role is frequently overlooked by contemporary Marxist scholars, with some exceptions such as Bryer (2004, 2005), who highlights landlords' shift from passive rent collectors to active proponents of capitalist accumulation.

Beyond the transformation of landowners, Varoufakis also neglects another key insight analyzed by Marx: the circulation of rent as revenue within the broader circuit of capital. In *Capital, Volume II*, Marx conducts a detailed analysis of what he calls the circuit of capital M–C…P…C′–M′. Value circulates by taking the forms of money capital (M), commodity capital (C) and productive capital (P), where value is expanded and transformed into a larger amount of commodity value, which is sold, and a larger amount of money is earned by the capitalist (Marx, 1984). Failing to consider this analysis, which emphasizes value forms and the time it takes for value to circulate and expand, results in a failure to understand the connection between value circulation and value production in the process of capitalist accumulation. This, in turn, leads to a failure to understand how class struggle both shapes and is shaped by the production and circulation of value. Marx's analysis of value circulating as capital can be used to investigate how value circulates as revenue in the form of wages, profits, and rents. From this perspective, rent can be defined as a portion of surplus value appropriated by landlords as revenue by forcing capitalists to pay for the right to use their land as a (non-reproducible) mean of production. Landlords can then choose to dispose of this portion of surplus value, which they have appropriated as rent, in various ways as revenue.

To understand this point, let us consider four different forms that rent in the hands of landowners can take. First, we can identify rent taking the form of a 'hoard' or what Marx called '*money simply held as money*'. However, in capitalism hoards are never permanent as they are eventually 'thrown' back into circulation. As rent is not kept as a hoard, we can then assume the second form that rent can take as *money used for purchasing final goods*. Alternatively, rent can be used by the landlord to invest in a new circuit of capital and take either the third form as *money capital* (M), starting once again a new circuit of industrial capital, or in a fourth form as *money loan* by becoming M in a new circuit of commercial capital or M–C–M′ without involving production P of commodities. The point is that contrary to Varoufakis' assertion that rent simply becomes money taken out of the circulation of capital on a permanent basis, Marx argues instead that rent can be taken out of the circuit of capital only *temporarily* as a hoard, but that hoards can never become a permanent form of value as capital accumulation is driven by value expansion.[7]

What is important at this point is to emphasize that for Marx rent is value (more precisely surplus value) that appears as a flow of revenue paid by the capitalists to the landowner for the right to use a non-reproducible mean of production. Rent is then the outcome of both production (a portion of surplus value extracted from workers) and circulation (value that circulates in the form of revenue that represents payment for the use of a non-reproducible mean of production). This important insight about value circulation and rent leads, in turn, to a particular theory of class struggle. Unlike Varoufakis' perspective, which assumes that capitalists and landlords have irreconcilable interests, Marx's analysis suggests a more complex relationship. While capitalists and landlords struggle over surplus value appropriation, they also share a common interest in maintaining the exploitation of the working class by maintaining control and ownership of both reproducible and non-reproducible means of production.

Class struggle from this perspective takes place in a context of class domination: the working class that produces value and surplus value is exploited and dominated by a class that owns and controls the means of production (capitalists own reproducible and landlords own non-reproducible means of production). In other words, class struggle in capitalism is at its core a struggle between owners and non-owners of the means of production. However, the owners' class is divided into two antagonistic and yet dependent-on-each-other sub-classes (capitalists and landowners) that confront each other over the appropriation of surplus value. The capitalist class is forced to accept the existence of the landowning class since surplus value extraction depends on the enforcement of the law of private ownership of the means of production, which the landowning class is the embodiment of. The landlord class, in turn, is forced to accept the existence of the capitalist class because its own economic survival in the form of rent appropriation depends on the ability of the capitalist class to extract surplus value from the working class. In the capitalism envisioned by Marx – where capitalists and landlords struggle against each other over the appropriation of surplus value but are also united in their struggle against workers – we can see how capitalists and landlords can in some instances act as a united front against workers and in some other instances confront each other by adopting each other's strategies or by simply becoming the 'other'.

This dynamic relationship enables capitalists and landlords to alternate roles, adopting each other's strategies to maximize the appropriation of surplus value. For example, a capitalist may purchase land to extract rent, effectively becoming a landlord. Conversely, a landlord may invest rent revenues into industrial capital, effectively becoming a capitalist. Historical examples include 18th-century English factory owners who used profits to acquire land and become landlords. Similarly, contemporary tech corporations like Apple and Amazon, while functioning as capitalist enterprises, also act as landlords by charging rents (e.g., seller fees on digital marketplaces). In this light, capitalism allows the owners of the means of production to employ both profit-maximizing and rent-maximizing strategies to appropriate surplus value, contradicting Varoufakis' rigid separation of landlords and capitalists as adversarial classes.

Ultimately, Marx's framework provides a more nuanced understanding of rent and class struggle than the one presented by Varoufakis. Rather than depicting landowners as static victims of capitalist expansion, Marx illustrates their active participation in capitalist accumulation. Furthermore, his analysis highlights the fluidity between capitalists and landlords, showing how both groups can interchange roles in their pursuit of appropriating surplus value. The fundamental class struggle, then, remains between those who own and control the means of production and those who do not, with landlords and capitalists maintaining both cooperative and competitive relations in their exploitation of the working class. In contrast, Varoufakis' perspective lacks this dialectical complexity, resulting in an incomplete interpretation of rent and class relations within capitalism.

TECHNOFEUDALISM OR CAPITALISM AS USUAL?

Varoufakis argues that Technofeudalism has fundamentally altered modern capitalist economies in three key ways:

(1) Traditional markets have largely disappeared, resulting in a state of economic stagnation.
(2) Rent extraction has supplanted profit generation as the primary source of revenue for Technofeudalist firms.
(3) State intervention, particularly through QE, has facilitated the entrenchment of these firms' dominance.

In what follows, I review some stylized facts about the US economy for the last few decades to test the validity of these claims.

Claim 1: The Disappearance of Markets and Economic Stagnation

Varoufakis contends that the conventional profit-maximizing behaviour of capitalist enterprises has been supplanted by passive rent-seeking, exemplified by major technology firms such as Amazon. He asserts that the monetization of digital platforms, which utilize cloud-based rent rather than traditional profit-driven investment, have rendered markets obsolete, leading to economic stagnation. This claim can be empirically tested in several ways. Snow (2023) critiques the argument that cloud capital is immune to market forces, emphasizing that digital advertising – the primary revenue stream for cloud-based businesses – remains market-driven and competitive.

Furthermore, historical analysis suggests that rather than disappearing, markets have evolved through the interplay of capitalist and landlord interests. A pertinent example is the shopping mall industry, where landlords create physical marketplaces and extract rent from retail firms. The shopping mall business model finds a parallel in digital platforms, where companies such as Amazon, Apple, and Google establish virtual marketplaces and levy seller fees. The existence of these markets suggests that rent-seeking does not preclude market dynamics but instead integrates them into new organizational forms.

Rent appropriation that results from the creation and ownership of markets is neither an invention of modern big-tech companies nor the radical outcome of Technofeudalism in its overthrowing of capitalism. In fact, privately created and privately owned markets have been around since at least the Middle Ages when in feudal Europe monarchs awarded 'charters', or permits, to local lords providing them with the authority to create markets, to collect rent from sellers (merchants or commercial capitalists) and to strictly regulate the behaviour of all market participants on their lands (Dyer, 1994). Today, the shopping mall industry exemplifies the symbiotic relationship between capitalists and landlords, who collaborate to maximize the appropriation of surplus value in the forms of profit and rents.

The sector's trajectory illustrates this very clearly. The first shopping malls were established in the 1950s, and the growth of mass consumption throughout the so-called 'Golden age of Capitalism' (1950s-early 1970s) brought both high levels of profitability to capitalist retail stores and high levels of rents to shopping mall owners. This success led to the establishment of an estimated 25,000 shopping malls in the United States by 1986. However, success in markets attracts competition and concentration, causing both profits and rents to fall. The problems within this sector were exacerbated by the emergence of e-commerce in the early 2000s and the COVID-19 pandemic, resulting in shopping malls closing at a rate of 1,170 per year between 2017 and 2022. Today, it is estimated that 700 large shopping malls remain in operation in the United States. In 2025, the sector remains highly profitable for the surviving participants, with approximately five large mall owners controlling the sector.

According to Statista, the average monthly asking rent for malls in the United States increased across all regions from 2020 to 2024. For the capitalist retail stores in malls, this translated into an average rent-to-revenue ratio range of 8%–20%. Similarly, the rents collected by big tech companies on their platforms, known as *sellers' fees*, vary from 8% to approximately 45%. The higher rent level results from the different services provided by platform owners to sellers. In the case of Amazon, for example, sellers can be charged *sale-related fees* (which include referral and closing fees), *seller account fees and shipping/fulfillment fees*. The shopping mall sector also provides evidence of how rent-seeking landlords can become the 'other' (i.e., profit-maximizing capitalists' retail stores) if the right opportunity to increase their revenues in the form of profits, rather than rents, is presented. The COVID-19 pandemic presented this opportunity to Simon Property Group, the largest shopping mall owner in the United States at the time.

The lockdowns caused by the pandemic in mid-March 2020 led to retail stores' apocalypse as customers remained at home and shopping mall attendance collapsed. However, for Simon Property Group, this crisis created a profitable opportunity to acquire retail stores and giant firms such as Brooks Brothers and Lucky Brand Jeans at deeply discounted prices out of bankruptcy for a meagre $325 million and $140.1 million, respectively. Just a few months later, in November of 2020, another profitable opportunity emerged. This time Simon Property Group joined forces with Brookfield Asset Management (the second largest mall owner at the time)[8]. Together they joined forces and purchased giant retailer JCPenney for $1.75 billion. Under the new owners, JCPenney closed nearly a quarter of its 850 stores, following a typical capitalist cost-cutting strategy to stop incurring larger losses and hoping to regain profitability in the near future. By 2025, JCPenney had not only regained profitability but also had less than $500 million in debt, down from nearly $5 billion at the time of its bankruptcy filing.

This provides evidence that rent, as surplus value in the form of revenue, is not necessarily transformed into unproductive consumption, as suggested by Varoufakis. In these cases, hoarded rent by Simon Property Group and Brookfield Asset Management (the two largest landlord rent-collecting shopping mall owners) became money capital (M) and was used to acquire bankrupt capitalists' retail stores, allowing these shopping mall giants to expand their appropriation of surplus value now in the form of profits. Techofeudalism fails to understand that 'landlords' and 'capitalists' share the same objective of maximizing the appropriation of surplus value, and if surplus value appropriation via rent is threatened, then surplus value appropriation via profits can be adopted. Furthermore, the claim that Technofeudalist firms are hoarding their cloud revenue is easily disproven by the recent wave of billions of dollars spent on artificial intelligence (AI) by tech firms. Amazon, Alphabet, Meta, and Microsoft all accelerated their AI spending in the first half of 2024, and this spending is expected to continue in 2025, likely reaching over $400 billion, with similar levels of spending anticipated to persist throughout 2026. These events provide evidence that members of the ownership class (capitalist and landowners) are adopting new and more sophisticated strategies to increase the appropriation of surplus value extracted from the working class. Although these strategies seem to contradict the nature of the capitalist system, the opposite is the case: they are, in fact, providing increasing success to the class of owners over the class of non-owners and keeping capitalism intact as a system of expropriators and expropriated.

Claim 2: The Primacy of Rent as a Revenue Source for Technofeudalist Firms

Varoufakis suggests that firms such as Amazon derive their primary income from rent rather than conventional profit-seeking activities. However, this assertion is contradicted by financial data reported by these companies. In 2023, ironically, the same year that Varoufakis' book was published, Amazon declared profits of $30 billion, turning around a $27 billion loss in 2022.[9] Amazon declared that these profits resulted from its provision of a unique type of service in high demand: Amazon Web Services (AWS). However, what Amazon management failed to acknowledg was that as an efficient profit-maximizing capitalist firm, the company achieved this high level of profitability by engaging in an aggressive cost-cutting strategy that involved laying off 27,000 employees. Amazon's strategies are far from resembling the passive rent-taking behaviour of landlords, as suggested by Technofeudalism, and more typical of throat-cutting, aggressive capitalists, as described by Marx. Amazon's high level of profitability was also the result of its management adopting aggressive anti-labour strategies. The Occupational Safety and Health Administration (OSHA) has routinely cited the company for exposing workers to hazardous conditions at its warehouse facilities. Workers denounced that Amazon demands such a high pace of work that there is little time for necessities such as bathroom breaks. In response to these poor working conditions, Amazon workers sought to unionize at warehouses in Bessemer, Alabama, and Staten Island, New York. Amazon management responded by spending more than $4.3 million on anti-union consultants (McNichols et al., 2023).

Far from being a passive rent-collecting landlord, as suggested by Varoufakis, big tech firms, such as Amazon, behave more like insatiable capitalist firms that seek to maximize their profits at any cost.

Claim 3: The Role of the State in Consolidating Technofeudal Dominance

Varoufakis claims that the state is helping Technofeudalist companies consolidate their dominant role by providing them with 'free' money via QE monetary policies, but this overlooks a critical point. The reality is quite different; instead of providing free financing, the capitalist state is helping big tech companies, such as Tesla (another Technofeudalist company), remain profitable. A review of Tesla's financial statements reveals that it is one of the few firms that enjoys government subsidies in the worst possible manner: a third of Tesla's profits in 2023 were due to the sale of carbon credits. That year, Tesla earned $1.79 billion in total credit revenue. This revenue comes at no cost to Tesla, making it what the business press calls a near-pure profit[10] stream. Even more impressive, the company's total carbon credit revenue increased by 54% the following year, in 2024, reaching $2.76 billion. In other words, the creation of a domestic carbon credit market by the Federal Government enables Tesla to remain profitable simply by selling carbon credits. The tragedy of this act is that the carbon credits sold by Tesla are purchased by combustion-engine carmakers, allowing 'dirty' companies to continue in business. The climate continues to be destroyed, but Tesla is profitable, and 'dirty' carmakers are allowed to remain in business. This is the direct outcome of the neoliberal strategy to solve climate change by creating 'carbon markets'. Rather than merely offering financial support, government policies have played a direct role in sustaining corporate profitability through regulatory mechanisms. This outcome highlights the contradictions of neoliberal environmental policies, which commodify sustainability initiatives rather than implement substantive regulatory changes.

CONCLUSION

In this chapter, I offer a critique of Varoufakis' hypothesis of 'Technofeudalism,' advocating for a reconsideration of Marx's writings on the circulation of value and rent, along with his analysis of class struggle. I contend that Marx's insights provide an alternative interpretation of the current stage of capitalism, diverging from the Technofeudalism framework put forward by Varoufakis. By conceptualizing rent as value circulating in the form of revenue and positioning class struggle as a dynamic value in which landlords and capitalists, while competing over the appropriation of surplus value, share common interests in their collective opposition to the working class, we obtain a theoretical framework that suggests modern capitalism has not morphed into Technofeudalism. Rather, the extractors and appropriators of surplus value are adapting and implementing new strategies of domination.

In addition, the empirical evidence presented and reviewed in this chapter challenges Varoufakis' characterization of Technofeudalism as a distinct departure from capitalism. Instead, contemporary economic developments suggest a continuation and evolution of capitalist mechanisms. Market structures persist, albeit in transformed digital and physical spaces. Rent extraction, while significant, does not preclude profit-driven competition. Finally, state intervention serves to sustain rather than subvert capitalist imperatives. These findings suggest that, while the dynamics of surplus value appropriation are shifting, they remain embedded within a fundamentally capitalist framework, rather than representing a transition to a novel economic system. Future research could employ Marx's theoretical framework to explore how contemporary technologies controlled by big tech companies for their own benefit might be appropriated and repurposed for the benefit of the working majority. At this critical juncture, it is essential to focus on fostering solidarity to realize the moment Marx envisioned long ago – the moment when 'the expropriators are expropriated'.

NOTES

1. Varoufakis' analysis of Technofeudalism is part of and a continuation of a broader (and in many cases non-Marxist) theoretical current, including Srnicek (2016), Wark (2019), and most recently Durand (2024) and Dean (2025).

2. In previous writings, Varoufakis (2019) has called himself an 'erratic Marxist', acknowledging his divergence from any strict Marxist paradigm. In a recent article (Varoufakis, 2024), he has stated that his book *Technofeudalism* '. . .falls squarely within the Marxist political-economic tradition. I wrote it as a piece of Marxist scholarship'.

3. Varoufakis mentions in Appendix 1 that his analysis draws, in part, from the work of Keynesian thinkers (e.g., Keynes, Galbraith, Minsky). Using standard Neoclassical/Keynesian economics (as found in most modern introductory economics textbooks) he defines profit as '*the portion of the revenue capitalists retain after they have paid wages to workers, ground rent to landlords, interest and financial rent to financiers, plus fees to professionals (e.g., marketers, advertisers), helping them build up brand rents*'. Similarly, capital accumulation is conceptualized from a Neoclassical perspective as having both micro- and macro-determinants. Micro-determinants are '*the level of investment (financed by past profits and new debt), R&D investment, innovative designs, managerial strategies,*

etc.', while macro-determinants are '*capitalist's motivation to accumulate capital depends on the anticipated level of demand for her or his output which, in turn, is largely determined by the level of aggregate (or economy-wide) demand*' (Varoufakis, 2023).

4. By relying on Marx's concept of capital, he states that capitalists are vested with the power to extract and appropriate surplus value from workers. However, the concept of value is defined differently than in Marx. For Varoufakis, value has two 'natures': '*experiential value* which is obtained from *experiential labor*, and *exchange value* which is "*the quantifiable value of a commodity under capitalism*"'. Regarding these concepts, Varoufakis clarifies that '*In classical political economics (e.g., Adam Smith, David Ricardo, Karl Marx), what I call experiential labour is referred to simply as labour. I add the adjective experiential in order to distinguish it (labour-as-an-experiential-activity) from labour-as-a-commodity. See commodity labour – which classical economists referred to as labour power. In short, while classical political economists made the distinction between labour and labour power, I find it less confusing (and more enlightening) to define the two natures of labour as experiential labour and commodity labour*'. Surplus value is defined as '*surplus exchange value, since experiential value is purely subjective and personal, and thus cannot be surplus to anything*' (Varoufakis, 2023, p. 229). He further states that '*The greater the competition between several sellers, the closer the price of a commodity reflects its exchange value, which, in turn, is determined by (or reflects) the total experiential labour ... expended in its production by every human involved, directly or indirectly, in producing it*' (Varoufakis, 2023, p. 188).

5. Varoufakis has claimed (without providing any evidence) that the cloud-rent hoarded by Technofeudal companies amounts to about 40% of US GDP, which, he further adds, translates into a loss of about $11 trillion in productive investments.

6. Manning (2022) argues, correctly from my perspective, that the Marxist tradition has almost completely replaced Marx's view on class struggle among the three major social classes with the view that, in modern capitalism, class struggle is only a struggle between the capitalist and working classes. We cannot, however, accuse Varoufakis of making this error.

7. See Campbell (1998) for a discussion of money hoards.

8. According to Statista (https://www.statista.com/statistics/1269370/largest-shopping-malls-property-managers-usa-gross-leasable-area/), Simon Property Group owns 241 million square feet of gross leasable land, and Brookfield Properties owns 155 million square feet of gross leasable land.

9. https://www.seattletimes.com/business/amazon/amazon-reports-30b-net-income-for-2023-reversing-loss-in-prior-year/

10. https://carboncredits.com/teslas-carbon-credit-revenue-soars-to-2-76-billion-amid-profit-drop/

REFERENCES

Bryer, R. A. (2004). The roots of modern capitalism: A Marxist accounting history of the origins and consequences of capitalist landlords in England. The accounting Historians'. *Journal, 31*(1), 1–56.

Bryer, R. A. (2005). A Marxist accounting history of the British industrial Revolution: A review of the evidence and suggestions for research. *Accounting, Organizations and Society, 30*(1), 25–65.

Campbell, M. (1998). In C. Arthur & G. Reuten (Eds.), *Money in the circulation of capital in the circulation of capital: Essays on volume two of capital*. St. Martin Press.

Dean, J. (2025). *Capital's grave*. Verso Books.

Durand, C. (2024). *How Silicon Valley unleashed techno-feudalism*. Verso Books.

Dyer, C. (1994). *Everyday life in Medieval England*. The Hambledon Press.

Manning, F. (2022). A defence of the concept of the landowning class as the third class. *Historical Materialism, 30*(3), 79–115. https://doi.org/10.1163/1569206x-20221938

Marx, K. (1981). *Capital: Volume I*. Penguin Books.

Marx, K. (1984). *Capital: Volume II*. Penguin Books.

Marx, K. (1991). *Capital: Volume III*. Penguin.

McNichols, C., Poydock, M., & Edayadi, M. (2023). *Employers regularly engage in tactics to suppress unions*. Economic Policy Institute. https://www.epi.org/blog/employers-regularly-engage-in-tactics-to-suppress-unions-examples-at-starbucks-amazon-and-google-illustrate-employers-anti-union-playbook/

Snow, H. (2023). We're still living under capitalism, not "Techno-Feudalism" *Jacobin Magazine. Fall Issue*. https://doi.org/https://jacobin.com/2023/10/cloud-capitalism-technofeudalism-serfs-cloud-big-data-yanis-varoufakis

Srnicek, N. (2016). *Platform capitalism*. Polity Press.

Varoufakis, Y. (2019). *Confessions of an Erratic Marxist in the Midst of a repugnant European crisis*. https://znetwork.org/znetarticle/confessions-of-an-erratic-marxist-in-the-midst-of-a-repugnant-european-crisis/

Varoufakis, Y. (2023). *Technofeudalism: What killed capitalism?* Bodley Head.

Varoufakis, Y. (2024). Are we transitioning from capitalism to Silicon Serfdom? *Jacobin Magazine*. https://jacobin.com/2024/02/yanis-varoufakis-techno-feudalism-capitalism-interview. February 18, 2024.

Wark, M. (2019). *Capital is dead*. Verso Books.

'WHAT IS IT?' MARX'S THEORY OF EXPLOITATION AND THE CLOSURE OF THE TRANSFORMATION PROBLEM

Riccardo Bellofiore[a] and Andrea Coveri[b]

[a]*(Formerly) University of Bergamo, Italy*
[b]*University of Urbino, Italy*

ABSTRACT

In this work, the authors first critically discuss key contributions from Michael Heinrich, Isaak Ilyic Rubin and Claudio Napoleoni to emphasize the essential categories of Marx's critique of political economy and lay the ground for an original assessment of the transformation of values into prices. Moreover, the authors give a sketch of Marx's monetary value theory of abstract labour in the early chapters of Capital I, *highlighting the crucial challenges to be addressed. In particular, the authors propose a reconstruction based on the 'method of comparison' Marx presented in Chapter 5 of* Capital I. *Exploitation is there defined as the 'consumption' of workers as human living bearers of labour power, giving foundation to the identity between the money value added in the period and the direct labour as the objectification of the fluid of living labour. The authors also stress that, in Part 7 of* Capital I, *Marx viewed capitalist reproduction as a monetary circuit. Taking inspiration from Augusto Graziani, the authors claim that 'labour' is monetarily ante-validated by money as finance to production and that in this macro-monetary perspective, the real wage of the working class must be taken as given. It follows that the individual price determination can alter the allocation of the direct labour exhibited in the money value added but cannot affect neither the constitution of the new value by living labour nor the macro-class division of surplus value. Accordingly, the transformation*

Money, Value and Marx's Circuit of Capital
Research in Political Economy, Volume 41, 211–230

ISSN: 0161-7230/doi:10.1108/S0161-723020260000041028

problem turns out to be a misconstruction due to a misunderstanding of the very content of Marx' value theory.

Keywords: Absolute value; money as commodity; abstract labour; monetary (labour) theory of value; macro-monetary theory; exploitation; transformation problem

INTRODUCTION

We are convinced that most of the discussion on the transformation problem, both by those who thought it led to the rejection of Marx's value theory and by those who reclaimed that it had to be maintained, is marred by a profound misunderstanding of what Marx's value theory is about and of where it has a problematic status. This is particularly true for the debate going on in English.[1]

The reasons are manifold. With not too much an exaggeration, they can be traced back to the circumstance that hardly anyone bothers to thoroughly examine how the theory was constructed and to the circumstance that the English translations are systematically the worst around, even when they are good.[2] Nor the reading of *Capital* and the other Marx's economic texts is possible in English, or actually almost everywhere, in a *variorum* edition.[3] This also means that, in the current state of the scholarship, Marx's economic works should be made available in a parallel textual version.[4] Last but not least, what is a stumbling block in the discussion is that some interpreters pretend to find a consistent Marx – without ambivalences, indecisions or contradictions – to defend or reject. We instead favour a problematising attitude, which is the only one letting to go to the bottom of the question: what is truly fundamental in Marx's value theory, and therefore what are the significant difficulties to be dealt with, if any.

Consistently, in Section 2 we discuss a few authors who shared this attitude and whom we consider fundamental in highlighting the key Marx's categories that are worth focusing on. We refer above all to Michael Heinrich, Isaak Ilic Rubin and Claudio Napoleoni. Though we do not agree with some of their conclusions, we believe a serious discussion of their contributions is essential to move the debate forward. In Section 3, we examine what really is the value theory of abstract labour about in Marx's own formulation, and lay bare its complications, related to the key concepts of 'absolute value' and 'money as a commodity'. In Section 4, we propose a reconstruction grounded on Marx's alternative way to give reason for his theory of value in the method of comparison presented in Section 2 of Chapter 5, stressing a living labour perspective and clarifying the originality of Marx's notion of 'labour' (which encompasses labour power, living labour, direct labour, living labour power). In Section 5, we show that Marx's monetary value theory of abstract labour is at the same time a macro-monetary theory of capitalist production. In this theoretical setting, the transformation of values into prices is not a problem, as we clarify in Section 6. Section 7 concludes.

PROBLEMATISING MARX

Michael Heinrich On Ex Post Socialisation of Labour and the 'Two Worlds'

Until the 1960s, the theory of value as a theory of relative prices rested on a concept of socially necessary labour exclusively as a technical average and on an understanding of value as an equilibrium category. Money played no essential role. Michael Heinrich's book *Die Wissenchaft vom Wert* (*The Science of Value*)[5] is welcome on both counts because in it socially necessary labour is not understood as a technical-material category, and money is a constituent of value. Heinrich's standpoint stands in direct antithesis to all pre-monetary approaches: Classicals, Neo-Classicals, Neo-Ricardians and most Marxists as well. At the same time, Heinrich is in dialogue with the heterodox Marxian stream since the 1970s that emphasised capitalism as a unique and historically specific social form and was questioning the equilibrium paradigm. All these alternative strands had however to confront the problem Heinrich rigorously insists upon: what is it that makes labour commensurable before circulation? And what truly means the 'real' abstraction of labour?

Heinrich's believes that production is the world of the concrete, the private and the incommensurable while circulation is the world of the abstract, the social and the commensurable. Between these two worlds, there is no bridge. The very core of Marx's labour theory of value is considered to be the exposition of the specifically social qualitative form of labour. The difficulty Heinrich correctly disclosed may be staged in the following way. In a society of universal commodity exchange – which is capitalist, as the first sentence of *Capital* declares – labours are immediately private. The sanction of their sociality is *a posteriori* through money. The *differentia specifica* of capital is the *nachträgliche Vergesellschaftung*: the *a posteriori* socialisation of separate and independent labours. It is in circulation that abstract labour and value come into being, when the product is confirmed as use value for others and becomes a commodity.

This implies a twist in the notion of *socially necessary labour*. In the new conception – which, as Heinrich recalls, was introduced by Helmut Reichelt in 1970 – what counts beyond the technical average is that the use values produced must correspond to a social need represented by some monetary demand on the market. Without the monetary ex post validation, products do not become commodities, labour contained remains just concrete labour and the abstraction of labour is not accomplished. The commodity, before and independently of circulation, is not an 'objectuality' (rendered in the following as objectivity) of value: a *Wertgegenständlichkeit*.[6] The real abstraction of labour is only actualised in circulation, where the immediately private labour has to be revealed as a share of social labour. Value certainly has a quantitative dimension in the magnitude of value which brought up in production, but the ascertainment of the objectivity of value can only be completed in circulation, because value is eventually fixed there.

Heinrich expunges any reference to labour as already 'abstract' in production, where he insists that only concrete labour could be found. Benetti and Cartelier arrived at similar conclusions during the 1970s, but they were more radical and abandoned Marx's value theory at the end of that decade.[7] Heinrich tries instead to maintain Marx's value theory as a monetary theory of value. One of the authors of this work published an article in 1989 titled 'A Monetary Labor Theory of Value'. It is not by chance that 'labour' is missing from Heinrich's expression. The quantitative bringing back of profit to unpaid labour, which old and new Marxism holds so dear, is secondary to Heinrich. The defence of the labour theory of value as a theory of exploitation would transform Marx into a Ricardian socialist, he says: Marx's approach would be degraded to nothing else than a *moral* critique of capitalism from an *idealised* view of bourgeois society. After all, Heinrich contends, exploitation is a phenomenon common to different social formations, what is specific is domination by value.

For Heinrich, there is no quantitatively determined value system except *concomitantly* as the quantitatively determined price system. It will come then as no surprise that he reaches two conclusions. The first is that individual prices and individual values are not comparable and that these latter cannot precede the former. The second is that if socially necessary labour is to be understood according to the technical definition alone, then the redundancy critique of the Marx's dimension of value must be accepted. Both conclusions are right. Heinrich provocatively suggests that the aforementioned objections can be argued against Marx's own solution in Volume 3 of *Capital*. A pre-monetary value theory is entirely *unnecessary* to determine the pre-monetary prices of production, and here again, he is correct.

Unfortunately, when he argues that value and surplus value are essential, not so much for the calculation, but for the understanding of the categories of price and profit, this is a petitio principii. The validity of Marx's theory of value is implicitly assumed.[8]

Isaak Il'ijč Rubin and the Abstraction of Labour as a Process

Heinrich was partially anticipated in his questioning by Rubin. This author in his 1924 second edition of *Essays on Marx's Theory of Value* was bringing back value to the *moment* of exchange as such. Not anymore so in the *third edition* (1928) and fourth edition (1930), where the determination of value refers to the *unity* of content (i.e., labour) and social form (value).[9] The content, it is argued, is not something to which the form attaches itself from the outside. Rather, it is the content itself that in its development gives rise to the form. When we take as our starting point not the finite form, value as a determinate social form, but the content itself from which the form must necessarily arise, we must include in the concept of labour the social form of its organisation as it is given in commodity production, i.e., we must recognise abstract-universal labour as the hidden content of value already in production.

Rubin's message here is that abstract labour is latently already present in production before the final circulation of commodities. Abstract labour does indeed only exist in 'exchange', Rubin writes, but this latter is to be understood no longer as a 'moment' but as the *totality* encompassing production *and* circulation. In this way, Rubin endeavours to maintain Marx's movement of expression from the inner to the outer. In his unpublished *Essays on Marx's Theory of Money* of the second half of the 1920s – only recently printed in the original Russian and translated in German and English – Rubin writes that, before the final metamorphosis of value within the circulation of commodities, 'value-as-content' (i.e. labour) is *monetarily pre-formed* by 'value-as-form': ideal money that must materialise into real money, 'absolute value'. It must be stressed that Rubin's approach was dependent on Marx's view of money as a commodity.

Heinrich is fully aware that for Marx money is value embodied in a commodity: that is, that the bearer of the universal value form for him is a commodity, i.e., money is a product of labour. This is for Heinrich just an assumption that can and should be dispensed with. Marx was misled by the payment system of his time and unduly transferred an accidental historical circumstance into the necessary categorical succession. We don't think that Heinrich is right here.

Claudio Napoleoni on Absolute Value, Money as a Commodity, and Labour

Before discussing more specifically about Marx's way of articulating this issue, it is useful to discuss Claudio Napoleoni's position in the early 1970s.[10] He saw in abstract labour and value the same thing, first regarded as activity, and afterwards as its product or result. Exchange values, which we understand as the simple/direct prices proportional to the amount of labour 'contained' in commodities, are the necessary form of manifestation of value on the market.[11] There is a basic connection between the notion of abstract labour and that of money as the essential output of the capitalist process. The emphasis is on money as 'absolute value'.

On the definition of 'absolute value', there is a revealing uncertainty in Napoleoni. He sometimes argues that absolute value is value 'as such' made autonomous in exchange, divorced from commodities and existing alongside them, which is right, some other times that it is 'exchange value' made autonomous in exchange, which is wrong. Why this confusion, besides the circumstance that it is induced by the absence of the distinction between value and exchange value before the second edition of *Capital I*? We will have to return to this. For the moment, we anticipate that in Marx the 'commodity' as the product of concrete labour is a use value, and as the product of abstract labour, it is 'intrinsic value'. This latter, however, is also ideal money *before* final circulation.

In fact, this is the point that we already saw in Rubin. It is because of that ex ante 'monetisation' of intrinsic value that labour is the 'content' of value and that the money measure may be translated in time units. Money, as the external measure of value within actual exchange, is the necessary phenomenal form of the immanent measure of value, namely (abstract) labour time. In other words, money, as absolute value, is the intrinsic value incarnated in gold as money.

Napoleoni did not yet know Rubin, but his thought (as well as Colletti's after 1967) is in many ways parallel to that of the Russian economist. A decisive clarification from Napoleoni in the early 1970s went however beyond Rubin.

The universal exchange of commodities analysed by Marx in the first chapters of *Capital* has nothing to do with a 'simple commodity society' where independent producers, owners of the means of production, exchange their commodity output after the production process. The reason is that commodity production is universal rather than occasional only when labour power itself becomes a commodity. Capital is what posits the universalisation of commodity exchange.

Napoleoni's interpretation goes beyond Rubin's because the former explains why Marx deduced abstract labour not just from universal commodity exchange as such (as in *Capital*), but also from capital as a social relation, as the living labour of the wage workers (in the *Grundrisse*). The 'ambiguity' of the two definitions is deceptive since the two definitions are not alternatives to each other, but complementary. Napoleoni's position needs to be integrated with Rubin, in this way: the living labour of the wage worker should be interpreted exactly as latent abstract labour. It is a 'potentiality' which 'comes into being' in the eventual metamorphosis of the produced commodity with money. Note that this reading does not assert that value is created in exchange, but rather that it is actualised in the unity of capitalist production and commodity circulation.

The Rubin-cum-Napoleoni argument becomes that the living labour of the wage workers as the 'potentiality' of abstract labour – namely, the 'social form' taken by human activity in capitalist production – is the determining element of the capitalist totality leading to the 'actualisation' of abstract labour in the moment of circulation as a separate phase in the capitalist circuit.

The determinations of abstract labour in Marx lead us from the *final* commodity market (where labour, as direct labour, is *objectified* living labour), back to the *initial* labour market (where labour is labour *power*: workers become a predicate of their own capacity to work) and forward to the *centre* of the valorisation process, the immediate process of production (where labour is the *living* labour of the wage workers as 'other-directed' work: workers are a predicate of abstract living labour as value in process). Rubin and Napoleoni provide us with a *processual* understanding of the notion of abstract labour, which is lacking in Heinrich.

The peculiarity of labour power (that its use value, living labour, is that of being the source of value-as-content) parallels the one about money as the universal equivalent or the form of value (that its use value, gold, is the materialisation of value-as-form). The dialectics of 'value-as-content' and 'value-as-form' internal to the commodity is made external in the use values of these two 'special' commodities. In capitalism, money is capital; hence, it stays at the opening and at the closure of the economic process – it remains within circulation (until it is partially or totally extinguished), going in a 'cycle' or 'circuit' (the German word is the same, *Kreislauf*), which has money both as the starting point and as the end product.

The capitalist process is a monetary circuit where money first buys labour power on the labour market, and afterwards, the output of the living labour extorted from workers takes the form of value on the commodity-market. The real counterpart of money-capital in the preliminary exchange on the labour market is its purchasing power in terms of wage workers, the human living bearers of labour power, which is known once the value of labour power is given.

Unlike Heinrich, Napoleoni was fully aware of the essential internal connection between money as a commodity and Marx's theory of value. If money is a commodity and its value is given ex ante, the price tags of commodities anticipate the amounts of the substance of value within the commodities so that value exists before final circulation. But if money is not anymore conceived as a special (excluded) commodity, Heinrich's difficulty is still there: the occurrence of a seemingly unbridgeable gulf between production (which remains the realm of the concrete and incommensurable) and circulation (which remains the realm of the abstract and commensurable).

'WHAT IS IT?' MARX'S FOUNDATION(S) OF THE VALUE THEORY OF (ABSTRACT) LABOUR

To get rid of this *impasse*, the best thing is going back to Marx: to see from where the difficulty stems from and to check if there was an alternative path that Marx implicitly suggested to ground his value theory (as a theory of surplus value and exploitation). We think that as a matter of fact, this is precisely the case.

At the opening of *Capital I,* we find the 'commodity' as a singularity articulated in an internal duality.[12] The 'body' of the product to be sold on the market is declared to be the 'bearer' of an exchange value. In a first definition, exchange value manifests itself as the quantitative ratios in which use values are exchanged according to proportions that seem arbitrary and that may vary randomly with the perpetual fluctuations of supply and demand. According to Samuel Bailey, an 'intrinsic value' conceived as an exchange value immanent to the commodity would be a *contradictio in adiecto*.[13] Marx disagrees and qualifies this opinion as a 'semblance'. This opens to the concatenated series of arguments that lead Marx to a second, more appropriate definition of 'exchange value'.

One can twist and turn a commodity at will, but it remains immaterial as 'value'. While the natural 'objecthood' (its being an object) of the individual commodity as a use value is immediately accessible and tangible, its peculiar 'objectivity' of value, on the contrary, is different from that of Mrs Quickly in Shakespeare's *Henry IV*: one does not know where to possess it. At this moment in the exposition value is nothing other than a 'ghost': an ethereal presence that does not yet exist. Marx, however, does not stop there but goes on to show how the ghosts in commodities 'take possession' of a body through a real 'incorporation' or 'embodiment'.

In what? The body which is possessed is that of 'money as a commodity': money as a 'thing' produced by labour. Indeed, money is defined by Marx as 'embodied value': this is nothing other than absolute value, which has a 'fetish-character'. Marx intends to dissolve the 'fetishism' that spontaneously arises from the fetish. How? By showing, firstly, how this 'thing of value' necessarily springs from the social relationship that commodities entertain with each other.

And then, secondly, by clarifying how this reified social relationship hides another specific social relation between human beings in the 'form of life' that is given under capital as universalised commodity production.

To accomplish this task, and thus unravel the enigma of money, Marx turns to the form of value as the polar relation that unites and opposes commodities. The body of gold as money ('exposed' or 'exhibited' in circulation as that embodied value which is absolute value) acts as the 'phenomenal form' of the value 'as such' of the commodities which have been sold and thus as the phenomenal form of their 'intrinsic' values. At the same time, the concrete labour that produces money as a commodity acts as the phenomenal form of the abstract labour contained in the commodity sold against money. In a sense, it can be said that gold as money is 'the' commodity since abstracting from it leaves only the product as residue.

The (non-Ricardian) commodity nature of money cannot be so easily removed because the key role of 'money as a commodity' has little to do with the organisation of the national or international monetary system at the time. Rather, it provides the answer to the decisive Marxian question: *what is it?*[14] What is it that constitutes the qualitative unity that grounds the equivalence relation among the commodities exchanged on the market? Marx's response is: labour. In circulation, the abstract labour contained within commodities is 'expressed'[15] in the concrete labour embodied in money as a commodity.

In Chapter 3, Marx writes: 'Money is the absolutely alienable commodity because it is the *disembodied* shape of all other commodities, the product of their universal *externalization, alienation*'.[16] Alienation, as transferring to others a property by sale in commodity exchange, is an 'externalisation', and the embodiment in money follows a 'dis-embodiment' from the commodities. Money can be a 'thing of value' precisely insofar as it is itself a commodity, a 'materialisation' of labour. In the value relation among commodities, the universal equivalent, and therefore also gold as money, is at the same time the 'common body of commodities' and the 'ghost made flesh'.

It is important to understand that in these deductions, Marx is pursuing two movements at once: not only the 'exposition' or 'exhibition' of value in the unity of production and circulation, as stressed by Heinrich and Benetti & Cartelier, but also that of an 'expression' of value from the inner to the outer, as Rubin and Napoleoni highlight. Likewise, it is also important to understand that Marx saw no contradiction between the two movements because of his conception of 'money as a commodity'. From the moment that gold enters the circuit and its commodity shape takes on the figure of money, the value of money is fixed as a determinate quantitative amount.

The relative value of money is established at the source of its production, where it is engaged in 'immediate barter': that is why as soon as gold enters circulation as money, its value is already to be taken as a given. From this moment on, *price fixing* makes it possible to translate the notional (ideal) expectation of the value that will come to light in circulation into amounts of labour. This is a point on which Marx insists several times. If this 'representation' were to be disproved, this would simply result in a discrepancy between the value amount already existing as expected value at the end of production and the value amount that will be realised in circulation.

MARX ON EXPLOITATION AS THE 'CONSUMPTION' OF 'LIVING LABOUR POWER' IN THE HIDDEN ABODE OF PRODUCTION

Marx's argument we have summarised is established on the basis of the deduction of value from exchange 'as such'. There is, however, another line of reasoning in Marx that we believe can and should be articulated with the absolute value approach and that is based on the deduction of value as something that capital 'sucks' from the living labour of wage-earners: that is, from the 'squeezing' of the use value of labour power of which they are the human carriers. It is the argument that we find in the *Urtext*, but also in the *Economic Manuscripts of 1861–1863*, and then in Chapter 5 of *Capital I*.[17]

Marx's theory of value was concerned with explaining how valorisation is possible: that is, to account for the source of the money value added and thus also to understand the generation of surplus value. His answer lies in the 'consumption' of the human beings as living bearers of labour power (or 'living labour power')[18]: that is, in the (antagonistic) extraction by capital of living labour from their labour power. This argument – while providing a justification of Marx's value theory of (abstract) labour since it is the reason for the proposition that the money value added has its source in nothing else than the expenditure of living labour under the control and manipulation of capital – does not require money as a commodity.

Let us give some more details of how this view can be structured. The 'consumption' by capital of workers means that these latter are 'worked over' in production to generate the money value added within the period. After the buying and selling of labour power and before immediate production, the value of labour power is seen by Marx as already-determined while the living labour performed in the capitalist labour process is yet-to-be-determined.[19] In Chapter 5 of *Capital I*, Marx proposes a 'method of comparison'. If the living labour sucked from the living bearers of labour power were equal to the necessary labour required to reproduce them, there would be no surplus labour, no surplus value and no profits. Although hypothetical and capitalistically impossible, this situation is nevertheless capitalistically meaningful: a capitalist process, to be viable, must reproduce the working population at the historically given standard of living. In this kind of Marxian analogue of the Schumpeterian circular flow (it is a zero-profit reproduction), relative prices are proportional to ratios between labour values (simple/direct prices). However, the living labour that can be 'sucked up' from living labour power is not a technical constant but a social variable.[20] Being the labour time extracted from workers a 'fluid', it can be extended *beyond* necessary labour, thus generating what Napoleoni, in an unpublished note written in 1973, calls *profitti originari* [original profits].

Marx assumes that the length of the working day is the same for each worker so that original profits are proportional to employment. Their sum is total surplus value. In order not to confuse the study of the origin of capitalist surplus value with that of its distribution among competing capitals, Marx maintains the same price rule as in the circular flow. If we subtract from the total amount of living labour forced in capitalist labour processes (and objectified in the money value added within the period) the smaller amount of labour that workers must perform to produce the equivalent of the commodities they receive as wages (and objectified in the value of labour power), we obtain surplus labour (expressed monetarily as surplus value).

The peculiarity of labour power is that it is inextricably linked to the bodies of workers as 'living labour power', human beings supposedly 'free' and 'equal': they may resist the coercion of capital.[21] In this social uncertainty (which is not a given, but a result of social and political interventions) lies the ultimate ground for the fact that 'living' labour is the only source of money value added. Value as objectified labour, 'dead' in the commodity output and exhibited in monetary form, is causally dependent on the extraction from the wage-earners of living labour in the capitalist labour process as a 'contested terrain'.

What we have here is a viewpoint according to which in capitalism, the generativity of surplus is endogenously determined. It springs from the social form that production takes as the production of a surplus value to be actualised in circulation. Exploitation is nothing other than the 'use' of workers because getting labour power in motion is inseparable from the 'consumption' of living labour power. The whole of the new money value added is a monetary expression of the objectification of living labour. The inquiry moves from the 'inner' (the exploitative social relation between capital and labour, which takes place in the labour market and in the immediate labour process) to the 'outer' (the intersection of production and circulation and then the market relations between many capitals in competition).

Contrary to the usual assertions, exploitation is not just another variant of personal oppression after slavery and feudalism: it is rather the other side of the coin of the impersonal domination of capital. The opposition that many interpreters draw between Marx's theory of value as a theory of exploitation or as a theory of domination is unjustified.

It may be asked if our reconstruction of Marx dispenses of the notion of absolute value altogether. We don't think so. It is true that absolute value is no longer expressed monetarily in a particular (excluded) commodity like gold. It is however expressed in the monetary exhibition of the abstract labour, which is contained in the entire world of commodities. After all is what Sraffa writes in §10 and §12 of *Production of Commodities by Means of Commodities*, before being getting bogged down in the search for an invariable measure of value, which in our perspective is an altogether different, and not so interesting, problem.

A NEW WAY TO LOOK AT THE TRANSFORMATION

This way of framing the question of valorisation leads to a new understanding of Part 7 on reproduction and accumulation in *Capital I*. In these pages, the rate of surplus value is identified as the 'macroscopic' register of class exploitation in the social and monetary relation going on between capital as a whole and the working class. From this perspective, exploitation can only be accounted for in terms of the labour contained in the commodities that is required for their production.

When the argument is about the macro-monetary dimension, this 'value' rate of exploitation does not need to be adjusted because individual prices diverge from simple/direct prices. In fact, once it has been theoretically grounded in the way we have proposed, the basic macroeconomic identity between direct labour (i.e., the living labour objectified) and the new value originated in the period (i.e. the money value added) cannot change, whatever the price rule governing individual exchanges.[22] What can change is only the allocation of the direct labour according to the labour 'commanded' by commodity prices, i.e. the objectified labour obtained by producers in circulation in exchange of what they sell. The transformation of values into prices is shown to be a *false* problem, no less than the search for an invariable measure of value.

It may seem that the transition from a price rule in terms of labour contained to a price rule in terms of labour commanded has changed the mass of surplus value, redistributing part of it from one class to another. This is not so. The fact that the objectified labour which is 'commanded' (obtained) by commodities on the market differs from the labour which is 'contained' in them cannot affect the macro- and class distribution but only the amount of labour commanded allocated through firms' pricing, that is according to a micro and individual perspective.

In Part 7 of *Capital I*, Marx posits a logical priority of the macro-dimension over the micro-appearance (which may be both a phenomenal manifestation or a seeming). The rate of surplus value as the ratio between the labour congealed in surplus goods over the labour congealed in wage goods depends on class struggle in production, and it must remain invariant to changes in distribution and its consequences on pricing (it rather depends on capitalist class autonomous choices about level and composition of output). The ratio of (the labour equivalent of) gross profits over (the labour equivalent of) the money wage bill depends on the microeconomic price rule, which in turn depends on a multitude of institutional factors and above all on the form of competition between capitals.

TOWARDS A MACRO-MONETARY RECONSTRUCTION OF MARX'S VALUE THEORY OF LABOUR

For these conclusions to be valid, it is necessary to reconstruct Marx's monetary labour theory of value as a macro-monetary theory of surplus value extraction[23] and take as given the composition of output, which is determined by the capitalist class.[24]

In 1983, Augusto Graziani published an article titled 'Let's rehabilitate the theory of value'.[25] Valorisation must be looked at not from the point of view of individual capitalists struggling against their competitors but in a macro-perspective that sets the entire class of capitalists against the class of workers. It follows that the valorisation of capital for capitalists as a class can come only from the only exchange 'outside' that class: which means from the buying and selling of labour power and the ensuing production process. If the profit of capitalists as a class is born solely from the relation established between capitalists and workers, it can only come into being as a product of the difference between the total sum of the living labour extracted from and the sum of labour returning to the workers in the form of the real wage.

It is from the autonomous capitalist decisions (on expenditure and production) that derives the share of the output that is allocated to the working class. The assumption that the real consumption of the working class is given is perfectly reasonable, at least at this level of abstraction: agents' freedom of choice in consumption cannot be raised as an objection, since it is something that concerns workers as individuals, not the working class as such. This latter has no freedom at all: what they can get comes from social struggles outside the market arena, first of all within production.

Marx's depiction of the macro-class capitalist process is transparent in this quote from *Capital I*:

> The illusion created by the money-form vanishes immediately if, instead of taking a single capitalist and a single worker, we take the whole capitalist class and the whole working class. The capitalist class is constantly giving to the working class drafts, in the form of money, on a portion of the product produced by the latter and appropriated by the former. The workers give these drafts back just as constantly to the capitalists, and thereby withdraw from the latter their allotted share of their own product. The transaction is veiled by the commodity-form of the product and the money-form of the commodity. *Variable capital* is therefore only *a particular historical form of appearance* of the fund for providing the means of subsistence, or the *labour fund*, which the worker requires for his own maintenance and reproduction, and which in all systems of social production, he must himself produce and reproduce. (Marx, [1867]1976, p. 713; Marx's italics, our underlining).[26]

The capitalist monetary circuit is 'opened' by a transaction, which takes place within the capitalist class: industrial capital (i.e., the firm sector as a whole) has a preferential access to the initial finance provided by money capital (i.e., the banking system) who create bank credit ex nihilo. This financing is advanced as capital by the entrepreneurs as a class to include within the capitalist labour processes workers as human bearers of labour power and thus to get hold of workers' labour power as the potentiality of living labour.[27] In a true basic macro-monetary outlook the economy is 'closed', the firm sector is vertically integrated, and there is no state: initial finance condenses into the money wage bill.[28]

As anticipated, the capitalist class autonomously decides not only the level but also the composition of output, fixing the 'given' class real wage. When production prices diverge from simple/direct prices, the given (unchanging) real wage for the working class must be accounted for in terms of the former and not of the latter price rule. The money capital advanced (i.e., the initial finance as the flow of banking loans to firms, equal to the money wage bill) must be evaluated accordingly so that workers are allowed to buy the same subsistence class real wage, which has been fixed by class struggle. If we divide the money wage bill (W) for the price of the wage-basket, we have N, the number of workers employed within the period:

$$N = \frac{W}{pb} \tag{12}$$

Note that $p = [p_j]$ is the row vector of the production prices of wage goods and $b = [b_j]$ is the column vector of the wage goods basket; thus $pb = w$ is the individual money wage, thanks to which every worker buys his/her lot of the wage-bundle (we assume as Marx a given subsistence real wage). It is important to understand that we are not 'adding up' the individual wage-bundles to get the class real wage: logically, it is the opposite, and we just assume for the sake of simplicity that the 'given' *class* real wage is allocated uniformly among workers.

Bank credit money as the initial finance to production, i.e., the money wage bill, translates into a determinate number of workers as human living bearers of labour power. Since workers must obtain the class real subsistence wage from capital, the advanced wage bill – which at first glance appears to be 'valueless' advanced money capital – once it is regarded as finance to production, translates a 'labour content' corresponding to the labour required to produce the class real subsistence wage. It is therefore not 'valueless' at all. This makes it possible to quantify the total necessary labour time 'contained' in wage goods (i.e., the necessary labour, NL) even outside the 'money as a commodity' case as follows:

$$NL = (\lambda b)N \tag{13}$$

where $\lambda = [\lambda_j]$ is the row vector of the quantities of labour 'contained' in commodities.

Total variable capital exhibits NL in simple/direct prices. In other words, the definition of 'necessary labour' in terms of labour contained is not erased when the price rule changes, as long as the assumption of a given real wage for the class and a macroscopic viewpoint in maintained. Marx is crystal clear in the 'Results of the Immediate Process of Production' about what is going on:

> The buyer of labour power is nothing but the personification of *objectified* labour which cedes a part of itself to the worker in the form of the means of subsistence in order to annex the *living labour power* for the benefit of the remaining portion, so as to keep itself intact and even to grow beyond its original size by virtue of this annexation. It is not the worker who buys the means of production and subsistence, but the means of subsistence that buy the worker to incorporate him into the means of production. The *means of subsistence* are a particular form of material existence in which capital confronts the worker before he acquires them through the sale of his labour power. (Marx, [1867]1976, pp. 1003–1004; italics are in the text; underlining is ours).

Note that in this macro-monetary perspective, the 'two worlds' divide is circumvented from the start because initial finance acts as a monetary ante-validation of the forthcoming expenditure of living labour within production. Heinrich's challenge has no reason to emerge.[29] Money as finance (to production) is the monetary imprinting of labour power as potential labour in motion when workers are incorporated in the capitalist labour process through the buying and selling of labour power. Class struggle within the immediate process of valorisation results in an actual extraction of (both concrete and abstract) living labour, which is then crystallised in the objectified direct labour monetarily exhibited through the price tags that capitalist firms append to the output.

Marx very often assumes – though it is crucial to the critique of political economy that this cannot be taken for granted – that the ex ante expectations of capitalist entrepreneurs about the extraction of living labour are confirmed ex post. The resulting expected money value added corresponds to a determined amount of abstract labour turned into actual social labour in final commodity circulation. Marx also assumes – and it is crucial to the critique of political economy that this too cannot be taken for granted – that the ex ante expectations about the sale of commodity output are fulfilled ex post. Because of these assumptions, it is possible to quantify the money value added and exploitation even before the final circulation of commodities.

What is the qualitative significance of this disarticulation between labour 'contained' versus labour 'commanded' by commodities? Or, if you wish, between the ratio of surplus value on the one hand and the ratio of gross profits over money wage bill in terms of labour equivalent on the other hand? It should be evident that the second ratio distorts and disguises the exploitation of labour in production. From a class point of view, the only adequate measure of class exploitation remains the rate of surplus value accounted for by labour contained, which is invariant with respect to distribution.

A transfer of value seems to take place in circulation because capitalists and workers consume different kinds of commodities.[30] If workers were the main consumers of commodities whose production prices are higher than labour values, it would seem as if they receive a 'refund' (of part of what they have been robbed as producers) equal to the labour equivalent lost by gross profits compared to surplus value. In this configuration, workers would be less exploited than expected: under-exploited, as it were. If, on the other hand, workers were the main consumers of commodities whose prices were lower than their labour values, it would seem as if they are more exploited than expected: over-exploited, as it were.[31] Nothing of the sort, of course, since the real wage of the working class is given. What is going on is merely a redistribution of money value added so that total gross money profits may end up being less or more than total surplus value. It is not a redistribution between classes, just a change in the price form tagged by firms in different sectors: the fact that workers get more or less than labour contained in terms of labour commanded is irrelevant to the fundamental categories of capitalist exploitation: how much living labour (and hence how much *money value added*) capital as a whole is able to extract and how much necessary labour is required for the production of the commodities needed to reproduce the working class.

The (individual) price dimension adds to the 'fetishism' of bourgeois society and erases any trace of exploitation from the surface since the labour exhibited by the money wage bill is 'displaced' relative to the (unchanging) labour content of the real wage going to the working class. These 'displacements' and 'distortions' should not be ironed out. They are integral to Marx's analysis of capitalism as governed by what Hans-Georg Backhaus (quoting Marx himself) calls the *Verrückte Formen*, the 'deranged' forms which are value, money and capital as 'fetishes'.[32]

FINAL REMARKS

In this work, we engaged with the contributions of three scholars who, we contend, are fundamental to a proper understanding of Marx's critique of political economy: Michael Heinrich, Isaak Ilyic Rubin and Claudio Napoleoni. Heinrich provided an interpretation in terms of a monetary value theory. Rubin moved the first steps towards a view of the abstraction of labour as a process. Napoleoni contributed to the understanding of the key role of absolute value and of money as a commodity and showed the complexity of Marx's notion of 'labour': not only as labour power and as living labour but also as living labour power. While pointing out the reasons why we cannot agree with some of their conclusions, we argued that a serious discussion of these authors is also essential to unravel the alleged problem of the transformation of values into prices.

Going back to Marx, we gave a sketch of Marx's monetary value theory of abstract labour in the early chapters of *Capital I*. To this regard, we identified the following two difficulties: first, that intrinsic value has a real (and not only ideal) existence only as absolute value and that absolute value seems inseparable from money as a commodity.

To overcome these obstacles, we proposed a reconstruction grounded on an alternative line of reasoning, which is based on the 'method of comparison' Marx presented in Section 2 of Chapter 5 of *Capital I*. Exploitation is there defined as the 'consumption' of workers as human living bearers of labour power. In other terms, the Marxian notion of exploitation is founded on the peculiar feature that, under capitalism, the *whole* living labour extracted from 'free and equal' wage workers is a 'forced' and 'abstract-alienated' performance of labour as activity. It is in the pumping out of living labour of capital as a vampire that we find the most important meaning of Marxian exploitation: the direct compulsion to do labour and surplus labour. Capital must secure for itself labour 'in action' from potentially recalcitrant workers, who somehow can still claim control over their own activities. This 'Other' from Capital must be 'embodied' – the meaning here is that living labour power must be made internal to capital – so that value begets (more) value, money brings about (more) money.

The distinction in the notion of 'labour' between its various determinations (living labour power, labour power, living labour and direct labour), on the one hand, and the insistence on the 'variability' of the living labour made liquid by capital within the period, on the other hand, fundamentally confirm Marx's value theory of abstract labour as a theory of exploitation. This is indeed the ultimate foundation for the argument that the new value added in the period originates from nothing else than direct labour as the objectification of the fluid of living labour.

The serious stumbling block for this theory is not really the transformation problem. As argued, exploitation must be understood, first of all, as the consumption of workers as living labour power commanded by capital and then, as a consequence, as the prolongation of living labour over necessary labour. Its 'macro-monetary' and 'class' accounting in terms of 'labour contained' (values) is perfectly adequate. To support this, we stressed that in Part 7 of *Capital I* Marx viewed capitalist reproduction as a monetary circuit. Expanding his argument, and taking inspiration from Augusto Graziani, we claimed that 'labour' is monetarily ante-validated by money as finance to production and that in this macro-monetary perspective, the real wage of the working class has to be taken as given. The only thing that the individual price determination can do is to alter the allocation of the direct labour exhibited in the money value added: but this variation has to do only with the (objectified) labour amounts which are commanded on the market by prices. It can affect neither the constitution of the new value by living labour nor the macro-class division of surplus value: both are adequately accounted in terms of labour contained in money value added, surplus value and value of labour power.

In order to grapple with the distortions imputable to the 'micro' individual price setting, these must be grasped as part of the 'deformations' bound to appear in the reified exteriority of circulation, mystifying the reification process that originates in production. It follows that the transformation problem turns out to be a misconstruction due to a misunderstanding of the very content of Marx's value theory.

NOTES

1. For an article like this the references may easily explode. That is why we do not list all the contributions which are common knowledge among the scholars and limit ourselves to register the important few to develop what we think may be our novel or lesser-known inputs to the debate.

2. Translations in English usually want to allow a sensible comprehension of the individual phrase, not taking care of the systematic recurrence of the terms (which may carry a peculiar connotation) nor of their possible change of meaning as the argument move forward. That is why translations in other languages are usually better: they may be wrong on some concepts, but the mistakes are recurrent, and this is a great advantage for serious scholars. A new translation recently appeared by Princeton University Press, edited by Paul North and Paul Reitter (Marx, [1867] 2024a), which looks better but we did not check it properly yet.

3. This is the great advantage of the Italian translations edited by Roberto Fineschi for La Città del Sole (Marx, [1867] 2011) and Einaudi (Marx, [1867] 2024b).

4. The only translation of *Capital I* with a side-by-side translation, unfortunately incomplete, is Ehrbar (2010).

5. Cfr. Heinrich (1999).

6. *Gegenständlicheit* is the objectivity standing *in front of* human beings, as something which has its *origin* in the *processual* moment of *labour as activity 'becoming' objective*.

7. Cfr. Benetti and Cartelier (1980).

8. For a more detailed critical engagement with Heinrich's *Science of Value* see Bellofiore (2025), which is an English version of the latter author's introduction to Heinrich (2023).

9. Cfr. Bellofiore (2021) and Rubin (2025).

10. We base ourselves mostly on Napoleoni's 1972-73 *Lectures on Marx's Theories of Surplus Value*, that one of us has just edited in Italian (Bellofiore, 2024a), and on the 1973 second edition of *Smith Ricardo Marx* (Napoleoni, 1975).

11. We borrow de Vroey's expression defining commodity prices proportional to 'labour values' as 'simple prices', while Shaikh called them 'direct prices.'

12. It is essential to understand that we use translations of German terminology in an accurate way, that we cannot specifiy here as it should be: we avoid entirely 'appear', and distinguish 'seeming' (*Schein*) and 'phenomenal manifestation' (*Erscheinung*); we articulate the movement from 'representation' (*Vorstellung*) to 'exposition' or exhibition (*Darstellung*) to 'revelation' (*Offenbarung*), as well as from 'inner' to 'outer'; we separate 'fetishism' from 'fetish-character', the different meaning of 'embodiment', the complex articulation of the notion of 'labour', and so on. To go deeper, the reference is to the writings of Bellofiore since at least 2011. Since almost all the secondary literature (especially in English) is blind to these aspects, the Marx which is discussed is a Marx which is not Marx. To be sure, we are only now approximating an accurate, if tentative, appreciation of Marx's value theory.

13. The adjective (intrinsic, as proper to the individual commodity before exchange, absolute in this sense) predicates something contradictory to the noun (value, as something which cannot but be relative).

14. This question is posed repeatedly by Marx in English in the pages on Bailey to establish labour as the unity behind the 'world of commodities'.

15. 'Expression' here means a movement from the inner to the outer.

16. The best translation here is that by Ehrbar (2010) at p. 774 of his *Annotations*. Here we disagree with both the Princeton U.P. and the Einaudi translations: 'divested' or 'spogliato' instead of 'disembodiment' is too weak (though we may understand the translators rejonder that it is good enough: but it obscures the point we are raising about absolute value). As Ehrbar notices, Marx plays on the dual meaning of *entäußern* and *veräußern*: disembodiment and alienation. Marx's enquiry on absolute value is reconstructed in detail in Bellofiore (2024b).

17. According to the numbering of the chapters in the fourth edition. It would be Chapter 7 in the third edition.

18. The reader has only to check the many translations of *Capital* to see that almost always 'living labour power' is translated as either 'labour power' or 'living labour': they are not the same. In the Penguin edition of Volume I, paradoxically, the translation is wrong, but in the appendix including the *Results* it is correct.

19. As Rosa Luxemburg clearly understood in the chapter on 'Wage-labor' in her *Introduction to Political Economy*.

20. '[T]he feature that distinguishes labor power from all other input commodities is that *technical conditions do not determine the mass of use-values* (days of labor) that the capitalist receives when he purchases a unit of commodity (a worker for the production period). Given a specified technology, when a bushel of corn is purchased as an input for a particular industry, the quantity of other inputs and the quantity of output is determined. *When a unit of labor power is purchased* (e.g., a worker for the production period), *the quantity of other inputs required and the quantity of output remains indeterminate*, "a

circumstance [that] is without doubt, a piece of good luck for the buyer"' (Schweickart, 1989, p. 295; our italics; the quote in the quote is from Marx, *Capital I*, Chapter 5).

21. This does not in any way exclude the possibility that they may adopt a collaborative approach to production.

22. Messori (1978) was probably the first who argued for a normalisation condition based on the invariance of the social net product when it is computed in production prices or simple/direct prices, even before the authors associated with the New Interpretation. Cfr. Bellofiore and Coveri (2022) on this issue.

23. The reader is alerted that 'macro-monetary' in our sense is quite distant from the meaning in other Marxist approaches.

24. In the following we assume (as Marx does in *Capital III*, Chapter 10) that 'ordinary demand' drives production, an assumption which corresponds to Keynes's first hypothesis that short-term expectations of firms are fulfilled: the expected money value added is validated ex post on the commodity market. This equality between supply and demand is due to the fact that effective demand drives production (as in Luxemburg and Kalecki), not to the fact that supply creates its own outlets (as in Say's Law). At the same time, the employed workers receive the (expected) real wage. It is at this point that in Marx's exposition it can be argued that 'intrinsic value' will be fully actualized in circulation, so that abstract labour (i.e., the immediate private labours yet to be validated on the market) is also the labour socialised ex post on the commodity market.

25. It has been translated in English as Graziani (1997a).

26. See also in *Results*: 'It is not a case of the worker buying means of subsistence and means of production, but of the means of subsistence buying the worker, in order to incorporate him into the means of production' (MECW, vol. 34, p. 411).

27. As Arthur (2022, Chapter 16) wrote, we have here labour as an 'internal other', while land is an 'external other'.

28. We cannot delve into a description and an analysis of the monetary circuit (cfr. Bellofiore, 2019). Let we just remind a point which is usually unnoticed, and which can be misunderstood because of an important error of translation (due to the odd similarity of 'money' with 'moneta'). In 'La teoria marxiana della moneta' [The Marxist Theory of Money], Graziani (1997b) points out that in Marx a distinction must be made between 'money' (*Geld, denaro, argent*) and 'currency' (*Münze, moneta monnaie*). *Geld* is what exhibits abstract wealth, 'wealth in general'; *Münze* is the universally accepted intermediary of exchange and is one among many representatives of wealth in general. The valorisation process is defined money–commodity–more money, M-C-M′, the reference is to *Geld*, while the monetary circuit is defined as currency–commodity–currency, C-M-C, the reference is to *Münze*: '[i]f therefore the specific end of the capitalist is to acquire money in the sense of wealth in general, it still does not follow that the purpose of the capitalist is to accumulate currency' (Graziani, 1997b, p. 28; the translation has been amended). Why is the monetary circuit given by C-M-C [beware, C is currency!]? Because bank credit financing production is currency 'standing for' money capital. What Graziani is actually saying here is that the theory of the monetary circuit fully respects Marx when it represents the capitalist sequence in such a way that the 'currency' recovered at the closure of the circuit is (at best) equal to the 'currency' injected at the opening, and that this is perfectly compatible with the sequence money–commodity–more money. Graziani adds a quote by Marx confirming that when Marx discusses the nature of profit, he makes it clear that profit is acquired by the capitalists taken collectively solely in the form of commodities and not money as such.

29. Backhaus (1997) – who, like Heinrich, dissents with pre-monetary theories of value – significantly writes that although pre-monetary value 'as such' cannot be realised in a pre-monetary exchange value, it is, in its own pre-monetary character, extremely real. What is more: paraphrasing Adorno, Backhaus thinks of pre-monetary value as the *ens realissimum* ('the most real being'), i.e. the driver of the dialectical development that takes place in the movement of capital in the world market. We agree with Backhaus, yet his position does not surmount Heinrich's conundrum, until the *ens realissimum* cannot be

thought as monetary. To do that, a parallel between a processual vision of abstract labour and the monetary circuit must be constructed.

30. One of the very few authors who came near to understanding the issue was Eduard Heimann in his *History of Economic Doctrines: An Introduction to Economic Theory* (Heimann, 1945, pp. 151–152). Unfortunately, he concluded that the redistribution of portions of the value added in the period, so that total gross money profits may end up being less or more than total surplus value, means that the labour theory of value is thereby 'invalidated'. In this reading, Marx's value theory would fail because (gross) profits would stem not only from the process of production, at the expense of workers, but also from the process of commodity distribution or circulation, at the expense of consumers. Our take is very different.

31. Cfr. Bellofiore and Coveri (2022) for an analytical formalization.

32. The attribution of 'social powers' to value, money, and capital as fetishes is by no means an illusion. Even the 'productivity of capital' is a phenomenal manifestation of 'things as they are' within the capitalist historical determinacy. Fetishism, on the other hand, has to do with the naturalisation of these social powers, as if they emerged from things as things. Fetishism has its roots in the fetish-character of value, money, and capital. The attribution of social powers to the fetishes can be shown to be illusory only at a more profound layer of investigation, by ripping the veil of reification and going back to 'labour' as the source of the reification process.

REFERENCES

Arthur, C. J. (2022). *The spectre of capital: Idea and reality*. Brill. Historical Materialism Book Series. https://brill.com/display/title/15466

Backhaus, H. G. (1997). *Dialektik der Wertform. Untersuchungen zur marxschen Ökonomiekritik*. Freiburg: ça ira.

Bellofiore, R. (2019). Augusto Graziani and the Marx-Schumpeter-Keynes 'cycle of money capital': A personal look at the early Italian circuitism from an insider. *Review of Political Economy*, *31* (4), 528–558.

Bellofiore, R. (2021). Isaak Illich Rubin (1886–1937). In A. Callinicos, S. Kouvelakis, & L. Pradella (Eds.), *Routledge handbook of Marxism and post-Marxism* (Ch. 49, pp. 495–502). Routledge.

Bellofiore, R. (2024a). *La passione della ragione. Scienza economica e teoria critica in Claudio Napoleoni*. Mimesis.

Bellofiore, R. (2024b). Absolute value. In R. Bellofiore & T. Redolfi Riva (Eds.), *Marx: Key concepts* (Ch. 5, pp. 67–107). Edward Elgar.

Bellofiore, R. (2025). On some problems in Marxian theory. A discussion of Michael Heinrich's science of value. *Ethics & Politics*. forthcoming.

Bellofiore, R., & Coveri, A. (2022). The transformation problem. In S. R. Farris, B. Skeggs, A. Toscano, & S. Bromberg (Eds.), *The SAGE handbook of marxism* (Ch. 10, Vol. 1, pp. 171–187). SAGE Publishing.

Benetti, C., & Cartelier, J. (1980). *Marchands, salariat et capitalistes*. F. Maspero.

Ehrbar, H. (2010). *Annotations to Karl Marx's 'Capital'*. University of Utah. https://content.csbs.utah.edu/~ehrbar/akmc.htm

Graziani, A. ([1983] 1997a). Let's rehabilitate the theory of value. *International Journal of Political Economy*, *27*(2), 21–25.

Graziani, A. ([1986] 1997b). The Marxist theory of money. *International Journal of Political Economy*, *27*(2), 26–50.

Heimann, E. (1945). *History of economic doctrines: An introduction to economic theory*. Oxford University Press.

Heinrich, M. (1999). *Die Wissenschaft vom Wert. Die Marxsche Kritik der politischen Ökonomie zwischen wissenschaftlicher Revolution und klassischer Tradition*. Westfälisches Dampfboot.

Heinrich, M. (2023). *La scienza del valore. La critica marxiana dell'economia politica tra rivoluzione scientifica e tradizione classica*. Italian translation of Heinrich (1999) by R. Bellofiore & S. Breda (Eds.), trans. by S. Breda. Pgreco.

Marx, K. ([1867] 1976). Results of the immediate process of production. In *Capital* (Vol. I). Penguin Classics.

Marx, K. ([1867] 2011). *Il Capitale, Libro I* (edited by R. Fineschi). La Città del Sole.

Marx, K. ([1867] 2024a). *Capital* (Vol. I). Princeton University Press.

Marx, K. ([1867] 2024b). *Il Capitale, Libro I* (edited by R. Fineschi). Einaudi.

Messori, M. (1978). *Sraffa e la critica dell'economia dopo Marx*. Franco Angeli.

Napoleoni, C. (1975). *Smith Ricardo Marx*. John Wiley (Halsted Press).

Rubin, I. I. (2025). *Essays on Marx's theory of value: Conceived as a variorum edition* (edited and translated by S. Takenaga). Brill.

Schweickart, D. (1989). On the exploitation of cotton, corn and labor. In R. Ware & K. Nielsen (Eds.), *Analyzing marxism*. University of Calgary Press.

WHERE DOES THE MONEY COME FROM? MARX'S COMMODITY CAPITAL CIRCUIT AND THE REPRODUCTION OF TOTAL SOCIAL CAPITAL

Guido De Marco

Association for the Redistribution of Labour, Italy

ABSTRACT

Many scholars emphasise the centrality of the money capital circuit *in exposing the monetary* nature *of capitalist production relations,* thereby distinguishing it from *mainstream, neo-Ricardian and Sraffian* approaches. *Additionally, monetary circuit theorists dispute Marx's reference to* commodity money, arguing *that* only credit can monetise profits. *In doing so, however, they overlook the layered structure of Marx's dialectical method, which encompasses* not only the circuit of capital analysed in Volume I of Capital, but also *the* two further circuits of capital introduced *in Volume II of* Capital *and the analysis of capitalist credit forms in Volume III. Marx* maintains *that only the* commodity capital circuit *provides a suitable framework for moving from the analysis of individual capitals to that of total* social *capital and* its *relations. Within this perspective,* the monetisation of surplus-value is not inherently problematic, *as it* relies on capitalists' consumption and on their *monetary advances,* which actively finance *new production. Marx's choice to begin* Capital, *Volume I, with commodity money reflects a theoretically* grounded *view of capitalist relations, overlooked by Circuitist theorists who conflate the distinct levels at which monetary realisation and credit become relevant. He defers the* analysis *of capitalist credit* forms *to Volume III,* consistent with *the historically grounded premise that capital initially emerged where commodity money*

Money, Value and Marx's Circuit of Capital
Research in Political Economy, Volume 41, 231–251

Published under exclusive licence by Emerald Publishing Limited
ISSN: 0161-7230/doi:10.1108/S0161-72302026000041032

predominated. Only when expanded reproduction surpasses what *the* existing mass of *commodity money* in *circulation* can sustain *does credit become necessary. Reinstating the* commodity capital circuit *also* clarifies *the nature of capitalism as* inherently prone to crises, *the inadmissibility of treating social reproduction as a* sequence *of* self-contained static periods *and the* inadequacy *of theorising the formation of prices of production under the* constraints of simple reproduction.

Keywords: Commodity capital circuit; circulation of surplus value; expanded reproduction; capital accumulation; monetary circuit theory; capital reproduction

INTRODUCTION

Capitalist social relations are inherently monetary. This insight is central to Marx's critique of political economy and plays a crucial role in understanding the process of capitalist reproduction. Yet, fully grasping the monetary nature of these relations – especially at the level of total social capital reproduction – requires returning to a largely neglected element in *Capital*, Volume II: the *circuit of commodity capital.*[1] This circuit plays a pivotal role in Marx's account of the *overall accumulation process*, as well as in the connected problem of the monetisation of *expanded reproduction*, providing a perspective that challenges much of the contemporary debate.

Several reconstructions of Marx's analysis have rightly emphasised the monetary character of capitalism and the analytical relevance of the *money capital circuit*. By foregrounding the monetary nature of capitalist relations, these approaches challenge the assumptions of neo-Ricardian, Sraffian and mainstream traditions.[2] A central claim in this literature, especially in Augusto Graziani[3] (1982, 1990, 1992, 1997), a leading theorist of the monetary circuit, is that *commodity money* (gold) *cannot monetise profit* with credit created by banks or other financial institutions being essential to sustaining the reproduction of capitalist social relations.[4] This chapter challenges this interpretation.

Graziani's critique rests on a crucial methodological misunderstanding: it overlooks the layered structure of *Capital*, the movement from abstract to concrete, and assumes – mistakenly – that the *money capital circuit* provides Marx's principal framework for analysing the reproduction of *total capital*. In doing so, it neglects the *commodity capital circuit*. Moreover, it also fails to account for the historically determined nature of capitalist social relations, where the market is the outcome of a specific historical process.

The argument developed here is that the *money capital circuit*, while suitable for analysing the reproduction of *individual capitals*, is inadequate for understanding the reproduction of *total social capital*. When Marx shifts his focus to the interrelations between different capitals and the dynamics of accumulation as a social process in Volume II, it becomes evident that – unlike the money circuit – only the *commodity capital circuit* allows for an adequate representation of these dynamics.

Precisely by adopting the *commodity capital circuit* as his framework for the analysis of total reproduction, Marx shows that the monetisation of surplus-value as such does not pose a theoretical problem. What matters is the monetisation of *additional* commodity capital generated through accumulation – a question that emerges only at a more concrete level of analysis. It is here that the role of credit appears, not as a foundational element but as historically developed forms for financing circulation under conditions of continuous *expanded reproduction.* Marx's theoretical move from commodity money to capitalist forms of credit is therefore consistent, reflecting both a methodologically grounded shift across levels of abstraction and a historically grounded presupposition, since the development of markets presupposes a long historical process in which commodity money played a central role.

Building on the central questions posed by Circuitist theorists – where does the money for surplus-value come from? Should the analysis not begin with credit? Is Marx's assumption of commodity money in Volume I flawed? – this chapter demonstrates how these questions are resolved once the commodity capital circuit is properly restored. In doing so, these criticisms of Marx's monetary theory dissolve, while the primary challenge shift to understanding the monetary implications of the overall accumulation process and the related issue of realising *expanded reproduction.*

When the debate about why Marx begins with commodity money in the first chapters of *Capital* is framed within the broader theoretical framework of the commodity capital circuit developed in Volume II,[5] its function as a historically rooted expression and product of capitalist relations becomes clear. This framing also highlights Marx's postponement of his analysis of credit, as well as the shortcomings of the monetary circuit theory when applied to the total reproduction of capital. Ultimately, restoring the *commodity capital circuit* as a key analytical tool not only elucidates how the reproduction of total capital unfolds but also exposes three major theoretical issues: the nature of capitalism as *inherently prone to crises*; the inadmissibility of conceiving social reproduction as a series of static periods; and the inadequacy of deriving the formation of prices of production within the constraints of simple reproduction – a framework which among other crucial assumptions, treats these prices as constant, thereby undermining any rigorous comprehension of its dynamics.

GRAZIANI AND THE THEORY OF THE MONETARY CIRCUIT REVISITED

In Chapter 4 of *Capital*, Volume I, titled 'The General Formula for Capital', Marx introduces the money capital circuit, M ... P ... M′, building on the analysis developed in the preceding chapters. This formula distinguishes the circulation of money as capital from that of money as money. In the circulation of commodities C–M–C, money functions merely as a medium of exchange – 'selling in order to buy' (Marx, 1990, p. 247) – where money is spent and exits circulation (Ibid., p. 255). By contrast, when money circulates as capital, it begins with a purchase and ends with a sale (Ibid., p. 249):

> the buyer lays out money in order that, as a seller, he may recover money. [...] He releases the money, but only with the cunning intention of getting it back again. The money therefore is not spent, it is merely advanced [as capital].

This process unfolds in three interconnected phases, linked by valorisation over time (De Marco, 2023, 2024). First, capitalists advance M to acquire the necessary conditions of production – means of production, raw materials and labour power. Second, these elements are employed in the production and valorisation process. Third, the commodities produced, C′, are sold, realising M′. Successful valorisation means C′ > C and M′ > M. Here, Commodity capital is not merely a physical product but potential value, to be validated only through sale.

Graziani and other monetary circuit theorists adopt this view but criticise Marx's reliance on commodity money, arguing credit alone can monetise profits. If capitalists only advance M, where does the additional money required for M′ to realise C′ come from? I will now examine his critique of this alleged deficiency in Marx's analysis, which frames the issue I intend to challenge (Bellofiore, 2005).

In his essay L'Analisi Marxista e la Struttura del Capitalismo Contemporaneo (1982), Graziani identifies a difficulty in using the circulation of commodity money to describe total capital reproduction. When firms sell commodities, 'there is a problem regarding *the realization of profit in its monetary form*' (1982, p. 720) [emphasis mine].[6] This arises when firms and banks are treated as distinct sectors, even though all monetary income is spent within the system (pp. 724–725).

With banks providing funds for wage payments and workers spending their wages on consumption goods, firms can repay the borrowed capital. The difficulty, however, arises with the payment of interest (pp. 725–726):

> If firms must pay interest to the banks, they need to obtain a corresponding sum through the sale of goods. [...] For this to occur, there must be an equivalent monetary demand in the market. [...] This requires that the banks themselves have injected an equivalent amount of money into the circuit.

Graziani concludes that the issue 'can only be overcome if, for other reasons, an additional money injection occurs during the economic process' (Ibidem, p. 727). Still, he finds this unsatisfactory, as such mechanisms are 'completely independent of the monetary circuit, which, in itself, lacks endogenous elements that guarantee its equilibrium' (Ibidem). If a solution to the monetary realisation of interest cannot be found within the circuit, capitalism's self-sustaining nature is questioned. Graziani then acknowledges that firms typically cannot repay interest on their debt without external interventions (Ibidem, pp. 728–729). Banks, in their financing function, shift from a short-term credit position to long-term positions. Over time, firms may convert short-term debts into permanent obligations, merging the bank's credit position and ownership positions. The distinction between industrial and banking sectors collapses, which Graziani does not consider problematic. If firms and banks form a unified sector, and assuming all monetary income is fully spent, we get the following scenario (pp. 724–725):

> at the end of the production process, the firms would find themselves in this position: a) the total salary disbursed (equal to the initial loan received from the banks) would have returned entirely to the firms' coffers due to workers' spending [...]; b) the banks, which have earned interest on the loans they provided, [...] would also spend their entire income, thus enabling companies to repay their debt to the banking sector.

Graziani's approach ultimately rests on assuming a single sector, omitting exchanges between capitalists. This reveals a deeper theoretical issue: Graziani conflates the analysis of the monetary circuit of individual capital with that of total capital reproduction, overlooking the methodological distinction carefully delineated by Marx. The money capital circuit, precludes a complete analysis of circulation and bilateral relationships established in commodity exchanges – a limitation inherent in the circuit itself, which depicts the reproduction of individual capitals – whereas, when the focus shift on total capital reproduction a complete analysis demands the framework of the commodity capital circuit.

Although Graziani's framework may seem to resolve the monetisation problem, it implicitly assumes a planned economy, since capitalists must act as buyers and sellers in mutual exchanges. As long as the analysis focuses on individual capital's reproduction, as Marx does in the first volume of *Capital*, it may be valid to abstract from the specific distribution and composition of the produced commodity capital, and from the amount of commodity money needed to complete its circuit. This methodological decision mirrors the behaviour of individual capitalists, who may invest in any sector with favourable valorisation prospects. Thus, *analysing individual capital solely in terms of the money capital circuit is appropriate*. However, a full analysis of *total* capital reproduction must consider how capital is distributed to align with social reproduction needs. At least two sectors must be taken into account. Neglecting exchanges between capitalists amounts to assuming a planned economy rather than a capitalist one.

This confusion resurfaces in 1997, with similar theoretical inconsistencies. In this later article, Graziani briefly considers commodity money for capitalist exchanges (1997, p. 27) but subsequently downplays its significance, stating (p. 31):

> If, as seems logical [...], we consider the capitalist class as a unified whole, the transactions from firm to firm cancel each other out since they are within the sector, while all that remains are payments the firms make outside their own group, and, in a closed economy, these can only be to pay wages.

This point is reiterated a few pages later (Ibidem, p. 41). Yet, even accepting Graziani's class-level analysis, monetary circulation cannot be confined to capitalist-worker relations. Capitalists' expenditures before production include not only labour power but also means of production and raw materials acquired from other capitalists. Similarly, subsequent sales, which will eventually lead to the realisation of the surplus value produced, must involve purchases by both workers and capitalists. If the money capital circuit fully represented total capital reproduction, only the purchases and sales in the circuit's initial and final stages could be considered. Since workers receive their wages from capitalists, commodity circulation begins with capitalist purchases. If M–C were to represent total circulation, it would imply that all market participants are buyers. Likewise, the final stage assumes that all are sellers. Clearly, it is not possible for all capitalists to be buyers in one phase and sellers in the next, as they would have no one to buy from or sell to, respectively. In each phase, they must be both buyers and sellers. The money capital circuit, by definition, excludes the full analysis of circulation and the *bilateral* relationships established in commodity exchanges. Hence, the limitation of the money capital circuit is structural: it reflects the circuit own form, which confines the analysis to individual capital's reproduction. By contrast, the analysis of total capital reproduction demands a transition to the commodity capital circuit, where exchanges among capitalists – and between capitalists and workers – constitute the crucial link in social reproduction. Graziani ultimately argues as though employing the *commodity capital circuit*, examining the exchange of pre-existing commodities, seemingly unaware of this (Ibidem, p. 32). This oversight results in a contradictory account of the circulation phase, undermining the coherence of his overall argument:

> It is useful first to analyse the phase of circulation. In this phase, when firms exchange commodities *produced earlier* [my emphasis], nothing prevents us from regarding money as one commodity among others, and in view of its nature as a commodity, is best suited to function as an intermediary in exchange.

The crucial aspect here is that exchanging these pre-existing commodities in the circulation phase constitutes the initial stage of the commodity capital circuit. Graziani fails to recognise this, which results in a shift in his perspective without adequate justification (1997, pp. 32–33):

> The case of the initial exchange between capital and labour is different. In this case, as we have seen, what occurs is not the exchange of commodities already produced, but the initiation of an economic process that is suited to realizing commodity production. At the ideal moment in which the production phase begins, since no commodity exists, commodity money also cannot exist. Money must be therefore the purchasing power without being a commodity: The only nature it can therefore have then, is that of a valid and accepted promise of payment – in other words, credit money.

The idea that 'the production phase begins, since no commodity exists' – at least in terms of consumption goods for workers – appears unsubstantiated. In fact, 'the commodities produced earlier' (Ibidem, p. 32) that he mentioned previously must include these consumption goods. Nonetheless, Graziani adds (Ibidem, p. 34):

> as observed earlier, the real problem of money is raised only in relations between capital and labour, whereas in the circulation phase nothing prevents money from assuming the form of commodity if firms, which must regulate their own reciprocal relations, so deem. Thus, the international money may be gold without in any way altering the nature of the problem.

The claim in the last sentence casts further doubt on the coherence of Graziani's argument. If commodity money plays a central role in the international market, then the strict necessity of credit money at the level of total capital becomes not only less evident but entirely questionable. This raises the question of how the international market is formed and whether it has always existed, a reasoning dangerously verging on the assumption of the market as an ahistorical form of productive relation. Essentially, Graziani's argument that credit money arises from the exchange between capitalists and workers, with credit injections managed by banks, echoes his 1982 article.[7]

The contours of the issue are now clear. As I will show, Marx's distinction between individual and many capitals is fundamental (Rosdolsky, 1977, p. 26) to understanding total reproduction. At a more concrete level of abstraction – namely, that of total capital – the assumptions made in analysing individual capital's reproduction become the central issue (Marx, 2015, p. 295). This methodological shift, necessary for moving from the reproduction of *individual capital* to that of *total capital*, involves the passage from the analysis of the *money capital circuit* to that of the *commodity capital circuit*.

THE CONDITIONS FOR THE REPRODUCTION OF TOTAL CAPITAL

As previously argued, especially with reference to Graziani's work, scholars advocating the monetary circuit – or relying on the money capital circuit to describe total capital reproduction – often overlook the commodity capital circuit. When Marx designates the money capital circuit as *the general formula* for capital (Ibid., pp. 256–257), he is explicit:

> M–C–M is in fact therefore the general formula for capital, in the form in which it appears directly in the sphere of circulation.

This is Marx's first reference to a *general formula* that encapsulates the *reproduction of individual capital within circulation*. However, after completing *Capital*, Volume I, he drafted the manuscripts later forming Volume II, published by Engels in 1885. Here, he extends the analysis beyond the money capital circuit (Chapter 1) to the circuits of productive capital, P . . . P' (Chapter 2), and commodity capital circuit, C' . . . C′ (Chapter 3). Ultimately, he argues that individual industrial capitals operate through the unity of all three circuits (Marx, 1992, pp. 181–3). Why does Marx emphasise this unity at the *individual level*? Many Marxist scholars do not address this question. Instead, they assume that the money capital circuit either constitutes the sole or the most appropriate general form for analysing the circulation and reproduction of total capital. This view has also influenced the debate on the transformation of values into prices of production. For example, Moseley (2016, p. 377) argues:

> The meaning of 'general' is that this formula [of money capital, M . . . M'] applies *to all capitals together* [my emphasis], and thus applies to the total social capital and the total surplus-value.

Yet, *general* could equally mean that it applies to each individual capital. If Moseley is correct, why does Marx outline three *general* formulas in Volume II?

Marx explicitly designates each circuit as *general*, meaning these formulas describe the reproduction of any individual capital (Marx, 1992, pp. 176–7). Indeed, Marx argues that only the *commodity capital circuit* captures the *movement* of *total social capital* – the totality of individual capitals and their interrelations. The shift from individual capitals to total social capital cannot be reduced to the mere aggregation of *individual money capital circuits*. Many Marxist scholars and monetary circuit theorists, despite their familiarity with the first four chapters of Volume II, continue to prioritise the money capital circuit when analysing social reproduction. Why? Given the fundamental role of money in Marx's analysis, this may seem obvious. However, the issue is more complex.

While the money capital circuit is essential for understanding the reproduction of individual capitals, it is inadequate for grasping the broader dynamics of total capital in Volume II. At this more concrete level of abstraction, the overall accumulation process and the relations between capitals must be explicitly considered, making the distribution of commodity capital crucial – an aspect secondary when analysing individual capital through the money circuit. Marx argues that only the *commodity capital circuit* can adequately describe total capital reproduction and reveal its essential structure and dynamics (1992, pp. 176–7):

> But precisely because the circuit C' ... C′ presupposes in its description the existence of another industrial capital in the form C (= L + mp) (and mp comprises other capitals of various kinds, e.g., in our case machines, coal, oil, etc.), it itself demands to be considered not only as the general form of the circuit, i.e., as a social form in which every individual industrial capital can be considered (except in the case of its first investment), hence not only as a form of motion common to all *individual industrial capitals*, but at the same time as *the form of motion of the sum of individual capitals* [my emphases], i.e., of the total social capital of the capitalist class, a movement in which the movement of any individual industrial capital simply appears as a partial one, intertwined with the others and conditioned by them.

The commodity capital circuit must be seen 'as the form of motion of the sum of individual capitals'; it addresses problems 'whose solution *must be presupposed in considering the circuit of a single individual capital*' (my emphasis) (Ibidem p. 177). This passage clarifies why the commodity capital circuit is necessary: it brings into view the relations among different capitals, a condition the money capital circuit fails to capture, an issue further substantiated throughout *Capital*.

Marx also contrasts his approach with that of classical economists, who mistakenly used the productive capital circuit to describe total reproduction (Ibidem, p. 166), and instead praises Quesnay's *Tableau économique*, which employs the commodity capital circuit for this purpose. His preference for this circuit is reaffirmed in Chapter 20 of *Capital* Volume II, where he examines simple reproduction (Ibidem, p. 468). In the money capital circuit, M ... M′ (= M + m), the specific use value of the produced commodity capital and the capital and the distribution of surplus value are irrelevant since the circuit is concerned only with the movement from c to m. In contrast, for total capital, 'it is necessary to demonstrate what becomes of each part of the value of this overall product C″' (Ibidem, p. 469). The commodity capital circuit fully encompasses the circulation of previously produced surplus product, which is why Marx's reproduction schemes begin with the total commodity capital, including surplus value generated in the prior circuit.

The key point is that the commodity capital circuit encompasses the total circulation of the product, incorporating the final stage of accumulation from the prior circuit. In this process, capitalist ownership of both the objective and subjective conditions of production constitute the fundamental precondition for social reproduction in its capitalist form. Thus, the commodity capital circuit is not merely a supplementary element – it is the necessary foundation for accurately describing the total capital reproduction process.

THE COMMODITY CAPITAL CIRCUIT

The circulation of commodity capital (C′) comprises two segments: (C) and (c), as shown in the following Figure 1. The first segment covers productive consumption necessary to reproduce (C′). Capitalists sell commodities to acquire (Mp) (means of production and raw materials) from other capitalists and labour power (L), with the money advanced as constant capital and variable capital, respectively. Workers sell their labour power for wages to buy consumer goods. Capitalists then undertake production and valorisation, generating new commodity capital that re-enters circulation in the next circuit.

The second segment of total circulation concerns the disposition of surplus value (c), split into (c°) and (c*). The circulation of (c*) represents the portion of surplus value directed toward individual consumption, circulation costs, or rent — unproductive uses that do not re-enter the production process. If (c*) equals (c), no accumulation occurs (c° = 0), and the subsequent circulation of new commodity capital proceeds with the same amount of money (M′). If (c*) is less than (c), the money (m°) obtained from selling (c°) is advanced for additional labour power (l), means of production and raw materials (mp), enabling accumulation. If (c*) exceeds (c), circulation contracts as part of the commodity capital (C) required for simple reproduction leaves the reproduction process.

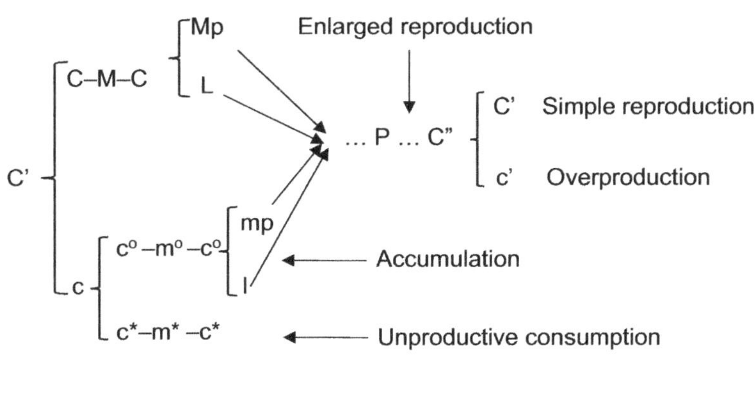

C' = M' = M + m° + m*; C' > C and c' > c°.

Fig. 1. Circuit of Total Social Capital Reproduction.

Enlarged reproduction ($C'' > C'$) occurs when accumulation ($c^{\circ} > 0$) takes place, valorisation intensifies or productive capacity improves (e.g. via faster turnover). Conversely, if reproduction contracts ($C'' < C'$), a crisis may ensue. Realising (C'') requires a *new* circulation, starting a new commodity capital circuit. Here, 'overproduction' (c') is the additional commodity capital produced over what was realised in the first phase.[8] (C'') may ultimately be realised only in the circulation phase of the next or subsequent circuits.[9]

Taking commodity capital as the reference framework does not imply disregarding that the three circuits of each individual industrial capital 'are continuously executed alongside one another' (Marx, 1992, p. 181) or that their succession is essential to their coexistence, which 'is itself only the result of the succession' (Marx, 1992, p. 183):

> The coexistence which determines the continuity of production, however, exists only through the movement in which the portions of capital successively describe the various stages. *The coexistence is itself only the result of the succession* [my emphasis].

To address specific issues, one may set aside the full complexity of the three circuits and focus on the most relevant one. The conditions ensuring the regular succession of phases within a given circuit, such as that of the commodity capital, also guarantee the coexistence of the three forms in which industrial capital reproduces itself.[10]

A superficial examination of the first phase of this circuit might suggest erroneously that a general equilibrium model, using simultaneous equations, capture some circulation aspects. Such a model sees exchange as a closed system, where commodities are redistributed and prices are set simultaneously. Yet, at this stage, the conditions for the next production process are merely posited, while the new commodities produced can circulate only in a later circuit – a crucial feature this approach misses, along with the temporal dimension of circulation that affects the turnover of the capital advanced.

Moreover, the essential purchase of labour power and its impact on subsequent production are misrepresented. Class structure, surplus value, and accumulation dynamics are absent. At this stage of circulation, there is no single price for each commodity but rather fluctuating market prices driven by supply and demand.

The general equilibrium approach also fails to recognise that capitalists, beyond withdrawing commodities for their (unproductive) consumption, have the money used for these purchases flow back to them (Marx, *Capital*, Volume II, p. 550). Finally, as Graziani (1977) argued, mainstream economists neglect money's role in the capitalist process; as Bellofiore summarises (2002, p. 121): 'From where does money enter the capitalist process? This issue remains an embarrassment for "bourgeois" general equilibrium theory, as the debate from Patinkin to Arrow-Debreu-Hahn to Clower to overlapping generations models clearly shows.'

The commodity capital circuit thus highlights the intertwined relationship between production, distribution, circulation, and accumulation, revealing how surplus value is either reinvested, devoted to consumption, or withdrawn from reproduction. By analysing the conditions ensuring the regular succession of phases within the commodity capital circuit, we gain a clearer understanding of how industrial capital reproduces itself as a whole.

WHERE DOES THE MONEY COME FROM?

In *Capital* Volume II, Marx convincingly outlines the historical role of commodity money and the reasons for choosing to begin his analysis with this form instead of credit money (1992, p. 192):[11]

> In considering the general forms of the circuit, and throughout this second volume in general, we take money to be metal money, excluding symbolic money, mere tokens of value which are specific to particular countries, as well as credit money, which we have not yet developed. Firstly, this is the course taken by history: credit money played no role, or at least not a significant one, in the early period of capitalist production. Secondly, the necessity of this course can be proved theoretically, in so far as everything critical that has so far been said about the circulation of credit money by Tooke and others compelled them time and again to look back at how the matter would present itself on the basis of mere metallic circulation.

Marx's choice proves its soundness precisely when addressing surplus value circulation, the issue Graziani highlights. In the money capital circuit, the initial commodity money is insufficient to close the circuit, as additional commodity capital must circulate. Graziani thus argues that any analysis of capital should begin with credit, as it can be readily expanded. Though his approach has limits, he raises a crucial question: How can surplus value be monetised without new credit?

Marx's Approach to the Circulation of Surplus-Value

Marx addresses this issue several times, first in Volume II of *Capital*, Chapter 17, 'The Circulation of Surplus-Value', where he distinguishes between the creation of surplus value and the amount of money required for its circulation (Marx, 1992, p. 404):

> An opponent of Tooke, who supports the form M–C–M′, asked him how the capitalist always managed to withdraw more money from circulation than he cast into it. Let us be clear that what is involved here is not the formation of surplus-value. ... [T]he question is not: where does surplus-value come from? But rather: where does the money come from which it is turned into?

Marx later asks 'Where does the money for this [surplus value] come from?' (Ibidem, p. 405) and answers by referring to the general analysis of commodity circulation (Ibidem, p. 407):

> The general answer has already been given: if a mass of commodities [. . .] is to circulate, it in no way affects the quantity of money needed for this circulation [. . .] *Thus the problem itself does not exist*. [. . . Any real problem here] coincides with the general problem: where does the sum of money needed in a country for the circulation of commodities come from?

This question matters as it concerns monetary circulation and value realisation in capitalist production. Under simple reproduction, using the commodity capital circuit, there is no fundamental issue in realising surplus value. Each new circuit begins at the same level as the previous one, and the money capital in the hands of capitalists is sufficient for monetary circulation. The issue of monetary circulation becomes relevant only in *expanded reproduction*, where, *ceteris paribus*, greater commodity capital requires additional money to complete the circulation phase. The presence of overproduction (c') at the end of the commodity capital circuit implies a monetisation issue only in the first stage of the enlarged new circuit, not in relation to surplus value itself but to the monetisation of the commodity capital produced as a consequence of the previous accumulation.

Initially, Marx provides the same response as in simple reproduction (Ibidem, pp. 418–419) and then considers ways to increase the money in circulation to facilitate the purchase of the 'increased commodity mass of a greater value' (Ibidem, pp. 418–19):

> The additional money required for the circulation of this increased commodity mass of a greater value must be created either by a more economic use of the quantity of money in circulation – whether by directly balancing payments, etc., or by means that accelerate the circulation of the same pieces of money – or alternatively by the transformation of money from the hoard form into the circulating form.

Finally, after pages reflecting the provisional state of his manuscript for *Capital* Volume II, Marx reaches a key theoretical point: beyond certain flexible limits, expanded capitalist reproduction would be impossible without credit (Ibidem, pp. 420–421):

> This also disposes of the pointless question of whether capitalist production *on its present scale* would be possible without credit [...] It would clearly not be possible. It would come up against the limited scale of precious-metal production. On the other hand, *we should not get any mystical ideas about the productive power of the credit system* [my emphases], just because this makes money capital available or fluid. But the further development of this point does not belong here.

Credit is essential for capitalist development. While metallic money allows limited expansion, *continuous* growth in commodity circulation needs credit. Marx identifies a theoretical limit to capital growth in the absence of new credit, yet this should not be mistaken for the claim that credit is indispensable to the very existence of capital reproduction.

Marx identifies several historical factors that underpinned the early expansion of commodity capital circulation before the full development of credit relations: the discovery of new mines, colonisation, wars, shorter turnover times, rising productivity, faster circulation, improved transport, balanced payments, the use of monetary hoards, capital devaluation, the diffusion of fractional reserves and the increasing use of commodity money as a means of payment rather than of purchase. These developments spurred – often unintentionally – the rise of capitalist relations based on commodity money. Early arrangements required the presence of a trusted intermediary, as the absence of a structured market made transactions precarious. Fully capitalist credit could only fully develop once industrial capitalist relations had been consolidated, relying primarily on commodity money for a long period. The gradual establishment of financial institutions – such as central banks and discount markets – was made possible by an economic environment in which commodity money circulation remained the foundation of mercantile exchanges. This monetary base provided the framework for both the initial formation and the progressive expansion of wider market relations among previously unrelated productive centres. Credit emerged slowly on this foundation. Independent, competing merchants and emerging capitalists gradually developed and consolidated lending and borrowing relationships, despite the absence of a stable, common institutional structure. Periodic crises, however, repeatedly exposed the inherent limits of both credit expansion and the circulation of commodity money.

For Marx, credit is not simply a mechanism for reallocating purchasing power but a structural component of accumulation. Banks do more than intermediate: they actively create credit *ex nihilo* to finance expanded reproduction, supporting both the acquisition of production conditions and the realisation of enlarged reproduction. Yet, while credit contributes to the reconstitution of the conditions of reproduction, it cannot produce them autonomously. Although credit drives the enlargement of capital, it ultimately rests on and is limited by the commodity capital previously realised, offering no guarantee that the expanded production it finances will be sold or valorised. If it helps sustain accumulation it also amplifies its contradictions. This is because the credit system pushes accumulation beyond its limits, it 'appears as the principal lever of *overproduction* [my emphasis] and excessive speculation in commerce' (Marx, 2015, p. 539) since much of the capital is operated by those who do not own it and thus take greater risks. As Marx notes, this dynamic accelerates both 'the material development of the productive forces' and 'the violent outbreaks of this contradiction', that is, the crises that periodically disrupt accumulation and expose the inherent limits of capital.

The Historical Intertwining of Credit and Commodity Money

Scholars of the monetary circuit approach have consistently stressed the need to move beyond commodity money when analysing the money capital circuit. However, their emphasis on credit often leads to an underestimation of the role of commodity money and the commodity capital circuit in the reproduction of total capital. This oversight neglects not only Marx's foundational analysis of commodity money in the first three chapters of *Capital* Volume I but also the historical development of credit *in its capitalist forms*, discussed in Volume III.

Marx's theoretical presentation did not follow the chronological sequence in which economic categories historically emerged. Instead, it was structured according to their hierarchical role within the capitalist mode of production.[12] He deferred the analysis of credit and financial capital to Volume III, privileging the logical organisation of his categories over a mere historical narrative. This methodological choice can be properly understood in light of his critique of political economy, first developed in the *Grundrisse* and later in the *Manuscript of 1861-1863* (Fineschi, 2013; Heinrich, 1989).

Credit, as a fundamental production relation, could only take specifically capitalist forms once commodity money had laid the groundwork for market formation and capitalist relations had become dominant. A crucial distinction must therefore be drawn between long-standing forms of commercial credit and the historically specific credit forms characteristic of capitalism. Yet this difference is frequently overlooked by those who maintain that credit alone enables monetary circulation. This issue has been the subject of a longstanding debate. For a historical account of the role of commodity money and its relation to credit, see Polanyi (1944), Bloch (1939) and Braudel (1979). On the distinction between pre-capitalist and capitalist credit relations, see Schumpeter (1954), Amato and Fantacci (2012).

The progressive formation of local, national and international markets has been driven by commodity money, leading to the rise of capitalist production relations, wage labour and capital competition.[13] Under the gold standard, paper currency temporarily replaced metallic money, which retained its commodity value. The system fundamentally depended on confidence in the availability of commodity money: in times of crisis, doubts about the currency's stability triggered runs on precious metals. Banks held large gold reserves, practicing fractional reserve banking; for example, in the 1920s, the Italian central bank was legally required to hold specific gold reserves covering 40% of banknotes in circulation (Article 4 of R.D.L. 21 December 1927, No. 2325). England maintained the gold standard for over two centuries, and most advanced economies adhered to it until 1971 when Nixon closed the gold window (Deleplace and Nell, 1996, p. 305). After the gold window closure, Italy still pledged its gold reserves as collateral for a 1976 loan from Germany.

State entities, financial institutions and central banks facilitated the issuance of paper money to support commodity circulation. While credit expanded, partly through government deficits and the formation of new national entities, the historical role of metallic money remained crucial in unifying markets and enabling credit expansion. Before the unification of Italy in 1861, more than 200 different metallic coins circulated, representing 78% of the means of payment (Banca d'Italia, 2011, pp. 25, 66).

In summary, the historical intertwining of commodity money and credit reveals how the latter's development was contingent upon the former's establishment. While the transition to a purely credit-based monetary system is often highlighted, the pivotal role of commodity money in enabling capitalist exchange relations should also be acknowledged.

Thus, we can answer the key question posed earlier. Marx had already addressed Graziani's concern: the issue lies not in the monetisation of surplus value per se but in the overproduction caused by accumulation in extended reproduction. This is evident in the circulation underpinning *simple reproduction* via the *commodity capital circuit*, where no particular problem arises in the circulation of surplus value. Difficulties emerge only because of overproduction generated by the overall accumulation process. In *extended reproduction*, circulation circuits expand and have historically been completed largely through commodity money circulation, which facilitated market formation and credit development.

SOME CONSEQUENCES WORTH EXAMINING

Using the commodity capital circuit to describe social reproduction provides decisive insights. Capital reproduction is never fully complete, as unsold commodity capital may encounter bottlenecks during the next circuit's circulation. Realisation is never guaranteed, and prices may fall short of expectations shaped during prior circuits. Cost-cutting, productivity gains, capital migration, and shifting accumulation rates influence turnover times and reproduction conditions (De Marco, 2023, 2024). These dynamics can obstruct the full realisation of value, meaning the completion of one circuit does not ensure success in the next, particularly when considering fixed capital, realised over multiple circuits and central to business cycles.

While reproduction on a given scale poses no inherent difficulty, the accumulation process drives both expansion and crisis: overproduction (c') exacerbates realisation challenges. When subsequent circulation fails to absorb prior output, accumulation hits its limits, potentially triggering a crisis. The commodity capital circuit thus reveals that the very forces propelling accumulation and development simultaneously generate the conditions for crisis within the dynamics of capital reproduction (Marx, 2015, p. 539).

Another decisive consequence concerns the so-called transformation problem, as the commodity capital circuit clarifies the debate over input-output price consistency. For most scholars, inputs and outputs prices must necessarily be equal. As Steedman (1977, p. 31), cited by Kliman (2007, p. 153), argues:

> A theoretical system in which a given commodity has different prices according to whether it is being sold or being purchased just does not correspond to any real capitalist economy.

At first glance, one might be tempted to assume that a commodity should have a single price since each exchange necessarily involves two parties. However, the commodity capital circuit shows that outputs from one circuit become inputs in the next. Within the same circuit, input and output commodities are temporally distinct. This temporal separation exposes how equating input and output prices misrepresents the actual process of capital reproduction and price formation – even under the provisional assumption that all production is realised at its value. In one of his criticisms of Moseley's macro-monetary theory—which assumes equality between input and output prices under equilibrium conditions—Freeman (2019, p. 2) employs the commodity capital circuit to emphasise the temporal distinction between input and output prices and to challenge equilibrium-based interpretations:

> The prices and values of commodities produced as outputs are not equal to the prices and values of these same commodities consumed as inputs at the start of the same period, but instead are equal to the prices and values of these same commodities when purchased at the start of the next period, prior to being consumed in that period.

Approaches insisting that input and output prices are necessarily equal fail to recognise that, in the commodity capital circuit, input and output prices refer to two distinct phases of circulation. On the other hand, approaches that assume equality only in equilibrium treat this condition as a convenient abstraction, which in reality can serve only as a provisional analytical tool. Both perspectives overlook the historical and structural determinants that shape production prices. Marx's analysis of commodity capital, by contrast, emphasises the centrality of accumulation and shows why input and output prices cannot be assumed equal, casting doubts on the simple reproduction framework that underpins the debate on the transformation of values into prices of production.

Assuming capitalists consume all surplus-value negates capitalist production itself (Marx, 1992, p. 199):

> *[The assumption that the capitalist consumes the entire surplus-value] is equivalent to assuming the non-existence of capitalist production and therefore the non-existence of the industrial capitalist himself* [my emphasis].

Adopting the framework of simple reproduction – along with its logically consequent assumptions, such as constant prices, constant values, constant productivity, equal exploitation rates, uniform turnover times and uniform rates of surplus value and profit – inevitably misrepresents the conditions under which production prices are formed. It overlooks the role of capital inflows and outflows between sectors, as well as changing accumulation rates – key factors in understanding capitalist dynamics, even without technological changes – which impact production prices. Yet these factors are typically disregarded as prices are treated as fixed.[14]

The history of science abounds with examples where complexity is simplified for the sake of convenience. A flat map may suffice for short distances, yet it proves inadequate for longer journeys, where only a great-circle route provides the shortest path. Debating how best to measure straight-line distances is ultimately futile: the constraint imposed by using a flat map nullifies any sophisticated attempt to capture the true geometry of Earth's surface.

Similarly, accepting a static model of simple reproduction – not only provisionally but as the sole definitive framework of analysis – prevents the understanding of the tendency towards the equalisation of profit rates and production prices formation. Capitalists relentlessly pursue accumulation, driving capital across sectors to maximise profit. The tendency of profit rates to equalise is thus one aspect of a dynamic process, not a static equilibrium, constantly counteracted by the equally powerful tendency for profit rates to diverge as capital relentlessly seeks the highest attainable return. The tendency to equalize does not lead to any actual equalisation, but to a declining frequency and amplitude of divergences. If the dynamism of this process is eliminated from the analysis, it becomes impossible to explain or even foresee the actual movement.

CONCLUSIONS

Most scholars regard the *money capital circuit* as the most suitable framework for analysing capital's social reproduction, focusing on monetary circulation. While they emphasise the essential role of credit, they overlook the *layered structure* of Marx's analysis, particularly his treatment of commodity money in

Capital, Volume I, and the use of different general circuits to describe the reproduction of capital. In fact, the money capital circuit is primarily suited for analysing the reproduction of individual capitals. At the more concrete level of abstraction that addresses total capital reproduction, the *commodity capital circuit* provides the only appropriate alternative. It clarifies circulation relationships, the accumulation process as a whole and addresses the crucial question: Where does the money for *expanded* circulation come from?

This analysis shows that starting from commodity money allows Marx to avoid the mistake made by monetary circuit theorists, who, starting from credit, end up assuming the money capital circuit as the reference framework for understanding the reproduction of total capital. The commodity capital circuit, on the other hand, reveals capital's social reproduction as an ongoing, incomplete process. Each circuit generates commodity capital that must be realised in subsequent circuits, making it impossible to treat reproduction as a series of isolated, self-contained periods. Commodity capital not yet realised, in turn, drives either expanded reproduction or crisis, thereby embedding both development and crisis within the dynamics of capital.

Another implication is that the commodity capital circuit highlights potential price differences between inputs and outputs, reinforcing and clarifying a point long emphasised by proponents of the temporal single system interpretation (TSSI).

Outputs produced with inputs from one circuit are sold in the next, and the temporal gap – across production and circulation – justifies price differences due to varying reproduction conditions. Moreover, since Marx's analysis centres reproduction on the spiralling accumulation process and the relations between capitals, the tendency to profit rate equalisation must be understood within the framework of expanded reproduction. This renders attempts to explain production prices under simple reproduction untenable.

Capitalism's market formation and expansion has historically relied on production relations anchored in reliable commodity money. Marx's methodological decision to first analyse the circuit of money capital, based on the use of commodity money, for the reproduction of individual capital and then to shift his focus to the level of total capital reproduction – thereby adopting the commodity capital circuit – highlights the historical role of commodity money in shaping the world market and clarifies the limits and possibilities for credit expansion. Ultimately, the commodity capital circuit proves essential for understanding capitalist accumulation and dynamics, as it underscores the crisis-prone nature of capitalism while exposing the inadequacy of static accounts of total capital reproduction.

ACKNOWLEDGEMENTS

I am deeply grateful to Giovanni Mazzetti for introducing me to Marx during my years at the University of Calabria, and for his lasting influence through ARELA (Association for the Redistribution of Labour). This chapter revisits some of his key insights on the analytic role of the commodity capital circuit and the limits of monetary circuit theory. I am especially thankful to Alan Freeman for his encouragement and support, as well as to José Tapia, Fabian Balardini, Gabriele Serafini, and two anonymous reviewers whose comments were very helpful. I am also grateful to Rama Manoharan for the patience and for very insightful editing. Any remaining errors are mine alone.

NOTES

1. Exceptions include Freeman, 1984; Murray, 1998; Arthur, 1998; Harvey, 2013; Foley, 1982.
2. See, for example, Nell in Deleplace and Nell, 1996, p. 251; Wray, 1990, p. 110. I will use the term 'money' to refer specifically to commodity money – gold, for the purposes of this chapter – unless otherwise indicated (Shaikh, 2016, p. 168, p. 194).
3. Graziani, along with Bernard Schmitt and Alain Parguez, is 'one of the recognised founders of the contemporary version of the theory of the monetary circuit' (Bellofiore, 2019, p. 2). This article by Bellofiore also provides an excellent summary of Graziani's thought as a Circuitist. I do not have the space to directly discuss the relevant literature produced by proponents of the theory of the monetary circuit, also denominated 'The circulation approach' (Deleplace and Nell 1996), so I will mention only a few key scholars. Readers can refer to the literature cited by these scholars, such as Rochon's chapter and Rossi's chapter, both in Ponsot and Rossi eds (2009); see also Graziani (2003).
4. On this basis, some scholars develop a seemingly justified critique of Marx's theory of money and question the early analysis in *Capital*, Volume I, where commodity money is introduced from the outset (Bellofiore, 1989, 2002, 2019; Bellofiore and Realfonzo, 1997; Graziani, 1997).
5. See, for example, Lapavitsas, 1994; Bellofiore, 2002, 2018; Campbell, 1998, 2019; Heinrich, 2021; Moseley, 2023.
6. The translations of this and subsequent passages from Graziani (1982) are mine.
7. In his restatement of Graziani's description of the monetary circuit of capital, Bellofiore reiterates that commodity money should be excluded at the outset: 'Currency cannot be thought of as a commodity [...] because the capitalist production of gold requires finance, as any production process: [... this] would implicate a vicious infinite regression'. There is no theory without presuppositions; Marx characterises capitalists as owning the means of production and possessing the monetary resources to initiate commodity circulation – historical presuppositions that avoid any problematic infinite regression. Conversely, using the same reasoning, the banking sector could not be assumed from the outset, as its specific power to create credit would remain unexplained.
8. The term 'overproduction' is typically understood as the production of goods that cannot be sold, often contrasted with 'underconsumption.' I retain it here because it fundamentally captures the real basis of any potential crisis. While all commodity capital must be sold to complete the circuit, the portion corresponding to simple reproduction has already found demand in previous circuits of circulation and is thus expected to do so again. In contrast, the excess portion exceeds the requirements of simple reproduction encompassing not only goods produced beyond immediate demand but also underutilised fixed capital. This additional capacity increases the potential for overproduction and points either to the expansion of capital base or to a crisis, should no additional demand emerge.
9. A more complex description, including the exchanges between industrial capital and capital of circulation (commodity-dealing, money-dealing capital), as well as interest-bearing capital and rent is not immediately relevant to the issue at hand. For a description of these relationships, see Lapavitsas (2017), De Marco (2023) and Balomenos (2024).

10. This choice distinguishes my analysis from that of Foley and Alemi (1997) and other scholars such as Basu (2011) and Chatzarakis (2024).

11. The arguments Marx uses to justify his decision to begin his analysis with the circulation of metallic currency are well summarised by Campbell (1998, pp. 129–157).

12. 'There was borrowing and lending in earlier situations as well, and usury is even the oldest of the antediluvian forms of capital. But borrowing and lending no more constitute credit than working constitutes industrial labour or free wage labour. . . . Although usury is itself a form of credit in its bourgeoisified form, the form adapted to capital, in its pre-bourgeois form it is rather the expression of lack of credit.' (Marx, 1973, p. 535).

13. See Balomenos (2024), Lapavitsas (2017), Itoh and Lapavitsas (1998), Shaikh (2016, Chapters 5 and 15), Argitis et al. (2014, pp. 7–11), Hall (2012), De Cecco (1975 [1971]) and De Brunhoff (1973). The importance of credit as the money of capitalism is addressed by Marx in the third book of *Capital*, Chapters 25–30.

14. I cannot address here the alleged inconsistency in Marx's theory of value, which continues to fuel the debate surrounding the so-called problem of the transformation of values into prices of production–an inconsistency that has been questioned and rebutted by several Marxist scholars (De Marco, 2021, 2023).

REFERENCES

Amato, M., & Fantacci, L. (2012 [2009]). *The end of finance*. Polity Press.

Argitis, G., Trevor, E., Michell, J., & Toporowski, J. (2014). *Finance and crisis: Marxian, institutionalist and circuitist approaches* Working Paper, No. 45. Institute for International Political Economy Berlin. https://hdl.handle.net/10419/105260

Arthur, C. J. (1998). The fluidity of capital and the logic of the concept. In C. J. Arthur & G. Reuten (Eds.), *The circulation of capital. Essays on volume two of Marx's Capital* (pp. 95–128). MacMillan Press Ltd.

Balomenos, C. (2024). A theoretical and archival investigation of Marx's analysis of interest-bearing capital and credit in the Manuscript of 1864-65 and its editing by Engels. *Paper presented at the 17th WAPE Conference*, Panteion University, on August 3rd, 2024.

Banca d'Italia. (2011). *La moneta dell'Italia unita, dalla lira all'euro*. Centro stampa della Banca d'Italia.

Basu, D. (2011). *Comparative growth dynamics in a discrete-time Marxian circuit of capital model*. Department of Economics, University of Massachusetts,

Bellofiore, R. (1989). A monetary labour theory of value. *Review of Radical Political Economy*, *21* (1–2), 1–25.

Bellofiore, R. (2002). Transformation' and the monetary circuit, Marx as a monetary theorist of production. In M. Campbell & G. Reuten (Eds.), *The culmination of 'Capital'. Essays on volume III of Marx's 'Capital'* (pp. 102–127). Palgrave.

Bellofiore, R. (2005). The monetary aspects of the capitalist process in the Marxian system: An investigation from the point of view of the theory of the monetary circuit. In F. Moseley (Ed.), *Marx's theory of money: Modern appraisals* (pp. 124–142). Palgrave MacMillan.

Bellofiore, R. (2018). Forever young? Marx's critique of political economy after 200 years. *PSL Quarterly Review*, *71*(287), 353–388.

Bellofiore, R. (2019). Augusto Graziani and the Marx-Schumpeter-Keynes 'cycle of money capital': A personal look at the early Italian circuitism from an insider. *Review of Political Economy*, *31* (4), 528–558. https://doi.org/10.1080/09538259.2020.1748306

Bellofiore, R., & Realfonzo, R. (1997). Finance and the labour theory of value. Toward a macroeconomic theory of distribution from a monetary perspective. *International Journal of Political Economy*, *27*(2), 97–118.

Bloch, M. (1961 [1939]). *Feudal society*. Routledge & Kegan Paul.

Braudel, F. (1979). *Civilization and Capitalism, 15th-18th century, Volume III, the Perspective of the world*. University of California Press.

Campbell, M. (1998). Money in circulation of capital. In Arthur and Reuten eds, *The circulation of capital. Essays on volume II of Marx's Capital* (pp. 129–157). MacMillan.

Campbell, M. (2019). Marx's transition to money with no intrinsic value in *Capital. Continental thought & theory: A journal of intellectual freedom*, *1*(4), 207–230. 150 years of *Capital.*

Chatzarakis, N. (2024). Stagnation and cycles in Marx's circuit of capital. *Paper presented at the 17th WAPE Conference*. Panteion University. on August 3rd, 2024.

De Brunhoff, S. (1973). *Marx on money*. Édition Sociales.

De Cecco, M. (1975 [1971]). *Money and empire: The international gold standard, 1890-1914*. Rowman and Littlefield.

De Marco, G. (2021). A Critique of Moseley's *Money and totality*. *World Review of Political Economy*, *12*(1), 106–132.

De Marco, G. (2023). Marx's general rate of profit – how turnover time, accumulation, and rate of surplus value affect the formation of prices of production. *Capital & Class*, *48*(4), 567–598.

De Marco, G. (2024). Turnover time and Marx's decomposition of profit adjustment in the process of equalization. In R. Herrera (Ed.), *Research in political economy, value, money, profit, and capital today* (Vol. 39). Emerald Publishing Limited.

Deleplace, G. & Nell, E. (Eds.). (1996). *Money in motion. The post Keynesian and circulation approaches*. MacMillan Press.

Fineschi, R. (2013). The four levels of abstraction in Marx's concept of 'Capital'. Or, can we consider the *Grundrisse* the most advanced version of Marx's theory of capital? In R. Bellofiore, G. Starosta, & P. D. Thomas (Eds.), *In Marx's laboratory. Critical interpretations of the Grundrisse*. Brill.

Foley, D. (1982). Realization and accumulation in a Marxian model of the circuit of capital. *Journal of Economic Theory*, *28*, 300–319.

Foley, D., & Alemi, P. (1997). *The circuit of capital, U.S. Manufacturing and non-financial corporate business sectors, 1947-1993*. ResearchGate. https://www.researchgate.net/publication/247809264_The_Circuit_of_Capital_US_Manufacturing_and_Non-Financial_Corporate_Business_Sectors_1947-1993

Freeman, A. (1984). The logic of the transformation problem. In E. Mandel, & A. Freeman (Eds.), *Ricardo, Marx, Sraffa. The Langstone memorial volume*. Verso.

Freeman, A. (2019). *The inconvenient problem of exchange consistency: Why Moseley's price interpretation of Marx is not a monetary interpretation*. https://www.academia.edu/39088230/TheinconvenientproblemWhyMoseleyisnotamonetaryinterpretation

Graziani, A. (1977). Recensione a mo' di premessa. In Roberto Convenevole, *Processo inflazionistico e redistribuzione del reddito*. Einaudi.

Graziani, A. (1982). L'analisi marxista e la struttura del capitalismo contemporaneo. In *Storia del Marxismo*, Volume 4: *Il Marxismo oggi*, Torino: Einaudi (pp. 701–741).

Graziani, A. (1990). The theory of the monetary circuit. *Économies et Sociétés, Monnaie et Production*, (1), 7–36.

Graziani, A. (1992). Production and distribution in a monetary economy. In H. Brink (Ed.), *Themes in modern macroeconomics* (pp. 98–114). The MacMillan Press Ltd.

Graziani, A. (1997). The Marxist theory of money. *International Journal of Political Economy, Summer*, *27*(2), 26–50. Marxian Theory: The Italian Debate.

Graziani, A. (2003). *The Monetary theory of production*. Cambridge University Press.

Hall, M. (2012). On the creation of money and the accumulation of bank-capital. *Capital & Class*, *16* (3), 89–114.

Harvey, D. (2013). A companion to Marx's *Capital* Volume Two. Verso.

Heinrich, M. (1989). Capital in general and the structure of Marx's *Capital*. *Capital & Class 38*, *13*(2), 63–79.

Heinrich, M. (2021). *How to read Marx's capital*. Monthly Review Press.

Itoh, M., & Lapavitsas, C. (1998). *Political economy of money and finance*. Macmillan.

Kliman, K. (2007). *Reclaiming Marx's capital: A refutation of the myth of inconsistency*. Lexington Books.

Lapavitsas, C. (1994). The banking school and the monetary thought of Karl Marx. *Cambridge Journal of Economics*, *18*(5), 447–461.

Lapavitsas, C. (2017). *Marxist monetary theory, collected papers*. Brill.
Marx, K. (1973 [1857-8]). *Grundrisse*. Penguin Books.
Marx, K. (1990 [1867]). *Capital: A critique of political economy* (Vol. 1). Penguin Books.
Marx, K. (1992 [1885]). *Capital: A critique of political economy* (Vol. 2). Penguin Books.
Marx, K. (2015). *Marx's economic manuscript of 1864-1865*. Brill.
Moseley, F. (2016). *Money and totality. A macro-monetary interpretation of Marx's logic in 'Capital' and the end of the 'transformation problem'*. Brill.
Moseley, F. (2023). *Marx's theory of value in chapter 1 of capital: A critique of Heinrich's value-form interpretation*. Palgrave Macmillan.
Murray, P. (1998). Beyond the 'commerce and industry' picture of capital. In C. J. Arthur & G. Reuten (Eds), *The circulation of capital. Essays on volume Two of Marx's Capital* (pp. 33–66). MacMillan Press Ltd.
Polanyi, K. (1957 [1944]). *The great transformation. The political and economic origins of our time*. Beacon Press.
Ponsot, J. F., & Rossi, S. (Eds.). (2009). *The political economy of monetary circuits. Tradition and change in post-Keynesian economics*. Palgrave MacMillan.
Rochon, L. P. (2005). The existence of monetary profits within the monetary circuit. In G. Fontana & R. Realfonzo (Eds.), *The monetary theory of production: Tradition and perspectives*. Palgrave Macmillan.
Rochon, L. P. (2009). The existence of profits within the monetary circuit: Some unanswered questions revisited. In *Ponsot and Rossi*.
Rosdolsky, R. (1977 [1968]). *The making of Marx's 'Capital'*. Pluto Press.
Schumpeter, J. (1954). *History of economic analysis. New York*. Oxford University Press.
Shaikh, A. (2016). *Capitalism. Conflict, class, crises*. Oxford University Press.
Steedman, I. (1977). *Marx after Sraffa*. New Left Books.
Wray, L. R. (1990). *Money and credit in capitalist economies. The endogenous money approach*. Edward Elgar.

MARX'S THREE CONCEPTS OF CAPITAL COMPOSITION, COHERENCE OR CONFUSION?

Anders Ekeland

Northwest University, China

ABSTRACT

This chapter takes a critical look at the relationship between Marx's three concepts of the composition of capital: the technical, organic and value composition. Among this 'holy trinity' of concepts, the organic composition is the one almost always used, but just as another name for the value composition of capital (VCC). Very seldom is the relation between three concepts critically discussed in Marxian economics. This chapter argues that the concept of 'technical composition of capital' (TCC) should be discarded since it is impossible to aggregate a heterogenous collection of different means of production to reach a number. The chapter further argues that since Marx's concept of 'organic composition of capital' (OCC) is defined on the basis of this impossible TCC, the OCC cannot be defined in a coherent way. Discarding these two impossible concepts – the TCC and the OCC – will have no major consequences for Marxian economics: it is simply a long-time overdue spring cleaning of the conceptual apparatus.

Keywords: Organic composition of capital; technical composition of capital; value composition of capital; labour composition of capital; inerrancy

INTRODUCTION

There are four major reasons why this spring cleaning has not happened. First and foremost, that practically all Marxists used the value composition of capital (VCC) under the 'pseudonym' of organic composition of capital (OCC). Secondly, many economists are prone to the kind of 'sloppy thinking' that was attacked by Joan Robinson (Robinson, 1953). Thirdly, since most economists of

Money, Value and Marx's Circuit of Capital
Research in Political Economy, Volume 41, 253–269

ISSN: 0161-7230/doi:10.1108/S0161-723020260000041035

all schools would agree that there is a secular trend towards more and more physical capital in industrial production, there is no reason to be too critical to use 'the mass of means of production' in a ratio *on a macrolevel.* Finally, because among those who did really discuss Marx' three concepts, there has been and is a strong tendency to what I will call 'the inerrancy of Marx' attitude to *Capital.* 'Inerrancy' is a word from Bible studies and means a strong impulse to try to make the Bible coherent, stretching the imagination to extremes in order to not have to admit the fact that there are major contradictions in and among the Gospels. Among Marxian scholars, it is a very strong unwillingness to frankly say that Marx made a mistake, that Marx is confused and sometimes even directly contradictory.

The chapter is a critique of three key contributions to the debate of Marx's composition of capital concepts: Orzech and Groll (1989), Moseley (1991) and Saad-Filho (1993). All three are examples of this 'apologetic' tendency. This tendency is present in all the "classical" controversies in Marxist economics, the transformation problem, the reduction of complex to simple labour, the problem of productive and unproductive labour. This 'inerrancy' attitude is an important obstacle for solving these problems.

SLOPPY THINKING

Attacking the neo-classical macro production function, Joan Robinson (Robinson, 1953) wrote that the:

> The student of economic theory is taught to write O = f(L, C) where L is a quantity of labour, C a quantity of capital and O a rate of output of commodities ... measure L in man-hours of labour; he is told something about the index-number problem involved in choosing a unit of output; and then he is hurried on to the next question, in the hope that he will forget to ask in what units C is measured. Before ever he does ask, he has become a professor, and so sloppy habits of thought are handed on from one generation to the next. (Robinson, 1953)

In a similar manner, most Marxist economists have forgot to as in what unit *physical,* the 'mass of means of production', is measured in Marx's technical composition (TCC); they have just 'hurried on' to use the value composition (VCC), a calling it the OCC, while most of them not even mentioning that there is a trinity of composition concepts. This 'sloppiness' is in fact the starting point for the 'Bible scholars'.

The structure of such apologetics has a distinct pattern. The starting point for Orzech and Groll, Saad-Filho and Moseley is the existing confusion among Marxists. They agree that Marx on this topic seems confusing or even contradictory, but their 'fundamentalist' objective is to argue that it only seems so, because Marx is never 'really' incoherent. They offer a new 'correct interpretation', that is what they think Marx most probably meant. The immediate problem – which they do not discuss – is that if their coherent interpretation/solution is correct, why did Marx not just write that himself? The problem then becomes that this new interpretation not only lacks textual support, it is contradicted by what Marx actually wrote, which , of course, only reflects that what Marx wrote was contradictory.

The structure of the chapter is as follows: I first discuss the contribution of Orzech and Groll (1989), which gives the best chronological overview of development of Marx's concepts. Then, I discuss Alfredo Saad-Filho's contribution. The third contributor I discuss is Fred Moseley, and both Moseley (1991, 2016) and Moseley's 2016 magnum opus, 'Money and Totality', discuss the role of the conceptual trinity in relation to various solutions to the most fundamental problem in Marxian economics, the transformation problem. Moseley is also interesting since Mosely discusses Engels's editing and construction of Volume 3.

I do not wish to get into a false debate: I do not mean that these serious Marxist have a religious fundamentalist apologetic attitude to Marx in principle. They would 'in principle' agree that Marx could be incoherent, but in each concrete instance the is, as I will try to show, a too strong tendency to try to make Marx coherent. In this case their problem is that these authors are familiar with the core issue of the Cambridge capital controversies, the impossibility of aggregating 'machines' without using prices or hours worked. One of the authors, Mosely, (Moseley, 2016), summarises this key point as follows:

> Marx's concept of capital is very different from the concept of capital in neoclassical economics, which is defined in terms of heterogeneous *physical goods* – as quantities of material inputs to production (machinery, equipment, buildings, raw materials, etc.), i.e., as 'capital *goods*'. ... The neoclassical definition of capital in terms of heterogeneous 'capital goods' is the reason why neoclassical theory has an insoluble 'aggregation problem' – because different kinds of physical means of production cannot be meaningfully added together. Marx's concept of capital, on the other hand, has no such 'aggregation problem', because Marx's concept of capital is defined in terms of money, which is homogeneous by its nature, and thus there is no problem adding up quantities of money capital across the economy (p. 10).

Moseley does not mention the Cambridge capital controversies here, but in a footnote p. 227, he states that neoclassical 'marginal productivity theory' has been 'thoroughly discredited by the devastating Cambridge criticisms'. But this insoluble aggregation problem is not mentioned at all when Moseley discusses the TCC later in that book.

THE IMPORTANCE OF THE CONCEPT OF CAPITAL COMPOSITION

Marx develops his concepts of capital composition from the very start of his economic studies. Since the study of Orzech and Groll (1989) [1] goes through this in the quite some detail, I will only discuss the points relevant for the objectives of this chapter. The point I want to make is that they really want to argue, firstly that the composition of capital is a very important concept in Marx theory, that the 'trinity' almost was there from the start, the Grundrisse, and that the concepts and their relation became clearer and clearer; in other words, that Marx's treatment of the concepts was not 'sloppy'. They start their chronological discussions of the Grundrisse, the Theories of Surplus Value, the two first German editions of Capital, by stating that the concepts are getting better, but at the end of each part having to admit that much progress has not been made, and they are negatively surprised by Marx's final definition in the French Capital Vol. 1.

Orzech and Groll start out saying that 'The composition of capital is among the most important and basic ideas of Marx's economic theories. The concept is defined explicitly in the first volume of capital, and descriptively in his notebooks' (p. 57). First of all, is the trinity, the OCC in particular, really among his most 'important and basic ideas?' I would say no. For example, the 'law' of a declining rate of profit only needs a VCC, like all schools of economics, and the fact that generations of Marxist economist have used a straight forward VCC, calling it OCC shows that. Was it really explicitly defined in the first volume of Capital and descriptively in his unpublished material? If that was actually true, why do Orzech and Groll, just six lines below this bold statement, complain that 'Unfortunately, Marx does not sufficiently explain the meaning of his complex definition and leaves much room for interpretation'.

To explain why they think Marx's definition of the trinity is so complex, Orzech & Groll argue that:

> The basic difficulty in fully grasping the meaning and significance of the composition of capital is rooted in Marx's methodological approach to his economic research. Being strongly influenced by Hegel's method, Marx's concepts have a dynamic meaning in their appearances and transformations. His categories are rarely straightforward, unequivocal meanings so familiar to, and expected by modern economists. On the contrary, they usually have multiple, sometimes complementary and sometimes contradictory meanings. This applies in particular to the composition of capital (p. 57).

It is not necessary here to discuss how Marx was influenced by Hegel, which he clearly was, but as Paul Zarembka points out that Marx repeatedly recommended a reviewer of Capital Vol. 1 that explicitly stated that 'the method of Marx is the deductive method of the whole English school, a school whose failings and virtues are common to the best theoretical economists'. Zarembka concludes that 'In my reading, this observation cuts through much discussion about the Hegelian influence in Marx's Grundrisse and can be offered as a proof that Marx's mature work in political economy is not dependent upon Hegel and dialectics' (Zarembka, 2000).

In my opinion, it is even less so when we are dealing with such a one-dimensional concept as a composition of capital, not Marx's concept of the 'money-form', fetishism and alienation, which are rich and fruitful concepts, but clearly not one-dimensional. What set of prices to be used in empirical research is of course a discussion, but it is a practical statistical one, not one with Hegelian mystique involved.

Grundrisse

Orzech and Groll see the *Grundrisse* as a first rough draft of *Capital* that '. . .constitutes Marx's first attempt to construct his theory' (p. 58). I agree with Michael Heinrich that the 'Introduction' we now find in the *Grundrisse* was not an introduction to a rough draft of Capital. It could not be because it started as a polemical note essay against a follower of Proudhon, Alfred Darimon. An excerpt of Darimon was the starting point, which made Marx dive into very interesting and fundamental issues, but it was not a planned book, a first draft. A polemical note became a research manuscript: consequently, the *Grundrisse* was not a first draft of *Capital*.[2]

Orzech and Groll write that 'The basic elements of Marx's theoretical system are already delineated in *Grundrisse*, although in a very unpolished and unfinished form. There he makes extensive use of the concepts which are to become the building blocks of his later analysis in *Capital*' (p. 58). I think this as a big overstatement. They present two quotations which do not even contain the word 'composition' or express 'composition' with other words.

Indeed, Orzech and Groll admit that none of the three concepts can be found in the *Grundrisse*:

> To sum up, as early as 1857/8 Marx had developed the major part of the theoretical apparatus which was to serve him in his analysis in *Capital*. It is, therefore, the more surprising that so a basic concept as the composition of capital does not explicitly appear in the earlier work. Marx discusses the 'paid part of the living labour' and the 'material, physical conditions' – concepts which can be taken to presaging the value and the technical compositions of capital. Yet nowhere in the *Grundrisse* does Marx define these concepts or differentiate between them – nor, for that matter between them and the organic composition of capital (p. 59).

It would have been much simpler to conclude that, when Marx was writing the *Grundrisse*, he had either not yet formulated any of these concepts or he did not need then for his polemical purpose; after all, he was not drafting Capital.

Theories of Surplus Value[3]

In an article on the transformation problem, Orzech and Groll also discussed Marx's concepts of the composition of capital: 'Marx defines the composition of capital in *Capital* I. Identical definitions are given in *Capital* III, and in volumes II and III of *Theories*' (p. 594 in Shalom & Ze'ev, 1987). In a footnote, they give the following references to *Capital* III and *Theories*: *Capital* III, pp. 144–145; *Theories* II, pp. 275–289, pp. 379–384; *Theories* III, pp. 382–396. The critical reader should get a little suspicious because 'identical definitions' is a very strong claim. To be very generous, at least all three concepts must be contained in one paragraph, but the references span 14, 5 and 14 pages, respectively. There is no, by any stretch of imagination, 'identical definitions' here. The reader should keep in mind this 'bold' statement in the following discussion of Orzech & Groll's (1989) article.

Orzech & Groll's (1989) article starts with an assessment of the *Theories*:

> During the three-year period between *Grundrisse* and *Theories*, Marx succeeded in clarifying for himself most of the problems that had remained unanswered in *Grundrisse* and consolidating his theories into a coherent system. The terminology and meanings of most of the concepts we find in the *Theories* are similar to those used later in the three volumes of *Capital* (p. 60).

Orzech and Groll then analyse each of Marx's concepts. They, without any critical comment, see the TCC defined as 'the relation between the amount of the means of production and the amount of living labour necessary to 'set them in motion'...' and add that although Marx 'coins' the term TCC in the *Theories*, he continues to use the terms 'physical composition' and 'material composition' interchangeably (p. 60) but why should Marx stop using these terms interchangeably? Orzech and Groll quote Marx saying that the means of production ' ... which now, according to our assumption, consist of tons of coal or quarters of corn'. In the appendix where they comment on previous interpretations, they explicitly refer to page 59 (Fine & Harris, 1979) where Fine and Harris state that the TCC 'is a ratio of physical, material, quantities and hence unmeasurable by a single index'.

In the section on the OCC, Orzech and Groll state that:

> The term 'organic composition of capital' is used for the first time in the *Theories*, but it is not clearly defined there. On the one hand, Marx sees it as being identical with the TCC ... on the other, he considers the OCC as the 'proportion between the part existing as fixed capital and the part laid out in wages.' The latter is clearly not a technological relation since both fixed (i.e., constant) capital and wages (i.e., variable capital) are expressed in value terms (pp. 60–61).

With such an obvious contradiction in the definition of the OCC, *the* key concept, how can this be called a consolidated and coherent system? Why did they overlook Fine and Harris clearly stating that the technical composition cannot be a scalar? Orzech and Groll also argues that in the *Theories* Marx also defines the VCC, but they quote very partially and selectively, which is no surprise, there is no substantial textual evidence that Marx had the 'trinity' definition of the VCC in his mind in the *Theories*.

Orzech and Groll conclude their discussion of the *Theories* in this way: 'This notion [the VCC], which is essential for the completion of his model of the capitalist economy, Marx develops more fully in *Capital* III. However, he does not introduce the complete definition until the French Edition of Volume I' (p. 61). But why, if Marx had it more 'fully developed' in Capital III, why did he not use the 'completed definition' in the first and second German editions?

Capital *Vol. III*

Orzech and Groll state (p. 63) that in *Capital* III,[4] Marx:

> ... restates the relationship between TCC and OCC in the most unequivocal terms: 'the technical composition of capital ... is the real basis of its organic composition' (C 111, 145). He develops the link between the technically determined amounts of the factors of production employed and their appearance in value terms (p. 63).

In fact, Marx on the references page gives a clear definition but not between 'technically determined amounts of the factors of production and their appearance in value terms'. Marx writes:

> A definite number of labourers corresponds to a definite quantity of means of production, and hence a definite quantity of living labour to a definite quantity of labour materialized in means of production. This proportion differs greatly in different spheres of production, and

> frequently even in different branches of one and the same industry, although it may by coincidence be entirely or approximately the same in entirely separate lines of industry.[5]

This is a crystal-clear definition of the 'labour composition of capital', hereafter the LCC: The quantity of labour that was needed to produce the means production is a measurable quantity since it is only accumulated living labour. What Marx here also makes clear is that the LCC is not any 'loose' or historical, macro-economic trend, from home spinning to factory spinning, it is a measurable ratio, on the enterprise level. The LCC is just another way of consistently aggregating heterogenous use values.

As far as I know, Joan Robinson (Robinson, 1947) is the only one that argues that this is what Marx really meant. After defining the usual algebraic symbols, she writes: 'There does not seem to be any way of writing the third ratio – the organic composition of capital – that makes sense, for neither c/v nor C/V corresponds to the idea which it expresses. It is clear enough, however, that what Marx has in mind, when he is talking about organic composition, is the of past labour embodied in the stock of capital goods to labour time currently employed' (page xii–xii). Later, on page 10, she writes that 'The organic composition of capital, dictated by technical conditions ...', but an analysis of the development of Robinson's analysis of capital composition is far beyond the scope of this chapter.

If Marx really was 'unequivocal', if Max really had 'developed' the 'link' between the TCC and the OCC how could there be so much confusion? The problem with the quotes that Orzech and Groll presents from Vol. 3 is precisely that the existence of a sum, a number, a magnitude and a measurement of the means of production in *physical units* is uncritically, unconsciously taken for granted, which is a bit strange given their reference to Fine and Harris that state explicitly that such a physical aggregation in impossible. Fine and Harris are by no means the only authors that find this physical aggregation to be a problem. In their comments on previous interpretations, Orzech and Groll mention that R. P. Wollf 'defines the TCC ... as the vector of all inputs'.

Later in this section on *Capital* III, Orzech and Groll go into an analysis of what changes are possible in the TCC without a change in the OCC and/or the VCC. They find that Marx uses a value relation, and 'By now, the distinction [between OCC and VCC] is already clearly stated, though not given the summarized and consolidated form in which we encounter it in Volume I ...'

They then quote Marx saying that the VCC might change while the TCC is constant and vice versa. Orzech and Groll get a little upset by Marx: 'This passage cannot refer to the organic composition of capital, for it is impossible for the OCC to remain constant when the TCC changes and vice versa. This leads us to the conclusion that Marx here speaks of a different kind of value expression'. After more quotes, Orzech and Groll conclude that 'Thus Marx has two capital/labour-power relations, the OCC, determined by production conditions and VCC determined by market conditions'. The obvious that Marx in

Vol. III is still confused and that Marx's views are not ascending from initial confusion to final clarity cannot be spelled out by Orzech and Groll.

DID CLARITY FINALLY ARRIVE WITH CAPITAL VOL. I?

Before I get into Orzech and Groll's analysis of the three editions of *Capital* Vol. I, let me – as Orzech and Groll do – state clearly the 'primacy' of those three editions, and among them, of course the primacy of the French edition. As Orzech and Groll points out, Marx thought the French edition contained so important changes that he in the postface wrote that it 'should be consulted even by people who are familiar with German'. It is necessary to make this clear because – as we will see below – later authors wanting to 'save' Marx, trying to find a 'correct' interpretation quotes from *Grundrisse*, *Theories* and *Vol. 3* as if they carried the same 'weight', as Marx definition from the French *Capital*. Not only did Marx introduce a new definition, he moved the definition to the start of the chapter.

The Three Editions

In the first and second German editions, Marx's definition of composition of capital is almost identical, but that he changed it marginally shows that he cared about the formulation. Orzech and Groll quote both of them in German and translate the definition from the first edition into English:

> ... a great revolution takes place in the process of accumulation in the *relation* between the mass of the means of production and the mass of labour power that sets them in motion. This revolution is reflected in the *changing composition of the constant and variable components of capital*, or in the changing relations of the parts of the value of capital which are converted into means of production and labour power. (pp. 67)

In my opinion, Marx gets it roughly right here; it might be that this is the LCC, the accumulated mass of labour in means of production and the magnitude of living labour, both measured by labour time. It is not clear if this a more 'loose', long historical trend or a precise measurable ratio in each factory. The technical composition is not mentioned. There secular historical trend could be illustrated, not summed up to a number, by looking at increasing numbers of steam engines, tonnes of steel, computers and tonnes of cloth as economic historians routinely do. As the saying goes: 'better to be roughly right than precisely wrong'.[6] Orzech and Groll argue that despite the fact that Marx does not define the technical composition, 'He does, however, describe it when he speaks of the of the relation between the means of production and the living labour used to operate them, both expressed in their physical units', but I would argue that in German, there is no mention of physical/material masse. The German word is 'Kapitalwerth', directly translated to 'Capitalvalue' or 'Capitalworth' in Germanized English, so either a monetary or a labour value aggregation is more probable. It seems to me, that Orzech and Groll want to read the French definition back into the German editions.

MARX GETTING IT PRECISELY WRONG

Let's keep in mind that it was when he was correcting the draft translations for the publication of *Capital* Volume I into French, in installments, that Marx penned his final definition of the three concepts. It was the first time he brought all three together in one paragraph.

> The composition of capital is to be understood in a twofold sense. As value, it is determined by the proportion in which it is divided into constant capital... and variable capital... As material, as it functions in the process of production, all capital is divided into means of production and living labour-power. This latter composition is determined by the relation between the mass of the means of production employed on the one hand, and the mass of labour necessary for their employment on the other. I call the former the value-composition, the latter the technical composition of capital. There is a close [strict][7] correlation between the two. To express this, I call the value-composition of capital, in so far as it is determined by its technical composition and mirrors the changes in the latter, the organic composition of capital. (Quoted from Saad-Filho, 1993, p. 136)

Orzech and Groll sum up what's new in two points. Firstly, 'Marx now ***explicitly*** differentiates between a composition of capital expressed in physical units and one expressed in value terms. The former is now strictly defined as the technical composition of capital'. This is correct, but for Orzech and Groll and everybody else, this creates a problem, because if there is a close, strict the relation between the TCC and the OCC then the OCC is just a good proxy/ indicator for the TCC, not perfect, but more than good enough, and we use it all the time. Then there is no need for another value composition, Marx writes 'in so far' without giving any indication how far 'so far' is. Instead of just stating that Marx was still confused, that this attempt to make the definition more precise than in the second German edition, just brought back the confusion and contradictions from his unpublished manuscripts they start to invent concepts and interpretation that has no textual support and does not help empirical research. While in their first point, it is stated that the TCC is 'expressed in physical' units, in their second point, they state that 'The technical composition constitutes the *social cost relation*, the organic composition, on the other hand, constitutes the *capitalistic cost relation*'. ... so the TCC has 10 lines below become a cost, that is a value relation, but it can just be either a technical or value composition, not both at the same time.

Orzech and Groll then correctly point out that 'Marx's definition leads directly to the question: what, then, is the relation between constant and variable capital which is ***not*** determined by, and does ***not*** mirror, the changes in the technical composition of capital? Good question, but the answer cannot be found by fine combing and interpreting what Marx wrote. One has to state the fundamental problem: that one cannot aggregate an heterogenous collection of physical goods without using a common characteristic. As we know from Marx's analysis of the commodity in Chapter 1 of Vol. 1, it is being the result of human work that is the common characteristic, primarily measured by the clock, and after several 'intermediate steps' expressed in money'. Not drawing this conclusion, the theoretical/conceptual problems are piling up for Orzech and Groll. It is not fruitful to follow them on their long and winding road back to

Grundrisse, back to Hegel. They find the value composition 'a confusing name' (p. 69), and they find that 'The TCC expresses the universal conditions of production: the physical relation between the means of production and living labour required in any system. It represents the eternal and universal features of economic life, and as such belongs to what Marx calls the production forces (p. 70)'.

Nevertheless, this is still not admitting plainly that it is Marx himself that is confused and contradictory. This is the inerrancy attitude in action. They have no excuse for not being aware of the fundamental aggregation impossiblity, as it is spelled out by Ben Fine and Fine & Harris (1979) on a page they refer to.

SAAD-FILHO: DEEP INERRANCY

While Fine and Harris (1979) are focused on Marx's concepts of capital in order to solve Marx's transformation problem, Alfredo Saad-Filho's paper "A note on Marx's analysis of the composition of capital" (Saad-Filho, 1993) is focused on the trinity. Saad-Filho in his conclusions explicitly refer to Ben Fine's contributions so he is placed in a tradition that illustrates that even if a Marxist author explicitly formulates the impossibility of the TCC, he just cannot – that is, he will not – draw the obvious theoretical consequences, probably because he feels that it would be too devastating for the prestige of Marx's *Capital*.

Already on the first page of his article of 1993, we get an indication of how Saad-Filho is going to end his argument:

> Although several interpretations of Marx's composition of capital exists in the literature, its complexity and relevancy has not always been fully recognised". Saad-Filho like Orzech and Groll sees the composition of capital as an "extremely important concept because it is central to some of Marx's most relevant and polemical analyses (...) While the content of each term [of the trinity] is quite evident at times, there are moments when he [Marx] seems to use them randomly or in a contradictory way; as a consequence, large parts of his inquiry may look arbitrary and puzzling. (Saad-Filho, 1993, p. 128)

Saad-Filho then follows in the tradition of Orzech and Groll with a couple of pages devoted to examples of confusion in the Marxist tradition. The conclusion he then draws clearly points to an 'inerrancy' attitude:

> The problems mentioned above are merely a sample of the difficulties one encounters in literature concerned with the composition of capital. *I search for a correct interpretation of Marx's understanding of the concept* (p. 128).

Could that 'correct interpretation', that is, the conclusion, be that Marx is confused and contradictory? Is it a scientific Marxian attitude to a priori exclude the most probable hypothesis that when so many serious and deeply dedicated Marxist economists are confused, the root cause of the confusion is Marx? If this was not enough, Saad-Filho assures the reader that:

> The progressive introduction of these terms [TCC, OCC, VCC] reflects an *increasing refinement* of Marx's own perception of the matters at stake, and as will be shown, allows

> him to clarify the presentation of his view. As the argument progresses Marx's views on the composition of capital and the precise meaning will be clear. Although the form of Marx's arguments change, it will not escape the reader that the problems with which he deals and *the results he reaches are essentially unaltered through the years*. (Saad-Filho, 1993, pp. 129–130, my emph.)

Saad-Filho is really raising the bar here that after so many years in the foggy desert, clarity will be finally delivered. There is an *increasing refinement* of the concepts. At the end, the inner essence of what seemed 'arbitrary and puzzling' to generations of Marxists will be revealed because '*it will not escape the reader that the results he reaches are essentially unaltered through the years*'. Since in science we are standing on the shoulders of previous researchers, one would expect an evaluation of the Orzech and Groll 'Stages' article, but Saad-Filho discusses Orzech and Groll's 'Stages' only once, devoting to these authors one long sentence:

> Groll and Orzech (1987, 1989a, 1989b, 1990), in their detailed discussion of the composition of capital (one of whose merits is the careful distinction of the TCC, OCC and VCC from each other) argue that the OCC is a long-run value-concept while the VCC is measured in market prices and refers to the short run, something with which I believe Marx would not agree. (Saad-Filho, 1993, p. 129)

I don't think this is a correct, precise description of Orzech and Groll's confused views, but Saad-Filho is probably right that Marx would not have agreed to introducing dynamics, there is no time dimension involved in the definition, the OCC is not measured at one point in time and the VVC at a later point in time. Measuring the ratios, OCC and VCC, as time goes by would give us two time series, observations of the OCC and the VCC, if it was possible to know when the OCC reflects the TCC and when it does not. The reason why nobody has done that is of course that TCC is impossible.

Besides this critical comment of Orzech and Groll introducing time and introducing dynamics, there is just a footnote: 'I do not have space to make a more detailed critique of Groll and Orzech, who have a highly sophisticated understanding of the composition of capital. See, however, Fine (1990)'. Soon after Saad-Filho has criticized Orzech and Groll for their dynamics, he is differentiating between a 'static case' and a 'dynamic case' without any comment on how his dynamic case differs from Orzech and Groll's short and long-run.

In the very beginning of the section on the 'static case' he quotes from *Capital* III, the very familiar concept of 'a certain mass of means of production' and Marx stating that 'This proportion constitutes the technical composition of capital and is the actual basis for its organic composition'. Commenting on this sentence Saad-Filho makes the key statement of his article:

> As the TCC is a relation between a heterogenous bundle of use values (the material inputs) and a quantity of labour it cannot be measured by a single index; for similar reasons, a comparison of the technical composition of capitals engaged in distinct sectors (shipbuilding and goldmining, say, where the use value of the inputs processed per hour of labour is very different) *is impossible*. (Saad-Filho, p. 131, my emph.)

Saad-Filho is not the first to point out this impossible aggregation. He is building on Fine & Harris (1979) but not on the impossibility of aggregation of heterogeneous capital goods. Fine and Harris who in their turn references (Murray, 1973), which do not mention this impossible aggregation problem, but another article in the same issue by David Purdy, does mention the problem (Purdy, 1973). Maybe Fine and Harris did not read Purdy's article, or, in any case, I have not found any references to Purdy. Saad-Filho could have mentioned that Simon Mohun mentions the impossibility in Tom Bottomore's Dictionary of Marxist Thought: 'Since there is no way in which heterogeneous means of production and concrete labour can be measured, the TCC is a purely theoretical ratio, whose increase is synonymous with a productivity increase' (Bottomore, 1983). Maybe Saad-Filho did not read Mohun at the time, but I cannot find anyone else that discusses what a purely theoretical ratio means when the numerator does not exist. How can you tell when it increases or decreases? How can there be a close correlation between this purely theoretical rate and a value rate, the OCC. Is there any evidence that Marx and later Marxist saw the TCC as purely theoretical ratio. In another well-known Dictionary, *The new Palgrave: A dictionary of economics (1991)* Anwar Shaikh writes about the OCC and its relation to the TCC. This is clearly the best attempt so far to indicate the problem but not pose is squarely, to make it look like it is possible to aggregate use-values, all kind of different 'machines' without using prices or labour time, when actually using both. Shaikh's formulation 'the technical composition is the inner measure of the composition of capital' and 'we can view the ratio c/l as the outer measure' and since the c is a value (=prices) and l is labour Shaikh just confirms that heterogenous use values can only be aggregated by using the fact that they are products of labour which the market 'standardises' into homogenous abstract labour. But let's assume that Anwar really solved the problem: if so, why did nobody tell Saad-Filho that the aggregation problem had been solved? If not in 1993, then in all the books and articles over the next 30 years where Saad-Filho repeated the impossibility of the aggregation?

Getting back to Saad-Filho's (1993) article, what does he do after stating the impossibility of the TCC? He, like all others who mentions the impossibility, he just ignores the problem: 'We know however that in capitalism all inputs are commodities; because of that; the technical composition can be assessed in value terms. This value-assessment gives us the *organic composition of capital* (OCC)' (Saad-Filho, 1993, p. 131).

This statement is simply not true, as you cannot 'assess' a TCC you have just declared to be non-existent. What you can do, the only thing you can do and everybody does is to aggregate using prices, whether you call it OCC or VCC is a matter of aesthetics. None of these concepts has any mathematical relation to the collection of 'machines', neither strict nor loose.

After clearly stating the impossibility of the TCC as a ratio, Saad-Filho fills no less than five pages with the usual quotes from *Theories* and *Capital* III, which – as we already know from Orzech and Groll – did not bring neither gave clarity nor refinement. Remember that Marx in the first and second German editions of *Capital* Vol is most likely to be interpreted as Robinson does that the

OCC is a ratio of dead and living labour. Marx made no mention of the TCC. Saad-Filho must know this definition from the German editions, since he explicitly mentions Orzech and Groll's 'Stages' article. But Saad-Filho does not even mention the first and second German editions as a stage in Marx journey to the French definition; indeed, he does not even mention the French edition! One might wonder why the reviewers or any of those mentioned in the acknowledgements pointed out and 'forced' Saad-Filho to discuss the first German editions and the French edition or later commentators.

The innovation that Saad-Filho makes is to introduce the static and dynamic case, posing the question: '... which set of values is to be used in the calculation of the OCC and VCC; the older and higher or the newer and lower? For Marx the answer is unambiguous. The OCC reflects the TCC at the *initial* (and higher) values of the component parts of capital, *before* the new technologies affect the value of the output, while the VCC reflects the TCC at the *final* (and lower) values of the elements of constant and variable capital' (Saad-Filho, 1993, p. 139).

To say that there is very little textual support in Marx's final definition of the trinity for the OCC and VCC to be dynamic in this way is an understatement, it is clearly contrary because the OCC is the VCC when it reflects the TCC which Marx and other Marxist clearly think is the case most of the time. If it was not the case most of the time, what's then the function of the OCC?

Saad-Filho's next step is to declare that 'It is quite obvious at this stage that a proper distinction between the OCC and the VCC can only be made by means of a *comparison* between contrasting situations' (Saad-Filho, 1993, p. 139). I like this nice 'contrasting situations', which sounds like 'in different contexts', instead of the plebeian 'at different points in time'. This pleasant formulation does not make the problem go away, however, as Saad-Filho ends up declaring that:

> Despite the conceptual clarity of this distinction [between the OCC and the VCC], the values that should be used in calculation of the OCC *are abstractions*. The difficulty of *calculating* the OCC in the static case does not imply that it is without use as a concept, as it was precisely in a static comparison of capitals with distinct organic compositions that Marx developed, in Part II of *Capital III*, his transformation of values into prices of production ... (Saad-Filho, 1993, p. 141, my emph.)

What Saad-Filho means by 'the values that should be used in calculation of the OCC are *abstractions*' is, to say the least, unclear. If Marx meant that the prices used to calculate OCC were abstractions, in the sense that the OCC could not be calculated, why did he not just tell his readers? We do not of course directly observe prices of production; they are estimates, but they can be calculated. One can – and Marxists do – discuss how relevant they are when profit rates are very far from being equalized.

As with Orzech and Groll, Saad-Filho gets entangled into confused if not outright contradictory statements. In the last paragraph before the conclusion, he declares that: 'Marx defined the OCC as the means to assess the TCC, a technical variable, in value terms'. This is strange. We have a myriad of 'machines', a heterogenous bundle of use values, impossible to aggregate and suddenly the TCC is 'a technical variable' in singular!

The concluding part of Saad-Filho's (1993) paper is one that I find very confusing, and it is in my opinion, no surprise that in later versions the formulations are a bit less confused. The problem is, however, the impossibility of the TCC and as a 'collateral damage' the OCC remains. In his book from 2019 Saad-Filho writes:

> There is, however, a severe difficulty with the OCC. ... it seems impossible to tell whether differences or changes in the OCC are due to differences or changes in the TCC (and, consequently, to differences or changes in the productivity of labour in *this* industry) or from differences or changes in the value of the means of production used up (that reflect the circumstances in *other* industries). However, for Marx there was no ambiguity. (Saad-Filho, 2019, p. 92)

After stating that for Marx there was no ambiguity, Saad-Filho has page after page with quotes from Marx's unpublished pre-Capital Vol. 1 manuscripts, not relating them to the German editions, nothing about the French Capital, that is the context where Marx introduces of the holy trinity of concepts.

MOSELEY AND THE PROBLEMATIC FRENCH CAPITAL VOL. 1

Fred Moseley has an impressive knowledge of the development of Marx's concepts and ideas, but he is – as I will try to show – also clearly influenced by the 'inerrancy' syndrome. For Moseley, Marx cannot be plainly wrong and contradictory. Moseley has an extensive discussion of the trinity in the first chapter of his 1991 book on the falling rate of profit in Post-War US, (Moseley, 1991). Moseley defines the TCC as the stock means of production, MP, divided by the labour used in production in a given period, a year, PL, and then writes: 'This ratio cannot be given a precise scalar meaning because the "means of production" consists of many different types of producers goods ... which cannot be meaningfully added together in physical terms ... especially since technological change continually alters the types of goods added together'. Moseley have no problem with the VCC, but with the OCC, he finds Marx definition 'notoriously ambiguous'. After citing the French definition, Moseley has the following comment: 'The difficulty with this definition is that it is not entirely clear what is meant by "a close correlation" and "in so far as it is determined by" and "mirror changes, but if you as Marx certainly did, think as Marx certainly did, that MPs can be aggregated, and argues, this is not a part of the definition that "There is a close relation..." then it is very clear what is Marx's view'. One might question if there is a close relation, but Marx's hypothesis that there is, is clear enough. The 'in so far ...' and 'mirrors changes' is clear enough, but makes Marx's definition incomplete. He does not give us any hint about what is happening in the tails of the distribution, when the correlation is not close, but if you, as Moseley does, argue that the TCC cannot be given a precise scalar meaning this should not matter. How can you empirically measure if X is closely related to Y, if X cannot be defined in any order of magnitude 'precise' way.

Moseley then tries to find an escape route from the 'ambiguities' by giving his own definition of the OCC as 'equal to the VCC in so far as the latter is affected only by technological change', but while it for Marx was a description of what he saw as a 'stylized fact', Moseley impose the 'close correlation' by definition. How do you know when there is a 'close relation' when the TCC cannot be measured? As a 'stylized fact', there are many examples of new technology, demanding less work, less material resources and giving more output. When we went from the big mainframes to laptops, has the 'mass' of MP in a physical sense increased or decreased? When it comes to textual support for his definition, as with Orzech and Groll, we observe that Moseley references Marx unpublished research and that they span several pages. These manuscripts are not easy to interpret, so referencing several pages means that Marx did not give any definitions. More importantly, what Marx decided to publish on the basis of this research study is summed up in the first two German editions, which does not mention the TCC or the VCC.

Moseley, after stating that the TCC cannot be 'be given a precise scalar meaning', engages in page after page of algebra in a lengthy discussion of Fine and Harris's (1979) ending up criticizing Fine and Harris for a definition of the TCC, which 'depends not only on the level of technology...but also on the average real wage. This definition seems clearly contrary to Marx's intentions'. The last sentence is true, but how is the 'level of technology' measured? In X tons of steel and Y kilometres of railway? Can one do any algebra when the ratio is fundamentally impossible to measure. How would Marxists have reacted if Ian Steedman had ventured into this kind of algebraic exercise, with an unmeasurable ratio?

Speed forward to Moseley (2016). Although Saad-Filho's (1993) article is in his reference list and he refers to it four times in footnotes, Moseley declares 'As is well known, the *technical composition of capital* (TCC) is a ratio in *physical* terms: the ratio of the quantity of means of production to the quantity of living labour in the production process (MP/L)' (p. 337), but the fact is that Purdy, Fine and Harris, Mohun, Saad-Filho and Moseley himself decades ago (1991) had pointed out the obvious fact that the TCC is impossible as a ratio. As we saw above, Moseley repeats that 'devastating critique' in the on page 10 in the study of Moseley (2016). The sad truth is that all of them after stating that, they then just go on as if it was a ratio.

Blaming Engels?

Trying to make sense of Marx in his 2016 magnum opus, Moseley quotes one line of it from Vol. III, incorrectly attributing it to Engels: 'The next paragraph is another ambiguous one-sentence paragraph, which was added by Engels (it is not in Marx's *Manuscript of 1864–65*) and which again mentions the OCC without defining it clearly: 'The *organic* composition of capital is the name we give to its value composition, in so far as it is ***determined by*** its technical composition and ***reflects it***. Unfortunately, the meaning of 'determined by' and 'reflects it' is left vague and imprecise in Engels' sentence (Moseley, 2016, p. 346). It is true that Engels added the sentence, but as we know by now, this is Marx's sentence, his definition. Orzech and Groll (p. 63) also find this sentence, which they correctly characterise as an 'anachronism' because it is identical to the French definition. They contacted the International Institute of Social History in Amsterdam and got the only possible answer that the sentence was not in Marx's manuscript. That should not have been necessary because Engels also added a footnote: 'The above has already been briefly developed in the third edition of Volume I. Since the first two editions do not contain that passage, its repetition here is all the more desirable'. That Engels only referred to his German editions of Capital not the French had the regrettable consequence that the existence of the French Capital was not made explicit. There seems to be a problem in some of the versions of Vol. III which lack Engels footnote. The online version lacks it,[8] so if you are not familiar with the 'organic composition' controversy, you will conclude that Marx had formulated the French definition before the publication of Capital 1.

CONCLUSION: DISCARD THE TCC AND THE OCC

The question of capital composition as a scientific question is not a difficult one. To aggregate a heterogenous collection of use values in this case means of production, hours of labour or prices are the only common characteristic one can use to aggregate them. It is only in the Marxist theoretical 'canon' that the OC has become a problem since Marx thought that the TCC existed as a number.

The main conclusion is that those who are working in the Marxian tradition should stop using the TCC and the OCC. The TCC is 'impossible', and the OCC is defined on the basis of the non-existing TCC and becomes an ill-defined and confusing concept.

NOTES

1. Hereafter all page references are from Orzech and Groll's (1989) article unless explicitly stated otherwise.
2. See Michael Heinrich on YouTube: https://www.youtube.com/watch?v=VVW3eu164-hE&t=4396s, from 05:00 to 12:00.
3. The reader should keep in mind that the 'Theories' is not a book but part of (40%) a collection of research manuscripts, see https://en.wikipedia.org/wiki/Theories_of_Surplus_Value
4. The reader must keep in mind that the manuscripts that became edited by Engels into Vol. 3 was written 3–4 years before the publication of Vol 1, and Marx never returned to these manuscripts; hence, Vol. 3 is written before Vol. 1.
5. I quote here from the Marxists Internet Archive, avoiding the problem that the page number will be different in all the printed versions of Vol. 3.
6. Falsely attributed to Keynes, coined-a bit differently by English philosopher Carvet Read (1848–1931). (Oxford Dictionary Online).

7. Some authors, Orzech and Groll (1989), Wolff has 'strict correlation', in the French Capital 1, 'lien intime'.
8. https://www.marxists.org/archive/marx/works/download/pdf/Capital-Volume-III.pdf

REFERENCES

Bottomore, T. B. (1983). *A dictionary of Marxist thought*. Harvard University Press.

Fine, B. (1990). On the composition of capital: A comment on Groll and Orzech. *History of Political Economy*, *22*(1), 149–155.

Fine, B., & Harris, L. (1979). *Rereading capital*. Columbia University Press.

Harcourt, G. C. (1975). *Theoretical controversy and social significance: An evaluation of the Cambridge controversies*. University of Western Australia Press.

Moseley, F. (1991). *The falling rate of profit in the postwar United States economy*. St. Martin's Press.

Moseley, F. (2016). *Money and totality: A macro-monetary interpretation of Marx's logic in capital and the end of the 'transformation problem'*. Haymarket Books/Brill.

Murray, R. (1973). Productivity, organic composition, and the falling rate of profit. *Conerence of Socialist Economic Bulletin*, *II*(5).

Orzech, Z. e. B., & Groll, S. (1989). Stages in the development of a marxian concept: The composition of capital. *History of Political Economy*, *21*(1), 57–76. https://doi.org/10.1215/00182702-21-1-57

Purdy, D. (1973). The theory of the permanent arms economy—A critique and an alternative. *Conerence of Socialist Economic Bulletin*, *2*(5).

Robinson, J. (1947). *An essay on Marxian economics* (2nd ed.). Macmillan.

Robinson, J. (1953). The production function and the theory of capital. *The Review of Economic Studies*, *21*(2), 81–106. https://EconPapers.repec.org/RePEc:oup:restud:v:21:y:1953:i:2:p:81-106

Saad-Filho, A. (1993). A note on Marx's analysis of the composition of capital. *Capital & Class*, *17*(2), 127–146. https://doi.org/10.1177/030981689305000106

Saad-Filho, A. (2019). *Value and crisis: Essays on labour, money and contemporary capitalism*. https://doi.org/10.1163/9789004393202

Shaikh, A. (1991). Organic composition of capital. In M. Milgate, J. Eatwell, & P. Newman (Eds.), *The new Palgrave: A dictionary of economics* (Ed. rev). Macmillan Press; Stockton Press.

Shalom, G., & Ze'ev, B. O. (1987). Technical progress and values in Marx's theory of the decline in the rate of profit: An exegetical approach. *History of Political Economy*, *19*(4), 591–613. https://ideas.repec.org/a/hop/hopeec/v19y1987i4p591-613.html

Zarembka, P. (2000). Accumulation of capital, its definition: A century after Lenin and Luxemburg. In *Research in political economy* (Vol. 18, pp. 183–241). https://doi.org/10.1016/S0161-7230(00)18007-1

Printed and bound by CPI Group (UK) Ltd, Croydon, CR0 4YY

15/09/2026

14962485-0005